MW01038926

The Limits of Liberalism

The Limits of
LIBERALISM

TRADITION, INDIVIDUALISM,
AND THE CRISIS OF FREEDOM

MARK T. MITCHELL

University of Notre Dame Press
Notre Dame, Indiana

University of Notre Dame Press
Notre Dame, Indiana 46556
undpress.nd.edu

Copyright © 2019 by University of Notre Dame

All Rights Reserved

Published in the United States of America

Excerpts from Four Quartets by T. S. Eliot. Copyright 1936 by
Houghton Mifflin Harcourt Publishing Company; Copyright © renewed
1964 by T. S. Eliot. Copyright 1941, 1942. T. S. Eliot; Copyright ©
renewed, 1969, 1970 by Esme Valerie Eliot. Reprinted by permission of
Houghton Mifflin Harcourt Publishing Company. All rights reserved.

Library of Congress Cataloging-in-Publication Data

Names: Mitchell, Mark T., author.
Title: The limits of liberalism : tradition, individualism, and the crisis of freedom /
Mark T. Mitchell.
Description: Notre Dame : University of Notre Dame Press, [2018] |
Includes bibliographical references and index. |
Identifiers: LCCN 2018043824 (print) | LCCN 2018048894 (ebook) |
ISBN 9780268104313 (pdf) | ISBN 9780268104320 (epub) |
ISBN 9780268104290 (hardback : alk. paper) |
ISBN 0268104298 (hardback : alk. paper)
Subjects: LCSH: Liberalism—Philosophy. | Political science—Philosophy.
Classification: LCC JC574 (ebook) | LCC JC574 .M568   2018 (print) |
DDC 320.51—dc23
LC record available at https://lccn.loc.gov/2018043824

∞ *This paper meets the requirements of ANSI/NISO Z39.48-1992*
(Permanence of Paper)

The Limits of
LIBERALISM

TRADITION, INDIVIDUALISM, AND THE CRISIS OF FREEDOM

MARK T. MITCHELL

University of Notre Dame Press
Notre Dame, Indiana

University of Notre Dame Press
Notre Dame, Indiana 46556
undpress.nd.edu

Copyright © 2019 by University of Notre Dame

All Rights Reserved

Published in the United States of America

Excerpts from Four Quartets by T. S. Eliot. Copyright 1936 by
Houghton Mifflin Harcourt Publishing Company; Copyright © renewed
1964 by T. S. Eliot. Copyright 1941, 1942. T. S. Eliot; Copyright ©
renewed, 1969, 1970 by Esme Valerie Eliot. Reprinted by permission of
Houghton Mifflin Harcourt Publishing Company. All rights reserved.

Library of Congress Cataloging-in-Publication Data

Names: Mitchell, Mark T., author.
Title: The limits of liberalism : tradition, individualism, and the crisis of freedom /
Mark T. Mitchell.
Description: Notre Dame : University of Notre Dame Press, [2018] |
Includes bibliographical references and index. |
Identifiers: LCCN 2018043824 (print) | LCCN 2018048894 (ebook) |
ISBN 9780268104313 (pdf) | ISBN 9780268104320 (epub) |
ISBN 9780268104290 (hardback : alk. paper) |
ISBN 0268104298 (hardback : alk. paper)
Subjects: LCSH: Liberalism—Philosophy. | Political science—Philosophy.
Classification: LCC JC574 (ebook) | LCC JC574 .M568   2018 (print) |
DDC 320.51—dc23
LC record available at https://lccn.loc.gov/2018043824

∞ *This paper meets the requirements of ANSI/NISO Z39.48-1992*
(Permanence of Paper)

To George W. Carey

With Gratitude

Requiescat in pace

A culture survives principally . . . by the power of its institutions to bind and loose men in the conduct of their affairs with reasons that sink so deep into the self that they become commonly and implicitly understood—with that understanding of which explicit belief and precise knowledge of externals would show outwardly like the tip of an iceberg.

—Philip Rieff

Liberty lives in the context of order; and order, beneficial to liberty, is maintained by traditions of many sorts, some quite illiberal in their content.

—Edward Shills

Tradition is not the worship of ashes, but the preservation of fire.

—sometimes attributed to Gustav Mahler

CONTENTS

PREFACE

In July 2016, the British people voted to leave the European Union. In November of the same year, Donald Trump stunned many by defeating Hillary Clinton in the U.S. presidential election. In January 2017, Trump took office to the consternation of those who were convinced that the rhetoric of secure borders and America First trade policies were ideas rooted in a reactionary and long dead—or at least dying—past.

In March 2017, Charles Murray, a scholar at the American Enterprise Institute, attempted to give a lecture at Middlebury College in Vermont. A crowd of protestors—mostly students (and some of their faculty instigators) of that august liberal arts institution—shouted him down, violently intimidated Murray and his host, Middlebury professor Allison Stanger (who was pushed to the ground and concussed trying to protect Murray as they made their way out of the building), and surrounded their car, pounding it and rocking it so that they had to creep away through the crowd to prevent injuring anyone.[1]

In July, a Google engineer named James Damore used the company's internal discussion board to argue that Google's culture had become an "echo chamber," that dissent from, what Damore considered, a liberal bias was not allowed, and that perhaps the reason that there are fewer women programmers than men is not a result of inferior capabilities but a difference of interests. Damore was accused of fomenting a hostile work environment and fired.[2]

In August, white nationalists, Klansmen, and others convened a march in Charlottesville, Virginia, ostensibly with the purpose of protesting the removal of a statue of Robert E. Lee. There was a counterprotest led by the so-called Antifa. Things turned violent. A woman was killed.[3]

These events are related. The intent of this book is to try to explain what's going on.

———

Samuel Johnson once said that people need to be reminded more often than they need to be instructed. This book seeks to remind those who have forgotten some basic and indispensable truths. So what I have to say is not new. Long ago, Plato argued that freedom taken to an extreme—that is, freedom that seeks to eradicate all limits—will call forth a dramatic reversal resulting in tyranny. In the nineteenth century, Alexis de Tocqueville said much the same thing. We would do well to listen.

The task of reminding often involves stating things that, in retrospect, appear obvious. But that is precisely the problem: until we are reminded, we are left adrift, armed merely with hunches and a nagging feeling that we may have taken a wrong turn. Nevertheless, most of us intuit that something is seriously amiss. The land of the free seems to be grappling with the meaning of its freedom, and some are finding that there is a world of difference between paying lip service to noble ideals such as liberty, tolerance, and self-control and actually doing the hard work of living up to those ideals. We must be reminded. But given that history continues unabated, the manner of the reminding, and the way we see the content of truths long known, will be unique to our own historic and cultural moment. As we pass "through the unknown remembered gate," as the poet T. S. Eliot suggestively put it, our insight into what at first seemed new will turn into a more chastened acknowledgment that we actually knew these basic truths all along. We are, as St. Paul so starkly put it, "without excuse." But the fact of our responsibility is also an indicator of our hope. We can choose a better way. We can choose to recall what we have long forgotten. We can choose to submit to an order long denied. The voices echo through the centuries. The wisdom of the wise is instructive, but so is the folly of fools. And we are the fools if we ignore either.

ACKNOWLEDGMENTS

Many people contributed to this book (even if they didn't realize it at the time). I have profited greatly from conversations with, and books and essays written by, among others, Richard Avramenko, Steven Carne, Patrick Deneen, Rod Dreher, Michael Federici, Ron Laurenzo, Joshua Mitchell, Ken Myers, Jason Peters, and Les Sillars. Walter B. Mead (who passed away before this book made it to publication) and Jeff Polet graciously read and provided helpful commentary on parts of the manuscript. Roberta Bayer read a draft and provided excellent advice at a crucial time. Two anonymous readers provided helpful suggestions on an early draft. Patrick Henry College librarian Vickie Thornhill is always a cheerful and able locator of books and articles. Steve Wrinn and his staff at the University of Notre Dame Press has been a steady and competent hand guiding this project through to completion. Thanks to all.

I would also like to acknowledge the following publications in which parts of this book have previously appeared: portions of chapter 4 were previously published in different form in my book, *Michael Polanyi: The Art of Knowing* (Wilmington, DE: ISI Books, 2006); part of chapter 4 was originally published as "Michael Polanyi, Alasdair MacIntyre, and the Role of Tradition," in *Humanitas* XIX, nos. 1–2 (2006): 97–125; and parts of the introduction and chapter 5 were previously published as "Making Places: The Cosmopolitan Temptation" in *Why Place Matters: Geography, Identity, and Civic Life in Modern America*, ed. by Wilfred M. McClay and Ted V. McAllister (New York: New Atlantis Books, 2014). These are used here with permission.

And finally to my wife, Joby, and children—Seth, Noah, Scott, and Tana, along with a new daughter-in-law Annabelle—you make life sweet. Thank you for your graciousness to me. I love each of you dearly.

Introduction

Surveying the Landscape and Defining Terms

Thus saith the LORD, "Stand ye in the ways, and see, and ask for the old paths, where is the good way, and walk therein, and ye shall find rest for your souls." But they said, "We will not walk therein."
—Jeremiah 6:16

Liberation, as we all know, is a good thing. At least that is what we are told and what we feel is true in our collective bones. However, obvious truths are sometimes the very ones that need to be probed. Although being liberated from slavery or oppression is clearly a good thing, it is not as clear that liberation from *tradition*—by which we obtain knowledge of social, natural, and divine limits—is unequivocally good. In fact, such liberation might be harmful both in terms of our capacity to know and in our capacity to act individually and collectively. In other words, an errant account of tradition may entail an errant account of knowing, which in turn may give birth to social and political maladies. The aim of this book is to examine and evaluate (1) the modern attack on tradition, (2) the liberal self complicit in that attack, and (3) the political cosmopolitanism, along with the identity politics, that accompanies both. However, we first need to clarify some basic terms. In so doing, we will establish provisional definitions that will become more fully articulated as we proceed.

1

LIBERALISM

It is virtually impossible to designate with any precision the moment (or perhaps even the century) that the modern world began, but we can identify certain features that provide evidence of its emergence, including the following seismic shifts: the rise of the new science, the breakup of Christendom, the rise of nominalism, the epistemological turn in philosophy, and the development of the idea of a state of nature and the social contract. All of these are in one way or another related, either causally or conceptually. The different facets and nuances involved in each particular event are important, but in this book I want to focus on one particular feature that, I would suggest, best characterizes the modern mind: the denigration of tradition. This disposition has fostered a certain cast of mind by which the past is seen as a dark and benighted place inhabited by miserable and deeply errant wretches, while the future is seen as a bright and hopeful place populated by happy and wise individuals who have shaken off the constraints of the past. The autonomous self—independent and free from any obligations that have not been expressly chosen—occupies this future land. Choice is the coin of this realm, and the story these people tell each other is one characterized by the steady march toward independence, toward liberation from the strictures of tradition, custom, and even liberation from nature and God.[1]

This new emancipated self represents the ideal of what has come to be called "liberalism." Although today we often hear of different types of liberals—classical liberals and welfare liberals, for instance—I am concerned with the noun rather than the adjective, for it is my contention that even though there may be certain secondary differences and policy distinctions between types of liberals, they all share a common account of human nature. (In this regard many so-called conservatives are actually liberals).

The very word "liberalism" derives from the Latin *liber*, "free." Ours is an age where individual freedom is cherished and any impediment to that freedom is seen as an affront to be demolished. Social contract thinkers such as Thomas Hobbes, John Locke, and Jean-Jacques Rousseau (and more recently John Rawls) developed a conception of "natural" man existing in a prepolitical (and even presocial) state of nature (whether historical or merely conceptual) wherein each individual is completely unattached to other humans, and in such a context all are absolutely free and equal. Social and political associations are formed by choice alone, and any attachment or obligation formed without consent is deemed illegitimate.

The ideal of the autonomous individual, conceived in a thought experiment, serves as the centerpiece of the political theory of Rawls, the dean of twentieth-century liberal thought. According to Rawls, the "original position of equality corresponds to the state of nature in the traditional theory of the social contract." This original position is "purely hypothetical"—any rational creature can enter into it by an act of imagination. The original position consists of a "veil of ignorance" whereby "no one knows his place in society, his class position or social status, nor does any one know his fortune in the distribution of natural assets and abilities, his intelligence, strength, and the like."[2] In this original position behind a veil of ignorance, everyone is perfectly equal, rational, and free to choose. Rawls is convinced that in such a condition, certain principles of justice would invariably be chosen if people merely acted in a rational and disinterested manner.[3] Rawls calls this "justice as fairness." The crucial point for us is Rawls's notion that it is possible to strip away all the particularity from a person—the particularities of history, culture, relationship, and temperament, not to mention human nature—and retain a core identity capable of rational agency. Reason in this conception is autonomous, and the essence of human identity is the capacity to will in accord with reason. Although Rawls provides a novel reconception of the state of nature, he is, by his own admission, engaging in a line of reflection about politics and the human person that extends back into the seventeenth century.

According to Pierre Manent, Hobbes should be considered the founder of liberalism, for he begins his theoretical reflections with the atomistic individual and roots his account of sovereignty in consent.[4] Hobbes showed how individualism could lead to absolutism, but, perhaps because of his relentless consistency, he did not find a ready following. Locke, however, is often seen as a moderate. He followed Hobbes in theoretical terms by beginning with autonomous individuals in a state of nature. At the same time, unlike Hobbes, he continued to affirm a more or less traditional view of society and morality. He speaks—albeit cursorily—in terms of natural law, which at least seems to suggest a fidelity to a tradition of moral reasoning that traces its roots back to the medieval Scholastics and beyond them to Cicero, and in some fashion to Aristotle. Nevertheless, in following Hobbes, Locke rejects any notion that political society is the natural state of human affairs. Instead, he begins his reflections on politics with a state of nature in which each free and equal individual is subject to nothing other than the law of nature.[5] Owing to the inherent dangers in such a state to life, liberty, and property, these free individuals contract with each other to form a society for the purpose of security.[6] In so doing they cede a portion of their rights (specifically, the right to punish offenders) to the established authorities.[7] This contract is legitimate because of the consent granted—either explicitly or tacitly—by each individual party to the contract.[8] For Locke, the only reasonable standard for subsequent legislation is the majoritarian principle: "And thus every man, by consenting with others to make one body politic under one government, puts himself under an obligation, to every one of that society, to submit to the determination of the majority."[9]

Such concepts seem quintessentially American given the Lockean flavor of the Declaration of Independence. We almost instinctively think in terms of consent of the governed; of free and equal individuals; of the rights to life, liberty, and property; and of the legitimacy of majoritarian rule. At the same time, Americans tend to be skeptical of tradition, which carries with it the musty odor of the past. Instead, we tend to be a future-oriented people, boldly striving to ensure that tomorrow will be better than yesterday and optimistic that through hard work (and perhaps good fortune) brighter days will always be ahead. When Ronald Reagan declared that it was "morning in America," he was tapping into that future-oriented sentiment. The United States has always been the land of perpetual dawn. There is, of course, a countervailing wind of pessimism that emerges periodically, but it is not animated by any inclination to rediscover the wisdom of the past or to submit to limits manifest in that wisdom. Instead, it is a pessimism about the future, which still provides no positive orientation to the past, except, perhaps, a whiff of nostalgia.

The Lockean framework around which our political institutions are ostensibly built, however, may not be as stable as we imagine. What, for instance, prevents the majority from oppressing the minority? Clearly, if there is no limit to the will of the majority, gross injustices are only a matter of time. *If* Locke's "state of nature has a law of nature to govern it" and *if* that law of nature is "as intelligible and plain to a rational creature, and a studier of that law, as the positive laws of the commonwealth," and *if* that law of nature continues in force even after the social contract is initiated, then the majority is checked, at least theoretically.[10] But what becomes of justice if this law of nature is ignored or denied? It would appear that the social contract could, in fact, become a means of oppression rather than liberation, for in practical terms power is amplified as individuals join forces—and woe to those who run afoul of the majority.

Consider these same concepts in the hands of Rousseau. Like Locke before him, Rousseau begins with a state of nature in which all are perfectly free and equal. Rousseau sets out the problem: "Find a form of association which defends and protects with all common force the person and goods of each associate, and by means of which each one, while uniting with all, nevertheless obeys only himself and remains as free as before."[11] But unlike Locke, whose social contract included ceding only the right to punish, Rousseau's contract consists of "the total alienation of each associate, together with all of his rights, to the entire community."[12] In such a context, all remain equal, for all have alienated all rights to the community. Furthermore, in Rousseau's mind, all remain free, for "in giving himself to all, each person gives himself to no one. And since there is no associate over whom he does not acquire the same right that he would grant others over himself, he gains the equivalent of everything he loses, along with a greater amount of force to preserve what he has."[13] Freedom and equality are preserved, but citizens now possess force, derived from their collective strength, so they can better preserve the freedom and equality to which they are committed.

The sovereign, in Rousseau's scheme, is merely the collection of the individual participants in the compact; thus, the sovereign could never have an interest that is contrary to the interests of the people as a whole.[14] The will of the whole is the "general will," which, though it becomes a somewhat mystical element in Rousseau's thought, is "always right."[15] Practically speaking, "the vote of the majority always obligates all the others."[16] For Rousseau, there is no limit on the majority, but this is not a troubling prospect, for law is nothing other than the general will, and no one would tyrannize himself. Power becomes at once unlimited and benign.

In such a context, the Lockean rights to life, liberty, and property take on an entirely different appearance. To oppose the general will is to act contrary to not only the will of the whole but to one's own will. In this light, Rousseau can claim that "whoever refuses to obey the general will will be forced to do so by the entire body. This means merely that he will be forced to be free."[17] In terms of property, "each private individual's right to his very own store is always subordinate to the community's right to all."[18] Even life itself becomes the possession of the state: "When the prince has said to him, 'it is expedient for the state that you should die,' he should die. Because it is under this condition alone that he has lived in security up to then, and because his life is not only a kindness of nature, but a conditional gift of the state."[19]

For Rousseau, it is not necessary to ask "who is to make the laws, since they are the acts of the general will . . . nor whether a law can be unjust, since no one is unjust to himself, nor how one is both free and subject to the laws, since they are merely the record of our own wills."[20] Popular sovereignty has been combined with the elimination of any conception of law that transcends the will of the majority, and this created a seismic shift in the development of liberalism, for, as John Hallowell remarks, liberalism "was based upon an uneasy compromise between two conflicting principles: the idea of the autonomy of individual will and reason and the idea of a higher law."[21] Once the commitment to a higher law was removed, the stage was set for the dramatic expansion of political power. It is perhaps no wonder that Bertrand de Jouvenel remarks that democracy—and here we must include liberal democracy—is "the time of tyranny's incubation."[22]

Rousseau is obsessed with the unity of the polity, a unity that brooks no minority opposition, or what he calls "partial association," which is to say, local communities within a whole.[23] The idea of a pluralistic society where individuals are free to associate with whom they choose rather than be equally united to the whole is, for Rousseau, a sign of the decay of the political community: "When private interests begin to make themselves felt and small societies begin to influence the large one, the common interest changes and finds opponents. Unanimity no longer reigns in the votes; the general will is no longer the will of all."[24] Thus, strong and independent local communities are, for Rousseau, a measure of the weakness of the state. As Robert Nisbet puts it, "True community for Rousseau is not anything arising out of kinship, religion, ethnicity, or language. True community lies only within the purview of the state."[25] Tradition, in other words, is not the measure or the context of healthy communities. Instead, the unified state replaces these localized and particularized sources of attachment and serves as the locus of both affection and power.

There is a logic to this development. The first wave of liberalism (call it the "moderate" wave) began with a picture of autonomous individuals in a state of nature who join in an act of consent and thereby legitimate the exercise of power. Metaphysical speculation or religious dogma seemed both too questionable and too divisive to provide an adequate foundation for a human polity. An alternative was needed. As George Sabine puts it, "Convinced that it must start from what was self-evident, modern philosophy could find nothing apparently so solid and indubitable as individual human nature. . . . Not man as a priest or a soldier, as the member of a guild or an estate, but man as a bare human being, a 'masterless man,' appeared to be the solid fact."[26]

However, although this collection of concepts—the autonomous individual, state of nature, consent, and so on—was indeed radical, and any explicit fidelity to the authority of tradition was ostensibly rejected in favor of a purely rationalistic approach to human affairs, a complete rejection was not so easily accomplished. As Nisbet puts it, "The image of the people that glowed in the minds of such men as Jefferson was composed of elements supplied, actually, by a surrounding society strong in its social institutions and memberships. . . . The symbols of liberalism, like the bells of the church, depend on prejudgments and social tradition."[27] In other words, moderate liberalism could be moderate because it was nourished by a rich soil of nonliberal elements inherited from the past and embodied in habits and practices that provided limits to the impulse to liberation. The American Founding occurred in this context. The French Revolution, only a few years later, occurred in a milieu where the social soil was not nearly as healthy, and therefore the limits that served to temper the American Founding were largely absent. The ideals of liberty, fraternity, and equality (admirable ideals when they exist in a proper context) ran to extremes, and rather than giving birth to a new order of liberty, the French Revolution descended into chaos and bloodshed, and power returned with a vengeance in the form of a dictator, Napoleon.

Liberalism's second wave (the elements of which were present at the very beginning in the philosophical atomism of Hobbes) represents a more radical and thorough realization of the ideal of autonomy. In reality it is merely a more honest version of liberalism, for first wave liberalism depended in practice on habits and traditions that it denied in theory. Liberalism in its pure sense turns on the absolutely free and unencumbered choice of the autonomous individual. As Michael Sandel puts it, "For the liberal self, what matters above all, what is most essential to our personhood, is not the ends we choose but our capacity to choose them." The liberal self is conceived as "free and independent, unencumbered by the aims and attachments it does not choose for itself."[28]

On one level, it seems intuitively correct to claim that liberty is inseparable from some notion of self-determination. If I cannot choose what I will do, where I will live, and with whom I will associate, it is difficult to claim that I am truly free. However, the logic of liberalism turns out to be a caustic acid that burns away anything that could plausibly limit the infinite exercise of individual will. Thus, with the decline of Christianity, the theological limits that once served to moderate the impulses of liberalism were set aside. With the rejection of final causation, and therefore of any notion of teleology, the belief that nature was normatively ordered and that there were certain activities conducive to human flourishing (and therefore certain activities that thwarted flourishing) was rejected. In short, neither God nor nature was any longer seen as a reliable (or even real) guide to ordering a good life. The only legitimate guide was the unencumbered will. Choice became the exclusive currency, and anything that thwarted choice was seen as an affront to freedom.

This absolutism of choice is clearly manifest in the words of Justice Kennedy in his 1992 opinion in *Planned Parenthood v. Casey*: "At the heart of liberty is the right to define one's own concept of existence, of meaning, of the universe, and of the mystery of human life."[29] This all-encompassing affirmation of the infinite range of the autonomous self represents the apex of second wave liberalism where the autonomous self has rejected any authority, tradition, or limit. We see the implications of this expansive notion of liberty today when, for instance, the designations of male and female are denied as nothing more than social constructions, which is to say, the arbitrary imposition of a social limit to which I have not consented. All categories that were once seen as somehow rooted in nature or even in the divine order have been rendered fluid and subject to nothing other than my will. And, of course, my will can change, so a personal pronoun I insist upon today may be a source of grave offense if you employ it tomorrow. Freedom becomes, in this empire of liberation, unpredictable, capricious, and eventually tyrannical.

Another way to conceive of the difference between first and second wave liberalism is this: first wave liberalism, because it relied (despite its explicit claims) on resources rooted in tradition, entailed a general agreement about substantive goods, including some notion of the good life, both individually and corporately. Second wave liberalism is characterized by an increasingly explicit and energetic rejection of any claim to a universal, substantive good. What matters in second wave liberalism is merely a procedural framework that creates the maximal space for individuals to determine their own good. First wave liberalism had space (perhaps unintentionally) for both substantive and procedural goods; however, as the denigration of tradition continued to work its way through institutions, practices, and habits of mind, the substantive good necessarily had to give way to the good conceived merely in procedural terms. When second wave liberalism became fully mature, all claims to substantive goods had to be reduced to mere subjective and individual choice. The stage was set for the most sweeping conception of freedom imaginable, one completely bereft of any explicit limits, save those to which the individual voluntarily submitted.

In short, although first wave liberalism was moderate and in many ways beneficial to those living under its sway, it was inherently unstable, for what stability it enjoyed was the result of assets surreptitiously retained from a preliberal past. It was theoretically compromised but practically conducive to political freedom. Second wave liberalism, on the other hand, may initially appear more theoretically consistent, but it eventually becomes absolutist and thereby undermines the very liberty it ostensibly seeks to champion. Liberalism, in other words, when it matures beyond its conflicted adolescent version, consumes itself. When fully mature, it gives birth to a grotesque and deformed offspring of insatiable appetite that at least some of the inventors of liberalism—namely Hobbes and Rousseau—intuited: illiberal liberalism.[30]

COSMOPOLITANISM

Rousseau insists that his ideal republic must be relatively small and that "the larger the state becomes, the less liberty there is."[31] Thus, the notion of "an extended republic," as Madison puts it, where liberty is maximized, would be for Rousseau a misguided aspiration. Of course, today in the United States the ideal of a small republic—as championed by Rousseau, Montesquieu, and the Anti-Federalists—has faded, and the large republic, and even political institutions that extend beyond the nation-state, has emerged—despite Rousseau's insistence—as the logical corollary to liberalism.

The rise of individualism is an important part of this story. Individualism is today celebrated by people on both the Right and the Left.

People on the Right often speak of rugged individualism, by which they mean some form of can-do independence, and they often balk at the language of community, which sounds suspiciously like communism. People on the Left frequently speak of the right of individuals to choose, and this is generally most pronounced in the context of sex, identity, and reproductive issues. However, both Left and Right frame their political self-understanding in terms of individual rights and take offense at the notion of limits on individual liberty.

For Rousseau, and for Hobbes, the only two legitimate nodes of political existence are the individual and the unified state. Intermediate institutions, local affiliations, and traditions that suggest limits on the behavior of the individual or constraints on the power of the state are seen as impediments to both the freedom of the individual and the unity of the state. This combination of individualism and the monolithic state sets the stage for a toxic combination of liberty without limits and a cosmopolitan political and social ideal where local differences—embodied in particular traditions—are subsumed under the rubric of unity. Thus we have the ideal of the autonomous chooser combined with a cosmopolitan impulse that seeks to eradicate differences, even as it celebrates the unconstrained choices of individuals. This combination of ideals can be summed up as the *liberal cosmopolitan state*. Such a state champions individual liberty, despises limits, and at the same time seeks unity, even if that unity compromises the liberty of some, who will, in Rousseau's words, be forced to be free. Again, illiberalism lurks in the dark interior of the liberal edifice.

Of course, cosmopolitanism is not a new idea; it has existed since antiquity. However, the liberal self finds a natural complement in the cosmopolitan ideal that gives the latter a plausibility and a practical efficacy that is unprecedented. Cosmopolitanism is, in short, a natural corollary to liberalism. Cosmopolitanism is a dream that animates the liberal imagination and provides a unifying narrative of political and social progress toward a world no longer beset by the differences of particular localities, traditions, and ideas. It is the dream that drives globalization, that "inevitable" force that will one day soon unite us all. However galling it may be to those who are charmed by such a vision, there are some who reject it outright and many who instinctively recoil from it. The ongoing tension between those who advocate a universal, cosmopolitan state of affairs (where nation-states are subsumed into international bodies) and those who resist such a vision in the name of national sovereignty and the goodness of local autonomy suggests that it is appropriate to consider a discussion of tradition in light of what we might term the "liberal cosmopolitan dream."

When people use the term in casual conversation, "cosmopolitan" generally refers to a disposition of urbane sophistication, a person who is not blinkered by the prejudices and limited experience of the provincial, the uneducated, and the narrow-minded. The cosmopolitan is one who exhibits tolerance rather than xenophobia, reason rather than prejudice, universalism rather than localism. The cosmopolitan considers himself a citizen of the world and views other affiliations as secondary to his universal embrace. He is suspicious of patriotism and fearful of nationalism. His community knows no limits; rather, the embrace of his imagination, if not his actual affections, extends to all humanity. Tradition, for the cosmopolitan, is an impediment to the universalized future that is the object of his dreams. The liberal cosmopolitan dares to dream of a world that has broken free from the confines and local particularities of tradition. Unfortunately, the headlong attempt to ignore or destroy tradition in an effort to usher in a unified cosmopolitan age has set the table for both philosophical error and social disaster.

It is important to recognize, however, that the word "cosmopolitanism" is used in a variety of ways. On the one hand, this flexibility points to the usefulness of the term; however, it also invariably creates confusion as various meanings slide past each other making effective communication about the concept frustratingly elusive. In an attempt to clarify the concept, a bit of history is helpful.

The Stoics are generally recognized as the first to fully develop a vision of cosmopolitanism. Cicero, for instance, argues that all men are joined by a common law that is rooted in reason and ultimately born of God:

> Law in the proper sense is right reason in harmony with nature. It is spread through the whole human community, unchanging and eternal, calling people to their duty by its commands and deterring them from wrong-doing by its prohibitions. . . . There will not be one such law in Rome and another in Athens, one now and another in the future, but all peoples at all times will be embraced by a single and eternal and unchangeable law; and there will be, as it were, one lord and master of us all—the god who is the author, proposer, and interpreter of that law.[32]

Here we clearly see Cicero's ethical cosmopolitanism whereby all humans are understood to participate in a natural order, grasped by reason. We are bound by common moral standards and bound by common limits on proper human behavior. We inhabit together a single and unified moral universe. It is important to note, though, that the emphasis is on the moral cosmos. There is no suggestion that a political cosmopolitanism, an actual universal *polis*, is necessarily entailed in the moral claim.

Roman emperor Marcus Aurelius, a Stoic, affirms law's connection to reason, but he both secularizes it and emphasizes political cosmopolitanism along with the ethical: "If the intellectual capacity is common to all, common too is the reason, which makes us rational beings. If so, we share reason which tells us what ought and ought not to happen in common. If so, we are fellow-members of a republic. If so, the cosmos is like a city—for in what other single polity can the whole human race belong in common?"[33] By this time (the late second century AD), of course, the *polis* as the normative political entity had been replaced by the idea of empire. With this expansive political reality, the ethical and political elements join together into a form of cosmopolitanism that, at least imaginatively, links humans not only morally but also politically.

In the modern age, Kant is a key figure in the history of cosmopolitanism. He memorably argues for an ethical universalism in the form of his categorical imperative. Persons are to be treated as ends and never merely as means. These persons legislate as citizens in a kingdom of ends where each rational creature acts as both legislator and sovereign. However, Kant's ethical cosmopolitanism differs from Cicero's. Reason is severed from nature. Man is autonomous. The god of Cicero is replaced by reason alone. This secularized version of ethical universalism goes hand-in-hand with a political vision. In *Perpetual Peace*, Kant writes,

> The peoples of the earth have thus entered in varying degrees into a universal community, and it has developed to the point where a violation of rights in *one* part of the world is felt *everywhere*. The idea of a cosmopolitan right is therefore not fantastic and overstrained; it is a necessary complement to the unwritten code of political and international right, transforming it into a universal right of humanity.[34]

In Kant, both ethical and political cosmopolitanism emerge in bold relief.

One of the foremost advocates of cosmopolitanism today is Jürgen Habermas. For Habermas, the alternatives before us are few and stark. We can either actively and intentionally work to realize the Kantian vision of a peaceful cosmopolitan order, or we can descend into an aggressive and likely violent tribalism.[35] As Habermas puts it, "Even if we still have a long way to go before fully achieving it, the cosmopolitan condition is no longer merely a mirage. State citizenship and world citizenship form a continuum whose contours, at least, are already becoming visible."[36]

In addition to Habermas, Martha Nussbaum is a leading contemporary champion of cosmopolitanism. According to Nussbaum, the cosmopolitan is "the person whose primary allegiance is to the community of human beings."[37] Allegiances to what Burke called the "little platoons" is secondary, and even trivial, for the demands of universal justice trump anything less than universal membership in humanity itself. Nussbaum writes, "If we really do believe that all humans beings are created equal and endowed with certain inalienable rights, we are morally required to think about what that conception requires us to do with and for the rest of the world."[38] Nussbaum realizes that such an expansive claim makes her vulnerable to those who offer up a commonsense objection: Isn't it a good thing that mothers, for instance, prefer their own children over all the other children in the world? Are not particular affections and affiliations the necessary glue that holds communities together? That make life sweet? In reply, Nussbaum argues that we can, in fact, justify giving special care for those in our own limited spheres, but we must do so in universalist terms. Universal ends, she asserts, are more efficiently realized when individuals attend to the particular individuals within their narrow spheres of influence.[39]

Nussbaum bears her cosmopolitanism like a cross: "Becoming a citizen of the world is often a lonely business. It is, as Diogenes said, a kind of exile—from the comfort of local truth, from the warm, nestling feeling of patriotism, from the absorbing drama of pride in oneself and one's own. . . . Cosmopolitanism offers no such refuge; it offers only reason and the love of humanity, which may seem at times less colorful than other sources of belonging."[40] Apparently, only the strong and brave lovers of humanity can muster the courage to be cosmopolitans. The rest of us hunker down in the refuge of our patriotism, prejudice, traditions, and local affections. Of course, the love of humanity is a curious ideal. How is it possible to love an abstraction? Can one feed humanity? Can one embrace humanity? Can one console suffering humanity? No. One can only love, feed, and console particular human beings. Nussbaum's apparently high-minded assertions bring to mind the character in Dostoyevsky's *The Brothers Karamazov* who noted that he loves humanity but finds individual human beings intolerable.

More recently, apparently realizing that a moral system that cannot provide a stronger justification for particular affections than "it's a more efficient way to realize universal ends," Nussbaum has modified her position: "Further thought . . . persuaded me that the denial of particular attachments leaves life empty of meaning for most of us."[41] It is striking that such a banal conclusion would require "further thought." One would hope that the lived lives of humans the world over would make it obvious that a meaningful life necessarily requires "particular attachments." What, after all, is friendship?

As one who embraces the basic contours of Rawlsian thought, Nussbaum follows in his metaphysically austere footsteps: "I now think it crucial that the political principles of a decent society not include comprehensive ethical or metaphysical doctrines that could not be endorsed by reasonable citizens holding a wide range of comprehensive doctrines."[42] However, she admits that "the moral sentiments on which Rawls relies are a bit too transparently rationalistic."[43] Thus, even though she is somewhat dubious about the rationalist flavor of the Rawlsian cosmopolitan project, she remains committed to the general ends toward which it strives. Nussbaum ultimately attempts to argue for a "purified patriotism," one that defends the liberal state as the normatively decent society.[44] Nussbaum's purified patriotism, of course, shuns any hint of nationalism or prejudice and instead makes it possible to embrace one's nation only to the extent that it realizes the goals of liberty and equality as understood by the liberal cosmopolitan. Thus, the citizens of a modern liberal state could, in these terms, legitimately express a patriotic love of country, while a citizen of any other type of polity throughout human history could not. One is tempted here to accuse Nussbaum of her own brand of provincialism even as she attempts to outline the contours of her cosmopolitanism.

In addition to ethical and political cosmopolitanism evident in thinkers such as Kant and Nussbaum, there is another form that, though related, deserves a separate discussion. Some thinkers on both the Left and the Right have expressed concern about the homogenization of culture. The pervasive influence of the global economy, global politics, and the technological extension of the imagination makes it increasingly possible to see oneself as a citizen of a global culture, even as local and particular cultures are drowned in the wave of commonality and sameness. We might term this "cultural cosmopolitanism," and although neither ethical nor political cosmopolitanism requires cultural cosmopolitanism, both are potentially facilitated by it.

Of course, some degree of cultural cosmopolitanism has always existed. Through travel and trade, individuals have encountered other cultures and in the process have adopted practices foreign to their native ways. However, this kind of cultural exchange has exponentially increased with technologies developed in the twentieth century. Today a person can travel with relative ease and great speed to virtually any part of the world. The so-called global economy brings people and interests together like never before, even as it fosters common tastes and habits. Cell phones and e-mail have made instant communication possible, and television and the Internet have brought forth a common means of accessing and consuming information on a global scale.

Some of our most ubiquitous technologies complement and even exacerbate the liberal self. Consider the iPhone, whose very name suggests the isolated self as the locus of concern. The ubiquity of the "selfie" is a symbolic representation of the self-referential nature of some of our most pervasive technologies. The digitalization of time is another, perhaps less obvious, change that favors the autonomous self. The sweep of an analog clock that suggests the presence of both the past and the future is replaced by the immediacy of the moment delinked from any temporal context. Our digitalized technologies have increased our capacities but at the same time tutored our imaginations to see only discrete bits of time divorced from anything beyond the immediate. As a result, we are tempted to see ourselves as discrete atoms unattached to any temporal context—and certainly not as inheritors of cultural gifts and responsibilities.

One aspect of this increasingly globalized culture is the necessary triumph of pop culture. Of course, high culture has always been the purview of a minority. It requires work to grasp, and the rewards are not immediate. On the other hand, pop culture goes down easily, requires virtually no effort, and is consumed at the touch of a button. The ascendance of a global pop culture has seriously undermined local folk culture, which is necessarily tied to a particular locality and is rooted in local skill and participation in a set of local traditions. Folk music, folk dance, local arts and crafts require apprenticeship and a willingness to labor under the authority of a particular tradition. For this reason, folk culture can never be cosmopolitan.

What the rise of cultural cosmopolitanism suggests is the emergence of a vision that is not merely the abstract dream of a philosopher but one in which the brotherhood of humanity can be imagined in concrete terms, where barriers of language and culture—which is to say, the barriers of tradition—are gradually eroded by the ongoing influence of commercial, communications, and entertainment technologies. Surely this is a practical advance of the Kantian vision, one that can be appreciated not only by a philosopher but by anyone who eats a Big Mac while watching reruns of *Friends* on the Internet. In the cloud of euphoria, though, it would be well to ask if there are any drawbacks to one or more of these cosmopolitanisms.

To begin, it is my contention that we should move beyond conceiving the social and political landscape in terms of a struggle between left and right or even between liberals and conservatives, as those terms are popularly employed today. Instead, I want to suggest that our situation today is best conceived as a conflict between those who advocate some version of liberal cosmopolitanism (along with its reactionary offspring, identity politics) and those who instead uphold the idea of tradition along with the inherent limits—social, natural, and metaphysical—that such a position entails. Around the world we see tensions between local autonomy movements and the nation-state and between nation-states and transnational political entities. There are moral and political debates that reveal the depth of the philosophical divisions. It is not difficult to think of examples. Here are several:

(1) The vote in the United Kingdom in the summer of 2016 to leave the European Union is a practical illustration of the conflict between those who affirm the propriety of local or national distinctions and those who dream of a universal cosmopolitan state.

(2) We see the same division from a different angle in the tension between the techno-optimists, who believe that limitless technological progress will save us from whatever crises we may encounter (many created by our own technologies) and those who are skeptical that such limitless progress will lead to the happy outcomes imagined by the optimists.

(3) The current debates centering on marriage, sexuality, and gender identity are illustrative of a sharp philosophical divide with real practical

implications. One side affirms some notion of limits, rooted in tradition, nature, or metaphysics, while the other side denies any limits other than individual preference. One side, in other words, affirms the existence of a human nature that contains within itself ends proper to human flourishing and therefore certain limits on proper human behavior, and the other side denies such a nature and affirms a nominalist conception of the human person whereby all limits are perceived as arbitrary impediments to individual choice.

(4) The disruptions on college and university campuses by students (with the tacit or explicit aid of some faculty) should remind us that the spirit of Rousseau is alive and well, even (and perhaps especially) among those who have never read him but have nevertheless drunk deeply from the well of his thought. When speech codes, trigger warnings, and safe spaces proliferate, when free speech is permitted only when it conforms to the will of the most powerful (or most vocal), and when those advocating ideas that run contrary to the prevailing ideology are silenced by violence or the threat thereof, the spirit of illiberal liberalism has triumphed. Those in the minority will be "forced to be free," and freedom becomes a caricature of itself.

(5) The recent debate about national borders is a practical indication of the tension between those who advocate some notion of limits and those cosmopolitans who dream of a world without borders. Borders, of course, represent limits. The liberal cosmopolitan sees borders as an unjust physical limit on the free movement of individuals, which is to say, unjust limits on the free expression of the self. For those who recognize and submit to limits—moral, cultural, religious, and natural—borders represent a reasonable way of framing the political and social landscape.

These debates will not end soon or be easily resolved, for they go far deeper than prudential questions of how best to govern. These differences are ultimately rooted in two profoundly different ways of seeing the world and of two profoundly different ways of understanding the human condition.

The Brexit vote in July 2016 followed by Donald Trump's "surprise" win in November of the same year should be understood as part of the same movement that, though not a tsunami, represents a clear challenge to the liberal cosmopolitan agenda that champions internationalism over nationalism, promotes an abstract global community over concrete local affiliations, and celebrates the inevitability of globalization. The fact that globalization has suffered a series of recent setbacks must be galling (not to mention confusing) to those convinced that it represents the inevitable logic of history.[45] President Obama, in his farewell address to the United Nations, expressed his concern and laid out his vision for a more unified world: "I believe that at this moment we all face a choice. We can choose to press forward with a better model of cooperation and integration. Or we can retreat into a world sharply divided, and ultimately in conflict, along age-old lines of nation and tribe and race and religion."[46] There are, in Obama's mind, two stark choices: liberal cosmopolitanism or the violence and unrest of nationalism, tribalism, and wars motivated by race and religion; cosmopolitan peace or the violence of identity politics. However, as we will see, these are not opposite alternatives but different manifestations of the same impulse.

Admittedly, Donald Trump was an odd messenger of the working class left behind in the euphoria of globalization. But many who witnessed the decimation of their communities along with the flight of capital and talent were led to question whether what benefits the purveyors of abstractions is equally beneficial to the rest. It goes without saying that Trump was no defender of tradition and surely no coherent advocate of limits. However, his America First rhetoric touched a chord that lay long unsounded by national leaders. His emphasis on securing the nation's borders pushed against the cosmopolitan dream of a world without borders where citizens of the world (and therefore of nowhere in particular) wander the planet seeking wealth, pleasure, and diversion. His refusal to submit to the strictures of political correctness endeared him to many (or at least earned him a grudging respect of those) who intuit that sanity rooted in common sense has fled the field under an onslaught of powerful and self-righteous individuals and institutions hell-bent on compelling all citizens to conform to standards that grow increasingly bizarre.

In short, the rise of Trump and Trumpism represents a reaction against forces—both on the left and right—openly hostile to local communities, limits, and certain aspects of orthodox Christianity. These are the ones who, as President Obama put it, "cling to their guns and religion." Trumpism represents a reaction against both cosmopolitanism and identity politics, which together constitute the bulk of the Democratic Party (and elements of the Republican Party, albeit in different ratios). However, at the same time, Trump's victory does not represent a nonliberal reaction (except on the fringes) but rather a largely visceral attempt to recover the conditions and benefits of first wave liberalism.

At first blush it appears that identity politics is the polar opposite of cosmopolitanism. Identity politics is a plausible response by those individuals who perceive they have been left behind—economically, socially, or politically—by the advances of globalization, or who intuit the vacuity of the cosmopolitan dream. Seeking an alternative to a comprehensive globalizing vision, some retreat into identity groups and seek status by means of grievance. They seek membership rooted in actual or historically appropriated offenses. Identity becomes the lens by which all of reality is read just as the cosmopolitan dream imposes itself upon the historical narrative of its adherents. Both ideologies are totalizing. Both are pseudoreligions with confessions, catechesis, soteriologies (theories of salvation), ecclesiologies (theories of membership), eschatologies (theories of the future), heretics, and martyrs.

Identity politics represents a uniquely modern form of political action, and it spawns a reactionary image of itself. It is modern insofar as it employs moral categories that are universalist and emerge out of a consciousness that tacitly affirms the universal membership of humans in a single community, even as groups within that community condemn other groups for ostensibly denying some entrance into that community. Identity politics traffics in the heightened concern for justice—inherited from the Christian tradition—that is the mark of the modern world. It seeks to right historic wrongs that have provided ongoing advantages to certain groups and excluded others. Identity politics only emerges in a hyperegalitarian context whereby members aspire to universal liberation from the injustices of the past. It is born in a hypersensitive age where any inequality is seen as an affront to liberty or dignity. However, identity politics also has a reactionary side, and this is clearly seen in the revitalization of white supremacy groups who see themselves as the perpetual targets of the grievances of race-based identity politics. The identity politics of the Left complements, and even calls forth, this emerging identity politics of the Right, a reactionary version of identity politics that tends to embed itself in the rhetoric of blood and soil and has many characteristics of a neopagan revival rather than a secular church.

Herein lies the gambit. On the one hand we see the continued support, on both the left and the right, for some version of liberal cosmopolitanism. At the same time the identity politics of the Left, along with immigration without assimilation, is serving to energize a reactionary identity politics of the Right. For some time we have heard of the rise of ultranationalist parties, of neo-Nazism, and violence against immigrants in certain European countries. Many of the most ardent opponents of Trump argued that the same forces are incubating in the United States and were nourished by Trump's victory. To be sure, a new tribalism characterized by xenophobia, violence, and suspicion of "the other" is a real possibility. Is the only alternative to either left- or right-wing tribalism some version of liberal cosmopolitanism? Neither alternative is attractive. However, it may be possible to imagine a third way that avoids the pitfalls inherent in both tribalism and liberal cosmopolitanism. Carving out this third way is a central goal of this book.

TRADITION

This third way turns on a rediscovery of the epistemic necessity of tradition and of the value of resources latent in our inherited traditions. Consequentially, it turns on a recognition that the liberal self is a myth that, because of the nature of knowing, simply cannot exist. The bulk of chapters 2, 3, and 4 will be spent exploring the role of tradition in the knowing process, but it might be useful at the outset to consider some of the different ways tradition has been conceived.

According to the sociologist Anthony Giddens, tradition as a concept is a relatively recent invention. For most of human history, societies were so deeply embedded in tradition that it was, in effect, invisible.[47] Or to put matters somewhat differently, the fact that you are reading a book about tradition per se—rather than about a specific tradition or set of traditions—indicates that you occupy a particular place in history and a critical perspective that is relatively recent. According to Giddens, tradition "defines a kind of truth."[48] Traditions are essential to any society, for "they give continuity and form to life."[49] Today the concept of tradition has retreated, and we find ourselves with greater autonomy and freedom but also with unprecedented anxiety and an acute susceptibility to addictions, for the guidance provided by tradition has been lost and we find ourselves adrift on a boundless sea of autonomy.[50] For Giddens, tradition often suffers from commercialization that transmutes it into kitsch, and the rise of various fundamentalisms represents nothing other than "beleaguered tradition."[51]

The German philosopher Joseph Pieper emphasizes the active aspect of tradition. The Latin *tradere* means "to hand over or surrender." But as soon as we conceive of tradition in this way, it becomes clear that we are speaking of two partners in the process: one who transfers and one who receives.[52] The person transferring the tradition is the authority, and receiving the tradition requires submission to that authority. However, the tradition is not authoritative simply because it is "traditional" or "ancient." It is authoritative, and therefore the person transferring it is authoritative, precisely because "I am convinced that it is true and valid."[53] In theology, authority rests in the proximity of the speaker to an original revelation; therefore, the antiquity of the source is inseparable from its authority. On the other hand, in the practice of science, the authority is the one who has made the most recent discovery.[54] And whereas science is characterized by a continual development as new discoveries add to the body of knowledge that is transmitted, the goal of sacred tradition "is always to represent *identically* what was originally shared with mankind from a divine source.[55]

The theologian Jaroslav Pelikan distinguishes between a vibrant, living tradition that can accommodate change while maintaining its identity and what he calls "traditionalism," which is ossified and rigid. As he puts it, "Tradition is the living faith of the dead, traditionalism is the dead faith of the living."[56] A tradition is living, according to Pelikan, precisely because it is not a self-contained imposition of the past onto the present. Instead, it is "a mark of an authentic and living tradition that it points us beyond itself."[57] Tradition, in other words, embodies truth in a particularized form.

The sociologist Edward Shils defines tradition in a way that is, perhaps, most closely in keeping with common usage: "Traditions are beliefs, standards, and rules, of varying but never exhaustive explicitness, which have been received from the preceding generations through a process of continuous transmission from generation to generation."[58] However, for Shils, tradition is not merely habits and practices incidental to a particular community. Instead, tradition "establishes contact between the recipient and the sacred values of his life in society."[59] This is true even in secular societies, for "the sacred must be acknowledged to exist in 'secular' societies. It finds expression, together with other beliefs, in the laws and customs of a society, in the written constitution, and, above all, in the unwritten expectations which govern conduct."[60] At the same time, traditions require constant attention, for "traditions are not independently self-reproductive or self-elaborating. Only living, knowing, desiring human beings can enact them and modify them." According to Shils, "Traditions develop because the desire to create something truer and better or more convenient is alive in those who acquire and possess them." However, "Traditions can deteriorate in the sense of losing their adherents because those who once received and reenacted and extended them now prefer other lines of conduct or because new generations to which they were presented find other traditions of belief or some relatively new beliefs more acceptable, according to the standards which these generations accept."[61]

In the pages of this book much more will be said about tradition. Suffice it at this point to note that there are a variety of approaches, some more compelling than others.[62] However, there are common threads that connect these different views, and we will spend considerable time working through both the similarities and the differences, and in so doing we will seek to establish an adequate definition of the concept.

At the outset, though, it might be helpful to indicate three different senses of tradition, each employed throughout this work: (1) "tradition" will be used to describe an epistemic concept that is a necessary and unavoidable ingredient in the knowing process; (2) "tradition" will also be used to indicate an idea's participation in what some have called the "Great Tradition" or the "Western Tradition," where tradition in this sense aspires toward universality; and (3) "tradition" will also be used to indicate local traditions carried along in songs, stories, crafts, and folk art, which are typically limited, and their essence lost if they are forced into a universal mode. How are these related? I will argue that the main thrust of the modern mind is characterized by a rejection of the authority of tradition. The epistemic role of tradition is denied, and once that happens, the other forms of tradition are treated with suspicion or outright disdain. Or to put matters differently, the liberal self denies the epistemic necessity of tradition and therefore is inclined to deny the authority of both the great tradition and local subordinate traditions, and shuns the limits implied by both. The cosmopolitan aspires to a kind of tradition-free universality that does war against the great tradition and against the local traditions by which our self-understanding is framed and which ground our loves in local goods and thereby nurture affections that extend beyond the local. Although "Tradition" will be used in all three of these senses, I think it will be clear from the context what meaning is intended.

The West has, for several centuries, been moving steadily toward the liberal conception of the self and its attendant cosmopolitan vision, but we do well to consider the coherence of these related positions. To that end, I want to begin with two figures often associated with the rise of the modern world: Francis Bacon and René Descartes. What is striking about each (and these two are merely representatives of a general trend of the time) is that they despise tradition. They are convinced that if they simply throw off the false limits imposed by the past and apply a particular method, individuals will acquire the knowledge and therefore the control of the world that has hitherto proved elusive.

In this regard, it is useful to point out that Alexis de Tocqueville argued that the America he visited in 1831 was the country "where the precepts of Descartes are least studied and best followed."[63] This claim provides a vital intimation that he expands upon only a few paragraphs later: "In the seventeenth-century Bacon, in natural science, and Descartes, in philosophy strictly so called, abolished accepted formulas, destroyed the dominion of tradition, and upset the authority of masters."[64] However, Tocqueville admits that even though the method of Descartes (and by implication Bacon) was intended to be applied only in a limited field, it was eventually applied to everything.[65] Before the new methodology could be universalized, certain habits of mind had to be overcome. However, by the eighteenth century these impediments had been largely dissolved, and the United States, and the Western world as a whole, came under the sway of a totalizing methodology rooted in Baconian science and Cartesian philosophical assumptions. However, despite the apparent success of this new methodology—characterized by a concerted attempt to reject tradition root and branch—problems lurked beneath the surface. Tocqueville points out some of the social and political consequences, but I want to focus primarily on the philosophical incoherencies. To that end, I will explore in some detail the thought of three twentieth-century thinkers—Michael Oakeshott, Alasdair MacIntyre, and Michael Polanyi—whose work, in various ways, attempts to overturn the Baconian/Cartesian rejection of tradition. In the process it will become necessary to reconsider the liberal conception of the self—a figure more imaginary than real—who is unconstrained, unattached, and absolutely free.

I argue that there is a cancer at the heart of the liberal cosmopolitan dream and, by implication, there are practical consequences that serve as outward indicators of this disease. The fundamental flaw turns on a faulty conception of the human person, and this error is inseparable from the way the liberal self views tradition. The practical implications emerge as a dispute between those who acknowledge the authority of tradition—and therefore the reality of limits—and those who champion some version of liberal cosmopolitanism in which differences of practice and belief, rooted in particular traditions, are eradicated in an attempt to realize both the limitlessness and the unity for which the liberal cosmopolitans long. I will argue that finding an alternative to the liberal self is the only avenue by which we can escape the incoherencies and pathologies latent therein. In chapter 5, with reference to Edmund Burke and Augustine, I will outline a tradition-constituted account of liberty that avoids the fatal errors of the liberal self and then conclude with an appeal for what I term humane localism, which avoids succumbing to both cosmopolitanism and identity politics.

CHAPTER 1

The Seventeenth-Century Denigration
of Tradition and a
Nineteenth-Century Response

As soon as I reached an age which allowed me to emerge from the tutelage of my teachers, I abandoned the study of letters altogether, and resolved to study no other science than that which I could find within myself or else in the great book of the world.

—René Descartes[1]

The rejection of Aristotle presaged the wholesale rejection of tradition. The rise of the new science gave rise to suspicions that Aristotle got some things very wrong, which he did. In terms of theology, Martin Luther saw the pervasive influence of Aristotle, via medieval Scholasticism, as a cause of great harm to the Christian faith. Characteristically, Luther's advice was unambiguous. In 1520 he wrote,

My advice would be that Aristotle's *Physics*, *Metaphysics*, *On the Soul*, *Ethics*, which have hitherto been thought his best books, should be altogether discarded, together with all the rest of his books which boast of treating the things of nature. Moreover no one has so far understood his meaning, and many souls have been burdened with profitless labor and study, at the cost of much precious time. I venture to say that any potter has more knowledge of nature than is written in these books. It grieves me to the heart that this damned, conceited, rascally heathen has with his false words deluded and made fools of so many of the best Christians. God has sent him as a plague upon us for our sins.

Luther is especially hostile to *De Anima*, for it does not reflect the Bible's teaching on the immortality of the soul, and to the *Nicomachean Ethics*, which he claims is beyond understanding. However, while claiming that the *Ethics* is incomprehensible, he also claims he understands it better than Aquinas, and he flatly condemns it:

> Again, his book on *Ethics* is the worst of all books. It flatly opposes divine grace and all Christian virtues, and yet it is considered one of his best works. Away with such books! Keep them away from all Christians! Let no one accuse me of exaggeration, or of condemning what I do not understand! My dear friend, I know well whereof I speak. I know my Aristotle as well as you or the likes of you. I have lectured on him and heard lectures on him, and I understand him better than do St. Thomas or Scotus. This I can say without pride, and if necessary I can prove it.

Luther does admit that several of Aristotle's works provide some beneficial insights into logic and rhetoric, but he absolutely rejects the core of Aristotle's account of nature, teleology, ethics, and the soul:

> I should be glad to see Aristotle's books on *Logic*, *Rhetoric*, and *Poetics* retained or used in an abridged form as text-books for the profitable training of young people in speaking and preaching. But the commentaries and notes should be abolished, and as Cicero's *Rhetoric* is read without commentaries and notes, so Aristotle's *Logic* should be read as it is, without such a mass of comments. But now neither speaking nor preaching is learned from it, and it has become nothing but a disputing and a weariness to the flesh.[2]

Rather than seek to improve on Aristotle and thereby work within the tradition to develop it toward a better articulation of reality, Luther simply rejects the tradition. In short, Luther's approach is revolutionary rather than evolutionary, an approach that comes to typify early modern thought. And although Luther's rejection of Aristotle seems more visceral than systematic, he helps to set the table for a systematic and categorical rejection of tradition a century later in the works of Francis Bacon and René Descartes.

FRANCIS BACON AND THE QUEST FOR CONTROL

Francis Bacon (1561–1626) was a man of many talents. He made a career of public service, but his passion was the acquisition of knowledge. Acknowledged as one of the founders of the modern scientific method, Bacon sought to create a firm foundation for the pursuit of knowledge. To this end he proposed his inductive method, by which certain knowledge could be gained through properly guided experimentation. Because he did not assert the existence of innate ideas, as did Descartes, or the reliability of the senses (unless fortified by proper method), he does not fall readily into the rationalist or empiricist camp. Because his inductive method relies upon the proper implementation of experiments, he is perhaps best identified as an experimentalist.

Motive

Bacon frequently speaks in terms of power, domination, and control. He writes that better than seeking power for one's self or one's country is "to endeavor to renew and enlarge the power and empire of mankind in general over the universe."[3] Bacon understands man and nature in adversarial terms. He explains this relationship using the theological doctrine of the Fall, which deprived humans of their position of control. Thus, he begins *The Great Instauration* by explaining his project as an attempt to restore the relationship between "the mind of man and the nature of things" to their "perfect and original condition, or if that may not be, yet reduced to a better condition than that in which it now is."[4] Here we have the first hints of Bacon's high hopes for his new method: the effects of the Fall can, at least in part, be overcome by a proper approach to scientific knowledge. It is no large step, then, to viewing the scientist, who makes this great restoration possible, as the source of a sort of secular salvation. Indeed, Bacon,

in one of his rare agreements with the ancients, remarks that "the introduction of great inventions appears one of the most distinguished of
human actions, and the ancients so considered it; for they assigned divine
honours to the authors of inventions, but only heroic honours to those
who displayed civil merit."[5] The granting of "divine honours" to those who
make great inventions suggests Bacon's priorities and opens the door to
his utopian political vision in *New Atlantis*.

Because man and nature are at enmity with each other, and because
nature frequently exhibits her power over mankind, Bacon seeks "a safe
and convenient approach" so that "by art and the hand of man she is forced
out of her natural state, and squeezed and moulded."[6] But this attempt to
gain the upper hand over nature is not primarily for the purpose of understanding, which, he claims, is the end of traditional Aristotelian methodology; instead, he intends his approach "to command [conquer] nature in
action."[7] In Bacon we see the *vita contemplativa* replaced by the *vita activa*.
The highest form of human life is no longer a life of contemplation but of
action and production.

Thus, Bacon's goal is to assert human control over nature. As he puts
it, "be well assured that I am labouring to lay the foundation, not of any
sect or doctrine, but of human utility and power."[8] The power of which
Bacon speaks, though, is not the raw power of brute force, but rather the
intelligent application of a proper method. Nature, then, must be understood before she can be controlled, for the secret to her control is submission to her rules. Thus, in order to attain the desired ends, it is essential
that humans develop a trustworthy method by which to penetrate nature's
secrets and thereby harness her powers.

Ultimately, though, nature does in fact appear to hold all the cards, for
death is an inescapable certainty. In his essay "Of Death," Bacon opens
with the trenchant statement: "Men fear death, as children fear to go in
the dark."[9] If Bacon was motivated in large part by the desire to subjugate
nature, it follows that he would desire, above all, to bring this greatest of
all natural calamities to submission. Indeed, while briefly mentioning in
passing the Christian view of the afterlife, he seems to hold the view that
great deeds, which produce fame, will serve to perpetuate a person's
memory and thus produce a sort of immortality:

> He that dies in an earnest pursuit is like one that is wounded in hot
> blood; who, for the time, scarce feels the hurt; and therefore a mind
> fixed and bent upon somewhat that is good doth avert the dolours of

death. But above all, believe it, the sweetest canticle is *Nunc dimittis*; when a man hath obtained worthy ends and expectations. Death hath this also, that it openeth the gate, to good fame, and extinguisheth envy.[10]

If pursuing great scientific deeds is, indeed, the path to fame, it is for Bacon also the route to a sort of divinity, or at least the assignation of "divine honours."[11] This is especially relevant in light of Bacon's own justification for his work: "Francis of Verulam reasoned thus with himself, and judged it to be for the interest of the present and future generations that they should be made acquainted with his thoughts."[12] Thus, Bacon's fear of death—which represents the all-encroaching power of nature—at least in part motivated him in his pursuit of that by which nature could finally be overcome.[13]

Doubt

In order to clear the field of contending approaches to knowledge, Bacon begins by arguing that the thinkers preceding him were working according to faulty methods and thus their conclusions were, at best, constructed upon poor foundations and, at worst, false sophisms. Bacon, like Descartes, begins with sweeping skepticism. First, he expresses his doubt of the philosophical work of both the Greeks and the medieval Scholastics; second, he, at least at times, appears to doubt the truths of Christianity; and, finally, he frequently reminds his readers that the senses are not to be trusted, for they often prove unreliable, either by failure or deception.

First, Bacon makes no attempt to disguise his disdain for Greek philosophy: the value of the "wisdom which we have received from the Greeks is but like the boyhood of knowledge, and has the characteristic property of boys: it can talk, but it cannot generate; for it is fruitful of controversies but barren of works."[14] Not only does he target Greek philosophy, he is just as anxious to distance himself from all other schools of thought. In his famous description of the idols of his age, he identifies all prior philosophy as "Idols of the Theater." Of these idols he writes, "We regard all the systems of philosophy hitherto received or imagined, as so many plays brought out and performed, creating fictitious and theatrical worlds."[15]

Second, in spite of his pious rhetoric, Bacon's treatment of Christianity can be interpreted as subversive of traditional Christian belief. Indeed, it does seem plausible that the same person who wrote "they that reverence too much old times are but a scorn to the new"[16] would include antiquated religion in that indictment. Furthermore, Bacon's arguments, themselves, seem at times to lead one to such a conclusion. For example, in his essay titled "Of the Unity of Religion," Bacon argues that the disunity among the various Christian sects provides ammunition to those who would deny its truth. Such disunity, he claims, was "unknown to the heathen. The reason was, because the religion of the heathen consisted rather in rites and ceremonies, than in any constant belief."[17] Thus, according to Bacon, belief is the cause of division, and division is an argument for disbelief.[18] Unity, on the other hand, can be sustained through "rites and ceremonies." Bacon opens his essay "Of Superstition" by asserting that it "were better to have no opinion of God at all, than such an opinion as is unworthy of him." With that in place, Bacon goes on to compile a list of the causes of superstition, the first of which is "pleasing and sensual rites and ceremonies."[19] When the arguments of these two essays are taken together, we can conclude that rites and ceremonies produce (1) unity and (2) superstition. But superstitions must be avoided, for such are certainly opinions unworthy of God. Thus, rites and ceremonies must be dispensed with, for they produce superstition. But, according to his essay "Of the Unity of Religion," without unity atheism is warranted. Thus, since unity is only possible when rites and ceremonies are primary rather than "constant belief" and since rites and ceremonies produce superstition that should be avoided, it follows that agnosticism (if not atheism) is the only path available to the seeker of truth. Such agnosticism (if Bacon does mean to argue in this manner) fits well with the sweeping doubt that is the basis for all he subsequently attempts to construct.

If, on the other hand, we read Bacon as a Christian, whose incongruent arguments lack any unifying theme or intent, then it is at least correct to argue that Bacon believed that the domain of faith is completely removed from that of science, and vice versa. He writes of "the corruption of philosophy by the mixing of it up with superstition and theology . . . [which causes] . . . fantastical philosophy but heretical religion [to] spring from the absurd mixture of matters divine and human." He concludes by asserting an absolute separation of the two: "It is therefore most wise soberly to render unto faith the things that are faith's."[20]

Finally, not only does Bacon seek to cast doubt upon ideas that have developed in history, but he also argues that the very tools that facilitate human knowing are unreliable and therefore should be doubted. In fact, he claims that "by far the greatest impediment and aberration of the human understanding proceeds from the dulness, incompetency, and errors of the senses."[21] To remedy this shortcoming, he proposes not the abolition of all sensory data but the fortification of the senses by means of his method: "I contrive that the office of the sense shall be only to judge of the experiment, and that the experiment itself shall judge of the thing."[22] Furthermore, what he calls the "innate" phantoms of the mind are not produced by the senses, but instead "are inherent in the very nature of the intellect, which is far more prone to error than the sense is." These innate idols distort reality; thus, the mind itself cannot be trusted to accurately represent reality to the knower. Like the senses, the intellect must be supplemented. Thus, Bacon concludes, "the intellect is not qualified to judge except by means of induction, and induction in its legitimate form."[23] Trust in traditional philosophical systems, in the truths of religion, and even the adequacy of the senses and the intellect Bacon deems inadequate and subject to doubt. Bacon, of course, does not long remain mired in skepticism. Indeed, his radical and sweeping doubt merely prepares the way for his new and bold venture.

New Beginnings

The desire to overturn the old and to establish new and uncorrupted foundations is a recurring theme of the early modern philosophers. Bacon is unambiguous on this point. It is perhaps instructive of his intent that a word that occurs repeatedly in his writings is "foundation." Bacon was skeptical of any knowledge derived from traditional foundations: "It is vain to expect any great progress in the sciences by superinducing or engrafting new matters upon old. An instauration must be made from the very foundations, if we do not wish to revolve for ever in a circle, making only some slight and contemptible progress."[24] Because the received way of doing things was comparable to a "magnificent structure without any foundation," Bacon concluded that there "was but one course left, therefore,—to try the whole thing anew upon a better plan, and to commence a total reconstruction of sciences, arts, and all human knowledge, raised upon the proper foundations."[25] This bold declaration indicates the incredible scope of Bacon's ambition, for he is not merely speaking of a scientific reform, but rather of a reconstruction of all of the categories of human knowledge. In addition to the sweeping scope, we should also note

the depth of the proposed purge. He is not speaking of reformation or improvement; he is advocating a revolution. He is proposing something "entirely different from any hitherto known," for although others have
certainly attempted to extend human knowledge, "they have not ventured
to cast themselves completely loose from received opinions."[26]

Bacon's revolution is not primarily one of content but of method.[27] In
order to apply this method, people must first abide by two simple dictums:
"1) to lay aside received opinions and notions [tradition]; 2) to restrain
themselves, till the proper season, from generalization." If these two rules
are followed, and if the method is faithfully applied, Bacon is confident
that all people will "fall into our way of interpretation without the aid of
any art."[28] The results, Bacon assures his readers, will be significant, for no
one should "imagine that this Instauration of mine is a thing infinite and
beyond the power of man, when it is in fact the true end and termination
of infinite error."[29] The offer is tantalizing, for Bacon holds out the promise of certainty and the elimination of error if only the past is erased and
new foundations are laid according to his plan.

Method

One of the central problems with past thinkers, according to Bacon, is that
they "pursued a kind of wandering inquiry, without any regular system of
operations."[30] The key is to "penetrate the more secret and remote parts of
nature . . . by a more certain and guarded method."[31] Since the senses and
the intellect are subject to doubt, Bacon concludes that "our only remaining hope and salvation is to begin the whole labour of the mind again; not
leaving it to itself, but directing it perpetually from the very first, and attaining our end as it were by mechanical aid."[32] The Aristotelian method
of inquiry, which relied on the syllogism and proceeded deductively, was
held by Bacon to serve nothing but the ends of those who sought to win
arguments. Properly conducted experiments are the key; thus "our only
hope, then, is in true induction."[33]

This new method, Bacon admits, shares a common beginning point
with the skeptics, for both start with doubt. But, according to Bacon, "they
roundly assert that nothing can be known; we, that but a small part of nature can be known, by the present method; their next step, however, is to
destroy the authority of the senses and understanding, whilst we invent
and supply them with assistance."[34] Thus, the senses and the intellect,
which are weak and unreliable when left to their own devices, once forti-

fied by the inductive method, become capable of rendering sound judgments. Confidence, then, must be shifted from the senses and the intellect to the method by which they are made reliable.

Equality

Bacon is confident that this method is so universally applicable that its proper use "leads to the discovery of everything else."[35] With such sweeping power and scope, one might suspect that only the specially gifted would be capable of properly wielding this incredible tool. On the contrary, Bacon claims that if his method is correctly understood and applied, "strength and excellency of the wit has but little to do in the matter."[36] Since this method is a "mechanical aid," it need merely be applied consistently to various problems of knowledge. The intellect and the senses are removed from the field of play and are called upon only to read and interpret the results of the experiment. Anyone can proceed along these lines, and knowledge of the past, fidelity to a tradition, or submission to the authority of a master are not required. Instead, all that is needed is (1) doubt (in tradition, the senses, and the intellect) and (2) a method that anyone can employ. Certain knowledge of reality is sure to follow. The individual armed with doubt and a proper method is pitted against the world and, Bacon is confident, will emerge the victor. The political vision that emerges from this scientific instauration is the subject of Bacon's utopian novella, *New Atlantis*.

New Atlantis

Bacon's *New Atlantis* presents the fictional account of a South Sea island existing in what would appear to be Eden-like happiness and bounty. A European ship, its occupants preparing themselves to die for lack of food, happens upon this island paradise, which its inhabitants call Bensalem. The sailors are treated well, their sick cared for, and they slowly come to realize the wonder of this place they have chanced upon. Their leader, though, recognizes the precarious nature of their situation, for they are completely dependent upon their hosts. He reminds his crew that "we are but between death and life; for we are beyond both the old world and the new; and whether ever we shall see Europe, God only knoweth. It is a kind of miracle that brought us hither: and it must be little less that shall bring us hence."[37] (The imagery of being between the old world and the new is not coincidental. This is precisely how Bacon understood the world he inhabited.) Through a series of interviews with the governor, in which the history of Bensalem is described along with an account of a scientific society called Salomon's House, the sailors become convinced that Bensalem is, indeed, a paradise. Having been brought to the island through the uncontrollable forces of nature, they eventually realize that they are free men and determine to remain indefinitely in this place of wonder.

As the account progresses, though, hints of something less desirable begin to emerge. The reader is treated to a description of a ceremony called the "Feast of the Family," in which the father of a family is honored when his offspring reach thirty members. The father, we are told, is called the *Tirsan.* (*Tirsan,* incidentally, is a Persian word meaning "timid" or "fearful.")[38] The elaborate ceremony concludes with all who are present proclaiming, in a somewhat eerie fashion, "Happy are the people of Bensalem."[39] In a meeting with one of the Fathers of Salomon's House, the narrator is treated to an explanation of "the true state of Salomon's House."[40] This highly respected leader explains that the "end of our Foundation is the knowledge of Causes, and secret motions of things; and the enlarging of the bounds of Human Empire, to the effecting of all things possible."[41] He then goes on to describe the various and marvelous ways that nature is controlled for the purpose of scientific advancement. The reader, though, must be somewhat suspicious when the Father of Salomon's House goes on to state that the discoveries made by the scientists are not automatically given up to the public. For the scientists "all take an oath of secrecy, for the concealing of those [discoveries] we think fit to keep secret: though some of those we do reveal sometimes to the state, and some not."[42] They do, he explains, "publish such new profitable inventions as we think good."[43] When the interview is over, the Father of Salomon's House dismisses the narrator with permission to publish all he has learned "for the good of other nations."[44] For Bacon, knowledge is power, and it becomes clear that the scientists of Salomon's House firmly grasp that fact.

In an essay titled "Of Wisdom for a Man's Self," Bacon notes that "the referring of all to a man's self is more tolerable in a sovereign prince; because themselves are not only themselves, but their good and evil is at the peril of the public fortune."[45] Thus, whoever is in charge of the public good is justified in making himself the center, of referring all to himself. It appears, then, that Bacon believes that when his method is embraced, the scientists should control the power (knowledge), and they should assume the reins of authority, which under a less enlightened system are given to leaders based upon hereditary titles or even popular will. The fact that the patriarchs of each family are called *Tirsan* only serves to highlight the docile nature of the subjects who would willingly submit to this benign, though pervasive, form of control, which maintains its power through oaths of secrecy and by intentionally withholding information that might empower the people and thereby jeopardize the power monopoly of the scientists. Thus, if *New Atlantis* is any indication, it appears that Bacon's quest for dominance over nature ultimately also includes dominance of human nature.[46] Politically, the vision laid out in *New Atlantis* appears strikingly similar to what Tocqueville described as equality in servitude.

Conclusion

Bacon strongly criticizes the traditional approaches to inquiry, which he thought hopelessly inadequate. Furthermore, he expresses his distrust of the senses and the intellect. Thus, the starting point for his inquiry is pervasive doubt. To remedy this unhappy situation he offers his inductive method, which, if properly applied, will produce "certain" results. Because the method is simple, anyone is capable of applying it; thus, truth is simply and immediately accessible to everyone. There is no need for instruction in the content or values of a particular tradition; instead, one needs primarily to be educated in the proper application of the method. With that in hand, all else comes easily. But, the promise of a future in which knowledge is widely expanded and accessible seems to run headlong into the problem of power. Since for Bacon knowledge and power are synonymous, and since men are motivated by the desire for power—over nature, but also, it appears, over human nature—it inevitably becomes the case that some acquire power while others are subjected to the will of the powerful. In other words, Bacon's account of knowing has significant political implications.

René Descartes and the Quest for Certainty

Motive

If the words that characterize Bacon's thought are "power" and "foundation," the word most obvious in Descartes's writing is "certainty." René Descartes (1596–1650) received a classical education at the Jesuit college in the French town of La Flèche, but he later came to scorn what he perceived as the confused and inconclusive nature of school philosophy.[47] "I was convinced," he writes, "that our beliefs are based much more on custom and example than on any certain knowledge."[48] This lack of certainty became *the* compelling problem for Descartes, who admitted that "my whole plan had for its aim assurance and the rejection of shifting ground and sand in order to find rock or clay."[49] This problem compelled Descartes to locate some solid foundation upon which to construct a clear and rational system. There is a restlessness in Descartes, a dissatisfaction with the merely probable, that drove him in his quest for certainty: "I would not have been able to limit my desires or to be happy, if I had not followed a path by which, thinking I was certain of acquiring all the knowledge of which I was capable, I thought also that I was certain, by the same means, of acquiring all the true goods that would ever be in my power."[50] Certainty in philosophical matters would provide "the perfect peace of mind which I seek."[51] This peace of mind would manifest itself in wisdom, which Descartes defines as "a perfect knowledge of all that man can know."[52] Descartes is optimistic that his solution to the problem of uncertainty will produce significant results, for the "chief fruit of these principles is that one will be able, in cultivating them, to discover many truths that I have not dealt with, and thus passing gradually from one to another, to acquire in time a perfect knowledge of the whole of philosophy and to rise to the highest degree of wisdom."[53]

New Beginnings

Descartes employs the image of a building in order to establish what for him is a crucial point. When a building is designed and completed by a single architect, the end product is "usually more beautiful and better ordered than those that several architects have tried to put into shape, making use of old walls which were built for other purposes."[54] In the same way, Descartes argues, philosophy, which has been added upon by various thinkers throughout the centuries, is not likely to exhibit the beauty or order of a system designed by one person. Thus he concludes that simply adding to the work of others is inadequate. Certainty will only be possible if the old, dubious foundations are razed and new foundations erected that admit of no doubt. Descartes believes that he is the one to establish such foundations: "I think I can say without vanity that, if there is anyone capable of bringing them [his thoughts] to this point, it must be myself rather than any other."[55] He prepared himself for this undertaking by "rooting out of my mind all the false opinions that had been instilled into me earlier."[56] This purging is central to Descartes's progress toward certainty. In the first paragraph of his *Meditations*, in which he develops his "indubitable" foundation, he sweeps the decks clear, attempting to expunge all dubious notions from his mind. He deems it necessary to "rid myself of all the opinions I had adopted up to then, and to begin afresh from the foundations, if I wished to establish something firm and constant in the sciences."[57] Thus, at the heart of Descartes's approach is the conviction that truth could only be secured by abolishing the old and uncertain and embracing the new and certain.

Doubt

At its heart, then, Cartesian methodology, the goal of which is absolute certainty, is characterized by a radical and pervasive doubt. The doubt with which Descartes begins is not simply doubt about certain tenets of classical philosophy or a suspicion of the methods of the Scholastics. By sifting through his various writings, one quickly becomes impressed with both the depth and breadth of Cartesian doubt. First, like Bacon, Descartes attacks the Aristotelianism of the schools. According to Descartes, the stagnation of all philosophy rooted in Aristotle is sufficient proof of the falseness of that approach: "We could not better prove the falsity of the principles of Aristotle, than by saying that men have been unable to make any progress by their means during the many centuries that these principles have been followed."[58] This being the case, Descartes argues that a man lacking any exposure to school philosophy is better equipped to make real progress toward truth than one who has spent his whole life studying in the Aristotelian tradition.[59] "Hence, we must conclude that those who have learned the least of all that has hitherto been called philosophy are the most capable of learning the true one."[60] Included in his critique of Aristotelianism is a critique of Aristotelian logic. Like Bacon, Descartes held that the dialectical logic taught in the schools, which was based on the syllogism, "teaches the means of conveying to others the things we know already, or even of talking a lot without judgment about what we do not know and which, consequently, corrupts rather than increases good sense."[61] Thus, in order to begin anew, Aristotelianism, along with the logic entailed thereby, must be set aside.

Descartes was not merely concerned with overturning one school of philosophy—his doubt extended far beyond that. Rule #3 of his *Rules for the Direction of the Mind* succinctly makes this point: "Concerning objects proposed for study, we ought to investigate what we can clearly and evidently intuit or deduce with certainty, and not what other people have thought or what we ourselves conjecture. For knowledge can be attained in no other way."[62] To obtain certain foundations, one must refuse to take anything on the basis of authority; instead, one must accept as knowledge only that which is clearly and distinctly obvious to the individual knower.[63] Descartes took this step because he was struck by the contradictory nature of philosophy. He admits that philosophy "has been cultivated by the very best minds which have ever existed over several centuries and that, nevertheless, not one of its problems is not subject to disagreement, and consequently is uncertain."[64] Thus, he informs his readers that "as soon as I reached an age which allowed me to emerge from the tutelage of my teachers, I abandoned the study of letters altogether, and resolv[ed] to study no other science than that which I could find within myself or else in the great book of the world."[65] Having cast off not only Aristotelianism and its syllogistic logic but all that had come under the name of knowledge prior to him, one might imagine that Descartes's doubt had reached its outermost limits. But such is not the case, for having discredited all that constituted the tradition of learning, Descartes then turned inward and pointed his doubting eye upon the very faculties of human knowing.

Both the senses and the intellect come up short under Descartes's withering gaze: "Because our senses sometimes play us false, I decided to suppose that there was nothing at all which was such as they cause us to imagine it."[66] The senses, then, because they at times prove deceptive, are untrustworthy and ill-qualified to serve as the certain foundations for which he seeks. Furthermore, "because there are men who make mistakes in reasoning, even with the simplest geometrical matters . . . judging that I was as liable to error as anyone else, I rejected as being false all the reasonings I had hitherto accepted as proofs."[67] The intellect, therefore, does no better than the senses. Because the conclusions that the intellect renders are subject to contention and contradiction, it, like the senses, cannot be trusted as an adequate foundation.

Thus, Descartes, in employing his radical and systematic doubt, undermines all the traditional sources of knowledge. He, in effect, clears the way for the introduction of his method by which he believes knowledge can be restored—and vastly improved. He summarizes this sweeping movement in the second paragraph of his *Meditations*: "I shall apply myself seriously and freely to the general destruction of all my former opinions."[68] This general destruction, as we have seen, includes all authority both exterior to himself, in the form of previous learning, and interior to himself, in the form of the senses and the intellect. But this radical destruction left only ruin in its wake: "What, then, shall be considered true? Perhaps only this, that there is nothing certain in the world."[69]

It is important to understand that Descartes is not claiming that everything in the world is equally dubitable. He acknowledges that "we are often compelled to accept what is merely probable."[70] But, if we recall the motivation for his project—certainty—it becomes clear that probabilities are simply inadequate. They are so inadequate to his purpose of establishing certain foundations that he eliminates probability as a category of knowledge and collapses it into the false. As he puts it, "I took to be tantamount to false everything which was merely probable."[71] Thus, in order to establish an absolutely indubitable foundation, Descartes reduces knowledge to only one type—certain knowledge—while declaring all else, even the highly probable, to be "tantamount to false." He has, by virtue of his radical doubt, rendered his reader completely helpless, desperately in need of rescue in a sea of doubt. Descartes, of course, has no intention of concluding that since apparently all can be doubted, all hope of certainty is lost. It is at this point that his method steps in as a sort of epistemic savior.

Method

Descartes's great appreciation for mathematics and geometry provided him with a model of certainty that he aspired to apply to philosophy. Since mathematics provides certainty, why had mathematical principles not been applied to the study of philosophy? While considering the certain conclusions of mathematics, he says, "I was astonished that on such firm and solid foundations nothing more exalted had been built."[72] He thus applied himself to this very endeavor: "I promised myself that I would apply it [mathematical method] just as usefully to the difficulties of the other sciences as I had to those of algebra."[73] This faith in the universal applicability of mathematics is key to the Cartesian method.[74] Mathematics, Descartes believed, would provide the model for his philosophical method by which certainty would be secured. One question that we must keep in mind, of course, is whether or not all knowledge is simply reducible to mathematical reasoning.

In his "Rules for the Direction of the Mind," Descartes defines "method" as "reliable rules which are easy to apply, and such that if one follows them exactly, one will never take what is false to be true or fruitlessly expend one's mental efforts, but will gradually and constantly increase one's knowledge till one arrives at a true understanding of everything within one's capacity."[75] Descartes's method consists of four simple injunctions:

> The first was never to accept anything as true that I did not know to be evidently so: that is to say, carefully to avoid precipitancy and prejudice, and to include in my judgments nothing more than what presented itself so clearly and so distinctly to my mind that I might have no occasion to place it in doubt.
>
> The second, to divide each of the difficulties that I was examining into as many parts as might be possible and necessary in order best to solve it.
>
> The third, to conduct my thoughts in an orderly way, beginning with the simplest objections and the easiest to know, in order to climb gradually, as by degrees, as far as the knowledge of the most complex, and even supposing some order among those objects which do not precede each other naturally.
>
> And the last, everywhere to make such complete enumerations and such general reviews that I would be sure to have omitted nothing.[76]

The first rule, of course, reflects Descartes's definition of knowledge. Only that which is certain can be admitted as knowledge, but all appears uncertain; thus, nothing is certain. With this, though, he establishes the ground for his first positive move: the famous and concise *cogito ergo sum* (I think, therefore I am).

> I became aware that, while I decided thus to think that everything was false, it followed necessarily that I who thought thus must be something; and observing that this truth: *I think, therefore I am*, was so certain and so evident that all the most extravagant suppositions of the

sceptics were not capable of shaking it, I judged that I could accept it without scruple as the first principle of the philosophy I was seeking."[77]

With this one indubitable truth established, Descartes applies his method toward expanding his knowledge. And, unlike Bacon, he proceeds via deduction, for "we should bear in mind that there are two ways of arriving at a knowledge of things—through experience and through deduction. Moreover, we must note that while our experiences of things are often deceptive, the deduction or pure inference of one thing from another can never be performed wrongly by an intellect which is in the least degree rational, though we may fail to make the inference if we do not see it."[78] Certain knowledge, then, is attained by first establishing an indubitable first principle and from that beginning point employing deduction so that all that follows is as certain as the first indubitable principle. In each step nothing may be admitted as knowledge that is not "clear and distinct." This is highlighted by the second rule, which dictates that all objects of inquiry be divided into their basic component parts, for Descartes is confident that all reality can be treated as a mathematical problem to be solved in simple and logical steps.[79]

Mathematics can proceed in a purely deductive fashion because the rules of mathematics constitute a universe unto itself. Thus, if Descartes seeks to apply the methods of mathematics to all inquiry, he must simultaneously postulate a theory of the universal unity of knowledge, for unless such exists, his deductive method, proceeding from his first indubitable principle, will necessarily break down. His third rule makes this assumption quite clear, for he believes that it is possible to begin with "the simplest objects and the easiest to know" and to "climb gradually" toward the "most complex." Elsewhere Descartes speaks of establishing a "*mathesis universalis*" (universal mathematics), which is "a general science which explains all the points that can be raised concerning order and measure irrespective of the subject-matter."[80] Descartes employs a metaphor to drive home this point on the unity (and therefore deductibility) of all knowledge: "All philosophy is like a tree, whose roots are metaphysics, the trunk physics and the branches which grow out of this trunk are all the other sciences, which are reduced to three principle ones, namely, medicine, mechanics and ethics."[81]

The fourth rule emphasizes review. To ensure certainty, one must continually examine one's work lest some detail be overlooked. Related but not identical to this point is Descartes's attempt to gain a clear and distinct intuition of an entire process, thereby affirming the truth of the process and not merely the individual steps. This is accomplished by a sort of mental sprint:

> So I shall run through them [the elements of a deduction] several times in a continuous movement of the imagination, simultaneously intuiting one relation and passing on to the next, until I have learnt to pass from the first to the last so swiftly that memory is left with practically no role to play, and I seem to intuit the whole thing at once. In this way our memory is relieved, the sluggishness of our intelligence redressed, and its capacity in some way enlarged.[82]

Memory (or in a collective sense, tradition) plays no role and, according to Descartes, ought to be circumvented. Of course, in light of his disdain for all philosophy prior to his own, it is perhaps not surprising that Descartes should relegate memory to the sidelines. We are warranted in asking, though: Is it so easy to set memory aside?

The individual, stripped of everything—even memory—is the epistemic center from which all else proceeds. Descartes, of course, makes haste to demonstrate God's existence—employing versions of both the ontological and cosmological arguments—but his method raises an important and recurring question: If God cannot be demonstrated—that is, if the arguments ultimately fail to provide deductive proof—then God's existence is reduced from certainty to some degree of probability, and probabilities are, for Descartes, entirely unsatisfactory. Descartes believed that his method did, indeed, provide the certainty for which he longed. But, many of those who followed in his steps followed only to a point. They agreed that doubt is the proper starting point of epistemology and that epistemology is the starting point of philosophy, but they refuse to go further, and with that refusal the door is, of course, opened to skeptical conclusions that would have horrified the pious Descartes.

Equality

Like Bacon, Descartes believes that method—his method—provides the mechanism by which anyone, regardless of native intelligence, can proceed with confidence to certain knowledge. Descartes promises to "show the paths to be very easy, so that anyone who has mastered the whole method, however mediocre his intelligence, may see that there are no paths closed to him that are open to others, and that his lack of further knowledge is not due to any want of intelligence or method."[83] Descartes is not merely arguing that his method will provide people with the tools allowing them to push further than they would have without his method. Instead, he is arguing that armed with his method all people are equally capable of attaining certain knowledge in the highest possible degree. He writes that "there are almost none so gross or so slow as to be incapable of acquiring correct opinions and even reaching the highest knowledge, if they are guided correctly."[84] The correct guidance to which he refers is not training in the content of a discipline, say philosophy, but training in his method. Indeed, even that appears unnecessary, for Descartes seeks to explain "the order which it seems to me should be followed in order to instruct oneself."[85] Thus, method becomes the great equalizer, which, because of its leveling impact, reduces and ultimately eliminates any need for reliance upon an authority. The self becomes both master and pupil.

Isolation

This radical equality that indicates the superfluousness of a teacher implies a certain degree of isolation. If it is true that the opinions of others should not be trusted, then one has no choice but to "go it alone," and, indeed, Descartes seems to revel in his solitude, both physical and mental. In terms of physical isolation, Descartes famously sets the scene. While a soldier in Germany he found himself forced to winter without company: "I spent the whole day shut up in a room heated by an enclosed stove, where I had complete leisure to meditate on my own thoughts."[86] It was during this time that he began to develop his revolutionary method. Prior to this winter solitude, he had decided "to leave all those places where I had acquaintances, and to withdraw here . . . [and] . . . without lacking any of the conveniences offered by the most populous cities, I have been able to live as solitary and withdrawn as I would in the most remote of deserts."[87]

His mental isolation is no less significant and no less self-imposed. First, because prior attempts at philosophy were wrong and tend to corrupt and confuse those who read them, Descartes found himself "constrained, as it were, to undertake my own guidance."[88] Implied in guiding one's self is an underlying faith in one's own mental abilities divorced from any tradition or authority. Indeed, Descartes recognizes and relishes such detachment.

Since Descartes seeks to establish indubitable foundations, and since he hopes to ignore any previous teaching, it follows that the foundations he hopes to establish are purely the products of his own mental labors. He desires, as he puts it, "to build on a foundation which is wholly my own."[89] The radical nature of this enterprise is well summarized in the opening paragraph of his Third Meditation:

> I shall now close my eyes, stop up my ears, turn away all my senses, even efface from my thought all images of corporeal things, or at least, because this can hardly be done, I shall consider them as being vain and false; and thus communing only with myself, and examining my inner self, I shall try to make myself, little by little, better known and more familiar to myself.[90]

Thus, Descartes's method necessarily entails isolation—at least mental, but ideally of the physical variety as well. He willfully separates himself from received tradition and from any membership in a community that embodies those traditions. There is, in the writings of Descartes, a supreme confidence—even hubris—that is impossible to ignore.

Conclusion

Like Bacon, Descartes believed that Scholastic philosophy was strangling knowledge, both philosophical and scientific. Because of the entrenched nature of this stagnant Aristotelianism, he determined to begin anew upon foundations that he believed provided absolute certainty and admitted of no controversy. To establish this foundation, he began with radical and universal doubt. Like Bacon, he declared all prior knowledge doubtful and prepared the way for the entrance of a universally applicable method by which doubts could be overcome. Unlike Bacon's inductive method, Descartes's method proceeds deductively from the certain foundation provided by the *cogito*. Since the method is simple and readily accessible to all, it follows that all people will be able to apply it and obtain the same degree of certainty. Furthermore, because the method begins with the individual stripped of the resources of the past and stripped even of memory of the past and unsupported by any authoritative traditions or teachers, Descartes's way is a solitary path. Although all people may, and indeed should, follow this same path, there is no community in the process, for the way is open to all, but each must travel alone, shut up within the confines of his own mind, initially doubting even the existence of the very mind he attempts to shut.

TOCQUEVILLE AND THE DEMOCRATIC INDIVIDUAL

Tocqueville provocatively claimed that Americans are Cartesians and that "in the seventeenth [century], Bacon, in the natural sciences, and Descartes, in philosophy properly so-called, abolish the received formulas, destroy the empire of traditions, and overturn the authority of the master."[91] However, he admits that it was not until the eighteenth century that this new (and radical) methodology took full root in America. In order to better understand the dynamics involved in the full-scale adoption of the Cartesian methodology, it is necessary to consider more closely Tocqueville's arguments, the key to which is the collapse of the aristocracy and the emergence of equality in the West.

A New World

Tocqueville saw himself on the brink of a new world, a world in which the traditional aristocratic social forms were dissolving and being replaced by the equality of conditions. Where the old world was held together by rigid social conventions that prevented—or at least greatly impaired—both social and geographic movement, equality of conditions destroyed the social structures of the aristocratic world. People were no longer inexorably constrained by the social conditions or geographic places into which they were born.

This change, Tocqueville argues, represents nothing less than a democratic revolution, a revolution that has been building for centuries: "Running through the pages of our history, there is hardly an important event in the last seven hundred years which has not turned out to be advantageous for equality."[92] Inventions such as firearms, the printing press, and postal services all served to make power and information available to all, breaking the monopoly previously held by the aristocratic classes. The Crusades and the English wars divided lands previously held by only a few.

The Protestant Reformation advanced the idea that all men are equal before God and thus undermined the hierarchical institution of the Catholic Church. Ultimately, this movement toward equality is, in Tocqueville's assessment, an act of God. Thus, to resist the spread of democracy and the equality that necessarily accompanies it is to pit oneself against providence itself.

Although the progress and universality of equality (at least in the West) appears to be fated, Tocqueville is not fatalistic. He argues that democracy can manifest itself in one of two ways. The first is democratic freedom. The second is a form of government in which equality is present but the citizens are debased and isolated, members of a vast, paternalistic state. Tocqueville calls this democratic tyranny, or equality in servitude. Because the democratic revolution will clear the way for one of these two conditions, Tocqueville recognizes the need for social and political leaders to "educate democracy." As such, *Democracy in America* is a handbook for both leaders and concerned citizens. It points out the various pitfalls that block the road to democratic freedom and explains how equality tends naturally toward democratic tyranny. Tocqueville believes democratic tyranny can be resisted, but not without both effort and commitment informed by a clear understanding of the new situation facing the West. He writes his book to help provide the necessary understanding.

In order to grasp how the movement toward equality shaped the American mind, it is necessary to explain several intermediate steps. Equality tends to isolate individuals both from the natural constraints of social position and from the traditions transmitted from the past. Tocqueville understands that the resulting individualism induces a range of philosophical, social, and political effects.

Equality and Individualism

Many of the most important events of the last millennium have conspired to move society toward equality. Theologically, the Protestant Reformation served to break down the hierarchical structure of the Church. No longer were priests needed to serve as mediators between God and man. Individuals could now approach the divine quite apart from any ecclesiastical structure. Rather than a hierarchy that induced individuals to see themselves as parts of a larger whole and in which the very hierarchy tutored minds toward community and toward the verticality of transcendence, the world in the wake of the Protestant Reformation was dramatically flattened. Each individual stood naked and alone before God, and from that posture was responsible for working out his own individual salvation with fear and trembling. In the most radical versions of Protestantism—rejected even by most Protestants—the church faded into the background, and the individual emerged as a priest without hierarchy—a priest with a congregation of one.

This same flattening occurred in philosophy less than a century later. This is most vividly evidenced in the seventeenth-century anti-Scholastic reaction of thinkers such as Descartes and Bacon. They led the charge in attempting to sever philosophy and natural science from dependence on the traditions and strictures of the past. Both believed that it was possible, and indeed desirable, for individuals to come to absolutely certain conclusions completely independent of any reliance on authority. As such, the role of history as an invaluable resource necessary for properly understanding the world was diminished. In an attempt to throw off the shackles of medieval philosophy—a synthesis of Aristotle and Christian thought—both Bacon and Descartes sought to begin anew, unencumbered by the burden of the past. The individual was seen as sufficient in himself; thus, the authority of both masters and tradition were undermined. In this orgy of epistemological egalitarianism, the community was no longer seen as essential. If each man is sufficient in himself, then the community becomes purely optional. If individuals are no longer understood to be parts of a community in a fundamental sense—a sense that makes human flourishing possible—then individuals are clearly free to wander in search of a community that suits them, or perhaps eschew community all together. Association becomes purely optional.

Accompanying this theological and philosophical flattening was a collapse of the hierarchical social structure. Like the hierarchical structure of the Catholic Church, the aristocratic arrangement of society bound individuals together in a vertically ordered community. As a result, people were constantly reminded, by the very structure of society, that they were parts of a larger whole, rooted in a particular history and a particular set of traditions. They were integral members of a particular social class; they were socially rooted. Because social mobility was virtually unthinkable, the aspiration to move or change one's status was rarely strong. One understood one's place, both geographically—because multiple generations living on the same piece of land produces intimacy with that place—and socially—one is mindful of one's ancestors, contemporaries, and descendants. The individual, in such a society, was rooted to a place both spatially and temporally. As Tocqueville puts it,

> Among aristocratic nations [,] families maintain the same station for centuries and often live in the same place. So there is a sense in which all the generations are contemporaneous. A man almost always knows about his ancestors and respects them; his imagination extends to his great-grandchildren, and he loves them. He freely does his duty by both ancestors and descendants and often sacrifices personal pleasures for the sake of beings who are no longer alive or are not yet born.[93]

This social arrangement served to tutor the minds of its members in a manner that constantly reminded them that a line of authority and responsibility existed, and people were expected to understand their place in that line along with the obligations and privileges accompanying it. In other words, people were constantly reminded of the fact that they inhabited a particular tradition.

With the dissolution of the aristocracy, coupled with the philosophical egalitarianism articulated by Bacon and Descartes, the individual could now envision himself as separate from all other individuals, equally capable of being whatever he set his mind to be. No longer constrained by dependence on the past (either philosophically or socially) the individual could now view himself and his ideas as equal with all others. This egalitarian individualism—the necessary condition for the rise of the liberal self—emerged along with modern Western democracies. But to the extent that equality forces people to rely only on their own resources, they are induced (or perhaps seduced) to imagine that their own ideas and resources are sufficient. In short, as Tocqueville puts it, "aristocracy links everybody, from peasant to king, in one long chain. Democracy breaks the chain and frees each link."[94] But with the breakdown of the ties that previously bound individuals to one another, people tend to forget about the community to which they belong: in its present form, its past as embodied in shared traditions, and its future constituted by both hope and responsibility. Tocqueville writes, "Thus, not only does democracy make men forget their ancestors, but also clouds their view of their descendants and isolates them from their contemporaries. Each man is forever thrown back on himself alone, and there is danger that he may be shut up in the solitude of his own heart."[95]

Tocqueville calls this condition individualism. In a world character-ized by individualism, people tend not to concern themselves with their communities. Instead, they focus on the narrow circle of their own imme-diate interests, and in so doing, their isolation is constantly reinforced by their circumstances. Thus, equality tends to breed individualism, and in-dividualism tends to blind people to the importance of place: the people, history, and traditions of a particular locale. As focus is turned inward to the liberated self, the community tends to fade into the background and individual desire takes center stage.

Equality and Skepticism

Individualism, though, is not the only consequence of equality. A height-ened sense of freedom also accompanies the breakdown of hierarchies, for when the constraints that these structures provided were removed, indi-viduals found themselves not only isolated but emancipated. Limited only by imagination, individuals could now fancy themselves free to create a world of their own choosing. Unconstrained by social conditions or tradi-tion, they could pursue wealth, land, power, success, and fame, and because all people were now (at least in theory) on an equal footing, they could justly imagine themselves achieving successes that, in an aristocratic world, they would not have dared to dream. This newfound spirit of freedom, though, was tempered in the American context by the countervailing spirit of religion, namely, Christianity. Thus, although the spirit of freedom tended to throw everything into disarray and tempt individuals to ques-tion virtually all that was conventionally accepted as true, the spirit of re-ligion set limits on the extent of the questioning. As Tocqueville puts it,

> The barriers which hemmed in the society in which they were brought up fall before them; old views which have ruled the world for centu-ries vanish; almost limitless opportunities lie open in a world without horizon; the spirit of man rushes forward to explore it in every direc-tion; but when that spirit reaches the limits of the world of politics, it stops of its own accord; in trepidation it renounces the use of its most formidable faculties; it forswears doubt and renounces innovation; it will not even lift the veil of the sanctuary; and it bows respectfully be-fore truths which it accepts without discussion.[96]

Here we can see the interplay Tocqueville identifies between what he calls the "spirit of freedom" and the "spirit of religion," the latter borne along by a steady tide of tradition. The spirit of freedom seeks to throw open all questions that had, in an aristocratic age, been deemed settled. But this frenzy of questioning pulls up short at the gates of religion and goes no further. The spirit of religion stands guard, if you will, flaming sword in hand, and though the spirit of freedom has produced a riot, the spirit of religion ensures that the rioting occurs only within certain parameters. Being confined to the mundane world, the questioning is usually harmless (and often beneficial). Tocqueville is convinced that the spirit of religion harnessed the energies produced by the spirit of freedom and channeled them to benign ends. Ultimately, however, Tocqueville is not sanguine about the long-term prospects of the spirit of religion. Equality, it seems, tends to produce skeptics, and, of course, skeptics are not constrained by the limits imposed by religious belief.

In the America Tocqueville visited, Christianity was widely accepted as true even if the affirmation was unreflective and perfunctory for many. Because the Christian religion includes a substantial number of moral teachings, those moral principles were adopted by Americans in the same unreflective manner. Thus, even though many were not wholly committed to all of the doctrines of the churches, there was a critical mass of people who were, and even those who were not absorbed and lived according to the general moral principles derived from the Christian faith. Social limits, rooted in a tradition of religious belief, provided a context within which freedom could thrive, but one that served at the same time to limit the extent of that freedom.

As we have seen, though, equality tends to break down the very things that once linked people together. As people come to perceive themselves increasingly as isolated theologically, philosophically, and socially, they will of necessity come to believe that their own mental faculties are sufficient. They will tend to be dismissive of traditions and authorities that require an element of submission and trust. Such people will fancy that they can think thoughts never before thought and blaze new and unique paths never before trodden. They will become suspicious of beliefs that have not been thoroughly vetted by their private rational faculties. At the same time, though, it is clearly not possible for an individual to refuse to believe anything based on authority. If individuals in an age of equality tend to doubt those beliefs that have not been subjected to the test of reason, and if it is impossible for any one individual to apply his reason to every question, then it follows that, for practical reasons, the authority of the individual will be accompanied by a trust in the authority of the mass of mankind. Thus emerges the reign of public opinion and, in our day, the ubiquity of the public opinion poll, that scientific-sounding substitute for thought.[97]

This reliance on the self and public opinion, divorced from any metaphysical or religious commitments, will tend to produce a certain kind of person. Individuals in such a climate will gravitate toward skepticism. That is, they will be suspicious of the claims made by religions that postulate a reality beyond the visible. In the process, the "spirit of religion," which Tocqueville believed provided a check on the "spirit of freedom," is removed and freedom will reign unopposed and without limits.

Equality, Uniformity, and Centralization

There is another problem brought about by the rise of equality: perfect equality can never be attained. In ages where equality is the highest social ideal, differences will offend. The irony is that as conditions become more equal, differences will offend more readily. Furthermore, when equality is the goal, a longing for uniformity naturally arises, and here we can see another driver of the cosmopolitan impulse. Of course, the desire for uniformity runs into the hard rock of reality, for in many ways humans are not equal, and complex human relations seem to constantly reveal that fact. From a certain perspective, inequality is a more persistent fact than equality. This, as might be imagined, will cause serious problems for those driven primarily by a love of equality. First, if differences are endemic to the human race, then attempts to effect some semblance of uniformity will be frustrated. This is not to say that many differences cannot be eliminated. Theological, philosophical, and social changes have all served to bring individuals more nearly to a state of equality. But if some differences are rooted in nature, then those differences will be impossible to fully eradicate, and this will create a heightened sensitivity to any difference whatsoever. When an insatiable desire encounters a situation that precludes the satisfaction of that desire, the emotional toll will be high, and vast energy will be expended to alleviate the incongruity. In short, the autonomous individual will be restless, agitated, and continually thwarted. However, the stage is set for the emergence of the liberal cosmopolitan.

We see here two sources of dissatisfaction brought about by the historic movement toward equality. First, skepticism undermines any belief in limits that transcend individual will. But if certain limits are built into the very structure of reality, rejecting those limits is to pit oneself against reality itself. The second source of dissatisfaction is rooted in the sheer impossibility of perfectly achieving equality. If equality is the social ideal to which an individual or a society is committed, the individual and society will suffer a continual sense of failure. This second source of dissatisfaction conditions and ultimately induces individuals to seek political centralization, for the only imaginable hope of achieving equality is through a centralized state capable of promising equality of conditions for all members of the society.

Thus, equality leads to a desire for uniformity, and uniformity requires centralization. The scope of centralization, of course, is limited by practicalities. Geographical distances along with cultural and national boundaries have traditionally provided limits to centralizing impulses. But as technology makes these barriers less formidable, as the globalization of the marketplace makes people increasingly aware of each other, as Western culture, especially in the form of entertainment, is exported to a world hungry for American pop culture, the potential scope of centralization will increase. As cultural barriers are broken, the possibility of uniformity increases, and this uniformity has led toward an increasing homogenization of culture. This sort of cosmopolitanism is one in which local differences, embodied in traditions, are not appreciated but despised or at least denigrated as the benighted practices of unenlightened provincials. Thus, economic and cultural homogenization make political centralization increasingly possible.

This is not to suggest that all people directly favor centralization. But if a sort of liberated equality is the highest social ideal, and if centralization is perceived to be the most effective means of achieving that end, then centralization will be embraced as the best means to a cherished end. Thus, individuals will seek the uniformity that centralization promises, for they love equality above all else. At the same time, the state will be all too willing to take up the very same cause, for by embracing uniformity and the centralization it requires, the state gains power. For different reasons, then, both individuals and the state will cherish uniformity: the first out of love of equality, the second out of love of power. Tocqueville puts the matter succinctly: "This community of feeling which in democracies continually unites each individual and the sovereign in common thought establishes a secret and permanent bond of sympathy between them. . . . Democratic peoples often hate those in whose hands the central power is vested, but they always love that power itself."⁹⁸ To a significant degree, Americans today have lost their suspicion of power. Conservatives still occasionally decry the centralization of political power but seem blind to concentrations of economic power; liberals occasionally decry the centralization of economic power, but seem unconcerned with state power. Neither sees the danger inherent in the power centers they champion. Furthermore, both political and economic power are enhanced by the presence of the autonomous individual who is unconstrained by a fidelity to tradition and animated by the idea that the individual self is an unlimited agent in pursuit of ever greater liberty in the context of perfect equality.

Even though democratic people tend to love the power of the state, they are not necessarily inclined toward the complete centralization of power. One impetus for centralization is the isolation that equality tends to produce. When individuals are isolated, they are weak and quite powerless against the whole. If they seek to remain in their isolation and at the same time achieve the political ends they desire, they must enlist the power of the state in service of their private goals. Thus, Tocqueville writes,

> such men will freely admit the general principle that the power of the state should not interfere in private affairs, but as an exception, each one of them wants the state to help in the special matter with which he is preoccupied, and he wants to lead the government on to take action in his domain, though he would like to restrict it in every other direction. As a multitude of people, all at the same moment, take this particular view about a great variety of different purposes, the sphere of the central government insensibly spreads in every direction, although every individual wants to restrict it.⁹⁹

Thus, although centralization is not explicitly embraced as a general principle, individuals favor it when their special interests are at issue. In light of this dynamic, Tocqueville argues that it is merely a matter of time before a democratic people find themselves ruled by a centralized government.

In addition to a love of power, there is another reason the state will prefer uniformity: simplicity. Local particularities make governing difficult. They require that officials be familiar with local customs and practices, and such familiarity is undesired for two reasons. First, it takes time and effort to learn about local communities. Governing well requires willingness to vary laws, or at least vary the interpretation of particular laws, to accommodate local differences. But the larger and more centralized a state becomes, the more difficult it will be to govern while respecting local variations. Thus "every central government worships uniformity; uniformity saves it the trouble of inquiring into infinite details, which would be necessary if the rules were made to suit men instead of subjecting all men indiscriminately to the same rule."[100] The problem here is one of propriety. To the extent that people are unequal, local communities will also be unequal. If local communities are different from one another, a central authority imposing a uniform rule across the board will inevitably fail to govern in a way that is best for local communities taken individually. In short, local particularities limit the effectiveness of centralized political structures. They are the grit in the works that must be removed if, in fact, a uniform system is to be implemented.

Uniformity destroys the local and particular and replaces it with a bland veneer of commonality devoid of any unique attributes that make it lovely. The natural human affection for a particular place is transposed into an ideal of universality that simply cannot sustain a free people, for as limits to centralization—the spirit of religion, submission to nature, local particularities—are dissolved, the possibility of any other alternative is simultaneously jeopardized. The centralized state fills the void created by these various denials, and the result is haunting. As Tocqueville puts it, "The unity, ubiquity, and omnipotence of the social power and the uniformity of its rules constitute the most striking feature of all the political systems invented in our day. They recur even in the most fantastic utopias. The human mind still pursues them in its dreams. [Democratic citizens] all think of the government as a sole, simple, providential, and creative force."[101] It is difficult to miss the god-like attributes Tocqueville uses to describe this political power. Where in an age of religious belief God was vested with attributes of unity, simplicity, omnipresence, and omnipotence, these very attributes have, in a skeptical age, been transferred to the state. Thus, although belief in God may have been rejected, religion of a sort remains, and the state naturally assumes the role once played by God.

Tocqueville notes that "in ages of equality all men are independent of each other, isolated and weak."[102] These are the liberal selves who imagine themselves free without limit. Ironically, though, such individuals are weak relative to the centralized state or to the mass of other liberal selves represented by "society." Weak isolated people will be poorly equipped to resist the centralization of power when it occurs. But equality tends to produce that very centralization that these weak, isolated people find irresistible. Motivated by the insecurity born of weakness, citizens will be naturally disposed "to give the central government new powers, or to let it take them, for it alone seems both anxious and able to defend them from anarchy itself."[103] In such a state, the people might continue with the basic outward trappings of self-government, but such outward elements are illusory, for "the citizens quit their state of dependence just long enough to choose their masters and then fall back into it."[104] If there happens to be an individual who objects to the notion of a strong, centralized authority, he is too weak and isolated to halt the juggernaut. The result is that the "individual is isolated and weak, but society is active, provident, and strong; private persons achieve insignificant things, but the state immense ones."[105]

The effects of equality will produce a sovereign altogether different than the classical tyrant who rules by fear and threat of force: "If a despotism should be established among the democratic nations of our day, it . . . would be more widespread and milder; it would degrade men rather than torment them . . . [for] the same equality which makes despotism easy tempers it." A kinder, gentler despotism will arise in which the leaders are not "tyrants, but rather school masters."[106] At this point Tocqueville's prose becomes luminous and is worth quoting at length:

> I see an innumerable multitude of men, alike and equal, constantly circling around in pursuit of the petty and banal pleasures with which they glut their souls. . . . Over this kind of men stands an immense, protective power which is alone responsible for securing their enjoyment and watching over their fate. That power is absolute, thoughtful of detail, orderly, provident, and gentle. . . . It provides for their security, foresees and supplies their necessities, facilitates their pleasures, manages their principal concerns, directs their industry, makes rules for their testaments, and divides their inheritances. Why should it not entirely relieve them from the trouble of thinking and all the cares of living? . . . It covers the whole of social life with a network of petty, complicated rules that are both minute and uniform, through which even men of the greatest originality and the most vigorous temperament cannot force their heads above the crowd. It does not break men's will, but softens, bends, and guides it; it seldom enjoins, but

often inhibits, action; it does not destroy anything, but prevents much being born; it is not at all tyrannical, but it hinders, restrains, enervates, stifles, and stultifies so much that in the end each nation is no more than a flock of timid and hardworking animals with the government as its shepherd.[107]

Again, the god-like attributes of the state should not be ignored. Neither should the infantile disposition of the citizens. We hear in these words echoes of Bacon's sheep-like *Tirsan*. The irony is significant: as limits to freedom are eradicated, the likelihood of a sustainable freedom becomes increasingly tenuous. Liberty, it would seem, requires limits, and a push toward unconstrained and unlimited freedom will tend to produce the opposite.

Tocqueville's analysis shows how the Baconian/Cartesian project, rooted in an impulse toward liberation from the constraints of the past, has profound social and political consequences. This is a crucial point. False accounts of knowing are not necessarily limited to the halls of the academy, and more is at stake than an arcane debate over the role tradition plays in knowing. If that claim is even remotely plausible, then we are warranted in probing deeper into what may appear on the surface only an obscure philosophical question.

CONCLUSION

Tradition, if Bacon and Descartes are correct, is an impediment to knowledge and therefore an impediment to progress. The individual, unencumbered by the burden of the past, is the ideal they champion. The liberal self, liberated from tradition, represents the new ideal. The burden of religion was implicated in this wholesale action against the past and the limits entailed therein. The gradual secularization of the academy throughout the eighteenth century culminates in Hume's rejection of miracles and even the notion of causation. Nature itself came to be seen in a different light. For with the rejection of Aristotle came the rejection of a teleological conception of nature in general and human nature in particular. If humans have a *telos*, then there are ends proper to human flourishing, and to ignore those ends is to thwart the possibility of a happy life. In this sense, the limits imposed by nature actually facilitated the likelihood of happiness.

However, with the rejection of a teleological conception of human nature, the notion that limits could be helpful guides was summarily rejected. What remains is the unencumbered self, limited by nothing other than individual desire. In short, late-stage liberalism declares that history is bunk, God is dead, nature is merely matter, and the individual will prevails.[108]

The liberal self finds justification in the various rejections asserted by thinkers such as Bacon and Descartes. However, the question must be asked: Were these rejections warranted? By way of reply I want to turn to three thinkers whose work in different but complementary ways challenges the modern notion that the way forward is the wholesale rejection of tradition. The following chapters on Oakeshott, MacIntyre, and Polanyi, respectively, are aimed to establish a single point: tradition is indispensable and any attempt to eliminate the role of tradition from an account of knowing will result in confusion and error.

If, as I will suggest, the rejection of tradition was a serious mistake, then we will do well to consider an alternative approach, one that does not ignore or deny the obvious advances made in the modern world but one that simultaneously does not ignore the resources inherent in tradition or, even more fundamentally, the necessary role tradition plays in knowing. In the process we may find ourselves confronted with the inadequacy of the liberal self, for if tradition is an unavoidable component of knowing, then the liberal self is a myth constructed in service of a liberal project that is incoherent at its very heart.

CHAPTER 2

Michael Oakeshott and the
Epistemic Role of Tradition

The human predicament is a universal appearing everywhere as a particular.

—Michael Oakeshott[1]

In a review of Walter Lippmann's book *The Public Philosophy*, Oakeshott scoffs at Lippmann's claim that the free institutions of the West were derived by referring to some abstract theory of natural law:

> Nobody would deny that it is important to have our general ideas about government as straight as we can get them; but the notion that practice derives from theory in this simple manner is, I think, a mistake. When Mr. Lippmann says that the founders of our free institutions were adherents of the philosophy of natural law, and that "the free political institutions of the Western world were conceived and established" by men who held certain abstract beliefs, he speaks with the shortened perspective of an American way of thinking in which a manner of conducting affairs is inconceivable without an architect and without a premeditated "dedication to a proposition."[2]

The reference to "abstract principles" recalls Burke's suspicion that such principles could ever do the work of prescription and tradition. Although

Oakeshott is frequently identified as a conservative and an ideological descendent of Burke, it should be noted that he is not, as some suggest, simply a twentieth-century Burkean.³ This is obvious, for example, when we consider their respective understandings of "tradition." For Burke, tradition is primarily understood in terms of inheritance. By referring to tradition, weak individual men may tap into the accrued wisdom of human history. In a famous passage, Burke writes, "We are afraid to put men to live and trade each on his own private stock of reason; because we suspect that this stock in each man is small, and that the individuals would do better to avail themselves of the general bank and capital of nations, and of ages."⁴ Tradition, in this sense, resembles what Chesterton termed "the democracy of the dead."⁵

For Oakeshott, tradition is somewhat different. Tradition for him is not merely, or even primarily, a historic repository of valuable and time-tested truths that are ignored at our peril. Rather, tradition primarily serves an epistemological function. In other words, tradition in the Burkean sense can be ignored or set aside, but, according to Burke, such negligence will produce terrible social and political instability, as exemplified by the French Revolution. The content embedded in tradition is the primary (though not exclusive) focus for Burke. And although the content of tradition is certainly appreciated by Oakeshott, he is equally concerned with the epistemological role tradition plays.

In his last major work, *On Human Conduct*, Oakeshott intentionally stopped using the term "tradition" and began employing the word "practice." This was done in order to avoid the confusion that arose from his use of the term "tradition." According to Oakeshott, "if such changes are read back into what I had written earlier they make it more exact."⁶ Thus, in Oakeshott's writing, "tradition" and "practice" are taken to be generally interchangeable, but neither can be reduced to meaning simply a repository of wisdom acquired from our ancestors.

Another example of how Oakeshott differs from Burke is in their views of nature, human nature, and teleology. Burke, taking a position that finds its antecedents in the Thomist and Aristotelian tradition, affirms the existence of human nature and the teleology that such a nature implies.⁷ Oakeshott, on the other hand, denies any notion of human nature or human teleology. Man, he writes,

has a "history," but no "nature"; he is what in conduct he becomes. This "history" is not an evolutionary or teleological process. It is what

he enacts for himself in a diurnal engagement, the unceasing articulation of understood responses to endlessly emergent understood situations which continues until he quits the diurnal scene. And although
he may imagine an "ideal" human character and may use this character to direct his self-enactments, there is no ultimate or perfect man
hidden in the womb of time or prefigured in the characters who now
walk the earth.[8]

Oakeshott's views might not be completely clear at this point, but this
brief discussion ought to suffice to show that it is incorrect simply to lump
Oakeshott in with so-called conservative neo-Burkeans. In order to better
grasp Oakeshott's understanding of tradition, it is necessary first to examine his somewhat complex philosophical views.

Experience and Its Modes

According to Paul Franco, Oakeshott's work can be divided into three
major themes: (1) his theory of philosophy; (2) his critique of rationalism
along with his more positive account of the rationality of tradition or practice; and (3) his theory of civil association.[9] Oakeshott is of interest to this
project primarily for his critique of rationalism and his account of tradition, but it will be useful to briefly summarize his overall philosophic position, for there is a coherence to Oakeshott's thought that makes
extracting pieces a somewhat treacherous process.

Oakeshott's first book, *Experience and Its Modes*, was published in
1933 when Oakeshott was a mere thirty-one years old. In a review, the
British historian R. G. Collingwood could barely contain his enthusiasm:
"Mr. Oakeshott's thesis . . . is so original, so important, and so profound
that criticism must be silent until his meaning has been long pondered. . . .
I can, in this brief notice, only say that it is the most penetrating analysis
of historical thought that has ever been written."[10]

Oakeshott, like Collingwood, belonged to the school of British ideal-
ists who saw themselves carrying on in the tradition of Bradley and Hegel.
In fact, in his introduction to *Experience and Its Modes*, Oakeshott admits
that the two books from which he learned the most are Hegel's *Phänome-
nologie des Geistes* and Bradley's *Appearance and Reality*.[11] Oakeshott's idealism becomes apparent in his definition of experience. "'Experience,'" he

writes, "stands for the concrete whole which analysis divides into 'experi-encing' and 'what is experienced.'"[12] Building on this definition, Oakeshott develops the point further: "Experience is a world of ideas. And the con-dition of a world of ideas satisfactory in experience is a condition of coher-ence, of unity and completeness. Further, the world of experience is the real world; there is no reality outside experience. Reality is the world of experience in so far as it is satisfactory, in so far as it is coherent."[13] Thus, since the world of experience is the real world, and experience is a world of ideas, we can see that for Oakeshott, the real world is a world of ideas. The criterion for judging this world of ideas is not the degree to which it corresponds with an external reality (as claimed by classical realism) but the internal coherence of the world.[14] As he puts it, "Fact is what we are obliged to think, not because it corresponds with some outside world of existence, but because it is required for the coherence of the world of ex-perience."[15]

Oakeshott's idealism is ultimately monistic, for although experience can be glimpsed from a variety of standpoints, which may give the impres-sion of a multiplicity of realities, we are reminded that "it is important to understand that there is, in the end, only one experience."[16] This one ex-perience is what we call truth, for "what is true and all that is true is a co-herent world of ideas."[17] Coherence, for Oakeshott, is the primary criterion of truth; however, he emphasizes the coherence of the whole, which sug-gests some standard of comprehensiveness, which together with coherence elicits an increasing degree of satisfaction as comprehensive coherence is approached. Thus, "a world of ideas which is unified because it is complete and complete because it is unified is a coherent world of ideas. And such a world alone is satisfactory in experience."[18] At times, coherence and sat-isfaction seem to be synonymous for Oakeshott: "The condition of a world of ideas satisfactory in experience is a condition of coherence, of unity and completeness. . . . Reality is the world of experience in so far as it is satis-factory, in so far as it is coherent."[19]

Humans desire to know and comprehend experience, and we thereby engage experience by means of various modes. Oakeshott identifies three modes of experience, which he understands as self-contained worlds: his-tory, science, and practice.[20] He admits that there is "no theoretical limit to the number of such worlds, and the choice of which we are to consider in detail must, to some extent, be arbitrary."[21] But, the selection of the three is not entirely arbitrary, for, he explains, "these seem to me to represent the main arrests or modifications in experience, the main abstract worlds of ideas. Moreover, they may be said to be established modes of experience; and each is a sufficiently well-organized and developed world of ideas to present material for analysis."[22]

Modes of experience represent "arrests in experience" whereby one standpoint is used as a point of reference. Thus "a mode of experience is experience with reservation, it is experience shackled by partiality and presupposition."[23] It is important to understand, though, that these arrests in experience are not parts of a whole, but "the whole from a limited standpoint."[24] Each mode is comprehended as a coherent, self-contained world. There can be no communication between these various worlds, and attempts to effect such communication results in the fallacy of *ignoratio elenchi*, or irrelevance.[25] Thus, what is true in one world is neither true nor false in another; instead, it is meaningless. For example, in the world of science, we might state that a particular geometric theorem is true, but to inquire whether or not the statement is morally true is meaningless.[26] Or again, inquiring whether or not a moral truth is historically true is merely to create a confusion, to commit the fallacy of *ignoratio elenchi*.

History, or the mode of historical experience, is limited to that which can be comprehended as succession, as a series. But all that can be so understood does not fall immediately into the mode of history, for history must be recorded; thus, one must distinguish between the "historical series" and the "time series." Further, that which is recorded as a historical series necessarily passes through a critical filter whereby judgment is passed by the historian: "But judgment involves more than a series, it involves a world. And the view that history is concerned with what is merely successive breaks down. What was taken for a mere series has turned, in our hands, into a world."[27] Thus, history is never simply a series of events recorded by historians; instead, it represents a coherent world, and it follows then that "the historian's business is not to discover, to recapture, or even to interpret; it is to create and to construct."[28] The result of this work of construction is a self-contained world, which, though coherent, represents not reality as a whole but an arrest, "the whole from a limited standpoint."[29]

The mode represented by scientific experience again seeks to create a coherent, self-contained world. Regarding this mode, Oakeshott writes, "The entire history of science may be seen as a pathetic attempt to find, in the face of incredible difficulties, a world of definite and demonstrable experience, one free from merely personal associations and independent of the idiosyncrasies of particular observers, an absolutely impersonal and stable world. The sole *explicit* criterion of scientific ideas is their absolute communicability."[30] Absolute communicability requires that personal perceptions and prejudices be set aside. Scientific experience "is a world of purely quantitative experience . . . [that] involves the assertion of reality under the category of quantity."[31] Thus "whatever cannot be conceived quantitatively cannot belong to scientific knowledge."[32] Far from being a complete representation of reality, science, like the other modes, is an arrest, and thus is defective, for all arrests fall short of the totality of experience. The defective nature of this mode is clear, for scientific knowledge is "abstract, conditional, incomplete, self-contained but not self-sufficient."[33]

The mode of practical experience differs from both history and science, for we dwell primarily in the practical, and we only step outside this mode if we intentionally do so. As Oakeshott puts it, "Practical experience is the most familiar form of experience. We depart from it but rarely, and such departures are always excursions into a foreign country."[34] The mode of practical experience includes such things as morality, religion, and aesthetics.[35] But again this mode represents an arrest and is thus defective. The implications of this claim are significant, and Oakeshott is quite aware of this. There are those, he notes, who hold that ultimate truth lies in morality and religion, but if these are merely a mode of experience, then they too are defective arrests in experience and cannot be taken for the totality of reality.[36]

In a later essay, "The Voice of Poetry in the Conversation of Mankind," originally published in 1959, Oakeshott adds the poetic mode to the three described in *Experience and Its Modes*. He uses the term "poetry" to cover all artistic endeavors, including painting, sculpting, acting, dancing, singing, literary and musical composition, and so on. Like the other modes, poetry consists of activity, but the poetic mode is uniquely characterized by "contemplating" and "delighting."[37] Poetic activity is not focused upon problem-solving or winning an argument: "At every turn what impels the activity and gives it whatever coherence it may possess, is the delight offered and come upon in this perpetually extending partnership between the contemplating self and its images."[38] Poetry, like all other modes, is an arrest, so one must never fall into the error of mistaking that world for the totality.

Yet, humans do, in fact, seek to understand the whole. This, for Oakeshott, is philosophy. Philosophy "means experience without reservation or presupposition, experience which is self-conscious and self-critical

throughout, in which the determination to remain unsatisfied with anything short of a completely coherent world of ideas is absolute and un-
qualified."[39] Thus, Oakeshott's intention for his book is to identify the
main modifications or arrests of experience, to show how each represents
a coherent world, and ultimately to show their inadequacies by considering each from the perspective of philosophy.[40] This is not to suggest that
the various modes are avoidable, for "in experience what is incomplete
cannot avoid asserting itself as complete; and when it asserts itself as complete, it cannot avoid the destructive force of the criticism of what actually
is complete."[41] Thus, philosophy is a never-ending attempt to grasp the
totality of experience as a complete and coherent world of ideas. But at
the same time, philosophy cannot simply replace the modes of experience.
The vast majority of lives are spent in the mode of practical experience. It
would be impossible and even undesirable to completely abandon this
mode. Thus "philosophy can and must supersede practical experience; but
it cannot take its place."[42]

This brief summary of Oakeshott's first book should suffice to show
the major components of his philosophic thought. Although I am ultimately interested in his critique of rationalism and his positive account
of the rationality of tradition (or practice), Oakeshott's philosophical
idealism—and the coherence theory of truth entailed therein—is an essential underpinning to the rest of his work and, therefore, cannot be ignored. With the general concepts presented in *Experience and Its Modes*
laid out, we can now go on to consider Oakeshott's critique of rationalism
and his understanding of the epistemic role of tradition. To this end, I propose to examine four essays by Oakeshott, each one published in *Rationalism in Politics and Other Essays*: "Rationalism in Politics," "Rational
Conduct," "Political Education," and "The Tower of Babel." Since each of
these essays is written to stand by itself and because the topics addressed
overlap considerably, we should expect a certain amount of repetition, but
I see no better way of examining Oakeshott's view of rationalism and tradition than to read closely several of his most trenchant essays.

"RATIONALISM IN POLITICS" (1947)

Oakeshott calls the modern cast of mind "rationalism." In so doing, he is
not denigrating reason per se; instead, his target is a certain conception of

reason, and it is that conception of reason and its implications that is the theme of "Rationalism in Politics." To begin, the rationalist is characterized by a fierce independence of mind: "His circumstances in the modern world have made him contentious: he is the enemy of authority, of prejudice, of the merely traditional, customary or habitual."[43] Yet this contentiousness, as with Descartes, comprised an odd mix of skepticism and optimism. He is skeptical of everything—all opinions and beliefs are open to his withering gaze. On the other hand, he is fully optimistic that his reason, the tool of his trade, is completely competent to winnow the wheat from the chaff. Such a combination of dispositions makes him suspicious of anyone's experience, save his own; thus the rationalist "has no sense of the cumulation of experience."[44] Such a person despises that which is habitual or traditional. Thus, he will prefer the new and untested innovation over the familiar and traditional that may require reform. For this reason, "there is, of course, no question either of retaining or improving such a tradition, for both these involve an attitude of submission. It must be destroyed. And to fill its place the Rationalist puts something of his own making—an ideology, the formalized abridgment of the supposed substratum of rational truth contained in the tradition."[45] In addition to the rejection of tradition, Oakeshott identifies two other general characteristics of rationalism: the politics of perfection and the politics of uniformity—"the essence of rationalism is their combination."[46] Because the rationalist has so much confidence in the ability of his individual reason to come to grips with any problem, he is unwilling to settle for what Oakeshott terms the "best in the circumstances." Instead, he will only settle for the best—for the ideal. Furthermore, "there can be no place for preferences that is not rational preference, and all rational preferences necessarily coincide. Political activity is recognized as the imposition of a uniform condition of perfection upon human conduct."[47]

At its heart, rationalism consists of a theory of knowledge. This view of knowledge assumes "the superiority of the unencumbered intellect," for the rationalist believes that reason unconstrained by habit or tradition is capable of attaining "more, and more certain, knowledge about man and society than was otherwise possible; the superiority of the ideology over the tradition lay in its greater precision and its alleged demonstrability."[48]

According to Oakeshott, all knowledge can be divided into two types, which he labels "practical" and "technical."[49] Technical knowledge is required for every scientific or practical endeavor, and "its chief characteristic is that it is susceptible of precise formulation, although special skill and insight may be required to give it that formulation."[50] Practical knowledge, on the other hand, "exists only in use, is not reflective and (unlike technique) cannot be formulated in rules."[51] The modern rationalist, though, has an obsessive preoccupation with certainty,[52] and because of that need, he insists that all knowledge is technical knowledge, for if some knowledge is not reducible to rules, then certainty in its regard is not possible: "The sovereignty of 'reason,' for the Rationalist, means the sovereignty of technique."[53] Thus, the rationalist denies the existence of practical knowledge.

Oakeshott points to the early modern period as the source of this movement: "What appeared to be lacking [from Aristotelian methodology] was not inspiration or even methodical habits of inquiry, but a consciously formulated technique of research, an art of interpretation, a method whose rules had been written down."[54] Oakeshott identifies the early seventeenth century not as the origin of rationalistic tendencies but rather as the period when rationalism emerges as an unmistakable approach.[55] He finds the thought of Francis Bacon and René Descartes as exemplary of rationalism. Bacon and Descartes sought to overturn the authority of tradition and create in its stead a better, more certain approach to knowledge. A universally applicable method, articulated at length in their writings, was intended to provide access to truth to anyone who would merely apply his own rational capacities according to the dictates of a particular methodology. For Oakeshott, this effort to effect a consciously formulated method was the catalyst that produced the rationalist. For the rationalist, the written word—the method—is paramount, and there is no knowledge outside that which can be written. Thus, the rationalist demands a book, a written text to which he can refer. But, because there are certain truths that cannot be contained in a book, the knowledge of the rationalist is only partial and lacks an essential element that is unwritable. Thus, "their knowledge does not extend beyond the written word which they read mechanistically—it generates ideas in their heads but no tastes in their mouths."[56] The effects of this new cast of mind were not limited to the esoteric halls of philosophy professors. Indeed, according to Oakeshott, "neither religion, nor natural science, nor education, nor the conduct of life itself escaped from the influence of the new Rationalism; no activity was immune, no society untouched."[57]

Rationalist education differs significantly from a more traditional approach, and, needless to say, a rationalist education serves only to perpetuate the errors of rationalism. Since only technical knowledge can be contained in books, practical knowledge cannot simply be transmitted by rote learning. Of course, the connoisseur—the expert—cannot do without a certain amount of technical knowledge, but that alone is inadequate. Oakeshott remarks that apprenticeship—"the pupil working alongside the master who in teaching a technique also imparts the sort of knowledge that cannot be taught"—though not completely abandoned, is certainly on the wane.[58] The failure to recognize the value of training in more than mere technique is made evident in the surge in professional schools wherein it is presumed that a mastery of technique equates with a mastery of the subject studied. This same bias shows itself in the study of moral philosophy whereby it is assumed that mastery of moral theory is adequate moral training. The goal of rationalist ethics is to formulate the moral law into readily accessible rules. Morality is compressed into a purely rational structure and peddled as the whole truth. But if it is the case that the mechanism of moral and political understanding is grounded in practical (or traditional or tacit) knowing, then it will be the case that (1) all rationalistic attempts to describe the process of understanding will be inadequate, and (2) the rationalist will fail to recognize the viability of any solution that looks beyond technical knowledge. Thus, the rationalist will reduce politics and morality to mere technique "to be acquired by training in an ideology rather than an education in behavior."[59] Moral education reduced to such thin gruel fails to produce that for which moral education exists: morally sound individuals. But if it is the case that technical skill alone will not suffice, then we do well to ask how to recover knowledge rooted in practice. Oakeshott writes,

> Moral ideals are a sediment; they have significance only so long as they are suspended in a religious or social tradition, so long as they belong to a religious or social life. The predicament of our time is that the Rationalists have been at work so long on their projects of drawing off the liquid in which our moral ideals were suspended (and pouring it away as worthless) that we are left only with the dry and gritty residue which chokes us as we try to take it down.[60]

Thus, a recovery of a proper understanding of morality requires a proper understanding of the nature and elements of knowledge, and central to that recovery is a recognition of and appreciation for that which is inarticulable, but nonetheless real. Moral ideals require the abiding presence of a religious or social tradition. But since religious and social traditions are complex collections of habits, customs, beliefs, and practices that cannot be reduced to a purely technical account, the rationalist tends to discount their importance. Oakeshott argues that the rise of rationalism corresponded with a decrease of belief. Rationalism "is certainly allied with a decline in the belief in Providence: a beneficent and infallible technique replaced a beneficent and infallible God."[61] But in replacing God and the religious beliefs entailed therein, the suspending element necessary for a proper understanding of morality was undermined. Social traditions, too, suffer the same fate, for in denigrating tradition, respect for the past is replaced by a myopic perspective that appreciates only the new and young and feels considerable embarrassment about that which is antiquated.

"Rationalism in Politics" is important primarily for its description of the twofold nature of knowledge. That knowing includes an unwritable, practical element along with the technical part is a crucial distinction that cannot be overemphasized. The following two essays pursue the subject of rationalism in greater depth and describe more fully the nature and function of tradition.

"Rational Conduct" (1950)

It is important, again, to recognize that Oakeshott, in critiquing rationalism, is not disparaging reason per se. He is not suggesting a nonrational theory of knowledge, politics, or morality. Instead, his concern is with a theory of knowledge that admits only the technical elements. Knowledge consists of both technical and practical components, and to ignore either is to provide an account that is simply inadequate. Thus, rationality, understood in its proper sense, is an unmitigated good. It is only when rationality is reduced to the purely technical that it slips into the damaging guise Oakeshott identifies as rationalism.

"Rational Conduct" contains one of Oakeshott's most memorable illustrations. He asks his readers to consider the claim by Victorian clothing designers that bloomers represented the "rational dress" for female bicyclists. By making such a claim for a particular costume, the designers, according to Oakeshott, believed that they had merely to consider the obvious elements involved in the activity: the physics of propelling a bicycle and the anatomy of the human being. All prejudices and habits concerning female dress could be disregarded in the process: "Consequently, the first step in the project of designing a 'rational' dress for this purpose must be a certain emptying of the mind, a conscious effort to get rid of preconceptions."[62] What was sought by the designers was "an eternal and a universal quality"[63] that was not subjected to the particularities of history or culture, of habit or custom. But is such a rational solution actually possible? Oakeshott does not think so, and to this end he observes that "impeded by prejudice, their minds paused at bloomers instead of running on to 'shorts'—clearly so much more complete a solution of their chosen problem."[64] The obvious question that arises from this whimsical illustration is, Why did the designers of clothing believe themselves to be creating a "rational dress"? And if such a rational process is not actually possible, what is missing in the account that would adequately explain their arrival at bloomers rather than, as Oakeshott suggests, shorts? The dearth of women bicyclists donning bloomers today only serves to drive home the point that although they may have served their purpose admirably when introduced, bloomers do not enjoy the universal and timeless quality claimed for them by their designers.

The false assumptions of the bloomer designers provides a point of departure for a discussion of "rational conduct." Such conduct is generally characterized by a specific and simple purpose. The complexities that always accompany a course of action are not given proper consideration; thus, in attempting to formulate the problem simply, it is not formulated adequately. The goal of this truncated formulation is the desire to express the problem in such a manner that a definite and certain conclusion is possible: "'Rational' activity is activity in search of a certain, a conclusive answer to a question, and consequently the question must be formulated in such a way that it admits of such an answer."[65] Such an approach requires the rational assessment of the means necessary to procure the desired end and "a high degree of detachment."[66] The mind must abstract itself from the prejudices of its particular situation and attend only to the rational elements of the task it is considering: "The 'rationality' of conduct, then, on this view of it, springs from something that we do *before* we act; and activity is 'rational' on account of its being generated in a certain manner."[67]

Of course, such an approach will necessarily exclude certain types of knowledge, for unless knowledge springs forth out of an unencumbered and detached mind, it fails to meet the standards of "rationality." Such behaviors born of capriciousness, impulse, tradition, habit, and custom are simply disregarded as inadmissible to conduct that is rationally determined.[68] Only that which admits of clear and definite ends and correspondingly clear and definite means falls under the rubric of "rational."

This approach to behavior and the knowledge that motivates it implies two important presuppositions. First, it is assumed "that men have a power of reasoning about things, of contemplating propositions about activities, and of putting these propositions in order and making them coherent." Second, it is assumed that "this is a power independent of any other powers a man may have, and something from which his activity can *begin*."[69] Thus, according to this view, "'rational' conduct is conduct springing from an antecedent process of 'reasoning.'"[70] The implications of this approach are important, for, as Oakeshott points out, a particular theory of mind is assumed. Rational conduct, as described here, assumes that the mind exists as a "neutral instrument" that must be exercised regularly and, when considering the "rational" solution to a problem, must be properly detached from the particularities of place and time. According to this view, "the mind will be most successful in dealing with experience when it is least prejudiced with already acquired dispositions or knowledge: the open, empty or free mind, the mind without disposition, is an instrument which attracts truth, repels superstition and is alone the spring of 'rational' judgment and 'rational' conduct."[71] In this view the mind is separate and distinct from the objects it considers, and a properly functioning mind need merely to rid itself of prejudice and consider the world "objectively" in order to come to "rational" conclusions.[72]

The problem with rationalism stems, Oakeshott believes, from this errant conception of mind. The rationalist sees the mind as an instrument into which information, beliefs, prejudices, and so forth are poured. The mind is conceived as separate and distinct from that which it contains. This dichotomy should recall Oakeshott's discussion of ideas in *Experience and Its Modes*. "Experience," Oakeshott writes, "is a world of ideas. And the condition of a world of ideas satisfactory in experience is a condition of coherence, of unity and completeness. Further, the world of experience is the real world; there is no reality outside experience."[73] This being the case, Oakeshott, rejects the subject/object dualism implied in rationalism in favor of his idealist conception of reality with its criterion of coherence. This errant view of mind is, according to Oakeshott, the single support for the rationalist: "Remove that, and the whole conception collapses."[74]

This incorrect conception of the mind produces further errors. If the mind is an instrument that dispassionately chooses simple and certain ends and the proper means to secure those ends, then it follows that theory precedes action, and technical knowledge is the whole of knowledge, for in this view theory motivates the mind in selecting means and ends, and only that which can be explicitly formulated is capable of being directly employed in the service of the chosen ends. But in this view, practical knowledge—that which is not reducible to propositions—is inadmissible. This, as we saw in "Rationalism in Politics," is a false conception of knowledge, which, Oakeshott argues, is not only misdirected but is in fact impossible: "Doing anything both depends upon and exhibits knowing how to do it; and though part (but never the whole) of knowing how to do it can subsequently be reduced to knowledge in the form of propositions (and possibly to ends, rules and principles), these propositions are neither the spring of the activity nor are they in any direct sense regulative of the activity."[75] Although it is certainly the case that technical knowledge is necessary and indispensable for any action, it represents "an abridgment" of the whole of knowledge. Thus, learning rules "is never more than the meanest part of education in an activity. They can be taught, but they are not the only things that can be learned from a teacher."[76]

Oakeshott now returns to the bloomers. Because the "rational" activity to which the designers aspired is, according to Oakeshott, an impossible ambition, and because with the added perspective of more than a century we can quite easily see that the bloomer solution is not rational at all in the timeless and universal sense, it becomes apparent that the designers simply failed to recognize the prejudices and traditions to which they were committed. Thus, the solution arrived at by the clothing designers fails to answer this question: What is the rational apparel for propelling a bicycle? But, on the other hand, bloomers is a very good answer to the following question: "What garment combines within itself the qualities of being well adapted to the activity of propelling a bicycle and of being suitable, all things considered, for an English girl to be seen in when riding a bicycle in 1880?"[77] The designers of bloomers were blind to the prejudices, traditions, and tastes of the English typical of the historical period in which the question of the female bicycle rider arose.

Although it is true that an end was chosen and pursued, that end was far from simple, and the means to that end had to conform to a complex assortment of conditions. Of course, the anatomical and mechanical considerations could not be ignored, but neither could the habitual, the customary, the traditional, and that which pertains to matters of taste. Thus, purely "rational" conduct is a false ideal, which derives ultimately from a faulty conception of mind, but which induces the rationalist to ignore significant areas of knowledge, and in so doing, he merely multiplies his errors.

It follows, then, that no skilled activity, be it cooking or scientific inquiry, begins with mere theory and moves subsequently to action. Instead, every such action occurs always "in an idiom or a tradition of activity."[78] Oakeshott offers scientific inquiry as an example. It is important to understand that he sees the principles elucidated in this example to transfer to all other areas of behavior. In other words, he does not understand science as a special case enjoying a privileged position distinct from all other activities.[79] Thus, only a person who is a scientist—that is, who is trained in and submissive to a particular tradition of inquiry—can even formulate a properly scientific question. A person who attempts to do science outside of the tradition that constitutes science will simply generate nonscientific answers to nonscientific questions: "What he will formulate is a problem which a connoisseur will at once recognize not to be a 'scientific' problem because it is incapable of being considered in a 'scientific' manner. Similarly, a connoisseur in historical inquiry will at once recognize that a question such as, Was the French Revolution a mistake? is a non-historical question."[80] Science, understood as a tradition of inquiry, pursues ends that are not fixed beforehand; it is an open-ended endeavor guided only by the body of tradition in which it exists. It does not depend upon a set of preestablished rules of conduct, for such rules are "only abridgments of the activity which at all points goes beyond them, and goes beyond them, in particular, in the connoisseurship of knowing how and when to apply them."[81]

It is important to grasp that a tradition is not fixed and static; rather, a tradition is flexible and capable of change without losing its continuity and coherence. In his "Introduction of Leviathan," Oakeshott provides a useful definition of tradition, which may help at this point. He writes, "It belongs to the nature of a tradition to tolerate and unite an internal variety, not insisting upon conformity to a single character, and because, further, it has the ability to change without losing its identity."[82] Thus, science may "properly be called 'rational' in respect of its faithfulness to the traditions of scientific inquiry."[83]

Principles and rules of conduct are mere abridgments, the technical elements, of a complex whole the elements of which cannot simply be reduced to technique. Skills must be acquired that cannot be gained through the mere study of a written account of an activity. The expert, the connoisseur, acquires habits of conduct and taste by observing a master and seeking to imitate him. In this sense, apprenticeship, whether it be formal or informal, is a necessary component of all skilled knowledge. This is relatively easy to recognize in a field such as cooking or carpentry, but it is no less true in the area of morality. In this case, the apprentice (a child, for instance) observes the actions of the masters, those who have acquired some degree of proficiency in moral action. Normally, the parents of the child fill the role of the master, regardless of whether or not they have themselves fully acquired the moral skills befitting a teacher. The student submits himself to the master, and in so submitting enters into a tradition of inquiry and behavior. Obviously, only one who possesses some measure of expertise is capable of passing that skilled knowledge on to the next generation. Thus, a tradition of behavior is necessary for the proper formation of expertise, and such a tradition can become fragmented and confused if only one generation fails to master properly the skills and subsequently to inculcate the young entrusted to its care. According to Oakeshott, "rational conduct," properly speaking, is "acting in such a way that the coherence of the idiom of activity to which the conduct belongs is preserved and possibly enhanced."[84]

But inculcation into a tradition does not begin with learning a list of rules or principles that ought to be followed. If theory actually follows in the wake of action, then we must know how to act properly prior to the development of the theory that justifies our action. In other words, if rules are an abridgment of a larger and more complex whole, then that whole is logically prior to the abridgment. Thus, through inculcation into a moral tradition, we learn how to behave morally as we live and observe those who have more developed and refined moral skills than we. In a certain respect, then, we know before we can explain what or how we know.[85] And when we develop the conceptual tools necessary to begin to describe what we know, that description represents only an abridgment—the technical element—of what we have learned.

But what happens when the moral tradition begins to fray? This ultimately results in the failure to pass the truths of the moral tradition on to the next generation. Oakeshott notes that "it is remarkable how trivial are some of the apparent causes—an earthquake, a plague, a war, or a mechanical invention, each appears to have had the power of disrupting (more or less seriously) the current of moral activity."[86] Regardless of the exact cause, "the condition may be described comprehensively as a loss of confidence in the traditional direction of moral activity, which carries with it a failure of impetus in the activity itself."[87] If the condition results in a loss of confidence and failure of impetus, then obviously recovery must result in "a revival of confidence and a renewal of impetus."[88] But this is not as simple as desiring a recovery. It is a mistake to assume that a failed or failing tradition can simply be abandoned and replaced with another. This assumption separates the mind from that which it knows, thereby falling into the rationalist error that attempts to maintain the subject/object dichotomy that Oakeshott identified earlier as the root error of rationalism. If, on the other hand, the mind and what it knows comprise a coherent whole, then a loss of confidence in one's moral tradition represents a move toward incoherence. Thus, recovery requires the reestablishment of coherence, and the only tools possible for such a recovery are the ones already possessed. Thus, "in the end, the cure depends upon the native strength of the patient; it depends upon the unimpaired relics of his knowledge of how to behave."[89] In short, the cure depends on tapping into the resources native to one's tradition.

Oakeshott concludes with a brief attempt to summarize his findings in terms of this question: What, then, is rational conduct, in the proper sense? First, it may be simplest to say what it is not. Rational conduct is not pursuing simple and clear ends by means of simple rules and principles that are presumed to represent the sum total of the knowledge necessary to accomplish one's chosen ends. Rules and principles are merely abridgments of a body of knowledge that is far more complex and simply cannot be reduced to a list of written rules. Since rational conduct is something other than this, and since the practical knowledge necessary for a proper understanding of action comes not from learning a list of rules but from inculcation into a coherent tradition of behavior, we can conclude that "'rationality' is a certificate we give to any conduct which can maintain a place in the flow of sympathy, the coherence of activity, which composes a way of living."[90] Conduct that is rational in this sense is properly termed rational conduct.

"Political Education" (1951)

The essay "Political Education" was originally given as Oakeshott's Inaugural Lecture at the London School of Economics. As the title indicates, its main concern is politics, but Oakeshott implies that the concepts he develops here also apply to morality.[91] Like "Rational Conduct," it seeks to articulate the epistemic necessity of tradition.

Oakeshott begins with a definition of activity that is reminiscent of the philosophical position he expressed in *Experience and Its Modes*: "To understand an activity is to know it as a concrete whole; it is to recognize the activity as having the source of its movement within itself."[92] A proper conception of an activity, then, is entirely self-contained and not dependent upon resources drawn from the outside. In the course of his discussion, Oakeshott examines "the adequacy of two current understandings of politics"[93] and finds them inadequate. He then proposes a third option as the more coherent account.

The first modern approach to politics is what he terms "empirical." According to this view, politics is nothing more than "waking up each morning and considering, 'What would I like to do?' or 'What would somebody else (whom I desire to please) like to see done?,' and doing it." One might find something resembling this approach in the "proverbial oriental despot, or in the politics of the wall-scribbler and the vote catcher."[94] In reality, though, such an approach is not only foolhardy, but in fact philosophically impossible, for it fails to conceptualize the activity of politics as a concrete whole; instead, it merely gives snapshots of abstract moments that can never add up to a coherent whole. Thus, "from a theoretical point of view, purely empirical politics are not something difficult to achieve or proper to be avoided, they are merely impossible; the product of a misunderstanding."[95]

The second understanding of politics is what Oakeshott terms "ideological." This type of politics is added to the empirical approach and supposedly provides it with its motivating force, for it "purports to be an abstract principle, or set of related abstract principles, which has been independently premeditated. It supplies in advance of the activity of attending to the arrangements of a society a formulated end to be pursued, and in so doing it provides a means of distinguishing between those desires which ought to be encouraged and those which ought to be suppressed or redirected."[96] Many ideals, or collections of ideals, have been employed to this end. Today we see the ideal of liberty or equality (and often both) touted as the abstract principle around which a particular political body arranges itself. Larger systems, such as liberalism or democracy or Marxism, fit the same mold. What is common to all such ideologies is the belief that they have been premeditated. The principles can be written down and referred to as a concise and reliable guide to action.[97] In this view, theory precedes action; premeditation leads to political activity in keeping with the premeditated principles. But for Oakeshott theory is derived from practice, and not vice versa. Thus, "so far from a political ideology being the quasi-divine parent of political activity, it turns out to be its earthly stepchild. . . . The pedigree of every political ideology shows it to be the creature, not of premeditation in advance of political activity, but of meditation upon a manner of politics."[98] If this is the case, then it is clear that, like empirical politics, ideological politics is also theoretically impossible, for it fails to provide a self-contained theory of political action.

Oakeshott presents a series of examples, some political and some not, to demonstrate his point. As in "Rational Conduct," he turns to scientific knowledge. It may, he argues, appear that the scientific hypothesis represents a premeditated plan of action, which owes nothing to any prior activity. If so, then scientific activity would be an example of action motivated by an ideology. But is this, in fact, the nature of scientific knowledge? Oakeshott answers, "The truth is that only a man who is already a scientist can formulate a scientific hypothesis; that is, an hypothesis is not an independent invention capable of guiding scientific inquiry, but a dependent supposition which arises as an abstraction from within already existing scientific activity."[99] Thus, the ability of a scientist to formulate a scientific hypothesis requires a prior education in the tradition of scientific activity. A hypothesis is an abstraction from a large and complex body of knowledge, and without the existence of that body, the abstraction would be unintelligible.

Turning to politics, it is sometimes assumed that the French Revolution was the product of an ideological theory of action. The Declaration of the Rights of Man, for example, has the appearance of a premeditated plan of action that served as a guide to the actions of the revolutionaries. Oakeshott will have none of this. The principles laid down in this "revolutionary" document are merely the abridged and abstracted common law rights enjoyed by Englishmen for centuries. Thus, these principles were not the product of hard thinking and solitary premeditation; instead, they were abstracted away from a long and complex tradition. In the same vein, Locke's *Second Treatise on Civil Government* was read in America and France "as a statement of abstract principles to be put into practice, regarded there as a preface to political activity. But so far from being a preface, it has all the marks of a postscript."[100] Again, we find not an ideology worked out prior to action, but an abridgment, in the case of Locke a "brilliant abridgment" of the traditions and practices of Englishmen. Thus, the ideological approach to political action is confused, for it fails to comprehend the true manner in which rules and principles are derived. Ideological politics is actually "a traditional manner of attending to the arrangements of a society which has been abridged into a doctrine of ends to be pursued, the abridgment (together with the necessary technical knowledge) being erroneously regarded as the sole guide relied upon."[101] Of course, at times such an abridgment may be of some value, when, for instance, one is attempting to export a political ideal. But too often it is forgotten that the abridgment is derived from a more complex whole. The practical knowledge not susceptible of abridgment is disregarded as unimportant. But, as should be obvious by now, "the abridgment is never by itself a sufficient guide."[102]

If activity presumes a complex preexisting tradition, then a definition of politics begins to emerge: "Politics is the activity of attending to the general arrangements of a collection of people who, in respect of their common recognition of a manner of attending to its arrangements, compose a single community."[103] Political action, then, springs out of a tradition of behavior that is more or less coherent. Because coherence is the single criterion for Oakeshott's approach to philosophy, it is no surprise that it again emerges as the central standard for pursing political action. When a practice is found to be incoherent with the overall tradition of a community, the practice is eventually altered to bring about a greater coherence: "In politics, then, every enterprise is a consequential enterprise, the pursuit, not of a dream, or of a general principle, but of an intimation."[104]

Oakeshott turns to the changing legal status of women to prove his point. For a long time the rights and duties of women were in a confused state, for women enjoyed some rights but not others. This resulted in an incoherence remedied by the eventual full enfranchisement of women. In other words, the rights and duties enjoyed by women intimated a fuller enfranchisement, and the attempt to resolve the incoherence resulted in the change. Of course, "there is no piece of mistake-proof apparatus by means of which we can elicit the intimation most worth while pursuing," but the intimation is all we have along with a more or less coherent tradition of political activity. There is, in other words, no absolute standard by which to measure our actions, and no definite goal to be gained save a greater coherence of our tradition of political activity. From this Oakeshott derives his definition of political activity: "In political activity, then, men sail a boundless and bottomless sea; there is neither harbour for shelter nor floor for anchorage, neither starting-place nor appointed destination. The enterprise is to keep afloat on an even keel; the sea is both friend and enemy; and the seamanship consists in using the resources of a traditional manner of behaviour in order to make a friend of every hostile occasion."[105]

This conception of political activity requires a particular kind of education. Although an ideological approach to politics (never mind its theoretical impossibility) emphasizes training in the technical elements of an ideology, the traditional approach must attend not only to the technical but also to the practical elements. Education must be of "our tradition of political behaviour. Other knowledge, certainly, is desirable in addition; but this is the knowledge without which we cannot make use of whatever else we may have learned."[106]

It is appropriate, at this point, to seek to understand just what constitutes a tradition of behavior, for the concept of tradition is frequently misunderstood. According to Oakeshott, a tradition of behavior "is neither fixed nor finished; it has no changeless centre to which understanding can anchor itself; there is no sovereign purpose to be perceived or invariable direction to be detected; there is no model to be copied, idea to be realized, or rule to be followed. Some parts of it may change more slowly than others, but none is immune from change. . . . Everything is temporary, but nothing is arbitrary. . . . Its principle is a principle of *continuity*."[107] Thus, although for Oakeshott nothing specific is prescribed, and neither is there a sure guide to the intimations to be pursued, "at least it does not lead us into a morass where every choice is equally good or equally to be deplored."[108]

Furthermore, even though education in one's own political tradition is essential, it is also the case that it is inadequate, for "to know only one's own tradition is not to know even that."[109] A full understanding of one's own tradition is only made possible by the study of other traditions, for such a study helps to reveal hidden truths and intimations in one's own tradition that would not otherwise be discovered. Thus, such a study brings us into a better and clearer understanding of our own tradition. "And the more thoroughly we understand our own political tradition, the more readily its whole resources are available to us, the less likely we shall be to embrace the illusions which wait for the ignorant and the unwary."[110]

In the 1962 republication of *Rationalism in Politics*, Oakeshott included a short appendix to "Political Education" titled "The Pursuit of Intimations." In the span of three pages, he attempts to address five objections to his thesis that political activity consists of the pursuit of an intimation. First, Oakeshott emphasizes that he is not describing what motivates progressive politicians and revolutionaries or what they believe they are doing, but rather he is describing what they actually succeed in doing. Second, some have suggested that Oakeshott's approach to politics replaces political reasoning with "acting on hunches" or "following intuitions." Oakeshott denies this and argues that if politics is how he describes it, then certain approaches to politics "must be considered either irrelevant or as clumsy formulations of other and relevant inquiries."[111] Third, some have suggested that Oakeshott's approach includes no theory of the good by which to judge the relative merits of one project over another, but this "is an unfortunate misreading of what I said: 'everything figures, not with what stands next to it, but with the whole.'"[112] Oakeshott asks his opponents to consider a concrete case in which a barrister in a court of appeal argues that his client has been awarded an inadequate sum. Does he simply claim that the award represents a gross injustice? Or does he attempt to show that the award is out of keeping with what is generally awarded in similar cases? Since the latter is obviously true and even assumed in the former, it follows that appeals to abstract notions of justice or equality are incapable of producing the desired effects. Thus, Oakeshott repeats, "moral and political 'principles' are abridgments of traditional manners of behaviour, and to refer specific conduct to 'principles' is not what it is made to appear."[113]

Fourth, some point out that most complex societies actually consist of a plurality of traditions. If this is the case, then Oakeshott's position appears to fragment wildly and actually serve to fracture a society rather than add to its overall coherence. To this Oakeshott offers three terse replies. First, "the absence of homogeneity does not necessarily destroy singleness." Second, in a legally organized society it must be assumed that the legal authority operates according to a particular tradition and, because of its legality, cannot have a competitor. Third, in order to conduct business politically, one must assume the existence at some level of a single community. If that does not exist in some form, then political activity becomes impossible.

The fifth and final objection is that Oakeshott's rejection of general principles leaves no guide for detecting incoherencies in a practice or for determining which intimations to pursue when incoherencies are identified. But this, Oakeshott points out, stems from a demand for a mistake-proof method for determining what ought to be done. Why assume such a principle exists in politics when all other endeavors lack such a guide? The scientist, the artist, and the craftsman all pursue their respective activities without the aid of a sure guide. So, too, must one who seeks to practice politics (or presumably the one who seeks to behave morally).

Oakeshott concludes by invoking J. S. Mill's "theory of human progress" and his "philosophy of history": "The view I have expressed in this essay may be taken to represent a further stage in this intellectual pilgrimage."[114] Of course, in light of his conception of politics as men at sail on a "boundless and bottomless sea" with no harbor or "appointed destination," Oakeshott's theory of progress is nonprogressive, open-ended, and wholly contingent. It continually seeks a greater internal coherence rather than an identity with an abstract ideal of reality.

"THE TOWER OF BABEL" (1948)

Although chronologically it precedes both "Rational Conduct" and "Political Education," "The Tower of Babel" deals with concepts fleshed out in the other essays. Oakeshott writes that his concern in this essay is "what is called moral activity, that is, activity which may be either good or bad." And contrary to those who look to nature to provide a guide to moral action, he asserts that the morality of an activity is determined "not by nature, but by art."[115] Specifically, he is concerned here not with the content of morality but with "the form of the moral life, and in particular the form of the moral life of contemporary Western civilization."[116] To that end, Oakeshott identifies two ideal forms of morality represented in the West. Neither is capable of independent existence, for they are ideal extremes, yet an individual or a society will inevitably tend toward one or the other. According to Oakeshott, one tendency is far preferable to the other, and unfortunately, morality in the West has taken a bad turn.

The first of these two forms of moral activity "is *a habit of affection and behaviour*, not a habit of reflective *thought*, but a habit of *affection* and *conduct*. The current situations of a normal life are met, not by consciously applying to ourselves a rule of behaviour, nor by conduct recognized as the expression of a moral ideal, but by acting in accordance with a certain habit of behaviour."[117] This form of morality involves the "unreflective following of a tradition of conduct in which we have been brought up."[118] Oakeshott is quick to point out that he is not speaking of moral intuition or a moral sense or what some might call "conscience"; instead he intends to indicate the type of moral action that constitutes the majority of our lives and is perhaps best illustrated by the manner in which moral action occurs in times of crisis when there is no time for the luxury of reflection.[119] In such cases, action occurs out of habit and does not rely upon any consideration of moral principles, rules, or ideals.

Education in this form of morality involves primarily "living with people who habitually behave in a certain manner: we acquire habits of conduct in the same way as we acquire our native language."[120] This type of education is not the product of the close study of a system of rules. Like the child who learns his own language, not by reference to a grammar book but by constant exposure to its proper use, so too this form of morality is acquired by observation and practice: "What we learn here is what may be learned without the formulation of its rules."[121] Oakeshott's distinction between technical and practical knowledge should be apparent here. This first form of moral life is concerned primarily with practical knowledge, with what cannot be stated as rules or principles, that is, technical knowledge.

Oakeshott is impressed by the stability inherent in this form of morality. This stability is a function of its flexibility within a context of continuity and coherence. In the same way that a language is stable yet constantly changing, so too this form of morality is capable of change without losing its identity. Some have criticized tradition as being inflexible and rigid, but nothing could be further from the truth, because "custom is always adaptable and susceptible to the *nuance* of the situation." This adaptability ensures that a traditional form of action is neither rigid nor unstable. Furthermore, this flexibility allows for the variations that inevitably arise in particular contexts. Thus, "this form of the moral life is capable of change as well as of local variation."[122] The flexible nature of this form of morality insulates it against crisis, but if it "denigrates into superstition, or if a crisis supervenes, [it] has little power of recovery. Its defence is solely its resistance to the conditions productive of crisis."[123]

The second form of moral life is in "many respects the opposite of the first." Where in the first, habit and affection are primary, in the second "activity is determined, not by a habit of behaviour, but by *the reflective application of a moral criterion.* It appears in two common varieties: as *the self-conscious* [sic] *pursuit of moral ideals,* and as *the reflective observation of moral rules.*"[124] The common feature linking these two common varieties is the self-conscious reflection on a rule or principle. "Normally the rule or the ideal is determined first and in the abstract." Such a formulation involves the reduction of moral ideas to words in such a manner that the proper ends of moral activity are clear and unambiguous. Once the rules are put into a readily accessible formula, it is then necessary to apply them to the particular situation: "In this form of the moral life, then, action will spring from a judgment concerning the rule or end to be applied and the determination to apply it."[125] This approach to moral activity is identical to the so-called rational conduct sought by the designers of bloomers Oakeshott discusses in "Rational Conduct," in which a simple and definite end is chosen and the means to that end are selected—theory is thought to precede action. In "The Tower of Babel," Oakeshott seems to hold that this approach to action is theoretically tenable; although, of course, this is an ideal form that lacks empirical examples. On the other hand, as we saw in the more.philosophically developed "Rational Conduct" and "Political Education," he believes that so-called ideological action is a confusion, and that in reality all action is ultimately derived from traditional forms or concepts.[126]

The education necessary to produce this type of morality is quite different than that required to produce the first type. Rather than education consisting primarily in observation and practice, this form requires the identification and study of moral rules and principles that have been "separated and detached from the necessarily imperfect expression they find in particular actions."[127] The removal of a rule from the particularities in which it is found is an attempt to universalize it—to find within it the element that makes it applicable to all other people in similar circumstances. It is the desire for uniformity. Furthermore, this form of morality, because it seeks universal ideals uniformly applicable to all humans, "calls upon those who practice it to determine their behaviour by reference to a vision of perfection."[128] Recall that in "Rationalism in Politics" Oakeshott argued that the two identifying characteristics of rationalism (in addition to a rejection of tradition) are a commitment to perfection and uniformity.[129] Thus, this form of moral action is at its core rationalistic, and the problems of rationalism in politics are similar to the problems of rationalism in morality.

With regard to change and flexibility, Oakeshott points out an irony. Tradition is flexible and quite capable of change according to the circumstances or local preferences. On the other hand, "a morality of ideals has little power of self-modification; its stability springs from its inelasticity and its imperviousness to change."[130] The irony is glaring, for the rationalist's desire to bring about perfect and uniform moral practices results in the very inflexibility that the critics of tradition claim to find so troubling.

Furthermore, "every moral ideal is potentially an obsession; the pursuit of moral ideals is an idolatry in which particular objects are recognized as 'gods.'" In other words, a particular ideal can be overemphasized to the point that its pursuit is no longer moral, for "every admirable ideal has its opposite, no less admirable." Thus, if one ideal is pursued to the exclusion of all others, the result is moral chaos. For instance, chaos would result if the ideal of liberty is pursued while its opposite, order, is ignored, or the ideal of justice is pursued rather than charity.[131] A tenuous balance must be navigated, and a view of moral activity based on rules and ideals does not possess the tools necessary to strike a proper balance. The moral life is, in Oakeshott's phrase, "determined by art."[132]

All moral systems, Oakeshott claims, comprise varying degrees of these two ideal moral forms, but the various ratios will determine the overall structure of each particular system.[133] He writes, "In a mixture in which the first [habit and affection] of these extremes is dominant, the moral life may be expected to be immune from a confusion between behaviour and the pursuit of an ideal."[134] When habit and affection retain primacy, the centrality of action will never be usurped by an impulse to reflect on rules and principles. This is not to say that reflection plays no part, for "there is no doubt whatever that a morality in which reflection has no part is defective."[135] Reflection plays an important role in this conception of morality, for it provides the tools necessary to evaluate, criticize, and reform itself. This mixture will offer not only confidence in action but also "intellectual confidence in its moral standards and purposes." Thus, "the education in moral habit will be supplemented, but not weakened, by the education in moral ideology."[136] This combination, in which habit and affection are primary but rules and ideology are not excluded, provides the resources, practically and conceptually, to effect a stable though flexible approach to moral life that recognizes the reality of particulars and the contingency of action. It recognizes the need for rules and ideals but never elevates them above the contingencies of life itself. "In short, this form of the moral life will offer to a society advantages similar to those of a religion which has taken to itself a theology (though not necessarily a popular theology) but without losing its character as a way of living."[137]

On the other hand, a morality in which the pursuit of ideals and rules is dominant will, according to Oakeshott, "suffer from a permanent tension between its component parts." This is because a commitment to perfection and unity will overshadow the simple coherence provided by a morality informed by habit and affection. As a result "it will seem more important to have an intellectually defensible moral ideology than a ready habit of moral behaviour."[138] Since this approach to morality holds that a rule or a principle must be universal in order to have proper justification for itself, there will be a lack of appreciation for the particularities that arise in local contexts. Thus, "it will come to be assumed that a morality which is not easily transferable to another society, which lacks an obvious universality, is (for that reason) inadequate for the needs of the society of its origin."[139] Moral action is given a secondary position to the coherence of the ideological system (which can never be a self-contained coherent whole), and when this occurs, action tends to become confused, disjointed, and lacking the coherence of action rooted in a tradition. Returning to the religion metaphor, Oakeshott likens this to "a religious life in which the pursuit of theology offers itself as an alternative to the practice of piety."[140]

According to Oakeshott, modern Western society has to its detriment overemphasized the rule-based form of morality while at the same time neglecting the form that concerns habitual conduct. The result is the moral confusion so often lamented in modern circles. Oakeshott writes, "The moral energy of our civilization has for many centuries been applied mainly (though not, of course, exclusively) to building a Tower of Babel; and in a world dizzy with moral ideals we know less about how to behave in public and in private than ever before."[141] Not surprisingly, the ascendancy of a morality of rules and ideals did not produce the certainty and uniformity desired.

Oakeshott treats his readers to a brief historical account of the changing conception of morality in the West. Our modern moral understanding is the result of two streams of thought, Greek and Christian. In the Greco-Roman world morality, for a time, consisted primarily of a habit of moral behavior. Aristotle's *Nicomachean Ethics* is, presumably, an example of a moral theory that emphasizes habit and practice rather than explicit rules in service of an ideology. Eventually, though, the Greco-Roman morality lost its vitality. There were, doubtless, those who still acted out of habit in accordance with the older morality, yet "in general, the impetus of moral habit of behaviour seems to have been spent—illustrating, perhaps, the defect of a form of morality too securely insulated from the criticism of ideals."[142] Into this weakened situation swept Christianity. Christian communities were characterized by faith and hope, "faith in a person and hope for a coming event." And "the morality of these communities was a custom of behaviour appropriate to the character of the faith and to the nature of the expectation."[143] Habit and affection provided the impetus to moral activity, along with the notable lack of any explicitly formulated moral ideal save, perhaps, the command to love God and neighbor. But, a change came over Christian morality. In the first three centuries of Christendom "the habit of moral behaviour was converted into the selfconscious [*sic*] pursuit of formulated moral ideals—a conversion parallel to the change from faith in a person to belief in a collection of abstract propositions, a creed."[144] Oakeshott speculates that this shift was the result of the evangelistic impulse of Christianity whereby the "Christian" way of life had to be abridged (e.g., reduced to technical knowledge) in order to produce the "easily translatable prose of a moral ideal."[145]

Modern Western morality, then, is the product of two streams of thought, both of which centuries ago became moralities of rules and ideals. Ironically, though this fact ought to be mourned as a loss, "the remarkable thing about contemporary European morality is not merely that its form is dominated by the selfconsious [*sic*] pursuit of ideals, but that this form is generally thought to be better and higher than any other." Morality that emphasizes habit and affection is scoffed at as primitive, while the alternative is seen as progressive. Furthermore, a morality of ideals is optimistically prized "because it appears to hold out the possibility of that most sought-after consummation—a 'scientific' morality."[146] Such a consummation of morality is a Tower of Babel, which only leads to moral confusion, for scientific knowledge requires propositions, and propositions can include nothing other than technical knowledge. Thus, a "scientific" morality, a morality in which the rules and ideals are finally confined to a

formula that is both universal and perfect, is nothing more than the rationalist's dream, which, if Oakeshott is correct, is more akin to a nightmare
of confusion.

On Human Conduct

Oakeshott's last major book, *On Human Conduct*, was published in 1975,
eight years after his official retirement and fifteen years prior to his death
in 1990. The primary theme of *On Human Conduct* is civil association and
thus outside of the range of our present concerns, but Oakeshott does also
include a discussion of tradition. Since what he says is generally in agreement with the works we have previously analyzed, I do not intend to spend
much time here. Several main points will suffice.

First, Oakeshott replaces the word "tradition" with "practice." He
notes that "I have become much more strict with the word 'practice'
and . . . I have abandoned 'tradition' as inadequate to express what I want
to express."[147] This change reflects the significant difference between
Burke's notion of tradition and Oakeshott's. In abandoning the term "tradition" Oakeshott is attempting to prevent the confusion that frequently
surrounds his use of the term "tradition." Whereas tradition is generally
understood as a body of information accumulated over time and one
which represents (for Burke) the collected wisdom of the past, Oakeshott's
concept is philosophical rather than historical. Oakeshott defines "practice" as "a procedure proper or useful to be observed and therefore capable
of being neglected or violated and capable, also, of being observed only in
the chosen subscriptions of agents."[148] Thus, a practice requires freedom,
and as such can either be attended to or neglected. Of course, since this
notion has a strong epistemological element, a practice, in the deepest cultural sense, cannot simply be ignored or rejected, for since the practice provides the original resources available to a community, even the rejection of
a particular practice is done within the context created by the practice; a
rejection of a practice is accomplished using the tools afforded by the practice itself. Oakeshott continues his definition:

> A practice may be identified as a set of considerations, manners, uses,
> observances, customs, standards, canons, maxims, principles, rules, and
> offices specifying useful procedures or denoting obligations or duties

which relate to human actions and utterances. It is a prudential or an authoritative adverbial qualification of choices and performances, more or less complicated, in which conduct is understood in terms of a procedure. Words such as punctually, considerately, civilly, scientifically, legally, candidly, judicially, poetically, morally, etc., do not specify performances; they do postulate performances and specify procedural conditions to be taken into account when choosing and acting.[149]

These "adverbial considerations" may "acquire the firmness of an 'institution,' or they may remain relatively plastic."[150] In no case, though, are they set in stone. They are capable of change and can adapt to accommodate local particularities. Furthermore, they "specify procedural conditions" rather than substantive goods. That is, they do not inform an individual of *what* ought to be done, but *how* something ought to be done. In Oakeshott's words, a practice "does not impose upon an agent demands that he shall think certain thoughts, entertain certain sentiments, or make certain substantive utterances. It comes to him as various invitations to understand, to choose, and to respond. It is composed of conventions and rules of speech, a vocabulary and a syntax, and it is continuously invented by those who speak it and using it is adding to its resources. It is an instrument to be played upon, not a tune to be played."[151]

According to Oakeshott, "The two most important practices in terms of which agents are durably related to one another in conduct are a common tongue and a language of moral converse."[152] Employing a metaphor that appears throughout his writing, Oakeshott likens moral conduct to a language. A moral practice is a "vernacular language of colloquial intercourse."[153] Like any living language, it is amenable of change, but in changing it is capable of retaining its identity. Thus, a moral practice is "never fixed or finished, but (like other languages) it has a settled character in terms of which it responds to the linguistic inventions, the enterprises, the fortunes, the waywardness, the censoriousness, and sometimes the ridicule of those who speak it. It *is* its vicissitudes, and its virtue is to be a living, vulgar language articulating relationships, responsibilities, duties, etc., recognizable by its speakers as reflections of what, on earth, they have come to understand themselves to be."[154] By likening moral practices to a vernacular language we can recognize Oakeshott's emphasis on coherence. A language only makes sense to others who speak it. The language acts as a coherent, though malleable, self-contained whole and can only be critiqued, judged, or altered by the speakers—that is, from the inside, by the speakers themselves.

Moral rules are mere abridgments of the practices from which they are derived. These rules "are to be recognized as densities obtruded by the tensions of a spoken language of moral intercourse, nodal points at which a practice turns upon itself in a vortiginous movement and becomes steadier in ceasing to be adventurous." As abridgments, they do not constitute the practice itself, but only make the practice more explicitly available. Moral rules, of course, are not undesirable, but it must always be remembered that although they "may help to keep a practice in shape . . . they do not give it its shape." Thus, rules and principles and duties can aid in articulating the basic structure of a practice, but "no moral practice can be reduced to the rules, the duties, or the 'ideals' it obtrudes."[155] In other words, a practice consists of both technical and practical knowledge, and to formulate the practice exclusively in writable rules or principles (technical knowledge) is to forfeit the essence of the practice itself.

OAKESHOTT'S CRITICS AND LIMITATIONS

Although Oakeshott's work has provoked a significant amount of criticism directed at the various aspects of his thought, I want to look only at two lines of criticism. First, I want to address an objection centering on whether or not rationalism is possible, for some have accused Oakeshott of confusion on this point. Then I want to consider accusations that his thought cannot avoid some version of relativism.

First, if moral rules are abridgments of a larger and more complex whole that constitutes a practice, then it would seem that a morality composed exclusively of rules is simply a confusion. Thus, it would follow that contrary to his essay "The Tower of Babel," there are not two ideal types of moral forms, the habit-based and the rule-based. For if rules are an abridgment of something more primary, then they require the prior existence of a whole practice, and it follows that a form of moral activity based on rules is ultimately untenable. In this regard a number of commentators have noted that Oakeshott appears confused as to whether rationalism is a possible though undesirable condition, or whether it is philosophically impossible.[156] Oakeshott, though, does not suffer from such a confusion.[157] As he notes in "Political Education," "to try to do something which is inherently impossible is always a corrupting enterprise."[158] Thus, Oakeshott argues that although a pure rule-based morality is logically impossible, it is possible for a society to look to rules and principles *as if* they did constitute a wholly coherent moral system. But such an attempt results only in a confused moral philosophy in which equally important moral rules find themselves at odds, or in which one particular moral rule is elevated above all the rest. In either event, morality becomes either an incoherent collection of competing rules or an idolatry in which one rule or ideal group of rules is pressed beyond what it can bear. Thus, to pursue a morality based exclusively on rules or an ideal is a "corrupting" endeavor that for a society is "mere folly."[159]

Second, Oakeshott has come under criticism for not being able to avoid moral relativism. His denial of any notion of natural law or any moral knowledge with a metaphysical referent;[160] his denial of anything resembling a correspondence theory of truth; his use of language as a metaphor for morality; his claim that politics (and presumably morality) consists of nothing more than the pursuit of intimations; his claim that one's tradition provides the only resources, the only referent, for moral action—all of these seem to point ultimately toward an inescapable moral and political relativism. In the following paragraphs I want to consider some of the specific objections and then determine to what extent they actually apply to Oakeshott's thought.

In a review of *Rationalism in Politics*, moral philosopher D. D. Raphael argues that Oakeshott's notion of politics as the pursuit of intimations provides no standard by which to judge whether or not a particular intimation ought to be pursued. Oakeshott, in his well-known example of the status of women, argues that women received the franchise in England because in most aspects they had already been enfranchised, and the persisting incoherence provided the impetus to move to full enfranchisement.[161] Raphael objects: "This is like arguing that if the lot of elderly people in our society has been deteriorating in most respects, that is a cogent reason for making it deteriorate in other respects too. Why should we say that one growing tendency in our society should be hastened, and another tendency checked? Only because we evaluate the one as desirable or just, and the other as undesirable or unjust."[162] Of course, Oakeshott refuses to acknowledge any abstract, universal principle of justice. There is for him no "mistake-proof"[163] method, no "steady, unchanging, independent guide to which a society might resort."[164] In response to just this sort

of objection, Oakeshott invokes his coherence criterion as the only existing standard.[165] There is no principle to which our action must correspond.
Instead, we must do the best we can with the resources we possess in our
particular moral tradition. We must, Oakeshott writes in his reply to Raphael, determine "the relative importance, in the given circumstances, of
the numerous, competing normative and prudential considerations which
compose our 'tradition.'" For this task we possess no "unique and undeni-
able norm." Instead, "what is sought is a decision which promises the most
acceptable balance in the circumstances between competing goods."[166] For
Raphael this is simply inadequate: "If the incoherence to be remedied is
simply between the legal status of women in some respects and their legal
status in others, coherence can be produced either by giving them addi-
tional rights or by taking away the rights they have. Incoherence between
the helplessness of elderly people in some respects and not in others can
be removed either by providing help where it does not now exist or by
taking it away where it does."[167] One might respond in Oakeshott's defense that the pursuit of intimations includes an awareness of the direction
in which the intimation is moving. Thus, since the liberties of women were
moving in the direction of full enfranchisement, it was reasonable to resolve the incoherence by granting full enfranchisement. But this does not
really solve the problem, for it is certainly imaginable that momentum
could at times move in an undesirable direction. To imagine an extreme
example, if Jews in Nazi Germany were deemed responsible for political
and economic troubles, to allow them to continue unbothered would result
in an incoherence. To resolve the incoherence in the direction suggested
by the momentum of events would be to go down the road pursued by the
Nazis. Of course, Oakeshott would reply that one cannot simply consider
one element in reality, for what matters is the coherence of the whole. But
this is not very satisfying. It appears that Raphael is justified in criticizing
Oakeshott for possessing an inadequate account of moral value.

For Oakeshott, in pursuing an intimation, one possesses only the resources made available by one's tradition. Thus, the question of intimations
rests ultimately upon a larger question of the meaning and content of tradition. Neil Wood notes that Oakeshott's conception of tradition is "the
most critical and yet the weakest ingredient of his political thought. It
would seem rather incongruous that while rejecting the mysticism of
natural law, he accepts an almost mystical conception of tradition."[168]
Wood locates the central issue in Oakeshott's apparent lack of any stan-

dard by which to evaluate competing traditions and concludes that "there is no reason why the well-established, just because it is well-established, should prescribe our conduct."[169] Since tradition is far from univocal and often quite vague, it "is hardly a satisfactory guide."[170] Hanna Fenichel Pitkin finds Oakeshott's conception of tradition wanting, for "Oakeshott simply has nothing to say to people without a tradition to preserve." John Gray criticizes Oakeshott's conception of tradition as "parochial." Oakeshott, he argues, does not take into account the plurality of traditions within a particular society.[171]

The problem with Oakeshott's conception of tradition, which his critics find so objectionable, does not lie primarily with Oakeshott. Instead, the trouble stems from a misunderstanding of his use of the word "tradition." This tendency toward misunderstanding, we can assume, is what provoked him to cease employing the term altogether and replace it with "practice." The confusion, as I have already pointed out, results in the assumption that Oakeshott means by "tradition" simply a repository of knowledge accumulated from the past and passed on from generation to generation. In this view, tradition is a source of information. Those critics of Oakeshott who find his notion of tradition insufficient misread Oakeshott. As I have tried to indicate, Oakeshott's concept of tradition does not primarily indicate a repository of knowledge; instead, Oakeshott's understanding of tradition is at its heart epistemological. Tradition is those assumptions, habits, customs, and procedures that provide us with the conceptual framework by which we engage the world. We see the world through the tradition into which we have been inculcated. We can do nothing else. Therefore, the resources afforded us by our tradition are the only tools available to us. We have access to nothing else, for we can see nothing else. Individuals are embedded within the particularities of their traditions; thus, any theory of morality or politics must recognize that we theorize and act *from* some particular place rather than from a placeless Cartesian abstraction. This place is constituted by prejudices, habits of mind and action, a history, tacit presuppositions that rarely if ever find explicit expression, stories and myths particular to the tradition, and the collected wisdom of those who have gone before.

Thus, objections that Oakeshott is too parochial and that his notion of tradition does not afford the resources to deal with new situations or produce necessary innovation simply miss Oakeshott's point. Such objections assume a rationalist theory of mind in which the mind is conceived as a neutral instrument separable from its contents. But for Oakeshott, when an innovation is needed, one simply cannot find a solution outside of what is available. And what is available constitutes one's tradition. Of course, it might be claimed that one can borrow resources from other traditions, and Oakeshott would quite agree. But in borrowing, one of two things must necessarily occur. First, in studying other traditions, we may actually bring to light resources in our own that were hidden.[172] Second, if we do find a resource present in another tradition that is conspicuously absent in our own, we must never forget that the manner in which we recognize, appropriate, and apply that new resource will inevitably be conditioned by our own tradition. Thus, although a person may gain inspiration from the traditions of others, the end result, once the particular resource is assimilated, is quite unique to one's own tradition.

Oakeshott's theory of coherence plays a key role here, for a tradition represents a more or less coherent whole—it provides the conceptual framework by which one sees the world. Thus, the question of relativism *between* traditions is simply not a relevant question for Oakeshott. Each person sees the world in terms of the tradition to which he belongs. No one can avoid that. And, thus, no one can avoid belonging to a tradition. For Oakeshott, neutrally evaluating traditions implies the possibility of getting outside of one's tradition and judging it against a standard that is independent of the tradition. This, for Oakeshott, is simply impossible. Each person and society must do the best it can with what it has inherited, and what it inherits is its tradition. There is nothing more—no external standard, no perfect, foolproof method by which to arrange one's life:

> A depressing doctrine, it will be said. . . . A tradition of behaviour is not a groove within which we are destined to grind out our helpless and unsatisfying lives. . . . But in the main the depression springs from the exclusion of hopes that were false and the discovery that guides, reputed to be of superhuman wisdom and skill, are, in fact, of a somewhat different character. If the doctrine deprives us of a model laid up in heaven to which we should approximate our behaviour, at least it does not lead us into a morass where every choice is equally good or equally to be deplored. And if it suggests that politics are *nur für die Schwindelfreie* [only for those who don't suffer vertigo] that should depress only those who have lost their nerve.[173]

This account of tradition, though it serves, to some extent, as a response to those of Oakeshott's critics who claim that his approach cannot avoid a relativism *between* traditions, ultimately still leaves us with a problem of an adequate theory of value *within* a particular tradition. Let me try to make that distinction clearer.

Oakeshott employs the metaphor of language to describe morality. A language is a self-contained, internally coherent whole that is nonetheless capable of changing while at the same time maintaining its identity over time. Such an image of coherence, apparent in language and embraced by Oakeshott as the criterion for truth (along with comprehensiveness and the satisfaction that both together elicit), does not permit a person to claim that one language is better or worse than another. It is simply reflective of a mistake in concepts to claim, for instance, that Chinese is better than Spanish. One might be able to claim that a particular language is more effective than another language in a particular case or range of cases, but such a determination requires that a person know each language equally well.[174] For Oakeshott, this is impossible, for one's moral language is carried along by one's tradition, and one's tradition, as we have seen, is the reference point from which all knowing takes place. Thus, accusations of relativism *between* traditions is, for Oakeshott, simply a confusion, for there exists no tradition-independent position from which such an evaluation can be made.

Although the question of relativism *between* traditions is meaningless for Oakeshott, he also denies that his position implies relativism *within* a particular tradition, for "if the doctrine deprives us of a model laid up in heaven to which we should approximate our behaviour, at least it does not lead us into a morass where every choice is equally good or equally to be deplored."[175] Indeed, his position does not permit a radical relativism in which all choices are morally equal, for the pursuit of intimations guided by the criterion of coherence establishes some guidance for action. However, Oakeshott does not appear capable of adequately responding to Raphael's criticism, for, as Raphael argues, an intimation can lead in immoral directions and coherence is satisfied by solutions that are patently unjust. In Oakeshott's defense we might respond that a tradition (his own tradition, since that is what Oakeshott primarily addresses) contains within it standards of justice and morality that serve as guides for determining how best to pursue an intimation, and when these standards are respected, a higher degree of coherence is achievable than if they are not. At best this introduces a clarifying concept that is not obviously present in Oakeshott but which we might assume he intends, for without it, relativism within a particular tradition appears inescapable. At worst, this represents an addition to Oakeshott, and if this is the case, then we must conclude that his account of tradition is inadequate. In either case, Oakeshott's approach to tradition is not completely satisfying—he is either vague where he should be clear, or he is lacking an element that is indispensable.

Nevertheless, it should be obvious that certain key elements of his thought are vital and will serve as guides as we press further. First, his distinction between technical and practical knowledge is crucial. The belief that all knowledge is capable of explicit and accurate verbal articulation is an error of the rationalist that we do well to avoid. Second, Oakeshott's view of tradition, not primarily as a resource but as an epistemologically necessary condition for knowledge is equally important. This insight undermines the Cartesian belief that human knowers are capable of shaking off the prejudices, habits, customs, and tacit presuppositions that constitute the context within which all theorizing takes place. This is not to suggest that all knowledge is subjective. Instead, this merely indicates that all knowledge is necessarily mediated by the particularities of one's own tradition.

CHAPTER 3

Alasdair MacIntyre's
Tradition-Constituted Inquiry

> All morality is always to some degree tied to the socially local and
> particular and . . . the aspirations of the morality of modernity to a
> universality freed from all particularity is an illusion. . . . There is no
> way to possess the virtues except as part of a tradition.
>
> —Alasdair MacIntyre[1]

Alasdair MacIntyre has variously described himself as "an Augustinian
Christian,"[2] a "Thomistic Aristotelian,"[3] a "Thomistic Aristotelian" and a
"Catholic,"[4] and simply "a Thomist."[5] These self-descriptions are all the
more notable in light of his earlier commitments to Marxism. Indeed,
MacIntyre's intellectual journey has prompted one commentator to re-
mark that "what distinguishes Professor MacIntyre is not the number of
beliefs he has doubted, but the number of beliefs he has embraced. His
capacity for doubt we share or surpass; it is his capacity for faith which
is distinctive and perhaps unrivalled."[6] Although MacIntyre's thought has
undergone significant changes over the course of his lengthy and highly
productive career, his so-called virtue trilogy—*After Virtue*; *Whose Justice?*
Which Rationality?; and *Three Rival Versions of Moral Enquiry*—present
the views of a thinker generally committed to the tradition in which the

differing views of Aristotle and Augustine are synthesized in the work of
Thomas Aquinas.[7] Ironically, although MacIntyre's "capacity for faith" has
been criticized, the tone of his books, especially *After Virtue*, is decidedly
pessimistic about the possibility of recovering that which has been destroyed by modernity. Thus, within MacIntyre's work we initially encounter what appears to be a paradox: belief mixed with despair, optimism with
pessimism. Yet, it is in his trenchant critique of what he terms the "modern
project" that the seeds of a more positive program are sown. Thus, for
MacIntyre, the apparent paradox is not paradoxical at all, for in his account the possibility of bringing about a more positive conception of
morality—and society more generally—is only feasible after properly di-
agnosing our current troubles, and such diagnosis requires a confrontation
with the failures in which we are deeply mired.

As with Oakeshott, a central theme in MacIntyre's thought is the
concept of tradition. As we saw in chapter 2, Oakeshott eventually substi-
tuted "practice" for "tradition" in order to avoid some of the connotations
carried by the term "tradition." MacIntyre, on the other hand, employs
both terms separately, so it will be important to understand how Mac-
Intyre's conception of tradition differs from Oakeshott's. We saw that one
of the central problems of Oakeshott's approach is a seeming inability to
avoid a form of moral relativism, for a morality based on nothing more
than the pursuit of intimations and the satisfaction produced by coherence
does not appear to provide the tools necessary to escape such a conclusion.
Furthermore, for Oakeshott, the question of judging between traditions is
not one that he considers relevant. MacIntyre, on the other hand, recognizes and appreciates the differences between various traditions, and he is
convinced that it is possible to determine the rational superiority of one
tradition over another.

Since the theme of tradition is at the center of MacIntyre's so-called
virtue trilogy, I will primarily focus upon those three works. To begin our
discussion, we can turn to his groundbreaking 1981 book, *After Virtue*.

Modernity, Incommensurability, and Emotivism

According to Russell Hittinger, MacIntyre's *After Virtue* "was a bombshell
thrown in the sandbox of contemporary ethicians."[8] Echoing G. E. M.
Anscombe's sentiments voiced two decades prior that "it is not profitable

for us at present to do moral philosophy," MacIntyre declares that all modern moral philosophy is merely the incomplete and largely incoherent fragments of a premodern ethical system.[9] Employing a memorable metaphor that echoes the setting of Walter M. Miller Jr.'s novel *A Canticle for Leibowitz*, MacIntyre likens modern moral philosophy to a great scientific culture that undergoes an almost complete destruction from within. Science falls out of favor, and those in authority attempt to rid it completely from the society. Some generations later there is a revival of interest in the idea of science, but much has been lost, and that which remains is badly damaged and incomplete. Any attempt to reconstruct a complete science from the remains is doomed at its inception because of the inability of these new scientists to comprehend properly the context within which the information they have recovered was originally employed. The world of moral philosophy, argues MacIntyre, is in much the same situation as this fictional world of science. MacIntyre's goal in *After Virtue* is to point out how the abandonment of moral philosophy rooted in the Aristotelian tradition is the source of the breakdown, and only by recovering that which was lost, through a sort of intellectual archeology, can intelligibility be restored.

Modern moral discourse is characterized by its interminability. In most major moral disputes no resolution is reached; instead, parties continue (or break off in disgust) presenting versions of arguments that simply cannot, on their own terms, reach a conclusion whereby one is shown to be rationally superior to another. Invoking the term employed by Thomas Kuhn, MacIntyre argues that modern moral arguments are "incommensurable."[10] By way of illustration, MacIntyre presents three issues that in today's moral discourse admit of no resolution: war, abortion, and economic justice.

Regarding the first, there are those who agree with the just war tradition that a just war must distinguish between combatants and noncombatants, but the weapons and tactics of modern warfare make such distinctions impossible, so all modern wars are unjust, and the only moral course is pacifism. On the other hand, there are those who recognize the dangers of the modern world and argue that the only possible way to avoid war is to be well armed and willing to fight, even if that includes employing nuclear weapons. A third position holds that the only justifiable wars are those that seek to liberate those groups who are oppressed by the domination of wealthy countries.

The second set of arguments, those dealing with abortion, are no less intractable. First, there are those who claim that because all persons possess rights to their own bodies, it is morally permissible for a woman to abort a fetus. On the other hand, I cannot will that my mother had aborted me. But if I cannot deny this in my own case, universalizing this principle shows that I cannot deny to others the same right to life that I claim for myself; thus, abortion is immoral. Finally, there are those who argue that murder is wrong and abortion is murder, for it is the taking of an innocent human life.

Regarding economic justice, there are those who argue that justice demands that all people have an equal opportunity, and such opportunity requires equal access to education, health care, and other resources. But this sort of access requires money, so those who possess more are morally (and ideally, legally) required to give up significant portions of their wealth to ensure equality. In addition, all private schools, private medical practices, and any other organization or institution that makes it possible for one person to secure benefits not available to all must be eliminated. On the other hand, there are those who claim that all people possess the right to do as they wish so long as no one else is hurt. According to this view, individuals are morally free to make agreements, exchange goods and services, and enjoy the fruits of individual initiative (and luck of birth) in whatever fashion they choose. In this case, private schools and private medical practices should not only be allowed, but they should be unregulated and subject only to the pressures of the market.[11]

In the various arguments one can recognize positions taken by thinkers such as Marx, Locke, Kant, Rousseau, Adam Smith, Rawls, and Nozick. These arguments are indeed incommensurable, and it should be noted that the tenor of modern debates is frequently shrill. This is no doubt due, in part, to the emotional intensity with which various positions are held and defended. But, without any overarching theory of morality, nature, human nature, or the good upon which to base moral discussion, it turns out that the premises used to support the differing conclusions appear to be arbitrarily selected by those advancing them.[12] The resulting moral theory—MacIntyre calls it "emotivism"—has come to dominate modern moral debates. This is "the doctrine that all evaluative judgments and more specifically all moral judgments are nothing but expressions of preference, expressions of attitude or feeling, insofar as they are moral or evaluative in character."[13] Thus, "emotivism rests upon a claim that every attempt, whether past or present, to provide a rational justification for an objective morality has in fact failed."[14] If emotivism is, indeed, the common feature of most modern moral discourse, then it is easy to understand the seemingly arbitrary nature of the premises supporting each particular position and also the rapid speed in which so many moral arguments degenerate into shrill assertions and counterassertions incapable of rational resolution.

Emotivism as an approach to moral theory is the product of a badly damaged conception of morality rooted in Enlightenment thought, for, MacIntyre argues, there was once a time when moral philosophers could make headway in moral disputes. This suggests a historical decline, from an approach to moral questions that provided the means to resolve moral disputes to the modern situation in which resolution is virtually impossible. Indeed, MacIntyre argues that only a moral theory very much like Aristotle's is capable of providing the resources necessary for dealing adequately with the moral disagreements of our modern world. Aristotle's moral theory is founded upon the notion that human beings have a specific *telos* rooted in human nature. However, Aristotle in general and teleology in particular were rejected by the early moderns, such as Bacon and Descartes, and that rejection has continued and solidified so that the problems within moral philosophy today are a direct result of that rejection.

But, some have objected, is it necessary to embrace Aristotle's teleology? Why not construct a theory of morality on the much more obvious foundation of human reason? In other words, perhaps the notion of rationality itself is an adequate grounding for a theory of morality. Modern analytic philosophers, for example, have attempted to employ rationality per se as the foundation of morality. One need merely survey the writings of such neo-Kantians as Rawls, Nozick, Donagan, and Gewirth to see the various ways this is attempted. But, MacIntyre claims, none of these are, in fact, successful, and further, the fact that so much disagreement exists between these philosophers who generally share the same conception of rationality provides strong evidence that their approach is fatally flawed.[15]

What specifically was it about the Enlightenment that led to this degeneration of morality? Premodern European moral theory was broadly Christian in character. Thus, there existed, prior to moral considerations, certain presuppositions that virtually all people presumed as true: God exists and created a world with certain moral structures; humans have a definite nature, and thus a *telos*, and are capable of recognizing this structure and are therefore responsible for their choices. The moral tradition that emerged out of this Christian consensus provided a common conception of morality that continued in large part into the modern period. This consensus is seen in the shared moral beliefs of virtually all the contributors of the modern project in spite of the increasingly diverse justifications for those beliefs. Thus, we see such disparate figures as Hume, Kant, and Kierkegaard all affirming the moral goodness of such things as truth-telling, family, and justice, while at the same time justifying those positions on the basis of the passions, reason, and mere choice, respectively.[16] This breakdown of common justifications (common conclusions have not, nor do they ever, completely disappear) began when modern science, which was mechanistic, replaced Aristotelian science, which was teleological. This shift is more readily apparent when it is construed, as MacIntyre does, in terms of categorical and hypothetical statements. The belief that God exists and is concerned with human action provides the grounds for a categorical command the obligation of which derives directly from God. The belief that humans possess a specific nature and a *telos* that accords with that nature provides the grounds for a hypothetical moral statement. But the Enlightenment systematically undermined the belief in God. By making autonomous reason the sole criterion for morality, the existence of God became little more than a heuristic device that was eventually seen as superfluous and then eliminated.

On the other hand, when Hume denies that an "ought" can be derived from an "is" he is directly attacking the Aristotelian notion of teleology, which claims that because something possess a certain nature, it ought to behave in a particular manner—for Aristotle, to know the "is" is to also know the "ought."[17] For instance, if we know what a watch *is*, we also know what a watch *ought* to do. Thus, if a hard is/ought divide is legitimate, then any conception of teleology necessarily breaks down. We can see, then, that at both the categorical and hypothetical level, the premodern conception of morality was undermined and eventually overturned. Thus, "moral judgements are linguistic survivals from the practices of classical theism which have lost the context provided by these practices."[18] Hearkening back to his introductory metaphor of destruction and partial though incomplete recovery, MacIntyre notes that the modern debate between the deontologists and consequentialists is merely a relic of premodern moral philosophy devoid of its original and essential foundations. Within the context of classical theism, he writes,

Moral judgments were at once hypothetical and categorical in form. They were hypothetical insofar as they expressed a judgment as to what conduct would be teleologically appropriate for a human being: "You ought to do so-and-so, if and since your *telos* is such-and-such" or perhaps "You ought to do so-and-so, if you do not want your essential desires to be frustrated." They were categorical insofar as they reported the contents of the universal law commanded by God: "You ought to do so-and-so: that is what God's law enjoins." But take away from them that in virtue of which they were hypothetical *and* that in virtue of which they were categorical and what are they? Moral judgments lose any clear status and the sentences which express them in a parallel way lose any undebatable meaning. Such sentences become available as forms of expression for an emotivist self which lacking the guidance of the context in which they were originally at home has lost its linguistic as well as its practical way in the world.[19]

Thus, in the wake of the abandonment of theism and teleology as grounds for categorical and hypothetical moral statements, a search has ensued to replace these discarded concepts with others that do the same work but do not carry the same baggage. For categorical judgments, rationality itself was employed by Kant as a foundation. One manifestation of this is found in the prevalence of rights theories, which supposedly provide a moral foundation for categorical statements without the need to recur to God. MacIntyre notes that the concept of natural rights or human rights is a relative latecomer onto the philosophical stage. If this notion were as fundamental as some wish to make it, then it is curious that no premodern philosopher ever stumbled across it. He bluntly concludes this line of thought: "The truth is plain: there are no such rights, and beliefs in them is one with belief in witches and in unicorns."[20]

Hypothetical moral statements, on the other hand, are transferred to utilitarian theories that base morality on the maximization of happiness rather than the attainment of some good essential to one's nature. MacIntyre attacks the concept of happiness as a useful standard for moral inquiry by revisiting the now familiar objection to Bentham's version of utilitarianism: there are too many types of happiness to reduce them to a single scale. MacIntyre duly notes Mill's attempt to overcome this vexing problem by distinguishing between higher and lower pleasures, but rightly concludes that despite Mill's attempts to salvage it, utilitarianism, owing to the varied and incommensurable nature of happiness, is simply not adequate to provide a unitary standard of moral value.[21]

Thus, although certain themes remain intact despite the attacks of modernity, these remnants are ultimately groundless and are sustainable not by rational argument but by emotive affirmation. Individual will, which is the essence of emotivism, has replaced both the will of God and teleology. In the end, "each moral agent now spoke unconstrained by the externalities of divine law, natural teleology, or hierarchical authority; but why should anyone else now listen to him?"[22] Since emotivism is based solely on individual will, MacIntyre presents his readers with a dilemma: either Nietzsche or Aristotle.[23] In other words, morality is either derived from a teleological structure that is more or less similar to that described by Aristotle, or it is a function of individual will in the fashion described by Nietzsche. In light of such stark choices, MacIntyre seeks to defend an approach to morality that is essentially Aristotelian and Thomistic.

Virtues and Rules

According to MacIntyre, one of the most conspicuous features of modern moral philosophy is its emphasis on rules and its neglect of the concept of virtue. Aristotelian ethics is oriented around the virtues and in that context rules, though never discarded, take a decidedly secondary position in the overall scheme. MacIntyre notes that whenever the virtues lose their primary place within a moral system, a form of Stoicism with its emphasis on rules inevitably fills the void.[24] An ethics of virtue requires an underlying teleology. When inquiry begins with a conception of a human *telos*, the question that emerges is, "What kind of person ought I be in order to reach my *telos*?" When such a question is asked, the emphasis will be on the development of the virtues (excellences of character) necessary to attain one's *telos*. On the other hand, when teleology is abandoned, as in most of modern philosophy, the concept of virtue necessarily fades into the background, and a rule-based approach to morality takes its place. Thus, in the world of modern moral philosophy the emphasis on rules and the virtual absence of the concept of virtue is a direct result of the abandonment of any notion of teleology.[25]

This is not to suggest, MacIntyre is careful to add, that rules are unimportant in a system of virtues. Indeed, in any system of morality, rules are necessary, but they are not sufficient in themselves.[26] "Rules and virtues are interrelated."[27] And although it seems that a system in which the virtues are primary still allows room for rules, in a system in which rules are emphasized the role of the virtues is squeezed out. But is a moral system in which rules are primary and the virtues excluded feasible? In such a system the central question becomes, "How do we know *which* rules to follow?"[28] Unless one has a conception of the virtues, especially the virtue of prudence, such questions break down into the interminable emotivist debates that characterize modern moral inquiry. Thus, MacIntyre writes, "To progress in both moral enquiry and the moral life is then to progress in understanding all the various aspects of that life, rules, precepts virtues, passions, actions as parts of a single whole. Central to that progress is the exercise of the virtue of *prudentia*, the virtue of being able in particular situations to bring to bear the relevant universals and to act so that the universal is embodied in the particular."[29] Thus, rules cannot be coherently and rationally applied unless the virtues are present and serve to determine which rule ought to be applied in a particular situation. Virtues, then, are logically prior to rules and serve to provide guidance for the application of rules.

MacIntyre notes that for the modern reader, perhaps the most surprising aspect of Aristotle's ethical theory is that "there is relatively little mention of rules anywhere in the *Ethics*."[30] This is not to say that Aristotle has no conception of rules or does not believe that some acts are absolutely and universally wrong. Aristotle writes, "One part of the politically just is natural, and the other part legal. The natural has the same validity everywhere alike, independent of its seeming so or not."[31] Since, for Aristotle, there are some acts that are simply and universally prohibited—for instance, adultery—his view is not consequentialist, but it is teleological.[32]

Another central feature of Aristotelian ethics that is generally rejected in modern circles is the notion that the good of an individual is inextricably tied up with the common good. In an approach rooted in the liberal self, the individual is conceived as standing prior to any commitment to a community; however, Aristotle understood that in important ways, the *polis* served to constitute the individual and in so doing served to make one's *telos* comprehendible. In other words, since humans are by nature political animals, and since the *polis* is the natural end of all human communities (for its end is self-sufficiency), it follows that humans require the *polis* in order fully to achieve their *telos*. Thus, the *polis* is logically prior to the individual, for without the *polis* a person cannot fully achieve humanity.[33] Because human goods are tied up in the *polis*, one cannot consider one's own goods without at the same time considering the goods of the community, for they are inseparable.[34]

MacIntyre is quite aware that Aristotle's *Ethics* presupposes what MacIntyre terms a "metaphysical biology," and he attempts to present an account of morality that is essentially Aristotelian but one that does not require any allegiance to Aristotle's biology, which, according to MacIntyre, must be rejected.[35] It is important to note, at this point, that in a later work MacIntyre admits that considerations of biology cannot simply be ignored. Although he admits that aspects of Aristotle's biology are wrong and ought to be rejected, "I now judge that I was in error in supposing an ethics independent of biology to be possible."[36] By attempting to construct a theory of ethics apart from any consideration of the biological fact of human existence, one essentially veers toward a Cartesian dualism, which denies the essential unity of the human being. Therefore, an ethical theory ought to consider the biological nature of human existence as well as the teleological structure of human life. Properly conceived, then, human existence is a unity comprising the biological and the nonbiological (mental, spiritual, etc.). This unity, which is the human being, is further constituted by the teleological nature of existence whereby pursuing one's *telos* is an important feature of flourishing. Further, the good of each person is only comprehendible in terms of the common good. Thus, humans are essentially embedded in a rich and complex metaphysical, biological, and social structure, and thus the modern notion of radical individualism—which is to say, the liberal self—rests, according to Aristotle (and MacIntyre), on a grave error.

HISTORY, THEORY, AND TRUTH

MacIntyre follows Aristotle in affirming the essential social and biological aspects of human life, but he goes further, for unlike Aristotle, MacIntyre argues that humans are historical beings and as such we are embedded in our historical moment. Aristotle's conception of moral inquiry is, however, ahistorical. According to MacIntyre, Aristotle believed that "individuals as members of a species have a *telos*, but there is no history of the *polis* or of Greece or of mankind moving towards a *telos*."[37] MacIntyre, for his part, is conscious of history and its importance for any type of inquiry and employs the methodology of other historicist philosophers of history in service of his project. In describing the intention of *After Virtue*, MacIntyre remarks that he hopes to find "in the type of philosophy and history propounded by writers such as Hegel and Collingwood . . . resources which we cannot find in analytic or phenomenological philosophy."[38] In his first book, *A Short History of Ethics* (1966), he writes,

> Moral philosophy is often written as though the history of the subject were only of secondary and incidental importance. This attitude seems to be the outcome of a belief that moral concepts can be examined and understood apart from their history. Some philosophers have even written as if moral concepts were a timeless, limited, unchanging, determinate species of concept, necessarily having the same features throughout history. . . . In fact, of course, moral concepts change as social life changes.[39]

This general attitude toward the historical nature of all inquiry remains a constant throughout his work. MacIntyre believes that one of the mistakes of the Enlightenment is the belief that one's historical place is accidental and can, with the proper epistemological effort, be transcended. The Enlightenment aspiration to an objective, universal perspective that manages to shake off the limitations effected by tradition, culture, language, and history is, for MacIntyre, an impossible—and ultimately damaging—dream.[40]

Language serves in important ways to frame and limit the possibilities of inquiry. Far from being a simple and neutral system of signs signifying universal truths, a language carries with it particularities unique to that language, for it in many ways reflects the particular history and culture out of which it has grown. Thus, "every tradition is embodied in some particular set of utterances and actions and thereby in all the particularities of some specific language and culture. The invention, elaboration, and modification of the concepts through which both those who found and those who inherit a tradition understand it are inescapably concepts which have been framed in one language rather than another."[41] This being the case, it is not self-evident that all concepts are readily translatable from one language into another. Part of the modern belief in objective and unmediated access to universal truth is the opinion that all texts are simply translatable.[42]

This appreciation for the historical, social, and linguistic embedded-ness of the human experience has a direct influence upon the manner in which any inquiry ought to be understood. Since we are, in part, the prod-ucts of a particular historical and social context, there is no way of throw-ing off these limitations, for to throw them off is to cause the disintegration of our very identities.[43] Thus, all inquiry is tied to the particularities of time and cultural milieu. If so, then the goal of attaining universal, objective facts completely untainted by the particularities of one's situation is im-possible. The particular situation in which each individual finds himself provides the conceptual framework by which facts are interpreted and in-quiry is conducted. But if the human mind is constituted, at least in part, by the particularities of history and society, then the facts that are pre-sented to the inquirer are themselves interpreted by a mind that is oriented and shaped by forces particular to time and social context. Thus, all inquir-ers begin their respective inquiries with resources that are the products of a particular history and culture (we can in general lump these factors to-gether under the rubric of "tradition").

This understanding of inquiry throws us back into the long-standing discussion between the nature of universals and particulars. Optimistic Enlightenment thinkers believed it was possible to transcend the particu-lars and achieve knowledge of universals quite untainted by the vagaries of tradition. But if an individual's tradition provides the framework within which all knowing occurs, then universal truth (assuming such exists) is only grasped through the mediating function of particulars rather than apart from them. One's historical place and social context do matter, for "without those moral particularities to begin from there would never be anywhere to begin; but it is in moving forward from such particularity that the search for the good, for the universal, consists. Yet particularity can never be simply left behind or obliterated. The notion of escaping from it into a realm of entirely universal maxims which belong to man as such . . . is an illusion."[44] It is important to note here that this position does not necessarily imply that universals do not exist or that they are unknowable. If we begin with the assumption that a reality exists that is independent from any perception of it (a realist view that Oakeshott denies), and if we also accept the premise that human knowing can never completely tran-scend the particularities of time and place, then we may still claim that universal truth may be aspired toward. Indeed, for MacIntyre, "the concept of truth is timeless,"[45] and this timeless truth is the proper goal of philo-sophical inquiry. At the same time, "there are no general timeless standards" by which rival claims are to be judged.[46] Thus, although timeless truth is, indeed, the ideal toward which a philosopher ought to aspire, he ought never believe that this universal and timeless truth can be known in a purely objective fashion that completely transcends the time and place from which the inquiry takes place.[47]

Practice, Narrative, and Tradition

With the above features in place, it is obvious that any account of the virtues will include the "complex, historical, multi-layered character of the core concept of virtue."[48] MacIntyre argues that the logical development of an account of virtue includes three stages: an account of the concept of a practice; an account of the narrative order of a human life; and an account of the concept of tradition.[49] Regarding these three stages, "no human quality is to be accounted a virtue unless it satisfies the conditions specified *at each of the three stages*."[50] This section will get to the heart of MacIntyre's understanding of tradition, and at the same time it will help to uncover important similarities and differences between MacIntyre's approach and that developed by Oakeshott.

Practice

According to MacIntyre, the concept of a practice is an essential precondition for understanding the virtues. He begins by claiming that his usage of the concept "practice" "does not completely agree with current ordinary usage."[51] According to MacIntyre, a practice is "any coherent and complex form of socially established cooperative human activity through which goods internal to that form of activity are realized in the course of trying to achieve those standards of excellence which are appropriate to, and partially definitive of, that form of activity, with the result that human powers to achieve excellence, and human conceptions of the ends and goods involved, are systematically extended."[52] Such a definition requires a bit of unpacking. First, a practice is coherent and complex. By way of example, MacIntyre points out that such things as tic-tac-toe, throwing a football, bricklaying, and planting turnips are not practices—they do not specify activities that are both coherent and complex. Of course, a game of tic-tac-toe is a coherent whole, but it is not complex. On the other hand, throwing a football, bricklaying, and turnip growing are not coherent wholes;

rather, they are activities the meaning of which is not fully apparent apart from a larger whole. Thus, a game of chess, the game of football, architecture, and agriculture are examples of practices, for they satisfy both the complexity and the coherency criteria. Complex activities such as physics, biology, painting, music, and politics all count as practices.[53]

Second, the goal of a practice is the realization of goods internal to that particular practice. MacIntyre employs an illustration to help distinguish the difference between internal and external goods. Imagine that an adult wishes to teach a child to play chess. The child, though, has very little interest in learning the game but does have a (typical) affection for candy. The adult might strike a deal with the child. For each thirty-minute session of chess completed by the child, the adult will promise to give the child a certain amount of candy. The child agrees and submits to the lessons wholly motivated by the promise of candy. After the child has mastered the basic rules of the game, the adult now alters the bargain. The child must win in order to secure the reward. The adult stipulates that he will never play in such a way as to absolutely preclude the child from winning, but the child must play with full concentration in order to win. The child agrees and, still motivated by the candy, plays to win. But at this point, there is no reason for the child not to cheat whenever there is no chance of being caught, for the goods the child seeks are external to the practice in which he is participating. Eventually, or so the adult hopes, the child will begin to appreciate the game of chess, not for the candy that has served as an external, contingent good, but for the goods internal to the game itself—skill, imagination, competition. At that point, the child will no longer be inclined to cheat, for to cheat is to refuse to engage the practice on its own terms and simultaneously forfeit the goods internal to that practice. The goods internal to a practice can only be achieved through excelling at a practice in terms of the practice. On the other hand, external goods, be they power, status, money, or candy, are not essential elements of a practice, for such goods can be secured in numerous ways, and achieving them does not necessarily depend on participating in a practice.[54] Furthermore, it is frequently the case that external goods are of a limited supply and therefore are objects of competition. Conversely, the goods internal to a practice are such that their achievement "is a good for the whole community who participate in the practice."[55] Thus, for example, when a golfer pushes the game of golf to new levels of excellence, all golfers can appreciate the achievement, and all are spurred to greater excellence.

Third, in addition to the achievement of internal goods, "a practice involves standards of excellence and obedience to rules."[56] Before a person can enter into a practice, he must first submit himself to the rules and standards that constitute the practice. The novice must subordinate himself to those who are recognized as the masters and undergo a period of apprenticeship during which the rules and skills are learned and acquired.[57] MacIntyre also employs the term "craft" in a manner that is essentially synonymous with practice.[58] MacIntyre generally speaks of craft in conjunction with the concept of apprenticeship. Apprenticeship entails an unequal relationship between a master and a student in which the student, in an act that includes something resembling a step of faith, places himself in a posture of submission to the authority of the master. It is only through such a process of submission and learning at the foot of a master that the novice can be brought into a proper understanding of a craft or a practice so that he can enjoy the goods internal to it: "Those qualities of mind and character that enable someone both to recognize the relevant goods and to use the relevant skills in achieving them are the excellences, the virtues, that distinguish or should distinguish teacher from apprentice or student."[59]

Thus, a virtue can be defined as *"an acquired human quality the possession and exercise of which tends to enable us to achieve those goods which are internal to practices and the lack of which effectively prevents us from achieving them."*[60] MacIntyre appears to hold that a complex relationship exists between practices and virtues. On the one hand, in the definition directly above, the possession of the virtues is necessary for properly participating in a practice such that the goods internal to it are enjoyed. Subordinating oneself to the authority of a master requires the virtue of courage. The learning process that ensues leads one to recognize what is due to the particular participants of the practice—that is, justice. In learning to appreciate the goods internal to the practice, one must participate according to the rules governing the practice—honesty. Thus, in order to properly enter into and participate in a practice, one must possess the virtues of courage, justice, and honesty.[61] It would seem, then, that certain virtues must be possessed prior to fully entering into a practice. On the other hand, at times it appears that MacIntyre believes that the virtues are the products of participating in practices: "Just as the virtues are exercised in the whole range of our activities, so they are learned in the same range of activities, in those contexts of practice in which we learn from others how to discharge our roles and functions first as members of a family and household, then in the tasks of schoolwork, and later on as farmworkers or carpenters or teachers or members of a fishing crew or a string quartet."[62]

Thus, it appears that practices require the virtues, and the virtues require practices. This is not, I think, a vicious circle. A preliminary example could take the following form: All normally situated humans belong to a family. A child becomes aware of certain social practices through parental training and by observing older siblings and peers. Prior to engaging in familial social practices, a young child observes and mimics. He becomes aware of a rough conception of the virtues even though engaging in simple activities that do not fully fit the definition of a practice. Although the activity may occur as component parts of a practice, the child's perceptual awareness is such that he cannot yet comprehend the coherent whole of which the particular action is a part. With this partially formed understanding of the virtues, the child moves gradually toward engaging fully in familial practices. Thus, a form of the virtues is gained by observing, and that is adequate to begin the process of initiation into familial practices, and through participating in practices as an apprentice, the child acquires and refines the virtues. As the virtues are extended and refined, it is possible for the child more fully to engage in and appreciate the goods internal to a practice. Further, it eventually becomes possible for the child to seek inclusion in increasingly diverse and sophisticated practices and through them develop a better comprehension of the virtues. Thus, in a real and important way practices require the virtues and virtues require practices.

Two negative definitions of a practice should be noted. First, although a practice includes an element of technical skill, it is never simply technique. For "what is distinctive in a practice is in part the way in which conceptions of the relevant goods and ends which the technical skills serve . . . are transformed and enriched by these extensions of human powers and by that regard for its own internal goods which are partially definitive of each particular practice."[63] Further, unlike a set of definitive technical skills that can be mastered, "practices never have a goal or goals fixed for all time—painting has no such goal nor has physics."[64] Any goals that might be attached to a practice are subject to changes that are derived from the history of that particular practice. Thus, "to enter into a practice is to enter into a relationship not only with its contemporary practitioners, but also with those who have preceded us in the practice, particularly those whose achievements extended the reach of the practice to its present point. It is thus the achievement, and *a fortiori* the authority, of a tradition which I then confront and from which I have to learn."[65] It is clear, then, that a practice includes an element of technical knowledge, but is not merely that, and a practice is only coherent in terms of its own history.

Second, although practices often depend upon institutions for their ongoing existence, a practice is not an institution. To use MacIntyre's examples, the game of chess, physics, and medicine are practices. Chess clubs, laboratories, and hospitals are institutions. It is a characteristic of institutions that they are concerned with external goods, such as money, status, and power, and so forth. But although institutions are not practices in the sense defined by MacIntyre, they do play an important sustaining role in the life of a practice. But, at the same time, institutions tend to co-opt the internal goods of a practice in the service of the external goods of the institution. In other words, practices are threatened with institutionalization by the very institutions that help sustain them. A practice can avoid this fate only if those who engage in the practice possess the virtues necessary to perpetuate the practice through an appreciation of the goods internal to the practice.[66]

Narrative

The second concept necessary for a coherent account of the virtues is the notion of the narrative order of a human life. It is a feature of modern thought to divide a human life into a variety of parts corresponding to biological development, social roles, professional roles, and so on. We tend to distinguish sharply between a child and the adult he will become, and we distinguish between the adult and the frail elderly person who eventually emerges. We tend to distinguish between a person's role as a daughter, a mother, a professional, a church member, and so forth. Such sharp distinctions are incompatible with the Aristotelian conception of the virtues. It is the nature of the virtues to unify; thus, a proper accounting of the virtues requires "a concept of the self whose unity resides in the unity of a narrative which links birth to life to death as narrative beginning to middle to end."[67]

Actions are unintelligible when divorced from what MacIntyre calls a "setting": "A social setting may be an institution, it may be what I have called a practice, or it may be a milieu of some other human kind." Further, and importantly, "a setting has a history," and apart from that history the actions related to the particular setting will be unintelligible both to the actors and to any who observe.[68]

MacIntyre employs an example to further his point. Recipes in a cookbook are set out in a step-by-step series. The cook is expected to follow these directions closely in order to produce the desired results. But, apart from the concept of a setting, the individual directions—add 1 cup of flour, crack two eggs—are quite meaningless. Each element in the process is unintelligible apart from the other steps in the sequence; furthermore, "even such a sequence requires a context to be intelligible."[69] The setting provides the necessary integrating context whereby an individual act or a series of related actions are given coherence and intelligibility.

The setting that is perhaps most familiar yet most overlooked is that found in the simple act of conversation.[70] We conceive of different conversations in terms of varying genres— tragedy, comedy, farce. "Indeed, a conversation is a dramatic work, even if a very short one, in which the participants are not only the actors, but also the joint authors, working out in agreement or disagreements the mode of their production."[71] Human interaction, MacIntyre claims, is best understood in terms of conversation, in which the participants engage in a dramatic event in which the actors share authorship. The shared authorship, though, is not synonymous with complete control of the setting or outcome of the dramatic piece, for each actor is thrust onto a stage not of his own making and is part of a social and historical setting that is largely unchosen. In light of these very real constraints, it is all too true that "we are never more (and sometimes less) than the co-authors of our own narratives."[72] We share authorship not only with those engaged in a particular conversation but also with those who have gone before us, who have contributed to the historical development of the setting in which we now converse. In this sense, in order to understand properly the multitude of human interactions (understood as conversational dramas) we must comprehend the narrative nature of those interactions.

What has this to do with an account of the virtues? When a human life is conceived merely as a series of fragmented and partially related events, the concept of virtue becomes meaningless. Virtues are dispositions to act in a way that promotes the *telos* of the individual actor. Such a *telos* is a holistic notion that comprehends the entirety of the person. When a narrative account of a human life is exchanged for one that is fragmented and lacking in any unifying teleological structure, the virtues are replaced by rules. The modern rejection of an ethics of virtue and the dominance of rule-based theories, both deontological and utilitarian, merely indicates that a narrative conception of human life has been discarded, lost, or perhaps overlooked.

A human is "essentially a storytelling animal." If humans find themselves engaged in conversation in settings that are the product of a particular historical development, and if our roles (of which we are at best coauthor) are laden with moral implications, then it follows that "I can only answer the question 'What am I to do?' if I can answer the prior question 'Of what story or stories do I find myself a part?'"[73] Stories, then, play an indispensable role in moral education: "deprive children of stories and you leave them unscripted, anxious stutterers in their actions as in their words."[74]

It is the nature of conversation to increase understanding. Furthermore, conversations are ongoing. That is, they can be reopened and the issues reengaged for further consideration. Thus, a conception of the human as a unity includes the question, "What is the best way to live my life given the settings in which I find myself?" In light of this question, the purpose of a human life presents itself as a quest. The quest is an ongoing pursuit of what it means to live a good life: "The good life for man is the life spent in seeking for the good life for man, and the virtues necessary for the seeking are those which will enable us to understand what more and what else the good life for man is."[75] A narrative account that unifies a particular life makes the continuity of such a quest intelligible, and the possession of the virtues makes the quest itself possible.

Tradition

The intelligibility of practices and narratives requires a wider context; thus, the third component for an account of the virtues is tradition. In *After Virtue*, MacIntyre defines a tradition as follows:

> A living tradition then is an historically extended, socially embodied argument, and an argument precisely in part about the goods which constitute that tradition. Within a tradition the pursuit of goods extends through generations, sometimes many generations. Hence the

individual's search for his or her good is generally and characteristically conducted within a context defined by those traditions of which the individual's life is a part, and this is true both of those goods which are internal to practices and of the goods of a single life.[76]

Another definition is given in *Whose Justice? Which Rationality?*, and although it is quite similar, it highlights certain important points:

> A tradition is an argument extended through time in which certain fundamental agreements are defined and redefined in terms of two kinds of conflict: those with critics and enemies external to the tradition who reject all or at least key parts of those fundamental agreements, and those internal, interpretative debates through which the meaning and rationale of the fundamental agreements come to be expressed and by whose progress a tradition is constituted.[77]

Perhaps surprisingly, an essential element of a tradition, according to MacIntyre, is a certain degree of conflict. This does not mean that there is not substantial agreement within a tradition. Indeed, without the background of fundamental agreement setting the parameters of the conflict, disagreement between those sharing a tradition would be impossible. The internal conflict—part of the conversational aspect of human existence—is not necessarily destructive of the tradition. Instead, internal conflict is an indicator of a healthy tradition in which options are explored with vigor. The ongoing results of the conflict represent the progression of the tradition, for to engage in the debate is to participate in the authorial task of writing the history of the tradition. Thus, "to be an adherent of a tradition is always to enact some further stage in the development of one's tradition."[78]

A tradition provides the resources necessary for evaluating the rationality of its internal structure. There is no universal and objective—that is, Cartesian—standpoint from which to deliberate the rationality of a particular claim or tradition. In other words, there is no traditionless place to which the thinker can escape and from which he can make judgments. Thus, the "resources of adequate rationality are made available to us only in and through traditions."[79] Because a tradition is an extended argument or conversation through time which evolves according to the manner in which the argument plays out, and because that argument is conducted in a particular language by particular people possessing a particular history, "traditions are always and ineradicably to some degree local, informed by particularities of language and social and natural environment."[80] Again, all inquiry is framed to a certain degree by the particularities in which the inquiry takes place. Although it is certainly true that all traditions of inquiry aspire to universal and timeless truth, this goal must be understood as an ideal that time and culture-bound inquirers can only approximate and never achieve. This, of course, is not to say that all traditions are equally right or wrong. Indeed, the claim that objective, universal truth is unattainable does not entail the inference that one attempt is no better than any other. One of the chief goals of MacIntyre's project is to show how one tradition can be shown to be rationally superior to its opponents, thereby justifying its claim to a closer approximation of truth than its foes.

It is important to note at this point that tradition-constituted inquiry does not pursue an explicit and specifiable goal; instead, it is essentially open-ended, unpredictable, and always susceptible of revision. In this light, "no one at any stage can ever rule out the future possibility of their present beliefs and judgments being shown to be inadequate in a variety of ways."[81] In this regard, MacIntyre points out, his conception of inquiry is anti-Cartesian and anti-Hegelian. It is anti-Cartesian because every rational tradition "begins from the contingency and positivity of some set of established beliefs."[82] Unlike the radical doubt with which Descartes attempted to begin his inquiry, tradition-constituted inquiry begins with the resources provided by the tradition itself. In much the same manner that an apprentice must entrust himself to the authority of a master before he can learn the subtleties of a practice, so too the starting point for tradition-constituted inquiry is submission to the authority of the tradition, and it is only from this beginning point that the participant can engage in the internal discussion within a tradition. This approach is anti-Hegelian because there is no explicit and specifiable goal toward which all inquiry is intentionally moving.[83] This does not constitute an agnosticism regarding the existence of God or final causes. Rather it is a recognition of the contingent and fallible nature of human rationality. Thus, although MacIntyre's approach is a kind of historicism that agrees at important points with Hegel, his fallibilism provides an important distinction.[84]

MacIntyre describes three basic stages in the development of a tradition. In the first stage "the relevant beliefs, texts, and authorities have not yet been put in question." The second stage occurs when the inadequacies of those beliefs, texts, and authorities emerge. The third stage entails the response in which the participants of the tradition produce "a set of refor-mulations, reevaluations, and new formulations and evaluations, designed to remedy inadequacies and overcome limitations." As a part of this devel-opment, those texts or authorities that are considered divine enjoy a status apart from other texts and authorities. Of course, these may undergo pe-riodic reinterpretations, but they are exempted from repudiation.[85]

Traditions can founder and die, so we must inquire into what accounts for the success or the failure of a tradition. In *After Virtue*, MacIntyre ar-gues that the reason a tradition weakens and dies is, in part, because of the failure of those participants in the tradition to properly exercise the virtues necessary to sustain the health of the tradition: "The lack of justice, lack of truthfulness, lack of courage, lack of the relevant intellectual virtues—these corrupt traditions, just as they do those institutions and practices which derive their life from the traditions of which they are the contem-porary embodiments."[86] In *Whose Justice? Which Rationality?*, MacIntyre's account of the failure of a tradition focuses upon what he calls an "episte-mological crisis." Recall that a central feature of a tradition is the internal and ongoing conflict between the participants of that tradition. The con-flict involves a discussion "about the goods which constitute that tradi-tion"[87] and "the meaning and rationale of the fundamental agreements"[88] that comprise the essential elements of the tradition. This ongoing inter-nal conflict may at any point "by its own standards of progress . . . cease to make progress. Its hitherto trusted methods of enquiry have become sterile. Conflicts over rival answers to key questions can no longer be set-tled rationally."[89] In addition to a cessation of progress, internal incoheren-cies may appear that defy the resources of the tradition. At this point, one of two things can occur. If the failures of the tradition are unresolved, the tradition itself is in jeopardy and will eventually be replaced by another established tradition, or a new tradition will grow up out of the ruins. If the tradition is to survive, MacIntyre argues, three distinct questions must be addressed. First, the revitalized tradition must, by employing new or revamped conceptual resources, be able to overcome the challenges that brought the tradition to the crisis. Second, the new account must further-more provide an explanation of why the original approach failed. Finally, this process of explanation must take place within a structure whose con-tinuity with the original tradition remains fundamentally intact.[90]

According to MacIntyre, if a tradition's internal conflict ceases to be a vital and ongoing process, the tradition has become sterile and an epis-temological crisis is at hand or has already occurred. It is for this reason (among others) that MacIntyre believes Burke's account of tradition is representative of a sick and dying tradition rather than a healthy one. In chapter 5, we will return to Burke and see in what ways MacIntyre's understanding of him is inadequate.

At this point, two related questions ought to be raised. First, do all people participate in a tradition simply by virtue of the social and historical context into which they have been born? Second, can one voluntarily choose to abandon one tradition in favor of another? In addressing the first, it appears that MacIntyre is not completely sure. He seems to affirm the inevitability of tradition when he notes that "I find myself part of a history and that is generally to say, whether I like it or not, whether I recognize it or not, one of the bearers of a tradition."[91] On the other hand, there are times he appears willing to entertain the possibility that a person may, in fact, be traditionless. In fact, *Whose Justice? Which Rationality?* "is primarily addressed . . . to . . . someone who, not as yet having given their allegiance to some coherent tradition of enquiry, is besieged by disputes over what is just and about how it is reasonable to act."[92] In particular he seems to believe that a person with no identifiable tradition can be found in "the kind of post-Enlightenment person who responds to the failure of the Enlightenment to provide neutral, impersonal tradition-independent standards of rational judgment by concluding that no set of beliefs proposed for acceptance is therefore justifiable." Such a person "finds him or herself an alien to every tradition of enquiry which he or she encounters and . . . does so because he or she brings to the encounter with such traditions standards of rational justification which the beliefs of no tradition could satisfy."[93] Thus, a person without commitment to any set of beliefs is one who is without a tradition. The existence of such a person seems highly problematic in terms of MacIntyre's own thought—this despite his claim to be primarily addressing such persons.[94] However, according to MacIntyre, rationality is a function of a particular tradition; thus, to have no tradition is to have no conception of rationality, and to reject one's tradition is either to reject one's own rational framework and thereby forfeit all rational justification for the rejection, or to maintain one's rationality but in so doing maintain at least a remnant of the tradition one is attempting to reject. MacIntyre, in the end, seems to take the latter tack:

> There is no neutral standing ground, some locus for rationality as such, which can afford rational resources sufficient for enquiry independent of all traditions. Those who have maintained otherwise

either have covertly been adopting the standpoint of a tradition and deceiving themselves and perhaps others into supposing that theirs was just such a neutral standing ground or else have simply been in error. The person outside all traditions lacks sufficient rational resources for enquiry and *a fortiori* for enquiry into what tradition is to be rationally preferred. He or she has no adequate relevant means of rational evaluation and hence can come to no well-grounded conclusion, including the conclusion that no tradition can vindicate itself against any other. To be outside all traditions is to be a stranger to enquiry; it is to be in a state of intellectual and moral destitution.[95]

Thus, although MacIntyre appears to waver on this question, the logic of his overall position seems to require us to conclude that a traditionless person would be highly deficient and completely incapable of any type of rational inquiry. In short, if such a person could be found, he would be unable to speak in any comprehensible fashion, for it is not "possible to speak except out of one particular tradition in a way which will involve conflict with rival traditions."[96] Thus, like Oakeshott, MacIntyre holds that a tradition is not simply a repository of valuable truth; instead, it represents the intellectual, social, and historical milieu into which a person is inculcated. In this sense tradition plays an indispensable epistemic role, for it provides the framework within which all inquiry occurs.[97]

MacIntyre's position regarding the first question makes the possibility of a definite answer to the second—can a person change traditions?—more difficult. He does, though, grapple with the problem. MacIntyre notes that when an epistemological crisis occurs, "an encounter with a rival tradition may . . . provide good reasons either for attempting to reconstitute one's tradition in some radical way or for deserting it."[98] If a tradition entails the epistemological function MacIntyre has attributed to it, simply abandoning one's tradition will be no simple undertaking. Of course, figures such as Descartes sought to rid themselves completely of any vestiges of tradition, but we are warranted in asking if he succeeded. According to MacIntyre, he did not. Descartes attempted to cast everything he thought he knew under the cloak of radical doubt with the hope that he might from that starting point find some truth that was indubitable. But MacIntyre correctly points out that "of course someone who really believed that he knew nothing would not even know how to begin on a course of radical doubt; for he would have no conception of what his task might be, of what it would be to settle his doubts and to acquire well-founded beliefs." Thus, there is a logical problem at the very heart of Descartes's method. Furthermore, although Descartes claimed to be casting off all influences of tradition, MacIntyre again points out that he was less than successful. In this regard, Descartes accepted his own capacity to employ properly the French and Latin languages, both of which are the complex creations of particular traditions. In addition, he appears simply to have overlooked "how much of what he took to be the spontaneous reflections of his own mind was in fact a repetition of sentences and phrases from his school textbooks. Even the *Cogito* is to be found in Saint Augustine."[99] Thus, although Descartes attempted to rid himself of the constraints of his own tradition, it appears that he was actually working within the confines of a particular tradition and, MacIntyre argues, participating in an ongoing internal conflict that arose within his own tradition.[100]

Descartes's apparent failure to throw off completely his own tradition is not a conclusive argument for the impossibility of such an action, but his failure should give us pause. The manner in which one might conceivably abandon one's tradition in favor of a new one will be addressed in more detail in the next section. Suffice it to say at this point, if tradition is as complex and as deeply rooted as MacIntyre suggests, the task of successfully moving from one tradition to another will involve immense challenges. Yet, in the end, the logic of MacIntyre's overall account requires that the possibility exists, for MacIntyre believes it is possible to determine the rational superiority of one tradition over another. If that is possible, then it also must be possible for an individual to recognize the general superiority of a tradition and change allegiance to it.

Practice, narrative, and tradition must all be included in an account of an ethics of virtue. MacIntyre does not claim to be simply rehearsing Aristotle's position, for he denies (until eventually changing his position) Aristotle's "metaphysical biology" and affirms the historical nature of inquiry, something Aristotle denies. In spite of the differences, MacIntyre believes himself to be working within Aristotelian tradition. That is, according to the account of tradition just described, it is perfectly consistent to claim to be working within a tradition while at the same time engaging that tradition in constructive debate, which may produce changes in the tradition as it progresses in the unpredictable and open-ended fashion typical of a healthy tradition.

TRADITION AND TRANSLATION

MacIntyre holds that some traditions are rationally superior to others, but since according to his position all rationality is constituted by a tradition, and every tradition is the product of cultural, social, linguistic, and historical forces, it is, on his own terms, impossible to step outside of all tradition and adjudicate from a tradition-independent epistemic vantage point.[101] Thus we must inquire how MacIntyre can maintain his strong view of tradition while at the same time avoid sliding into some form of relativism.[102]

MacIntyre recognizes the significance of the problem and devotes considerable effort in describing a solution. He presents the problem as follows:

> There is always the possibility of one tradition of action and enquiry encountering another in such a way that neither can, for some considerable stretch of time at least, exhibit to the justified satisfaction of its own adherents, let alone to that of the adherents of its rival, its rational superiority. And this possibility will arise when and if the two traditions, whether embodied in the same language and culture or not, cannot find from the standpoint of either an adequate set of standards or measures to evaluate their relationship rationally.[103]

When such a confrontation occurs, an obvious solution is simply to deny the possibility of a resolution. MacIntyre describes this possibility: "If the only available standards of rationality are those made available by and within tradition, then no issue between contending traditions is rationally decidable. To assert or to conclude this rather than that can be rational relative to the standards of some particular tradition, but not rational as such. There can be no rationality as such. Every set of standards, every tradition incorporating a set of standards, has as much and as little claim to our allegiance as any other."[104] MacIntyre calls this the "relativist challenge." Another related hurdle is what he terms the "perspectivist challenge," which "puts in question the possibility of making truth-claims from within any one tradition."[105] Unless both of these challenges can be overcome, MacIntyre's position stumbles at the same point as does Oakeshott's.

MacIntyre rightly points out that both challenges rely in part on a false dilemma: either the Enlightenment ideal of direct access to universal, objective truth is valid, or the postmodern rejection of all truth is correct. Since the first horn of the dilemma is rejected (by MacIntyre and also by the postmodernist), then the second horn must obtain. Hence, both the relativist and the perspectivist challenges hold.[106] But the tradition-constituted account developed by MacIntyre claims that there is a third alternative that makes it possible to reject the Enlightenment version of universalism without succumbing to postmodern relativism. This position, as we have seen, acknowledges the social, cultural, linguistic, and historical embeddedness of all traditions of inquiry, but it also affirms the existence of a reality that is independent of human inquiry, a reality knowable (at least in part) and timeless.[107] Thus, tradition-constituted inquiry will affirm the particular nature of all inquiry while at the same time aspiring to knowledge of universal truth in an open-ended and contingent process of inquiry that progresses in unpredictable ways and is always open to revisitation and revision.

The relativist challenge fails to consider the possible implications of an epistemological crisis. Although a tradition may successfully overcome such a crisis as described in the previous section, such successful resolutions are not always the case. If a tradition fails to resolve a crisis, the tradition will crumble, for its rational center will prove inadequate to maintain the coherence of the overall structure. Thus, the tradition will be discredited on its own terms.[108] If a tradition fails to meet the challenges posed by an epistemological crisis while at the same time other traditions avoid or successfully meet such challenges, then it is necessarily the case that some traditions are more capable than others of rationally justifying their own positions in terms of their own internal rationality. Thus, some traditions are rationally superior to others, and if that is the case, the relativist challenge collapses.

The perspectivist, who questions the possibility of making truth-claims from within any one tradition, fails on slightly different grounds. This position assumes the possibility of attaining a position free of any tradition from which to make the claim that truth claims from within any one tradition are impossible. The perspectivist assumes it is possible to flit from one tradition to the next, trying on each in turn and determining that truth claims are untenable when made from within a tradition. Perspectivism, according to MacIntyre, "is a doctrine only possible for those who regard themselves as outsiders, as uncommitted or rather committed only to acting a succession of temporary parts."[109] Herein, though, lies the rub, for "genuinely to adopt the standpoint of a tradition thereby commits one to its view of what is true and false and, so committing one, prohibits one from adopting any rival standpoint."[110] Thus, if the perspectivist claims to move easily from one tradition to another, he is actually self-deceived, for participating in a tradition requires commitment and submission to the internal authority of that tradition. Furthermore, if "the resources of adequate rationality are made available to us only in and through traditions,"[111] then a person without a tradition is simply incapable of rationally justifying the perspectivist claim. Thus, the perspectivist challenge fails in multiple ways.

One tradition can be judged rationally superior to another if it is able to overcome or avoid epistemological crises where other traditions demonstrate their inadequacy by their failure to do so. But what conclusions can we draw if two traditions persist over a period of time without succumbing to the challenges of an epistemological crisis? Must we therefore conclude that both are equally true? This, it would seem, leads us back into the problem of relativism. Is there a way to determine what MacIntyre terms the "rational superiority" of one apparently successful tradition over another? MacIntyre believes that there is.

From the perspective of each successful tradition the other is wrong. If the inquiry could proceed no further than this, we seem to have something resembling emotivism at the level of traditions whereby commitments are merely the products of arbitrary, irrational choices, or, more accurately, accident of birth. The key, according to MacIntyre, involves learning the "language" of the other tradition: "One has, so to speak, to become a child all over again and to learn this language—and the corresponding parts of the culture—as a second first language."[112] Such a learning process enables the inquirer to understand the other tradition from the inside. It is an empathetic engagement in which one takes the time and effort to understand another tradition in its own cultural, historic, and linguistic terms. This approach admits that many concepts cannot simply be translated without a distortion or loss of meaning. This flies in the face of Enlightenment sensibilities, which hold that "all cultural phenomena must be potentially translucent to understanding, that all texts must be capable of being translated into the language which the adherents of modernity speak to each other."[113]

Once this process of language learning is completed, the inquirer is in a unique position to judge differing, yet apparently successful, traditions. By employing his "second first language" the inquirer can comprehend the challenges, the limitations, and the failures of the rival tradition in terms of the tradition itself. If those limitations and shortcomings can be overcome by resources supplied by the opposing tradition along with an explanation of why the limitations and shortcomings exist, there is good reason to conclude that one tradition is rationally superior to its rival.[114] Thus, only through gaining a sympathetic insider's look at the internal components of a rival tradition is it possible to attempt to demonstrate the rational superiority of one apparently successful tradition over another. This, of course, is no easy task, and such a process cannot occur overnight. Indeed, such attempts may prove, at least for a time, inconclusive. This does not, of course, indicate that the two traditions are equally true. It does, though, point to the open-ended and ongoing nature of inquiry and should spur further attempts to move toward the timeless ideal of truth rather than engender complacency.

Epistemology, Submission, and Faith

Tradition-constituted inquiry, it would seem, proceeds on a track that is epistemologically antithetical to what we have come to expect from more modern approaches. We should not expect the kind of epistemological first principles to which Descartes and his descendants aspired. As MacIntyre has made clear, there are no pretheoretical facts; there exists no tradition-independent rock upon which one can stake one's epistemological fortunes. In short, epistemological first principles in the Cartesian sense are "mythological beasts."[115]

If no absolutely indubitable epistemological starting point exists, then knowing must proceed on some other basis. But if we cannot begin with some sure knowledge, how can we go on to know anything at all? It seems that we are thrown into a paradox very similar to the one described by Plato in the *Meno*. Socrates, in reply to Meno, his interlocutor, formulates this paradox: "Do you realize what a debater's argument you are bringing up, that a man cannot search either for what he knows or for what he does not know? He cannot search for what he knows—since he knows it, there is no need to search—nor for what he does not know, for he does not know what to look for."[116] The solution suggested by Plato, his theory of recollection, though ultimately unconvincing, may contain more truth than we might at first suppose. In order to know, we must at least know how to know, else we could never begin. In short, we must begin with some knowledge or else the inquiry would never get under way.[117] This seems to produce something of a circular argument when we attempt to justify our knowledge: I begin with some semblance of knowledge; from that unsecured, unjustified starting point, I proceed to gain more knowledge; the adequacy of the knowledge I have gained serves retrospectively as a justification for the adequacy of the unsecured starting point. Thus, in an important way "the end is to some significant degree presupposed in the beginning, in which initial actualities presuppose and give evidence of potentiality for future development."[118]

Thus, we must begin at a point that is not foundational in the Cartesian sense. Along with this very un-Cartesian starting point, MacIntyre argues that we also need a teacher to show us the proper manner in which to proceed: "Hence there emerges a conception of rational teaching authority internal to the practice of the craft of moral enquiry, as indeed such conceptions emerge in such other crafts as furniture making and fishing, where, just as in moral enquiry, they partially define the relationship of master-craftsman to apprentice."[119] Here we take up again the discussion that was begun earlier when we explored the manner in which a practice is learned and mastered. Because of that prior discussion and because this topic will come up again in chapter 4, it will not be necessary to dwell on it here for long.

It is important to note, though, that when we originally encountered the concept of master and apprentice it was in the context of entering into a practice, such as agriculture or architecture. Now the field has expanded considerably to include moral inquiry itself, which MacIntyre conceives as a craft (or a practice). If moral inquiry falls under the rubric of a practice requiring submission to the authority of a master, then it is reasonable to assume that all rational inquiry requires the same learning process. But when one submits oneself to the authority of a master (be this an individual person or a tradition of inquiry or both), trust is essential. When one submits to the authority of another, one must by faith follow where the master leads without knowing fully the destination. It is only after this relational process has produced the proper moral and intellectual habits that the apprentice can look back and rationally comprehend the path that has been trod. Thus, "faith in authority has to precede rational understand-ing."[120] This requires, among other things, the virtue of humility, for only with such virtue is submission and trust possible. But if we must believe before we can understand, or, more properly, so that we can understand, it follows that "rational justification is thus essentially retrospective."[121] It is in light of this account that MacIntyre notes that "Anselm's arguments are in no way accidentally in the form of a prayer."[122] Thus, contrary to the false ambitions of Descartes, rational thought cannot ground itself in in-dubitable first principles. Like any other practice or craft, moral inquiry requires submission to authority, trust, and the wisdom of a teacher.

MacIntyre and Oakeshott

As far as I can tell, neither MacIntyre nor Oakeshott ever mentions the other in print. It is certain, though, that MacIntyre is familiar with Oake-shott's work. In 1967, MacIntyre published an article titled "The Idea of a Social Science."[123] The article is a review of Peter Winch's influential book of the same title published in 1958.[124] In the book, Winch includes a fairly substantial discussion of Oakeshott's view of a morality based on habit and affection rather than one that is primarily rule-based.[125]

Temperamentally, Oakeshott and MacIntyre could not be more dif-ferent. Whereas MacIntyre regularly informs his readers of his beliefs and has been accused of an excessive capacity for belief, Oakeshott consistently describes himself as a "sceptic."[126] Ironically, despite MacIntyre's inclina-tion for belief and Oakeshott's self-described skepticism, both men have been accused of rejecting reason.[127] These accusations are the result of both men's belief that thought cannot be properly conducted in a purely abstract and rationalistic manner. This belief can be summed up in the emphasis both put on the role of tradition. To be a part of a tradition is to submit oneself to the basic premises upon which the tradition rests. Apprentice-ship is an important element in the process of inculcation into a tradition, and apprenticeship requires that the student submit himself to the master in an attitude of trust.[128] But such notions as submission, trust, and the decided nonegalitarianism entailed in the relationship between a master and a student are concepts that find little favor in a world that celebrates the liberal self along with epistemic independence and autonomous ratio-nality. Thus, it should not be surprising that accusations of irrationality have been leveled against both by those who do not share their appreciation for the tradition-dependent nature of all inquiry.

According to Oakeshott, modern philosophy, which is characterized by a desire for certainty and uniformity, insists that all knowledge can be reduced to technical knowledge. MacIntyre, too, rejects this view when he notes that "a practice . . . is never just a set of technical skills."[129] However, he notes that "the success of the natural sciences has conferred prestige upon technique as such, and outside the natural sciences agreement on technique has often been allowed to substitute for agreement on matters of substance."[130] Technical skills are indeed necessary, but practical knowledge is less easily learned, for although technical knowledge can be gleaned from a book, practical knowledge is only obtained by participation. Oakeshott sees this neglect of practical knowledge as a harbinger of a crisis of the Western tradition, for practical knowledge, once lost, is not easily recovered.[131] MacIntyre's belief that modern moral philosophy is seriously damaged overlaps significantly with Oakeshott at this point. When morality is separated from practice, narrative, and tradition, it loses its rational coherence and descends into emotivism. Practice, narrative, and tradition produce a context in which moral action can be learned and in which the virtues can become habitual. When those contextual conditions are removed, all morality must be reduced to a consideration of rules. A morality of rules is nothing if not a morality of technique, while a morality that emphasizes the virtues within the context of practice, narrative, and tradition also leaves room for practical knowledge. In this respect, both MacIntyre and Oakeshott agree that one of the problems faced by modern philosophy is an elevation of technical knowledge at the expense of the practical. They agree further that this problem, which at its root is a problem of knowledge, has deleterious effects that extend outward from the realm of philosophy into the moral and political spheres.

An important similarity, and one that is the focus of this book, is the central role tradition plays for both Oakeshott and MacIntyre. What I have termed the "epistemic role of tradition" is crucial in understanding the thought of both. The centrality of the role of tradition points to the fact that the particularities within which each individual is embedded are in many ways constitutive of the individual, and thus such particularities as history, culture, language—which is to say, tradition—cannot be transcended in the quest for universals.

Whereas Oakeshott emphasizes the flexible, the habitual, and the procedural nature of tradition, MacIntyre speaks primarily in terms of conflict, rationality, and substantive goods. For MacIntyre, a tradition is "an argument extended through time."[132] The subject of the argument is in part "about the goods which constitute that tradition."[133] Thus, conflict takes center stage, and the subject of the conflict is the nature of the good. The argument or conflict is conducted in a rational fashion, for at the heart of tradition is a reasoned argument extending through time and participated in by all those who count themselves members of the tradition.[134] Like Oakeshott, MacIntyre understands the open-ended nature of all inquiry; thus, the argument that takes place within every healthy tradition is ongoing and contingent, even if some (or all) of the participants fail to recognize that fact. Furthermore, both Oakeshott and MacIntyre recognize that those who participate in a tradition contribute to its ongoing development.[135]

Central to MacIntyre's conception of a practice is the twofold distinction between internal and external goods. Whereas Oakeshott describes practices primarily in procedural terms, MacIntyre speaks in terms of securing goods internal to the practice. But since, for Oakeshott, "practices are themselves the outcomes of performances," a practice is the "by-product" of performances the goal of which are "the achievement of imagined and wished-for satisfactions other than that of having a procedure."[136] Thus, for Oakeshott, a practice is the procedure that emerges through the act of pursuing a desired satisfaction. It is not the achievement of the satisfaction; rather, it is the procedural conditions that make the realization of satisfactions possible. For MacIntyre, the practice itself contains goods internal to it, and those goods are realized through pursuing standards of excellence unique to the particular practice.[137]

The morality that both Oakeshott and MacIntyre affirm is one in which rules play a secondary, though indispensable, role. For Oakeshott, a morality based primarily upon "habit and affection" is preferable to one in which rules are primary. Since, according to Oakeshott, theory is derived from practice and not vice versa, moral rules (theory) are abridgments of habits and affections, which are the products of practice. Thus, a morality based primarily upon rules is a morality that is guided by abridgments that are erroneously believed to represent complete and unabridged truth— such a morality is based on a confusion of thought, and it is no wonder that moral confusion results. For MacIntyre, an ethics in which the virtues are given a central role is preferable to that in which rules are primary. Recall that, for MacIntyre, the rise of rule-based moral philosophy is the result of the abandonment of theology and teleology. In *After Virtue* he argues for a return to a teleological conception of human life in order to provide a rational framework upon which to construct an account of the virtues. In his *Three Rival Versions of Moral Enquiry*, MacIntyre acknowledges that the position he is defending includes "metaphysical realism," which "has as its core the view that the world is what it is independent of human thinking and judging and desiring and willing." Furthermore, the opponents of this view, MacIntyre notes, realize that "realism is inherently theistic."[138] MacIntyre's position also includes an affirmation that one's good is inextricably tied up with the common good. Thus, to pursue the common good is simultaneously to seek one's own good.[139] MacIntyre's account of morality, then, affirms a teleological account of human nature; metaphysical realism, which he believes implies theism; and the connection between the common good and individual good.

Oakeshott denies all three. First, Oakeshott strikes an existentialist note when he claims that man "has a 'history,' but no 'nature'; he is what in conduct he becomes. This 'history' is not an evolutionary or teleological process."[140] People become what they become as a result of the choices they make, and these choices are not guided by a teleology that provides the essential pattern to which humans ought to strive to conform. Next, although Oakeshott does not deny the existence of God, his skepticism requires that he consider moral and political questions without consideration of metaphysical or theological claims. In this regard, Oakeshott strikes a Humean note when he writes that if the "self-consciously conditional theorist . . . is concerned to theorize moral conduct or civil association he must forswear metaphysics."[141] Finally, Oakeshott rejects the Aristotelian notion that man's individual good is tied up with the common good. This understanding is a ramification of his rejection of any notion of teleology, for teleology postulates that there is a good that is good for all humans and (in Aristotle's view) that good is fully realized in the common good. Aristotle argues that all men pursue happiness (*eudaimonia*), yet Oakeshott denies that such a concept has any content. "I cannot want 'happiness'; what I want is to idle in Avignon or to hear Caruso sing."[142] Thus, there is no "common end" to which humans ought to aspire, for at the heart of Oakeshott's moral theory is individual choice, which is the product of autonomous persons pursuing self-chosen ends.[143]

Like Oakeshott, MacIntyre realizes that traditions can encounter crises, both internal and external, and for MacIntyre, an important indicator of the "rational superiority" of a tradition is its ability to overcome a crisis where other traditions fail. Another manner by which the rational superiority of a tradition can be established is through the painstaking process of learning the language of the rival tradition as "a second first language." In so doing a person can learn to speak the idiom of two traditions equally well and from that position evaluate the weaknesses of each from the inside. Although MacIntyre is careful to stress that such an investigation may prove (at least for a time) inconclusive, he is firmly opposed to any suggestion of a relativism of traditions. Thus, one tradition must be rationally superior to all others, even though we may not be able to determine with absolute certainty which one that is. Oakeshott, on the other hand, would never imagine that it would be possible to learn the idiom of another tradition as a "second first language." Since we are constituted by the ideas derived from our tradition, to imagine that we could grasp another tradition at the same fundamental level is, for Oakeshott, simply a confusion. He does not deny that the study of other traditions is beneficial, for "to know only one's own tradition is not to know even that."[144] Yet, such studies should provide us with a better understanding of our own tradition rather than serve as an opportunity to find a tradition that we believe is better. For Oakeshott, "to range the world in order to select the 'best' of the practices and purposes of others . . . is a corrupting enterprise."[145] This ought not to surprise us, though, for Oakeshott's emphasis on the coherence of a self-contained world, which is analogous to language, does not permit comparisons of one whole against another. To do so presumes a reality that is independent of both, and for Oakeshott no such thing exists.[146] From the above discussion it should be clear that whereas MacIntyre leaves open the possibility of switching allegiances from one tradition to another, for Oakeshott such a suggestion is unintelligible.

This brings us back to the basic philosophical orientation of both Oakeshott and MacIntyre. Oakeshott's idealism relies on satisfaction produced by a comprehensive coherence. MacIntyre's realism, on the other hand, holds that knowing requires that the mind adequately grasp a reality that is independent of it. Oakeshott's position leads him to conclude that it is simply a confusion to imagine that a person could switch from one tradition to another. One's tradition provides him with the only resources at his disposal; thus, to switch traditions would be to abandon all of one's intellectual resources. This is simply an impossibility. Instead, experience is a unified whole, and inquiry seeks to produce an ever-increasing level of coherence within that whole.

Oakeshott's approach produces a rather complex picture of conflicting traditions. First, the resources at each person's disposal constitute that person's tradition. Each person is born into a complex web of social, intellectual, political, and moral practices. These are inherited through inculcation into the milieu that produced them, and they become part of an individual's experience—they serve to produce a more or less coherent whole that represents the world of experience for that person. Second, it is a confusion to speak of evaluating different traditions and, having determined which is superior, committing one's self to that tradition. Since the experience produced by each respective tradition represents a more or less coherent world of ideas, and since one's resources for evaluating one's tradition and other traditions are the totality of one's own tradition, it is inconceivable that a person could move from one world of ideas to another. This point is clear if one understands that a world of ideas is a totality; there cannot exist more than one such world. Thus, when two comprehensive traditions collide, one is not presented with an either/or option. The resources by which the collision is comprehended are the product of one's tradition; thus, the particularities of one's own tradition will serve to define the features of the other tradition. If an opposing tradition appears to provide desirable resources (that is, desirable for effecting greater coherence of the whole), they are, in the very recognition of their desirability, incorporated into one's own tradition, and in being so incorporated, they become part of one's tradition. Thus, the either/or is transcended by a both/and whereby the resources of one tradition are subsumed into a larger whole of one's total experience, a whole which is continually seeking greater coherence.

In the end, the differences between MacIntyre and Oakeshott can only be adequately addressed when we consider the viability of their respective understanding of the nature of reality, and it is at this point that MacIntyre's realism seems to fare better. Oakeshott's theory of knowledge does not seem able to avoid sliding into a soft form of relativism, for as we saw in chapter 2, coherence alone does not appear adequate as a test of truth. In other words, coherence itself is not a good, for it is conceivable that a coherent tradition is at the same time an immoral tradition, unless, of course, one first postulates that the coherent whole is *morally* good. In this case, the goal of coherence makes moral sense, for in seeking coherence, a tradition is attempting to fashion itself in keeping with a reality that is morally structured. But at this point it becomes obvious that we are no longer relying completely upon a coherence test of truth, for we have introduced an independent moral reality that serves as a model. In attempting to avoid a relativism between traditions, we have inadvertently slipped into a realist mode of thought.

Furthermore, Oakeshott appeals to satisfaction as a constitutive part of coherence or, at times, even synonymous with coherence. Oakeshott writes, "Reality is the world of experience in so far as it is satisfactory, in so far as it is coherent."[147] But satisfaction as a measure or indicator of coherence—and therefore of truth—seems to be little more than an emotivist appeal, and MacIntyre's arguments against emotivism would seem to hold against Oakeshott's account insofar as it depends on satisfaction as a criterion.

It is here that MacIntyre's account seems more successful on its own grounds than does Oakeshott's. As a realist, MacIntyre recognizes that various traditions can and do exist, each one attempting with varying degrees of success to apprehend an independent reality. Because that reality provides the goal for rational discourse, and because in that reality rationality and morality converge into a single point, one can determine the morally superior tradition by determining the rationally superior tradition. However, the case is never completely closed, for questions are always susceptible of revisitation, and our conclusions are always provisional and fallible.

Neither Oakeshott nor MacIntyre provides us with what Oakeshott terms a "mistake-proof" method or technique by which to judge the tradition in which we find ourselves a part. In this they both agree: the human situation is full of uncertainty, and knowing resembles an art more than a well-formulated system of rules. It is at this important point that their traditionalism converges and presents a strong argument against those—like Descartes and Bacon—who would claim that human knowing is a purely objective, detached affair in which rationality exists prior to and apart from the particularities of one's tradition. For both Oakeshott and MacIntyre tradition is an epistemological necessity, and they would agree that to attempt summarily to throw off one's tradition and proceed free from all of the commitments entailed therein is, in a word, incoherent.

THE ACHIEVEMENT OF MACINTYRE

MacIntyre recognizes that an apparent dilemma seems implied by modern conceptions of moral inquiry: "*Either* reason is thus impersonal, universal, and disinterested *or* it is the unwitting representative of particular interests, masking their drive to power by its false pretensions to neutrality and disinterestedness."[148] According to MacIntyre, this dilemma is patently false, for what it

> conceals from view is a third possibility, the possibility that reason can only move towards being genuinely universal and impersonal insofar as it is neither neutral nor disinterested, that membership in a particular type of moral community, one from which fundamental dissent has to be excluded, is a condition for genuinely rational enquiry and more especially for moral and theological enquiry. . . . A prior commitment is required and the conclusions which emerge as enquiry progresses will of course have been partially and crucially predetermined by the nature of this initial commitment.[149]

MacIntyre employs the word "tradition" to describe this third way that avoids both horns of the dilemma. This is an important insight. If this alternative is viable, then we are justified in simultaneously denying both the universalistic aspirations of the Enlightenment, upon which the liberal project is founded, and the nihilistic conclusions of those who labored to overcome it. In chapter 4, I will explore the ideas of Michael Polanyi in an effort to supplement what we have achieved so far. It is my hope that the concepts with which he deals will provide a further dimension to the account of tradition that has emerged thus far.

A final comment. If our rationality is constituted by the tradition we inhabit, then the very manner in which we comprehend a historically embedded reality is inevitably conditioned by who we are and when, historically, we are. If that is the case, then simply to recover an Aristotelian or a Thomist ethics is impossible. However, the fact that we do aspire to recover concepts that have apparently passed into history indicates that the resources of the past are never completely lost. But if history is as pervasive as MacIntyre believes, then attempts at recovery are better understood as attempts to appropriate with the understanding that the appropriated concepts will, in the very process of appropriation, undergo a change by virtue of the historic moment into which they are drawn. Thus, it is only too true that one can never go home, for home exists only as a memory, and it can be resurrected only by the refurbishment that is the inevitable result of exposure to the present historical moment. The past, then, is indeed an indispensable resource, yet its goods are not simply appropriated, for in appropriating them we make them our own, and in so doing, we unavoidably color them with the present.

CHAPTER 4

Michael Polanyi and the
Role of Tacit Knowledge

We must now recognize belief once more as the source of all knowledge. Tacit assent and intellectual passions, the sharing of an idiom and of a cultural heritage, affiliation to a like-minded community: such are the impulses which shape our vision of the nature of things on which we rely for our mastery of things. No intelligence, however critical or original, can operate outside such a fiduciary framework.

—Michael Polanyi[1]

Michael Polanyi came to philosophy late and in a rather unconventional manner. Born in 1891 in Budapest into an upper-class Jewish family, Polanyi was initially trained as a medical doctor. He served in this capacity during World War I, but his first love was chemistry, and after the war he submitted a previously published paper as his doctoral thesis and dedicated himself to research. He took a post in Berlin, but in 1933 he, like many of his Jewish colleagues, left Germany, fleeing the increasingly anti-Semitic policies of Hitler's government. He accepted a position as head of Physical Chemistry at the University of Manchester in England. In addition to chemistry, Polanyi's interests ranged from economics to politics, and eventually to philosophy. By the mid-1940s Polanyi's scientific publications were outnumbered by his papers dealing with nonscientific topics, and in 1948 the University of Manchester agreed to change his status to Professor of Social Studies.[2]

Polanyi's thought is wide-ranging and encompasses a great variety of topics, but I am primarily interested in his epistemology, specifically the role tradition plays in knowing. The title of Polanyi's magnum opus suggestively sums up his project: *Personal Knowledge: Towards a Post-Critical Philosophy*. The title itself raises questions, for personal knowledge sounds suspiciously like a rejection of objective knowledge in favor of some sort of subjectivism. A postcritical philosophy alludes to Kant's so-called critical philosophy and suggests that this work is an attempt to transcend the Kantian framework.

Central to Polanyi's thought is his critique of modernist theories of knowledge, which he lumps together under the rubric of "objectivism." The objectivist holds that the ideal of complete objectivity, as is often assumed by the hard sciences, is possible. A corollary to objectivism is methodological doubt, which refuses to acknowledge any truth claims that are not demonstrable.[3] Such an approach to knowledge produces the so-called fact/value distinction in which empirical, explicit, objective facts are completely separated from the realm of values, which are merely subjective preferences. This separation of fact from value has produced, according to Polanyi, a false and ultimately harmful understanding of truth that manifests itself morally and politically. In place of objectivism Polanyi develops his theory of tacit knowledge, which he sums up in the pithy dictum "We can know more than we can tell."[4] In developing this postcritical theory of knowledge, Polanyi seeks to apply the findings of Gestalt psychology to epistemology and invokes the indispensable role of tradition, authority, and belief. Furthermore, his entire philosophy rests on the belief that an external reality exists that is knowable, although only partially and provisionally. The first four sections of this chapter will focus on four central elements of Polanyi's thought: tacit knowing, tradition, realism, and the objective/subjective divide. Once the core of Polanyi's theory of knowledge is laid out, I will turn to a discussion of his moral and political ideas. Finally, I will discuss Polanyi in relation to Oakeshott and MacIntyre.

A THEORY OF TACIT KNOWLEDGE

Gestalt Psychology

How do we recognize a face? This is an apparently simple question, but it is much more complex than it would at first seem. Humans can easily pick out a particular face—a friend, a spouse, or an acquaintance—from a lineup of a hundred or a million, but if we inquired into just how the recognition came about, the person who so readily identified the face would be hard pressed to explain *how* he knew. In other words, it appears that we can know more than we can tell. Of course, all faces are different, and the particular features of each—the shape of the nose, the size of the mouth, the spatial relationship of eyes to mouth, the curve of cheek, and lines of the chin—all combine to form the particular physiognomy that we instantly recognize. Polanyi appropriates the findings of Gestalt psychology to help provide a clue to the problem. Gestalt psychology, in Polanyi's words, claims that "the particulars of a pattern or a tune must be apprehended jointly, for if you observe the particulars separately they form no pattern or tune."[5] In terms of the present example, Polanyi writes that "Gestalt psychology has demonstrated that we may know a physiognomy by integrating our awareness of its particulars without being able to identify these particulars."[6] Although Gestalt psychologists understand this integration as a passive event, Polanyi disagrees: "I am looking at Gestalt, on the contrary, as the outcome of an active shaping of experience performed in the pursuit of knowledge. This shaping or integrating I hold to be the great and indispensable tacit power by which all knowledge is discovered and, once discovered, is held to be true."[7] This "tacit power," which serves as the foundation of all knowledge, is the heart of Polanyi's theory of knowledge.

Two Kinds of Awareness

Tacit knowing comprises two types of awareness. When we focus upon an object we are aware of it focally. It is the explicit object of our attention, and our awareness of it is the subject of our concerns. But all focal awareness is accompanied by subsidiary awareness. We attend focally to an object or idea while attending subsidiarily to particular clues that are not the object of our attention. The integration of these two kinds of awareness constitutes tacit knowing. Polanyi gives his readers several examples that serve to clarify this distinction.

(1) The particulars of a physiognomy are not immediately specifiable, yet the identity of a particular person is recognized without hesitation. The particular features of the physiognomy are subsidiarily known and their integration produces the recognizable face that is the focus of our atten-

tion. In other words, we do not focus upon any particular facial feature; instead, we focus upon the face as a whole and the joint relationship between the subsidiaries and the focal produce a recognizable face.[8] This joint integration is tacit knowing.

(2) A stereoscope is an instrument in which two pictures of the same object are observed, each by one eye. The pictures are taken from slightly different angles. The image produced by the tacit integration of the two pictures contains a three-dimensional depth that neither of the single pictures possesses. In this case, we attend subsidiarily to the two pictures and focus on their integration. The integration, of course, will be destroyed if focus is shifted to the particular pictures.[9]

(3) When a person employs a probe to explore a hidden cavity, or when a blind person uses a stick to find his way along an unknown path, the individual is aware of the impact the handle produces in his hand when the probe strikes an object, but the individual attends to these impacts subsidiarily. His focus is upon the end of the stick, and by attending focally to that while attending subsidiarily to the impact of the stick in his hand, he is able to comprehend objects by virtue of the stick. In a certain respect, the probe becomes an extension of his own body, and it is for this reason that subsidiary awareness and focal awareness can be understood in terms of physiology and identified as "proximal" and "distal." The proximal term is that which is closest to one's body—in actuality it is that which is either part of one's body (e.g., a hand or a limb) or that which becomes an extension of one's body (e.g., a probe or any other tool). We dwell subsidiarily in the proximal term in order to attend focally to the distal term.[10]

(4) A skillful performance requires the same tacit integration of subsidiary and focal elements. For example, if a piano player shifts the focus of his attention from the piece he is playing to the observation of his fingers, he very likely will become confused and have to stop. In the same way, an athlete will be unable to specify all that goes into a skillful performance of his particular sport, and if while performing he turns his focus on the particulars of that performance, his performance will likely fail.[11] Thus, "subsidiary awareness and focal awareness are mutually exclusive."[12] Furthermore, "focal and subsidiary awareness are definitely *not two degrees* of attention but *two kinds* of attention given to the *same* particulars."[13]

(5) When we use language, again, the dual structure of subsidiary and focal awareness is evident. When we read words we attend focally to the

meaning of the words and attend subsidiarily to the words and letters that comprise them. If we turn our focus to the words themselves, their meaning is lost. For example, if one repeats a particular word over and over, the word soon becomes meaningless noise. Once we return our focus to the meaning of the word and attend subsidiarily to the word itself, the integration is restored, and the word once again functions as a carrier of meaning. In a certain respect we look *through* the word to its meaning, and when looking through a word we employ it in the service of meaning that is beyond the word. When we shift our attention to the word itself we no longer look through it but *at* it, and the tacit integration is lost as the word becomes a meaningless symbol.[14] Thus, the subsidiary–focal relationship is one that can be characterized as a *from–to* relationship. We attend *from* the subsidiaries *to* the focal target.

It is important to recognize at this point that subsidiary awareness is not unconscious awareness. Instead, Polanyi writes,

> the level of consciousness at which we are aware of a subsidiary particular may vary over the whole range of possible levels. Some subsidiary things, like the processes in our inner ear, of which we are aware in feeling the position of our head, are profoundly unconscious, strictly subliminal. But we are not unconscious of a pointing finger the direction of which we are following, nor of the features of a face that we are seeking to recognize, nor of the paper and pen used with a bearing on the content of a written message we are composing.[15]

Four Aspects of Tacit Knowing

Polanyi identifies four aspects of tacit knowing; each reveals a manner in which the tacit integration of particulars produces more than the mere sum of disparate parts. First, the from–to aspect of tacit knowing by which we attend subsidiarily to certain things while we attend focally to the object of our attention can be called the *functional* structure of tacit knowing. Second, the integration of subsidiary and focal objects of attention produces a change of appearance of that which we know. Take, for example, the stereoscope. The tacit integration of particulars attended to subsidiarily produces a three-dimensional image. In Polanyi's words, "We are aware of the proximal term of an act of tacit knowing in the appearance of its distal term; we are aware of that *from* which we are attending *to* another thing, in the *appearance* of that thing."[16] This change in appearance can be termed the *phenomenal* structure of tacit knowing. Third, when the integration of subsidiaries and the focal elements occurs, new meaning emerges that was not available prior to the act of tacit integration. For example, when we employ a probe to explore the interior of a cavity, we attend subsidiarily to the impact of the tool in our hands as we focus on the meaning derived from the distal end of the probe. In Polanyi's words, "We are attending to the meaning of its impact on our hands in terms of its effect on the things to which we are applying it."[17] This new meaning that emerges in the wake of the integration is the *semantic* aspect of tacit knowing. Fourth, the functional, phenomenal, and semantic aspects of tacit knowing combine to reveal something that does not simply appear different or mean more but actually is more than the simple integration of particulars: "Since tacit knowing establishes a meaningful relation between two terms, we may identify it with the understanding of the comprehensive entity which these two terms jointly constitute. Thus the proximal term represents the particulars of this entity, and we can say, accordingly, that we comprehend the entity by relying on our awareness of its particulars for attending to their joint meaning."[18] This entity represents the *ontological* aspect of tacit knowing and comprises the fourth aspect of the tacit.[19]

Indwelling

The from–to nature of tacit knowing reveals some important features of the tacit dimension of human cognition. First, it puts the human knower at the center of the knowing process. This is the central motivating purpose of Polanyi's epistemological project. The modern ideal for knowledge is strict detachment in which complete objectivity is ostensibly achieved by removing the knower from the process. In his preface to *Personal Knowledge*, Polanyi admits that the ideal of detachment is perhaps a harmless (though false) ideal when dealing with the exact sciences, but "it exercises a destructive influence in biology, psychology and sociology, and falsifies our whole outlook far beyond the domain of science. I want to establish an alternative ideal of knowledge, quite generally."[20]

The tacit dimension of knowing consists of an integration of two elements: the subsidiary and the focal. In physiological terms these are proximal and distal elements. In order to focus on any object of intended knowledge, one must dwell in the subsidiary as one attends to the focal target. That which we hold subsidiarily we take as the proximal term of the tacit relationship. It becomes an extension of our body in the process of achieving a meaningful integration with the distal element. Thus, the probe becomes an extension of our hand; our visual perception of the particulars of a physiognomy extends to the integration of the particulars into a recognizable countenance; the bodily skills we achieve through repetitious practice produce a skillful performance; our comprehension of words extends to the meaning that they produce. Since the proximal component of tacit knowing resides in our bodies and extends out from them, "the bodily roots of all thought" becomes clear. We are generally aware of our bodies only subsidiarily, and those things we employ subsidiarily while attending to the focal target become essentially extensions of our bodies. Thus, "our body is the ultimate instrument of all our external knowledge, whether intellectual or practical."[21] Indwelling, then, indicates the extension of the body in the process of knowing. Polanyi writes, "The use of the term 'indwelling' applies here in a logical sense as affirming that the parts of the external world that we interiorise function in the same way as our body functions when we attend from it to things outside. In this sense we live also in the tools and probes which we use, and likewise in our intellectual tools and probes. To apply a theory for understanding nature is to interiorise it. We attend from the theory to things interpreted in its light."[22]

Since all knowledge is rooted in the subsidiary–focal integration, it is quite accurate to claim that "all knowledge is either tacit or rooted in tacit knowledge. A wholly explicit knowledge is unthinkable."[23] Furthermore, "the ideal of a strictly explicit knowledge is indeed self-contradictory; deprived of their tacit coefficients, all spoken words, all formulae, all maps and graphs, are strictly meaningless."[24] But if all knowledge consists of the subsidiary–focal relationship, and the subsidiaries represent the bodily indwelling of the knower in an active integration of the two elements, then it follows that "all tacit knowing requires the continued participation of the knower, and a measure of personal participation is intrinsic therefore to all knowledge."[25] By claiming that knowledge requires the active and continued participation of the knower, Polanyi separates himself radically from those who embrace the ideal of rational and passive detachment. Furthermore, by claiming that the body plays a central role in knowing, he sets himself up against the Cartesian dualism that conceives of the body as a mere physical extension and of the mind as related only accidentally to the body.

The Triad of Tacit Knowing

Tacit knowing can be understood as a triad consisting of three components, each performing a particular and essential function. We employ the (1) subsidiary elements in the process of focusing upon (2) the object of our attention. The individual (3) integrates the subsidiary and the focal in an active process that constitutes tacit knowing. But this triad is not necessarily permanent, for "the subsidiaries have a meaning to the knower which fills the center of his focal attention," thus "the knower can dissolve the triad by merely looking differently at the subsidiaries."[26] The image of a triad provides a useful framework, for in reflecting on this image it is possible to better comprehend the dynamics of tacit knowing. Polanyi describes this in the following:

> Suppose, then, that it is possible at least in principle, to identify all the subsidiaries of a triad; however elusive that may be we would still face the fact that anything serving as a subsidiary ceases to do so when focal attention is directed on it. It turns into a different kind of thing, deprived of the meaning it had in the triad. Thus subsidiaries are—in this important sense—essentially unspecifiable. We must distinguish, then, between two types of the unspecifiability of subsidiaries. One type is due to the difficulty of tracing the subsidiaries—a condition that is widespread but not universal—and the other type is due to a sense deprivation which is logically necessary and in principle absolute.[27]

None of the three elements of the triad can be removed without destroying the meaning created in the tacit integration. Thus, if this account of knowing is accurate, the ideal of objective detachment is rendered impossible, for the active participation of the knower is indispensable. Furthermore, if all knowing is formed in this triadic fashion, which necessarily includes elements that are unspecifiable, then we can agree with Polanyi that all knowledge is either tacit or rooted in tacit knowledge. Thus, the ideal of a purely explicit knowledge is also rendered impossible.

But to dwell in a subsidiary in order to attend to the object of our focus implies trust, for indwelling entails a degree of submission to the standards of that in which we dwell. This leads us to a second major part of Polanyi's epistemology.

Tradition

Modern Rejection of Tradition

According to Polanyi, modern philosophy is characterized by, among other things, a rejection of tradition. The early moderns initiated their inquiries by explicitly and categorically rejecting the authority of the Aristotelian and religious traditions. Those traditions were seen as oppressive and a hindrance to the pursuit of truth. Any reliance on belief or tradition as a starting point for investigation was rejected. This ideal has continued to our day. Polanyi writes, "To assert any belief uncritically has come to be regarded as an offence against reason. We feel in it the danger of obscurantism and the menace of an arbitrary restriction of free thought. Against these evils of dogmatism we protect ourselves by upholding the principle of doubt which rejects any open affirmation of faith."[28] The twin streams of early modern philosophy—rationalism and empiricism—both rejected any dependence on tradition and authority. As Polanyi puts it, "Cartesian doubt and Locke's empiricism . . . had the purpose of demonstrating that truth could be established and a rich and satisfying doctrine of man and the universe built up on the foundations of critical reason alone."[29] Polanyi believed that the modern descendants of Descartes and Locke were still pursuing their ideals in the twentieth century, and that they manifested themselves in the form of both logical positivism and skepticism. These modern empiricists and skeptics "are all convinced that our main troubles still come from our having not altogether rid ourselves of all traditional beliefs and continue to set their hopes on further applications of the method of radical scepticism and empiricism."[30]

The attempted rejection of all tradition and authority among the early modern thinkers gave rise to the ideal of explicit, objective knowledge. Tradition and authority are mediating elements that inevitably influence the mind subjected to them. A mind subjected to such influences cannot obtain the necessary distance to attain a purely objective and explicit grasp of the facts. Thus, the war on tradition is the attempt to rid the mind of epistemological mediaries that cloud and influence the mind and prevent the knower from accessing unmediated truth. According to Polanyi, "Objectivism has totally falsified our conception of truth, by exalting what we can know and prove, while covering up with ambiguous utterances all we can know and *cannot* prove, even though the latter knowledge underlies, and must ultimately set its seal to, all that we *can* prove."[31] The question that arises, then, is one we have encountered in previous chapters: Is tradition epistemologically necessary? If so, then the ideal embraced by modern philosophy is self-contradictory, and it would follow that those who embrace this ideal inevitably produce incoherence within their systems of thought. As with Oakeshott and MacIntyre, Polanyi, too, recognizes the epistemic role of tradition; thus, for him the rejection of tradition must be overcome. In Polanyi's phrase, a "post-critical philosophy" must be developed.

A Return to St. Augustine

Polanyi develops his account using broad historical brushstrokes. Philosophy was born in Greece, and Greek rationalism reigned until the spiritual fervor of Christianity reached a climax with the thought of St. Augustine. In his intellectual struggle leading up to his conversion, Augustine, who at one time expressed a great admiration for and interest in science, came to consider "all scientific knowledge as barren and its pursuit as spiritually misleading."[32] This sentiment solidified after his conversion, and his teaching on the matter "destroyed interest in science all over Europe for a thousand years."[33] According to Polanyi, Augustine "brought the history of Greek philosophy to a close by inaugurating for the first time a post-critical philosophy. He taught that all knowledge was a gift of grace, for which we must strive under the guidance of antecedent belief: *nisi credideritis, non intelligitis*."[34] Thus, for the ancient Greeks, reason was primary. Augustine overturned that tradition by arguing that faith preceded reason. Modern philosophy, in turn, rejected the Augustinian primacy of belief with its rejection of all forms of tradition. Polanyi's critique of modern thought reveals its incoherencies. Modern thought has reached a dead end, and in order to remedy the error, Polanyi claims "we must now go back to St. Augustine to restore the balance of our cognitive powers."[35] This call for a return to Augustine is a call for a postcritical philosophy.

Polanyi is quick to point out that he does not repudiate the incredible gains made in the modern period: "Ever since the French Revolution, and up to our own days, scientific rationalism has been a major influence toward intellectual, moral, and social progress."[36] Yet, in spite of the obvious progress, there has been a darker side. Writing as a European Jew, Polanyi was all too aware that the benefits produced by modern rationalism were offset by the horrors of the twentieth century. Thus, despite the obvious advances, the promises of inevitable progress brought on by the ubiquity of modern rationalism rang hollow. Although he is loath to discard all of the gains of modernity, he is also convinced that the moral and political tragedies of the twentieth century clearly reveal the practical consequences of modern rationalism: "The question is: Can we get rid of all these malignant excrescences of the scientific outlook without jettisoning the benefits which it can still yield to us both mentally and materially?"[37] For Polanyi, then, the obvious benefits produced by modern science have been accompanied by a corresponding crisis of knowledge, which has manifested itself in inhumane acts of unspeakable proportions. The problem must be dealt with at its roots, and so a new approach to knowledge must be proposed:

> Keeping these awful aspects of our situation tacitly in mind, I shall try to trace a new line of thought along which, I believe, we may recover some of the ground rashly abandoned by the modern scientific outlook. I believe indeed, that this kind of effort, if pursued systematically, may eventually restore the balance between belief and reason on lines essentially similar to those marked out by Augustine at the dawn of Christian rationalism.[38]

Notice here and elsewhere that Polanyi employs the phrase "restore the balance" when referring to his postcritical philosophy. The historical progression that he has described elicits the image of a pendulum. Greek rationalism was one extreme. It was rejected by Augustine, whose ideas forced the pendulum far in the opposite direction. Modern rationalism, in turn, rejected Augustine and forced the pendulum hard in the direction of rationalism. A balance implies a mix of the two—a proper relationship between reason and belief. Thus, Polanyi's call for a return to Augustine is not a call to reject all appeals to reason or to reject the importance of science or other secular pursuits. Instead, it is a call to recognize the indispensable role belief plays in all knowing, for the modern bias in favor of rationalism, which insists that all knowledge be either rationally or empirically demonstrable, has produced a discrediting of belief. All claims to knowledge that were not susceptible to demonstration were denigrated as subjective opinion. Polanyi is attempting to force the pendulum away from

the extreme of rationalism so that the role of belief can once again be recognized as indispensable: "We must now recognize belief once more as the
source of all knowledge. Tacit assent and intellectual passions, the sharing
of an idiom and of a cultural heritage, affiliation to a like-minded community: such are the impulses which shape our vision of the nature of
things on which we rely for our mastery of things. No intelligence, however critical or original, can operate outside such a fiduciary framework."[39]
The contours of this fiduciary framework must now be explored, and it is
here where we see the centrality of tradition in Polanyi's thought.

Tradition and Authority

Knowing is an art, and any art is learned by practice.[40] Thus, the learning
of rules is not the primary manner by which an art is acquired: "Rules of
art can be useful, but they do not determine the practice of an art; they are
maxims, which can serve as a guide to an art only if they can be integrated
into the practical knowledge of the art. They cannot replace this knowledge."[41] Practical knowledge precedes the knowledge of rules, for one must
possess a degree of practical knowledge in order to properly apply the
rules. But if practical knowledge is not learned by the study of rules, then
one must acquire it through practice. But how can a person practice an art
if he does not yet know how to do so? The answer lies in submission to an
authority in the manner of an apprentice—we learn by example:

> To learn by example is to submit to authority. You follow your master
> because you trust his manner of doing things even when you cannot
> analyse and account in detail for its effectiveness. By watching the
> master and emulating his efforts in the presence of his example, the
> apprentice unconsciously picks up the rules of the art, including those
> which are not explicitly known to the master himself. These hidden
> rules can be assimilated only by a person who surrenders himself to
> that extent uncritically to the imitation of another.[42]

In learning by submitting to the authority of a teacher, the pupil seeks to
grasp what he initially does not comprehend. In other words, the knower
dwells in the subsidiary awareness of particulars while focusing upon an
entity which the particulars jointly constitute: "In order to share this

indwelling, the pupil must presume that a teaching which appears meaningless to start with has in fact a meaning which can be discovered by hit-
ting on the same kind of indwelling as the teacher is practicing. Such an
effort is based on accepting the teacher's authority."[43]

But if knowing is an art, and if learning an art requires dwelling in the
practices of a master, then it follows that there must exist a tradition by
which an art is transmitted, and any attempts categorically and systematically to reject tradition are logically incompatible with knowing. But this
argument may be extended more radically, for, according to Polanyi, "all
human thought comes into existence by grasping the meaning and mastering the use of language."[44] If that is the case, then we must conclude that
the ideal of a tradition-free inquiry is simply impossible. "No human mind
can function without accepting authority, custom, and tradition: it must
rely on them for the mere use of a language."[45] A child must put his trust
in the language-speakers around him and seek to indwell the particulars
of the language before he can master it. He does not begin by learning
rules of grammar and syntax, for the rules themselves require language in
order to be formulated. In the same way, any skill must first be acquired
through submission to the authority of a particular tradition, for the skill
itself exists primarily in its practice and only secondarily in rules, which
are necessarily formulated subsequent to the practice. Tradition, then,
plays an indispensable role in the knowledge that we acquire, and it would
seem that Polanyi is justified in claiming that "traditionalism, which requires us to believe before we know, and in order that we may know, is
based on a deeper insight into the nature of knowledge and of the communication of knowledge than is a scientific rationalism that would permit
us to believe only explicit statements based on tangible data and derived
from these by a formal inference, open to repeated testing."[46]

Polanyi, whose epistemological concerns are primarily motivated by
political and moral issues, employs a political example to make his point.
Polanyi construes the modern political scene as a confrontation between
the followers of Edmund Burke and the followers of Thomas Paine.
Burke, of course, denounced the French Revolution as a dangerous and
destructive event, for its leaders sought to overturn all traditional practices
and values and construct *ex nihilo* a new and better society that would secure the rights of man and achieve progress relying on autonomous reason
alone. Paine, on the other hand, embraced the ideals of the French Revolution and agreed that each society ought to be free to begin anew, just as

the French did. Polanyi admitted that many of his contemporaries embraced the ideals of Paine against the traditionalism of Burke, but he argued that such an embrace was somewhat ambiguous, for although in theory most moderns advocate the radical liberty of Paine, in actual practice many—most notably the British and the Americans—are Burkeans.[47] "In actual practice it is Burke's vision that controls the British nation; the voice is Esau's, but the hand is Jacob's."[48] This is no doubt a strange inconsistency, but Polanyi argues that Britain retained its stability while the French suffered the throes of their infamous revolution, because the British generally "profess the right of absolute self-determination in political theory and [rely] on the guidance of tradition in political practice."[49]

The traditionalism that Polanyi advocates is dynamic. His high regard for scientific discovery leads him to comprehend tradition as an orthodoxy that enforces a kind of discipline on those subject to the tradition, but the orthodoxy is a dynamic one in that "it implicitly grants the right to opposition in the name of truth."[50] According to Polanyi this view of tradition "transcends the conflict between Edmund Burke and Tom Paine. It rejects Paine's demand for the absolute self-determination of each generation, but does so for the sake of its own ideal of unlimited human and social improvement. It accepts Burke's thesis that freedom must be rooted in tradition, but transposes it into a system cultivating radical progress."[51] This description of tradition points to the fact that even though Polanyi agrees with Augustine that knowing is rooted in belief, he is decidedly non-Augustinian in his view of social progress. On the one hand, his epistemological position emerges from his recognition that modern critical philosophy ultimately is a dead end, and "the balance of our cognitive powers" can only be restored by forcing the pendulum back toward Augustine. But, on the other hand, the obvious advances made in the modern era, at least in part due to modern philosophy freeing itself from certain constraints of the past, make him much more optimistic about the prospects for progress than was Augustine.

Furthermore, tradition for Polanyi is not a simple and stable resource that can be accessed in a purely objective fashion. Polanyi's traditionalism is dynamic in that it encourages a degree of dissent, but even more fundamentally tradition is dynamic in that we cannot participate in it without changing it: "Traditions are transmitted to us from the past, but they are our own interpretations of the past, at which we have arrived within the context of our own immediate problems."[52] Thus, each generation employs tradition, but the appropriation necessarily entails interpretation, and the interpretation is necessarily conducted in light of the concerns, biases, and problems of the particular generation appropriating the tradition. In addition, each person who participates in a tradition contributes to the development of the tradition itself. Thus, "every new member subscribing to a national (or general human) tradition adds his own shade of interpretation to it."[53] Tradition, in Polanyi's sense, then, is dynamic on several levels. First, while enforcing a degree of orthodoxy, it also permits—even encourages—dissent, for frequently dissent provides the impetus for progress. Second, tradition is dynamic in that each generation interprets it in its own particular terms in reference to its own particular problems. Finally, each individual contributes to a tradition simply by participating in it. Thus, tradition is constantly changing while at the same time maintaining its identity.

Community

A tradition requires the presence of a community committed to its perpetuation. Since knowing is an art that requires one to enter into a practice by virtue of submission to the authority of a master, and since practices exist in traditions by which they are transmitted, Polanyi concludes that all knowing begins in this traditional scheme. Traditions do not exist apart from the communities that embrace and transmit them to subsequent generations. The authoritative nature of a tradition does not, though, mean that a tradition cannot be rebelled against or rejected. But it is the case that "even the sharpest dissent still operates by partial submission to an existing consensus."[54] Rebellion is always in reference to some established body of knowledge; therefore, even rebellion is conditioned by the existing tradition against which the rebellion takes place.

Since all knowing rests on a fiduciary framework, belief precedes knowing. But belief cannot exist except within a community. At its most basic, language requires belief. When a child learns a language, he believes that the language-speakers who surround him are not uttering gibberish. In the same way, all skills require submission to a master, even though the novice does not yet comprehend the meaning of that which he is practicing. Science is no different, for the aspiring scientist must submit herself to the authority of a practicing scientist, and such submission requires belief. "Thus," in Polanyi's words, "to accord validity to science—or to any other of the great domains of the mind—is to express a faith which can be upheld only within a community. We realize here the connexion between Science, Faith and Society."[55] The connection, if I may spell it out, is that science, or any other area of knowing, depends on a fiduciary framework in which belief necessarily precedes all knowing. This belief, though, cannot be sustained apart from a community of believers who sustain the tradition by passing it to the next generation through a process of apprenticeship. Thus, all knowing requires the existence of a society committed to a particular tradition and engaged in passing it on. This is not to say that knowledge is only possible within a homogeneous community. Indeed, a particular society may be composed of a variety of competing traditions. But the social nature of knowing depends on the existence of social structures, each of which is committed to a particular tradition or set of traditions.

Of course, it is frequently the case that the adherents of a tradition are not explicitly aware of that to which they are committed, for often the premises of a tradition "lie deeply embedded in the unconscious foundations of practice."[56] These premises are tacitly passed to the next generation through education in the practices by which the tradition is constituted. Polanyi puts it this way:

> Articulate systems which foster and satisfy an intellectual passion can survive only with the support of a society which respects the values affirmed by these passions, and a society has a cultural life only to the extent to which it acknowledges and fulfils the obligation to lend its support to the cultivation of these passions. Since the advancement and dissemination of knowledge by the pursuit of science, or technology and mathematics forms part of cultural life, the tacit coefficients by which these articulate systems are understood and accredited, and which uphold quite generally our shaping and affirmation of factual truth, are also coefficients of a cultural life shared by a community.[57]

But Polanyi's thought as thus far described appears to provide no defense against challenges of relativism or subjectivism. In the next two sections I will show how Polanyi is able to affirm personal knowledge and the logic of traditionalism while at the same time affirming that truth exists and is knowable.

REALISM

Meno's Paradox

Meno's paradox is a recurring subject in Polanyi's work. The paradox can be summarized as follows: When we seek understanding, we either know what we are looking for or not. If we know what we are looking for, we need look no further, for we already possess the understanding for which we seek. On the other hand, if we do not know what we are looking for, how can we proceed? It is meaningless to pursue that which we do not know, and it is unnecessary to pursue that which we already possess.[58] Polanyi believes his theory of knowledge solves the paradox. According to Polanyi, "The *Meno* shows conclusively that if all knowledge is explicit, i.e., capable of being clearly stated, then we cannot know a problem or look for its solution. And the *Meno* also shows, therefore, that if problems nevertheless exist, and discoveries can be made by solving them, we can know things, and important things, that we cannot tell."[59]

Borrowing from the French mathematician Henri Poincaré, Polanyi lists four stages of discovery: *preparation, incubation, illumination,* and *verification.*[60] *Preparation* indicates the time spent immersed in the details of a problem. It is the necessary though not sufficient groundwork, for without adequate preparation, one is incapable of either adequately formulating a problem or of recognizing likely avenues to pursue its solution. *Incubation* is the period during which the mind works on the problem, often when explicit attention is focused on other things. This period is largely unspecifiable. The solution becomes clear in a moment of *illumination.* This is the moment in which we exclaim, "Eureka!" The particulars of the problem over which we have been working suddenly coalesce into a solution. The move to illumination is unformalizable. In Polanyi's words, a "logical gap" between the particulars of the problem and its solution is crossed: "'Illumination' is then the leap by which the logical gap is crossed. It is the plunge by which we gain a foothold at another shore of reality."[61] *Verification* comes last. This is the period when we confirm that which we already know. Polanyi is fond of pointing to such figures as Kepler and Einstein as examples of thinkers who, through a process that included much work, experienced an illumination that confirmed in their minds that they had made a significant discovery only to spend much subsequent time and effort attempting to verify that which they knew to be true.[62]

What guides this progression that climaxes in illumination? Meno's paradox is yet unsolved, for the account thus far only describes the steps by which a problem is solved and says little about what motivates the progression. Polanyi explains the solution as follows: "We can pursue scientific discovery [and by analogy all discovery] without knowing what we are looking for, because the gradient of deepening coherence tells us where to start and which way to turn, and eventually brings us to the point where we may stop and claim a discovery."[63] Thus, "we should look at the known data, but not in themselves, rather as clues to the unknown; as pointers to it and parts of it. We should strive persistently to feel our way towards an understanding of the manner in which these known particulars hang together, both mutually and with the unknown."[64] The integration of the known particulars with the unknown reality that is sought is best understood in terms of Gestalt psychology wherein the particulars combine to reveal a previously unknown reality. Sometimes this process is immediate and requires no period of incubation, as in the use of a stereoscope. At other times the tacit integration requires significant time and labor and may only be verified long after the discovery has been made.[65]

The knower is guided by a deepening sense of coherence. If that were not so, then the scientist, for example, would be compelled to attempt every possible solution to a problem. But that is simply not the case, for a good scientist is able to anticipate with some accuracy whether or not a possible solution is likely to be correct. Polanyi calls this power "intuition" or "foreknowledge." He writes, "But there exists also a more intensely pointed knowledge of hidden coherence: the kind of foreknowledge we call a problem. And we know that the scientist produces problems, has hunches, and elated by these anticipations, pursues the quest that should fulfill these anticipations. This quest is guided throughout by feelings of a deepening coherence and these feelings have a fair chance of proving right. We may recognize here the powers of dynamic intuition."[66]

Polanyi is not assigning a quasi-mystical status to intuition and foreknowledge. Instead, he is merely acknowledging the unformalizable element that accompanies discovery. Intuition, for Polanyi, "is a skill for guessing with a reasonable chance of guessing right; a skill guided by an innate sensibility to coherence, improved by schooling."[67] Because it is a skill, intuition is both fallible and not reducible to rules, yet at the same time, a well-developed sense of intuition tends to be right. Thus, a well-trained practitioner—be it a scientist, a politician, an ethicist, or an athlete—exhibits an ability to guess skillfully, which the novice simply does not posses.[68] Finally, "intuition works on a subsidiary level," which attests to its unspecifiability.[69]

Reality Defined

One of Polanyi's favorite phrases in describing the process of discovery is "contact with reality." He speaks of "contact with a hidden reality" and an "intimation of a hidden reality." Realism is central to the thought of Polanyi, and he regularly affirms his commitment to that philosophical position.[70] The view that reality is independent of the knower and at least partially hidden undergirds his account of discovery, for an intimation of an unknown yet knowable coherence explains how one can pursue an answer that is yet unknown and justifies his claim that we can know more than we can tell. He writes,

> We can account for this capacity of ours to know more than we can tell if we believe in the presence of an external reality with which we can establish contact. This I do. I declare myself committed to the belief in an external reality gradually accessible to knowing, and I regard all true understanding as an intimation of such a reality which, being real, may yet reveal itself to our deepened understanding in an indefinite range of unexpected manifestations.[71]

The above definition of reality contains at least four important points that recur throughout Polanyi's work when he defines reality. First, reality is external to the knower. In other words, reality is not dependent upon the mind of the knower. It exists even if it is not apprehended. Second, reality is knowable. We can establish contact with it. Our minds are such that they can comprehend the reality that is external to them. Third, contact is gradual. We continually attempt to extend or strengthen our contact with reality, but that is never a once-and-for-all event. Instead, it is an endeavor we share with those who have gone before and anticipate for those who will come after us. Finally, the real may manifest itself in "indefinite" and "unexpected" ways. Thus, "when we accept the discovery as true, we commit ourselves to a belief in all these as yet undisclosed, perhaps as yet unthinkable, consequences."[72]

A further aspect of reality is the relationship between tangibles and intangibles. Modern philosophy has created a bias toward that which is tangible, but "the belief that, since particulars are more tangible, their knowledge offers a true conception of things is fundamentally mistaken."[73] For Polanyi, intangibles are more real than tangibles. He writes, "I shall say, accordingly, that minds and problems possess a deeper reality than cobblestones, although cobblestones are admittedly more real in the sense of being tangible. And since I regard the significance of a thing as more important than its tangibility, I shall say that minds and problems are more real than cobblestones."[74] Recalling the various aspects of tacit knowing, the particulars are integrated in the act of tacit knowing, and their integration produces a phenomenal change that has semantic and ultimately ontological significance. In other words, when particulars acting as subsidiaries are integrated in the act of knowing, they become more than the sum of their respective parts. The gestalten, when integrated successfully, reveal an entity that is more real than the particulars of which it is composed. Thus, the intangible meaning of a tacit integration is more real than the tangible particulars of which it is comprised. Furthermore, tangible particulars do not admit of the same range of indefinite and unexpected manifestations as intangibles; thus, "the vagueness of something like the human mind is due to the vastness of its resources. . . . By my definition, this indeterminacy makes the mind the more real, the more substantial."[75]

In one essay Polanyi employs a description that is suggestive. He writes that we "gradually penetrate to things that are increasingly real, things which, being real, may yet manifest themselves on an indeterminate range of future occasions."[76] The image of gradually penetrating to that which is more real suggests a vision of reality in which the core is more real than the fringes. But there is a paradox at the center of this conception of reality, a paradox that Polanyi has no interest in resolving, for the further we advance, the more indeterminate and unexpected will be our findings. This indeterminateness is not due to an essential randomness at the heart of reality; instead, it points to the infinite richness of reality, a richness that produces unexpected manifestations because of this richness. We will never reach the core of reality, for we are finite, and reality presents us with infinite possibilities. The process of knowing presents us with continual surprises, and if the more real is that which is capable of manifesting itself in indeterminate and unexpected ways, the knowing process is open-ended and contingent, and because it is conducted by imperfect individuals who embody a particular tradition, it is both fallible and colored by our subjectivity.

Our Embeddedness

Modern critical philosophy (of which liberalism is a part) is characterized by a desire to destroy the influence that tradition exercises on each knower. Religious doctrine, moral maxims, trust in authority, to which premodern people quite willingly submitted, have come under fire. Individuals were "urged to resist the pressure of this traditional indoctrination by pitting against it the principle of philosophic doubt."[77] Demand proof. Believe nothing that has not been explicitly proven. Rid the mind of traditional belief, which is mere opinion, and obtain certainty by grounding all inquiry in reason. The ideal for this approach to knowledge is a virgin mind, one that is untainted by all belief that has not been derived from reason alone. But such a mind is not easy to produce, and, in fact, if one succeeded, the result would be something less than a human mind: "A virgin mind must be allowed to mature until the age at which it reaches its full natural powers of intelligence, but would have to be kept unshaped until then by any kind of education. It must be taught no language, for speech can be acquired only a-critically, and the practice of speech in one particular language carries with it the acceptance of the particular theory of the universe postulated by that language."[78] Polanyi concludes by stating what should be apparent: "An entirely untutored maturing of the mind would, however, result in a state of imbecility."[79] Thus, in order to avoid the absurd consequences of a virgin mind, we must acknowledge the fact that we all are embedded in a variety of ways. I will look briefly at three of those ways—linguistic, cultural, and historical—all of which make up aspects of tradition.

First, language is, according to Polanyi, that which separates humans from animals.[80] In fact, "all human thought comes into existence by grasping the meaning and mastering the use of language."[81] Language, though, is essentially social; thus, if all thought that is specifically human is the product of a language, and if language is necessarily social, it follows that human thought is essentially social.[82] But humans do not share a universal language. A language consists of a stable yet malleable assortment of words by which the speaker engages his society and his world. Thus, when we employ a particular language, "all questions we can ask will have to be formulated in it and will thereby confirm the theory of the universe which is implied in the vocabulary and structure of the language."[83] In other words, the language we indwell constitutes the framework by which we see the world. Thus, "our most deeply ingrained convictions are determined by the idiom in which we interpret our experience and in terms of which we erect our articulate systems."[84] Furthermore, since human thought does not exist outside of language, we cannot speak or even think except from within a language. But language is acquired a-critically—the learner (in the case of original language acquisition, the learner is the child) must submit himself to the authority of the language he aspires to master.[85] Thus, the a-critical nature of language acquisition implies that "the practice of speech in one particular language carries with it the acceptance of the particular theory of the universe postulated by that language."[86] All humans are, by nature of the linguistically based character of thought, necessarily embedded within a particular linguistic tradition that is at least initially accepted a-critically and which constitutes the framework by which the world is viewed and consequently establishes the parameters of thought.

Second, humans are embedded within a particular culture. As with language, we a-critically enter into a cultural framework when we are born: "Members admitted to a community at birth cannot be given a free choice of their premises; they have to be educated in some terms or other, without consultation of any preference of their own."[87] We initially accept, in an a-critical fashion, the habits, traditions, and religious and moral practices of a particular culture. Polanyi writes, "The whole universe of human sensibility—of our intellectual, moral, artistic, religious ideas—is evoked . . . by dwelling within the framework of our cultural heritage."[88] One's culture is comprehended by indwelling, and indwelling implies submission and trust; thus, to indwell a culture requires an initial movement of trust.

Third, human thought is constituted in part by the historical setting in which that thought occurs. The objectivist believes it is possible for the individual to transcend fully his historical situation and grasp truth unmediated by the vicissitudes of his historical moment. This is simply another error of the objectivist position. This point perhaps can be made clear if we remember that languages and cultures change and develop over time.

Therefore, the particular historical moment one inhabits will be framed by the particular language and culture into which one is a-critically inculcated. Thus, if linguistic and cultural frameworks change with time, and if language and culture provide the framework through which we see and interpret the world, then in an important way *when one is* serves to constitute in large part *what one is*.[89]

If we are indeed embedded within a language, a culture, and a historical moment, then it is foolishness to imagine the possibility of achieving a neutral stance from which to critique that very framework. The linguistic, cultural, and historical moment in which one dwells represents the particular tradition(s) to which one belongs. Tradition provides us with the tools by which we can mount a critique; thus, to imagine the possibility of evaluating one's particular tradition from outside all traditions is tantamount to critiquing one's particular language by standing outside any language.[90] It is self-contradictory.

It perhaps goes without saying that we are all limited by our personal capacities. Polanyi writes, "I must admit that I can fulfil my obligation to serve the truth only to the extent of my natural abilities as developed by my education. No one can transcend his formative milieu very far, and beyond this area he must rely on it uncritically."[91] Our individual capacities are fixed, but they can, however, be extended or directed by education. Polanyi writes, "Although our fundamental propensities are innate, they are vastly modified and enlarged by our upbringing."[92] Our upbringing consists of our education, broadly understood in both its formal and informal aspects. Thus, not everyone is capable of genius despite the best education. Furthermore, innate strengths in one area may be accompanied by weaknesses in other areas. Therefore, all humans possess a personal capacity that may be developed and directed but cannot be exceeded. In that way, people are limited by their basic capabilities.

In summary, we are both limited and empowered by the traditions we inhabit. Polanyi admits that his own thought is unavoidably colored by who he is. In other words, he admits that he is not attempting to begin his inquiry as a virgin mind or as one who begins from universal doubt, both of which are absurd ideals. Instead, he recognizes that all human inquiry is conducted within a fiduciary framework that is a-critically accepted by the inquirer:

> I must admit now that I did not start the present reconsideration of my beliefs with a clean slate of unbelief. Far from it. I started as a per-

son intellectually fashioned by a particular idiom, acquired through my affiliation to a civilization that prevailed in the places where I had grown up, at this particular period of history. This has been the matrix of all my intellectual efforts. Within it I was to find my problem and seek the terms for its solution.[93]

But, if we are thus so wholly embedded in these ways, how, despite our strivings to make contact with reality, can one avoid a slide into subjectivism?

Transcending the Subjective/Objective Dichotomy

Commitment

We have seen that Polanyi's position depends on a belief that an external reality exists and that it is provisionally knowable. Our attempts to establish contact with reality require an act of commitment. However, the notion of commitment as a necessary condition for attaining knowledge is an affront to those steeped in the ideal of objectivism: "Epistemology has traditionally aimed at defining truth and falsity in impersonal terms, for these alone are accepted as truly universal."[94] It is precisely this ideal that Polanyi seeks to overturn. As he explains it, the purpose of *Personal Knowledge* "is to re-equip men with the faculties which centuries of critical thought have taught them to distrust."[95] Objectivism seeks to remove the influence of the human knower from the knowing process, but if it is the case that all knowing is either tacit or rooted in the tacit, and if the tacit integration requires the active participation of the knower, then participation is an unavoidable component of all knowing. Thus, if the participation of the knower is eliminated, no knowing can occur—or, to put the matter differently, "to avoid believing one must stop thinking."[96]

In addition, as we saw in the previous section, the knower is necessarily embedded in a particular linguistic, cultural, and historical context, which is to say, the knower is unavoidably enmeshed in tradition. In order to function within the given parameters of his existence, the knower must necessarily submit himself initially to the framework produced by his language and culture in a particular historical moment. This submission is an a-critical commitment that is unavoidable. Thus, at the general level of language and culture, each person necessarily begins all inquiry within a fiduciary framework.

But commitment also runs on another level, for all assertions of fact implicitly carry with them the passionate commitment of the speaker. According to Polanyi, "If language is to denote speech it must reflect the fact that we never say anything that has not a definite impassioned quality."[97] Thus, a declaratory sentence, if it is to convey any meaning, must entail an implied assertion: "I believe." "Such a prefix should not function as a verb, but as a symbol determining the modality of the sentence. The transposition of an assertion of fact into the 'fiduciary mode' would correctly reflect the fact that such an assertion is necessarily attributable to a definite person at a particular place and time: for example, to the writer of the assertion at the moment of putting it to paper, or to the reader when he reads and accepts what is written."[98] This assertive quality of a declaratory sentence is that which gives meaning to the sentence, and thus, "an unasserted sentence is no better than an unsigned cheque; just paper and ink without power or meaning."[99]

If it is the case that all declarations of fact imply an assertion of belief, then it follows that no truth claims can live up to the dispassionate objectivist ideal.[100] The picture of the dispassionate thinker standing apart from the object of his attention and forcing it to submit to the universal laws of logical thought all while remaining completely detached from the process appears, in light of Polanyi's analysis, to be blatantly false. In truth, each individual participates passionately in the knowing process. This passionate knower asserts what he believes to be true, and in that assertion, he makes a claim about reality, but because reality is hidden and manifests itself in indeterminate and often unexpected ways, such a claim represents a commitment, for "a truthful statement commits the speaker to a belief in what he has asserted: he embarks in it on an open sea of limitless implications."[101] This connection to reality presents us with a clue to how personal knowledge both admits of the passionate nature of knowing and avoids a slide into radical subjectivism and relativism.

Universal Intent

Humans desire to understand. We possess an innate craving to make sense of the chaos, to pursue the intimations of coherence that bear on a hidden reality that is waiting to be grasped.[102] This desire to understand is strong and motivates our passionate pursuit of knowledge. But when we believe we have grasped a truth we do so with the belief that the truth we have comprehended is of universal scope. For if we believe that we have grasped a coherence bearing on reality, we "will expect it to be recognized by others."[103] Polanyi calls this claim to universality "universal intent." Universal intent entails a claim about truth, for a truth claim is an assertion of what I believe to be true of reality. Thus,

> an empirical statement is true to the extent to which it reveals an aspect of reality, a reality largely hidden to us, and *existing therefore independently of our knowing it*. By trying to say something that is true about a reality believed to be existing independently of our knowing it, all assertions of fact necessarily carry *universal intent*. *Our claim to speak of reality serves thus as the external anchoring of our commitment in making a factual statement*.[104]

This claim of universal intent can, though, embroil the individual in an unexpected tension, for it does happen that a person may make a claim with universal intent only to realize that his position is not universally accepted. Polanyi writes, "We suffer when a vision of reality to which we have committed ourselves is contemptuously ignored by others. For a general unbelief imperils our own convictions by evoking an echo in us. Our vision must conquer or die."[105] Earlier we discussed the logical gap that must be crossed in an integrative act of illumination. Such an illumination represents a newly discovered coherence in reality, and since it bears on reality, the person who travels across the gap will assert his newfound insight passionately and with universal intent. This passion that leads to discovery produces what Polanyi terms "persuasive passion" by which the individual attempts to convert others to his way of thinking.[106]

Conversion

Polanyi's use of St. Augustine as a model for a postcritical epistemology makes it especially apropos to speak in the idiom of conversion. Although Augustine's famous conversion was a religious one, and the type of conversion of which Polanyi speaks is primarily epistemological, the two are in many ways similar, for a conversion both in the religious and epistemological sense (and at times they may be one and the same) produces an alteration in one's fundamental interpretive framework, which necessarily alters the manner in which one views the world. Conversions may entail a radical shift in one's interpretive framework or a modest modification, but the "depth of the cognitive commitment may be measured in either case by the ensuing change of our outlook."[107]

Conversion occurs when one's interpretive framework is challenged by another interpretive framework. In such cases, one encounters "a new language" (that is, a conceptual language, not necessarily a linguistic one), which implies a different interpretive framework, which in turn implies a "new way of reasoning."[108] When the opposing frameworks are so different that adherents of one cannot even speak intelligibly to adherents of the other, the possibility of one partisan convincing another of the superiority of his position is slight. But when convincing becomes impossible, conversion remains viable.[109] Thus,

> the less two propositions have fundamentally in common the more the argument between them will lose its discursive character and become an attempt at mutually converting each other from one set of grounds to another, in which the contestants will have to rely largely on the general impressions of rationality and spiritual worth which they can make on one another. They will try to expose the poverty of their opponent's position and to stimulate interest for their own richer perspectives; trusting that once an opponent has caught a glimpse of these, he cannot fail to sense a new mental satisfaction, which will attract him further and finally draw him over to its own grounds.[110]

When two competing interpretative frameworks collide, partisans on both sides will seek to convince each other of the superiority of their particular approach. The persuasive passions will attempt to effect universal assent because those belonging to each side passionately embrace their commitments with universal intent and consequently feel threatened by those who do not share the same fundamental interpretive framework.

When a person's commitment to his interpretive framework is shaken, he may experience a "mental crisis which may lead to conversion from one set of premises to another."[111] But such a movement is not completely specifiable, for

> conversion seems to come "out of the blue." It seems clear that we do not become converted—whether to a political party, a philosophy, *or*

a religion—by having the truth of what we become converted to demonstrated to us in a wholly logical or objective way. Rather, what happens when we become convinced is that we see at some point that the particular party or religion or epistemology or world view (or even scientific theory) in front of us holds possibilities for the attainment of richer meanings than the one we have been getting along with. At that moment we *are* converted, whether we have ever willed it or not.[112]

Thus, epistemological conversion, like Augustine's religious conversion, occurs in some sense unexpectedly. That is not to say it cannot be desired, but in a sense it is a gift that arrives unbidden.[113] We tacitly come to dwell in subsidiaries that were previously unknown or rejected. The integrations made possible by this new orientation produce new possibilities for meaning, and the increasing coherence attests to the contact with reality that has been attained.

Subjective, Objective, or Personal?

Polanyi's main target in his epistemological writings is what he calls objectivism, which is shorthand for a collection of epistemological theories with roots in Descartes and Locke. "Objectivism"—or what he describes as the "crippling mutilations imposed by an objectivist framework"— "has totally falsified our conception of truth."[114] It has been assumed that absolute objectivity is an attainable ideal and consequently that all knowledge based on belief is merely subjective.[115] But aspiring to complete objectivity is a false ideal, which has exercised its "destructive influence in biology, psychology and sociology, and falsifies our whole outlook far beyond the domain of science."[116] It is a "Fool's Paradise,"[117] which is ultimately self-contradictory for two reasons. First, "any attempt rigorously to eliminate our human perspective from our picture of the world must lead to absurdity."[118] Thus, an attempt to develop a theory of knowledge without acknowledging the role played by the knower is logically impossible, and objectivism claims to do just that. Second, objectivism presumes that it is possible to construct a theory of knowledge apart from any belief. It attempts to rid itself of any a-critical elements and accepts as knowledge only that which can be clearly and distinctly known and verified. But in reality, all knowledge depends on a fiduciary framework; thus, though it is true that the objectivist claims to admit nothing as knowledge that depends on belief, it is more accurate to say that the objectivist "tolerates no *open* declaration of faith."[119] The contradiction in logic manifests itself in a contradiction of action:

> I do not suggest, of course, that those who advocate philosophic doubt as a general solvent of error and a cure for all fanaticism would desire to bring up children without any rational guidance or contemplate any other scheme of universal hebetation. I am only saying that this would be what their principles demand. What they actually want is not expressed but concealed by their declared principles. They want their own beliefs to be taught to children and accepted by everybody, for they are convinced that this would save the world from error and strife.[120]

We see precisely this contradiction today in those who claim a fidelity to moral neutrality, who claim that people should be free to do and believe whatever they want, but who at the same time show their absolute allegiance to the liberal conception of the self when they quite willingly compromise the liberty of those who dissent from the reigning orthodoxy, and they do so in the name of liberty.

If the ideal of objectivism is discarded and a new theory of knowledge is introduced, one that emphasizes personal commitment and the fiduciary framework of all knowing, it appears that the entire project rests on a circular argument. Polanyi makes this painfully clear when he sums up the implications of his account: "Any inquiry into our ultimate beliefs can be conducted only if it presupposes its own conclusions."[121] In other words, what Polanyi calls "our liberation from objectivism"[122] appears at first blush to be every bit as undesirable as that from which we have been liberated. Polanyi realizes the inevitable criticism that his theory of knowledge will initially receive: "The moment such a program is formulated it appears to menace itself with destruction. It threatens to sink into subjectivism: for by limiting himself to the expression of his own beliefs, the philosopher may be taken to talk only about himself."[123]

The key to the problem is to find a way to affirm the personal element in all knowing while at the same time affirming the objective nature of the thing known. In Polanyi's words, we may distinguish between the personal in us, which actively enters into our commitments, and our subjective states, in which we merely endure our feelings. This distinction establishes the conception of the *personal*, which is neither subjective nor objective. In so far as the personal submits to requirements acknowledged by itself as independent of itself, it is not subjective; but in so far as it is an action guided by individual passions, it is not objective either. It transcends the disjunction between subjective and objective.[124]

A key distinction between the merely subjective and the personal is the element of activity. Whereas the subjective is passive and entails no passionate commitment, the personal "is neither an arbitrary act nor a passive experience, but a responsible act claiming universal validity."[125] Here we see the centrality of Polanyi's realism, which combines with and fortifies personal knowledge to keep it from descending into subjectivism. Personal commitment results from a passionate resolve to make contact with a hidden reality. Thus, personal knowledge "implies the claim that man can transcend his own subjectivity by striving passionately to fulfill his personal obligations to universal standards."[126] In the sense that personal knowledge affirms the possibility of establishing contact with an independent, hidden reality, it is indeed objective knowledge.[127] But since the passionate participation of the knower is ineliminable, knowing is never objective in the sense of being impersonal and completely unconditioned by the knower.

The active element of personal knowledge cannot be stressed enough, for that element determines whether or not a particular assertion is personal or subjective. Polanyi writes, "*The fiduciary passions which induce a confident utterance about the facts are **personal**, because they submit to the facts as universally valid, but when we reflect on this act non-committally its passion is reduced to **subjectivity**.*"[128] In other words, if one passively assents to a particular position, observing it, as it were, from the outside as a dispassionate and disengaged observer (the objectivist ideal), one is indeed speaking in terms of the subjective. But, if one passionately commits oneself to a position because of its perceived universality, which is a function of one's belief that contact with reality has been achieved, then the knowing is personal. If one looks *at* the position, from the outside, it is subjective; if one looks *with* the position and all that it entails and does so with universal intent, it is personal.[129] The personal is comfortable partners with the objective, while the subjective and the objective are mutually exclusive. Thus, personal knowledge overcomes the objective/subjective disjunction by affirming the personal element in all knowing while at the same time affirming an objective reality toward which all knowledge strives.

The Fact/Value Dichotomy

By transcending the subjective/objective barrier, Polanyi's theory has obvious implications for the so-called fact/value distinction. If we agree with Polanyi that all knowing includes the personal participation of the knower and operates within a fiduciary framework, then it follows that all knowing, both scientific and humane, is on the same epistemological footing. Thus, "the moment the ideal of detached knowledge was abandoned, it was inevitable that the ideal of dispassionateness should eventually follow, and that with it the supposed cleavage between dispassionate knowledge of fact and impassioned valuation of beauty should vanish."[130] The obvious conclusion to be drawn is one that "denies any discontinuity between the study of nature and the study of man."[131] This conclusion flies in the face of modern thought, which, in its attempt to protect science from any subjective element, erected the fact/value barrier. But, in Polanyi's words, "it has now turned out that modern scientism fetters thought as cruelly as ever the churches had done. It offers no scope for our most vital beliefs and it forces us to disguise them in farcically inadequate terms."[132] Polanyi offers his postcritical theory of knowledge in an attempt to give legitimate voice to those things we value most even though they are not empirically verifiable.

If the fact/value distinction is, as Polanyi argues, based upon a mistaken conception of the nature of knowing, then it follows that truth—which Polanyi defines as contact with an independent and hidden reality that manifests itself in the future in indeterminate and unexpected ways—is not the sole purview of the empirical sciences. In his later work, Polanyi took to speaking in terms of "meaning," and this emphasis is clear as he describes the implications of breaking down the fact/value distinction:

> If . . . personal participation and imagination are *essentially* involved in science as well as in the humanities, meanings created in the sciences stand in no more favored relation to reality than do meanings created in the arts, in moral judgments, and in religion. At least they

can stand in no more favored relation to reality on a basis of the sup-posed presence or absence of personal participation and imagination in the one rather than in the other. To have, or to refer to, reality—in some sense—may then be a possibility for both sorts of meanings, since the dichotomy between facts and values no longer seems to be a real distinction upon which to hang any conclusions.[133]

By eliminating the distinction between facts and values, Polanyi seeks to reestablish the possibility for humans once again to embrace with confi-dence values such as truth, beauty, and justice. These are not merely sub-jective preferences; instead, they are ideals to which we may personally commit ourselves in the belief that they are truly meaningful, for they bear on an intangible reality that is actually more real than that which is merely tangible.

Relativism and Solipsism Refuted

It should be clear by now that Polanyi's theory of knowledge does not de-scend either into solipsism or relativism. First, it is not solipsistic because "it is based on a belief in an external reality and implies the existence of other persons who can likewise approach the same reality."[134] Second it is not relativistic because truth claims are made with universal intent. They represent what "I believe to be the truth, and what the consensus ought therefore to be."[135] Polanyi grants that a theory of personal knowledge must admit "the indispensable biological and cultural rootedness of all free actions," but it must also acknowledge "that each man has some measure of direct access to the standards of truth and rightness and must limit for their sake at some point his subjection to given circumstances."[136] This leads us to the question of responsibility.

Personal Responsibility

Because personal knowledge is based on a conception of truth grounded in reality, humans are not simply free to do as they please. With freedom to know comes responsibility to act in accordance with that knowledge. Objectivism, by insisting on the ideal of detachment, "seeks to relieve us from all responsibility for the holding of our beliefs."[137] Furthermore, by erecting the fact/value barrier, objectivism also greatly reduces the purview of our intellectual powers by seeking to dismiss all value judgments from the realm of legitimate knowledge. By insisting on the personal participation of the knower and by showing that all knowing consists of a fiduciary element, a much broader venue for knowledge is produced, but at the same time this significantly changes our conception of freedom. In Polanyi's words, "This reappraisal demands that we credit ourselves with much wider cognitive powers than an objectivist conception of knowledge would allow, but at the same time it reduces the independence of human judgment far below that claimed traditionally for the free exercise of reason."[138]

By affirming realism, Polanyi affirms that truth is timeless and universal; thus, "though every person may believe something different to be true, there is only one truth."[139] But that which we claim to be true may conceivably be wrong, for "personal knowledge is an intellectual commitment, and as such inherently hazardous. Only affirmations that could be false can be said to convey objective knowledge of this kind."[140] Personal knowledge is risky. It requires commitment to that which we believe is true even though we may be wrong.[141] But our innate desire for coherence forces us to pursue that which may not be demonstrated with absolute certainty. Our passionate commitment to ideals we hold with universal intent establishes our responsibility. Our craving for the universal precludes arbitrary or glib choices: "*The freedom of the subjective person to do as he pleases is overruled by the freedom of the responsible person to do as he must.*"[142] Thus, personal knowledge is a passionate commitment to universal truth made by limited and fallible knowers who strive to make contact with a hidden and indeterminate reality and embrace their findings with universal intent. Polanyi sums this up with the following provocative paragraph:

> The stage on which we thus resume our full intellectual powers is borrowed from the Christian scheme of Fall and Redemption. Fallen Man is equated to the historically given and subjective condition of our mind, from which we may be saved by the grace of the spirit. The technique of our redemption is to lose ourselves in the performance of an obligation which we accept, in spite of its appearing on reflection impossible of achievement. We undertake the task of attaining the universal in spite of our admitted infirmity, which should render the task hopeless, because we hope to be visited by powers for which we cannot account in terms of our specific capabilities.[143]

Our responsibility, then, is to ideals that we cannot achieve on the basis of our specifiable powers. But we pursue them nonetheless because of our belief that contact with reality is possible, and although we cannot articulate precisely how, we believe that our unspecifiable powers will serve to propel us further than we can imagine. This hope, Polanyi adds, "is a clue to God."[144]

MORALITY AND MORAL INVERSION

The Status of Moral Ideals

For Polanyi, the intangible is more real than the tangible, and the real is defined as that which is independent of the knower and reveals itself in indeterminate and unpredictable ways. We come to know the real through a process of tacit integration whereby the subsidiaries in which we dwell combine in the process of focusing on a particular target and produce meaning that is larger than the sum of the subsidiary particulars. How does this theory of knowledge address the status of moral truth? Modern objectivists believed that "the critical faculties of man unaided by any powers of belief could establish the truth of science and the canons of fairness, decency, and freedom."[145] However, all knowing depends on a fiduciary framework, and moral knowing is no exception. We come to accept moral teachings, like any other body of skillful knowing, by entrusting ourselves to a moral tradition or teacher in a process Polanyi calls interiorization: "To interiorize is to identify ourselves with the teachings in question, by making them function as the proximal term of a tacit moral knowledge, as applied in practice. This establishes the tacit framework for our moral acts and judgments."[146] Since the interiorization occurs within the knower, it is correct to understand "man as the source of moral judgment and of all other cultural judgments by which man participates in the life of society."[147] But although the tacit integration occurs in the human knower, it does not follow that morality is the arbitrary invention of human beings. Since intangibles are more real than tangibles, the tacit integration that produces moral ideals actually produces something that is more real than materiality.

Because moral ideals are the product of a tacit integration that, as do all integrations, bears on reality, the moral standards produced are embraced with universal intent.[148] This, of course, does not imply that they are universally known. Personal knowledge is inherently risky and carries with it the possibility that the truth claims we embrace with universal intent may in fact be wrong. Thus, "values which I deem to be transcendent may be known only transiently to a small minority of mankind."[149] Further, Polanyi believes that it is possible for men simply to deny the moral tradition into which they have been inculcated, as a result, for example, of a commitment to a theory of knowledge that renders transcendent moral ideals impossible. Thus, Polanyi does "not assert that eternal truths are automatically upheld by men. We have learnt they can be very effectively denied by modern man."[150]

Moral reality, like scientific reality, has a status that is independent of the knower.[151] Polanyi refers to the truths that direct our actions and to which we ought to submit as "transcendent obligations." These include truth, justice, and charity.[152] These cannot be derived as conclusions to a deductive argument. Instead, "belief in them can therefore be upheld now only in the form of an explicit profession of faith."[153] These ideals serve as subsidiaries in the active event of tacit knowing, and as subsidiaries they are largely unspecifiable when serving in that capacity:

> Indeed, we cannot look at our standards in the process of using them, for we cannot attend focally to elements that are used subsidiarily for the purpose of shaping the present focus of our attention. We attribute absoluteness to our standards, because by using them as part of ourselves we rely on them in the ultimate resort, even while recognizing that they are actually neither part of ourselves nor made by ourselves, but external to ourselves.[154]

But since moral ideals are real, they have indeterminate future manifestations. That is, the manner in which they reveal themselves in the future may be completely unexpected. Moral ideals may change in the future as contact with reality achieves new insights and greater coherence. But these standards do not change arbitrarily or explicitly. In the search for the solution to a problem, in the attempt to achieve greater coherence, we may alter our standards in practice in order to achieve that coherence. Thus, in seeking the solution to a problem "our intuition may respond to our efforts with a solution entailing new standards of coherence, new values. In affirming the solution, we tacitly obey these new values and thus recognize their authority over ourselves, over us who tacitly conceived them." This is, Polanyi concludes, "how new values are introduced, whether in science, or in the arts, or in human relations."[155]

Moral Inversion

Harry Prosch notes that Polanyi's "critique of contemporary epistemology was, in fact, generated by an ethical problem: the damage he thought this epistemology was doing to our moral ideals."[156] Indeed, the moral implications of objectivism are a frequent topic in Polanyi's writings. This, perhaps, is not surprising given Polanyi's firsthand experience with and lifelong concern about the philosophical roots of totalitarianism. Polanyi's account of the moral implications of objectivism begins with an account of the historic changes wrought by modern thought.

The scientific revolution led by such men as Descartes and Bacon included a disdain for any knowledge based on the authority of tradition.[157] At a certain level this rejection was warranted, for in the limited range of scientific investigation empirical observation must be given a prominent role. The success of science in the last three centuries attests to the positive impact of a rejection of certain assumptions that found their roots in Aristotelian metaphysics and biology. But even though a partial rejection of tradition was beneficial to the scientific enterprise, the momentum of modern philosophy continued to push toward the wholesale rejection of all tradition. This culminated in the intellectual and political events surrounding the French Revolution. Because of this radical shift in orientation away from tradition, Polanyi argues that history can be divided into two periods. First, all societies that preceded the revolution in France "accepted existing customs and law as the foundations of society." And although it is true that there "had been changes and some great reforms . . . never had the deliberate contriving of unlimited social improvement been elevated to a dominant principle."[158] On the other hand, the French revolutionaries embraced with zeal the ideal of the unlimited progress of man, both morally and materially: "Thus, the end of the eighteenth-century marks the dividing line between the immense expanse of essentially static societies and the brief period during which public life has become increasingly dominated by fervent expectations of a better future."[159] We live in a revolutionary age.

This optimistic and passionate drive toward human perfection, which was the product of a wholesale rejection of the authority of tradition, produced another equally significant result. The combination of Cartesian doubt and Lockean empiricism produced a theory of knowledge that precluded any truth claims that did not admit of empirical justification. Thus, religious and moral claims were a priori ruled out-of-bounds.[160] This effectively produced a skepticism about all claims to knowledge not grounded in empirical investigation. Thus, the authority of religion, specifically Christianity, which had held a dominant position for fifteen centuries, was undercut at its foundations. Scientism became the new religion, and its priests—the scientists and modern philosophers—employed epistemological objectivism as their instrument of worship.

Skepticism, of course, is not unprecedented. In antiquity there were those who embraced a skeptical view of the world, but modern skepticism is different because it occurs in a culture steeped in the residue of Christianity: "The ever-unquenching hunger and thirst after righteousness which our civilization carries in its blood as a heritage of Christianity does not allow us to settle down in the Stoic manner of antiquity."[161] Thus, although modern philosophy does not permit the consideration of the truth claims of Christianity, the memory of Christianity remains and produces a passionate urge to pursue righteousness even though modern philosophy has rendered the reality of moral truth impossible.

The result of this twofold change wrought by the wholesale rejection of the authority of tradition is a situation in which the deep moral impulses—which are the product of a Christian heritage—are combined with a skepticism that denies the reality of the very impulses modern humans feel most acutely. Polanyi describes this situation as follows:

> In such men the traditional forms for holding moral ideals had been shattered and their moral passions diverted into the only channels which a strictly mechanistic conception of man and society left open to them. We may describe this as a process of *moral inversion*. The morally inverted person has not merely performed a philosophical substitution of material purposes for moral aims; he is acting with the whole force of his homeless moral passions within a purely materialistic framework of purposes.[162]

Moral inversion, then, is the combination of skeptical rationalism and moral perfectionism, which is nothing more than the "secularized fervour of Christianity."[163] But, whereas moral perfectionism within a Christian context is moderated by the doctrine of original sin, the perfectionism of a post-Christian world provides no such moderating counterbalance. Thus, the passionate perfectionism of Christianity persists despite the rejection of the doctrines that, in times of belief, prevented it from wrecking havoc on the society committed to its ideal. Furthermore, skeptical rationalism prevents any rational justification for the moral impulses that animate modern Western citizens. This seemingly contradictory marriage of incompatible elements allows individuals and societies to commit the most immoral acts—which according to the skeptic are not really immoral since morality is an empty category—all in the name of a perfectionism that is a longing rooted in a Christian heritage that has been rendered unbelievable. Thus, the ideal of moral perfection, which in Christianity was rooted in transcendent reality, was immantentized because of the parameters established by modern epistemology. This new objectivist man attempted to bring about a purely immanent perfection without the hindrance of moral limitations on the means to that end.[164] But why, Polanyi asks, should such a doctrine, so obviously contradictory, be held, especially by moderns who pride themselves in their intellectual rigor? "The answer is, I believe, that it enables the modern mind, tortured by moral self-doubt, to indulge its moral passions in terms which also satisfy its passion for ruthless objectivity."[165]

Polanyi distinguishes between two manifestations of this combination of moral skepticism and moral perfectionism. The first is personal; the second is political. The first is found in the existentialist. In this view, traditional morality has no justification. Choice is all that exists apart from the bare facts of science. Thus, all moral ideals are discredited: "We have, then, moral passions filled with contempt for their own ideals. And once they shun their own ideals, moral passions can express themselves only in antimoralism."[166] This is the modern nihilist who denies any distinction between good and evil. Thus, on the personal level, moral inversion produces the individual nihilist, Dostoevsky's Raskolnikov, for example. The second manifestation is political. When moral skepticism and moral perfectionism are simultaneously embraced, the political restraints provided by traditional morality are destroyed. The perfectionist element demands "the total transformation of society," but because moral distinctions are denied, there is no limitation on the political means to achieve the desired result.[167] Thus, in political terms, moral inversion produces totalitarianism, and it might be legitimate to point out that totalitarianism can manifest itself in both Soviet and, ironically, liberal guises.[168]

Pseudo-substitution

One question remains in the present discussion: How is it that some modern societies were apparently (at least for a time) better insulated than others from the frenzied passion produced by moral inversion? This question is important because it appears that all modern societies have by and large embraced the twin elements that constitute moral inversion, namely, moral skepticism and moral perfectionism. The answer, according to Polanyi, is found in what he terms "pseudo-substitution." In short, some societies were less susceptible—at least for a time—of succumbing to immoral moralism because they continued to embrace traditional morality in practice, all while denying its reality in theory. This, according to Polanyi, merely indicates that "men may go on talking the language of positivism, pragmatism, and naturalism for many years, yet continue to respect the principles of truth and morality which their vocabulary anxiously ignores."[169] Polanyi argues that both Britain and the United States have managed to escape the grim inhumanity of moral inversion by virtue of this dichotomy between practice and theory. This achievement was rendered possible by a sort of "suspended logic" by which the British and the Americans did not pursue their theoretical positions to their practical ends.[170]

Although pseudo-substitution is a possible means of avoiding the negative consequences of moral inversion, it is clearly not ideal, for it does not dispense with the problem but only holds it at bay through a process of self-deception. It seems that what Polanyi refers to as a recovery of balance between man's moral demands and his critical powers indicates a more stable solution, for it attempts to overcome the epistemological shortcomings of objectivism, which have created the possibility of moral inversion in the first place. Thus, a recognition of the a-critical framework of our knowledge will reopen the philosophical possibility of obtaining real moral truth, and that recovery will destroy skepticism and thereby knock out one leg supporting moral inversion. Furthermore, such a recovery would once again make possible the legitimate discussion of religion and at least open the door to a more suitable religiously informed anthropology, which would knock out moral inversion's second leg. A return to orthodox Christianity is perhaps unlikely, but it is not, in Polanyi's argument, a necessary condition for avoiding the perils of moral inversion. A return to traditional religious forms might, though, be one of the outcomes produced by overcoming the objectivist epistemology that prevails in favor of a theory of knowledge that recognizes the fiduciary framework upon which all knowing rests.[171]

POLANYI AND OAKESHOTT

Oakeshott, born in 1901, was ten years Polanyi's junior. Polanyi was born and educated on the Continent, but they both spent the majority of their professional lives in England. As far as I can discern, Polanyi never refers to Oakeshott in print, but he must have been aware of his work. Oakeshott, on the other hand, mentions Polanyi on several occasions. His only sustained discussion of Polanyi comes in a review of Polanyi's *Personal Knowledge*.[172] Widely regarded as a superior stylist, Oakeshott criticizes Polanyi's presentation:

> It is a book full of side-glances into other matters; it is disordered, repetitive, digressive, and often obscure; as a work of art it leaves much to be desired. . . . Professor Polanyi's ambition to let nothing go by default, to surround his argument with an embroidery, not of qualification but of elaboration, and to follow his theme into every variation that suggests itself, make the book like a jungle through which the reader must hack his way.[173]

Yet, despite the stylistic shortcomings, Oakeshott finds much to appreciate. He notes with favor Polanyi's critique of empiricism, his denial of the moral neutrality of scientific investigation, and Polanyi's insistence on the personal element in all knowing. Oakeshott agrees that scientific knowing is an acquired skill that is obtained through practice and includes an unspecifiable element that cannot be reduced to specific rules.

Oakeshott, though, does detect a possible problem in Polanyi's theory of knowledge, for once absolute objectivity is denied, the danger of a slide into subjectivism becomes acute. Although Polanyi goes to great lengths to avoid this conclusion, Oakeshott is unsure of Polanyi's ultimate success, for he rightly understands that Polanyi's theory of knowledge escapes subjectivism only if Polanyi's realism is true. Thus, Oakeshott writes, "in the end a belief that our thoughts are moved by 'an innate affinity for making contact with reality' seems to be the only premiss, properly speaking, of scientific enquiry and the means by which it transcends merely personal conviction."[174] Oakeshott, the self-proclaimed skeptic, muses that this assumption seems to rest on excessive belief, for Polanyi's theory of knowledge "is as little sceptical as it is positivistic . . . [and] . . . Professor Polanyi doesn't do as much scepticism for himself as might have been hoped and as the occasion seems to demand."[175] Oakeshott goes on to suggest that Polanyi's lack of a skeptical demeanor indicates that "at the edges of his argument there is a suspicion of philosophical innocence."[176] This criticism should not surprise us given the fact that Oakeshott once wrote that "it is always more difficult to doubt radically and intelligently than to believe."[177] Here, at the very foundations of their respective theories of knowledge, a twofold disagreement emerges that, in large measure, sums up their differences: Oakeshott's idealism and Polanyi's realism; Oakeshott's skepticism and Polanyi's a-critical philosophy.

To accusations of excessive belief and inadequate skepticism, Polanyi, of course, would respond that the ideal of doubt as an epistemological device has produced the many philosophical confusions witnessed in modern thought. Indeed, in Polanyi's view, skepticism is not only an undesirable ideal, it is an impossible practical goal. Hume, for example, while advocating skepticism, "openly chose to brush aside the conclusions of his own scepticism at those points where he did not think he could honestly follow them. Even so he failed to acknowledge that by so doing he was expressing his own personal beliefs."[178] Thus, if Polanyi is correct and belief is the necessary framework within which all thought takes place, then it is Oakeshott rather than Polanyi who commits a philosophical error in claiming to be a skeptic, for skepticism is philosophically impossible. It would, perhaps, be more accurate to argue that Oakeshott is probably reacting to the excessive confidence of the rationalist, who believes that by applying a particular technical methodology certainty can be obtained. This, both Oakeshott and Polanyi recognize, is a false ideal, but Oakeshott overreacts by retreating into some degree of skepticism, which is as impossible an ideal as rationalism. Polanyi manages to avoid this result by denying the rationalist's (objectivist's) ideal while asserting the possibility of acquiring knowledge of reality in an open-ended, contingent, fallible process in which the knower must take personal responsibility for that which he claims with universal intent. One might add further that despite his self-professed skepticism, Oakeshott's heavy reliance on tradition seems to undercut his skepticism. Of course, Oakeshott's refined definition of tradition as practice is primarily procedural rather than substantive, but, nonetheless, in emphasizing the role of tradition (or practice), he does appear to accept some beliefs a-critically, which, as Polanyi insists, is necessary for all knowing.

Although Oakeshott disagrees with Polanyi on the question of the primacy of belief and on the assumption of an external reality with which we strive to make contact, there is much with which Oakeshott agrees. In his discussion of the two types of knowledge, practical and technical, Oakeshott remarks in a footnote that "some excellent observations on this topic are to be found in M. Polanyi, *Science, Faith and Society.*"[179] In another essay, Oakeshott points the reader's attention to the same work by Polanyi and calls it "brilliant."[180] Oakeshott obviously found much common ground between his emphasis on practical knowledge and Polanyi's discussion in *Science, Faith and Society* of the fact that scientific investigation cannot proceed on the basis of rules alone. In Polanyi's words, "the rules of research cannot be usefully codified at all. Like the rules of all other high arts, they are embodied in practice alone."[181] Thus, knowledge embodied in practice cannot be acquired except through a personal relationship consisting of a master and an apprentice in which the apprentice submits himself to the authority of the master and in so doing acquires the skills necessary to master the particular field of inquiry. Such practical, unformulatable knowledge exists only in traditions that exercise authority by requiring a degree of submission by those who seek to become full practicing members. Thus, Oakeshott's practical knowledge is quite similar to the unformulatable knowledge of which Polanyi speaks. Furthermore, Oakeshott's insistence that the modern rationalist relies excessively on technical knowledge maps onto what Polanyi calls "objectivism." Finally, both believe that a central problem of modernity is an erroneous theory of knowledge. In Oakeshott's understanding, the modern rationalist, in his zealous quest for rational certainty, denies any knowledge that is not technical, that cannot be formulated into explicit rules.[182] Similarly, Polanyi argues that the ideal of doubt in combination with the demand for strict verification destroys any possibility of knowledge of those ideals we hold most dear. It creates the erroneous ideal of rational detachment, which, it is believed, will produce universally certain knowledge.[183] In short, both

Oakeshott and Polanyi believe that an error in epistemology, which denies the possibility of any knowledge that is not explicit, is the root cause of much that has gone amiss in modernity.[184]

Both Polanyi and Oakeshott agree that tradition is both a resource that ought to be heeded and an indispensable component of knowing. Engaging fully in a tradition requires submission to an authority in the form of a master to an apprentice. Knowing is an art that requires skill. The skill necessary to know requires a relationship with a master whereby one can learn the unspecifiable elements of a skill and thus eventually become a connoisseur. All skills are comprised of two types of knowledge—technical and practical (in Oakeshott's terms), and the tacit and the explicit (in Polanyi's idiom). Since all skills contain an element that is unspecifiable, that element cannot be acquired apart from submitting one's self to the authority of a master who is himself working within a tradition. Thus, all skillful knowing requires the presence of a tradition, a master who has mastered the unspecifiable elements of the skill, and a willingness to submit to the authority of the master in order to engage the tradition and thereby acquire its unspecifiable skills.

A central concept in Oakeshott's critique of rationalism is his insistence that practice precedes theory. Therefore a theory is inevitably the abridgment of an already existing practice.[185] Thus, for Oakeshott, those who believe that it is possible to construct theories from a purely rational epistemological stance unhindered by antecedent traditions or practices merely demonstrate that they have succumbed to the rationalist's error. For in actuality all theory necessarily depends on antecedent practices as the conveyers of practical knowledge. Practical knowledge is essential to any skill, but despite its indispensability, it is not fully specifiable. Polanyi, too, but for other reasons, argues that practice precedes theory. Polanyi's theory of tacit knowing entails the integration of two elements, the subsidiary and the focal, with a third, the knower. This tacit triad underlies all knowing. Thus, the unspecifiable exists prior to that which we can specify. In other words, "we can know more than we can tell."[186] When we specify something, we do so using language. But because that which we specify depends on the tacit integration of the subsidiary and the focal, it follows that that which cannot be specified is antecedent to that which we can specify. Polanyi writes, "If everywhere it is the inarticulate which has the last word, unspoken and yet decisive, then a corresponding abridgement of the status of spoken truth itself is inevitable."[187] Moreover, even those premises that admit of formulation frequently serve as the unacknowledged foundation of a particular practice. Thus, Polanyi writes, "the adherents of a great tradition are largely unaware of their own premises, which lie deeply embedded in the unconscious foundations of practice."[188] The theoretical foundations of a tradition are often hidden within practices and only become evident when the practice itself is carefully studied, but even then, a fully explicit account remains impossible. Yet, this distinction is not as absolute with Polanyi as it is with Oakeshott, and it is in their respective views of scientific hypotheses that this difference emerges.

It is important first to point out that both Oakeshott and Polanyi employ scientific knowledge as a model for all knowing. This leads to a dissolution of the fact/value distinction, for once it is recognized that scientific knowing entails the personal participation of the knower, any pretense to a purely objective, value-neutral realm of facts must be abandoned. Further, both agree that only a person who has acquired the skills carried in the tradition of science is capable of recognizing a scientific problem or of formulating properly a scientific hypothesis.[189] Yet, it is at this point that a significant difference between Polanyi and Oakeshott emerges. Oakeshott argues that a hypothesis is a "dependent supposition which arises as an abstraction from within already existing scientific activity." This hypothesis is "inoperative as a guide to research without constant reference to the traditions of scientific inquiry from which it was abstracted."[190] For Oakeshott the process of science is always conducted in reference to the tradition out of which it emerges. In other words, Oakeshott's idealism with its coherence test for truth reduces science to an ongoing search for greater coherence of the whole. For Polanyi, scientific discovery is different, for as reality is encountered, new and often surprising manifestations of reality are grasped. Polanyi's account is progressive and forward-looking in that it entails the possibility of increasingly greater insight into reality itself.[191]

The difference lies in Polanyi's realism, for in Polanyi's understanding, reality exists independently of the knower and reveals itself in indeterminate future manifestations. Thus, although a scientist works within a tradition, he is not primarily motivated by a desire to achieve greater internal coherence within a tradition but by the possibility of making contact with an independent reality. Such contact represents discovery that is genuinely new and often unexpected. We can see, then, that the difference between Polanyi and Oakeshott on this point amounts to a difference between Oakeshott's idealism and Polanyi's realism.

It should be clear by now that the essential differences between Polanyi and Oakeshott can be traced back to their differences regarding the nature of reality and the manner in which the mind relates to that reality. Despite this fundamental difference, though, both agree that an incorrect view of knowledge has widespread implications that extend far beyond the merely theoretical. Both believe that modern theories of knowledge, which seek an ideal of purely explicit knowledge grasped by neutral minds, are mistaken. And although they disagree about the ultimate remedy—one grounded in a skeptical idealism, the other in an a-critical realism—they share much agreement as to the proximal causes of the modern problem.

Oakeshott characterizes the mistaken view of knowledge as modern rationalism; Polanyi finds the modern errors in what he terms "objectivism." The rationalist and the objectivist share some striking similarities that we do well to understand, for the amount of congruence on this point indicates the important ways Polanyi and Oakeshott are similar despite their fundamental differences. There are three important similarities. First the rationalist, it will be recalled, rejects all appeals to tradition. All appeals to authority are rejected save the authority of one's own neutral mind engaging the facts in a purely detached fashion. Second, the rationalist is committed to the goal of perfectionism. Since the rationalist is committed to finding rational solutions, he cannot imagine solutions that are imperfect. Third, the rationalist seeks uniformity, and this is a direct product of the rationalist's perfectionism, for the perfect rational solution must necessarily be equally perfect for all people and places. The rationalist believes that all differences caused by the particularities of culture, tradition, language, and history must be transcended in the process of directly engaging universal truths unmediated by particulars. In this way, it is clear how rationalist thinking paves the way for the cosmopolitan ideal. However, in Oakeshott's words, "a scheme which does not recognize circumstances can have no place for variety."[192] Thus, the rationalist rejects the authority of tradition and pursues his ideal of perfect uniformity employing only the resources of his unencumbered rationality in the process. But because it is impossible completely to throw off the particularities in which one is embedded, the rationalist ideal necessarily causes an internal incoherence and disarray in a person's understanding of morality and the world in general.

As a result, the rationalist knows less and less about how to properly behave and how to engage the world.

Oakeshott argues that the moral perfectionism of the West finds its roots in the early Christian centuries. The morality of the early Christian church emphasized habits and affections of behavior motivated by faith, hope, and charity. There were no formal moral ideals; instead, "the morality of these communities was a custom of behaviour appropriate to the character of the faith and to the nature of the expectation."[193] In the course of the first several centuries, though, there occurred a change. Christian morality began to become formalized in a collection of abstract ideals. Oakeshott suggests that this change may have been brought about in the process of attempting to package Christianity for audiences who lacked the traditions out of which Christianity was born. In other words, the message of Christianity had to be abridged in order to make it accessible to other cultural traditions. In the process though, "the urge to speculate, to abstract and to define, which overtook Christianity as a religion, infected also Christianity as a way of moral life."[194] But this abridgment of Christian habits and customs into a creed that could be translated across cultural and linguistic boundaries produced a morality corresponding to this change. Rather than emphasizing habits and customs rooted in a tradition, moral ideals were abstracted from the original traditional behavior. A morality of abstract ideals aimed at perfection calls forth the social and political energy of true believers who seek to transform society into the universal ideal to which they are committed. With the emergence of secularism and the corresponding decline of traditional religious belief, the stage was set for an energized, secular, moral, and political program, one in which the resources and limits inherited from tradition were summarily denied while the moralistic fervor remains.

Polanyi's account closely parallels Oakeshott's, but he goes into far more detail in describing the damaging consequences produced by an erroneous theory of knowledge. First, like the rationalist, Polanyi's objectivist rejects the authority of tradition and seeks to acquire a virginal mind, detached from any personal commitments or prejudice. This is accomplished by subjecting all opinions and prejudices to a universal and methodological doubt exemplified by Descartes. Second, universal and systematic doubt severely reduced the possible range of inquiry. This is especially so because of the caustic work of doubt on any beliefs that are not derived from rational deduction or empirical verification. Thus, religious belief eventually went the way of tradition, with which it was closely tied. When the possibility of knowing was reduced to only that which could be known with explicit certainty, the false ideal of scientific detachment and doubt was hailed as the standard for real knowing, while the areas of religion, morality, and the arts were, in effect, demoted to the realm of subjective opinion. Thus, the modern rejection of the authority of tradition coupled with the elevation of doubt as the ideal epistemological starting point produced a skepticism about all that could not be established using scientific methodology. The rise of science and the denigration of all other fields of inquiry relied on a uniform methodology by which all knowledge could be judged. The fact/value barrier was raised, and morality, religion, and beauty were relegated to a realm outside of objective knowledge. On the other hand, the exact sciences, it was believed, dealt only in the realm of objective facts and were conducted purely on the basis of a uniformly applicable methodology. Here we see an emphasis on uniformity emerging in Polanyi's account just as it does in Oakeshott's.

Like Oakeshott, Polanyi argues that Christianity has significantly influenced the development of morality in the West. From its inception, Christianity has included a standard of moral perfection, which was counterbalanced by the doctrine of original sin. Thus, the Christian is commanded to be perfect, yet because of his sinful nature, he cannot meet that demand. He needs grace, and that grace is imparted by God through Christ. Thus, moral perfectionism is a standard against which no man can stand blameless, yet by God's grace human nature will eventually be made perfect. This is the hope of the Christian. But the changes brought about in the early modern period produced a religious skepticism that ultimately resulted in the denial of the transcendent and consequently led to the denial of divine grace. But, Polanyi argues, the moral perfectionism of Christianity was so embedded in the Western heritage that despite both the overt denial of the theology that made such a standard plausible and a denial of the counterbalance of divine grace that made it livable, the moral perfectionism remained, detached from its roots and free to roam unconstrained by its theological antecedents. The result of this impulse toward moral perfectionism combined with a rational skepticism that denies any real status to moral ideals created a volatile tension within the Western psyche. This ironic combination of mutually exclusive forces is what Polanyi calls moral inversion. Immoral moralism is the practical manifestation of this toxic combination. Polanyi saw this in the politics of the

Soviet Union. We might, with a longer perspective, find the same sort of impulses emerging in a more subtle form in liberal democracies of our day.

Conclusion

To summarize, both Polanyi and Oakeshott agree on the source of the modern problem, which is an errant conception of knowledge. To some extent they agree on the solution, for against the modern rationalist/objectivist both argue for the recovery of concepts such as tradition, practice, commitment, submission, apprenticeship, and inarticulable truths. As we saw, Oakeshott's theory of knowledge does not seem able to avoid sliding into a form of moral relativism. This is because coherence alone as a test for truth is inadequate. Polanyi puts it this way: "Coherence as the criterion of truth is only a criterion of *stability*. It may equally stabilize an erroneous or a true view of the universe."[195] Without an independent reality that is knowable—albeit imperfectly and provisionally—there is no way to evaluate which of two stable moral traditions is preferable. Thus, at the very roots of their respective philosophical accounts they diverge, and it is at this point that Polanyi's realism appears preferable to Oakeshott's idealism. However, as Oakeshott points out, and as Polanyi would agree, such a position requires a step of faith—a commitment to a conception of reality that ultimately does not admit of definite proof. Such, Polanyi acknowledges, is the case with all of our most deeply held beliefs. Such, it seems, is the essence of the human condition.[196]

POLANYI AND MACINTYRE

MacIntyre mentions Polanyi with some frequency and discusses him on several occasions.[197] He criticizes him primarily for succumbing to irrationalism, which, according to MacIntyre, results from Polanyi's fideism. There is a double irony here, for MacIntyre himself has also been accused of irrationalism, and although there are differences between the two, in large part I find that Polanyi and MacIntyre are walking the same path and actually serve, in some ways, as complements to one another.[198]

MacIntyre writes that "Polanyi is the Burke of the philosophy of science." MacIntyre does not intend this comparison as a compliment, for he is quite critical of Burke, and by linking Polanyi to Burke he extends those same criticisms to Polanyi, for, as he puts it, "all my earlier criticisms of Burke now become relevant to the criticism of Polanyi."[199] Just what are those criticisms? According to MacIntyre, "Polanyi, of course—like Burke—combined with his emphasis on consensus and tradition a deep commitment to a realistic interpretation of science. Polanyi's realism rested on what he called a 'fiduciary commitment.' Feyerabend (and less explicitly Kuhn) have retained the fideism; what they have rejected is the realism and with it the objectivism which Polanyi held to as steadfastly as any positivist."[200] MacIntyre argues that Burke contrasted "tradition with reason and the stability of tradition with conflict. Both contrasts obfuscate."[201]

I do not, at this point, want to explore whether or not MacIntyre's reading of Burke is satisfactory. I will address that question in chapter 5. At this point, I want to show how MacIntyre is in error when he equates Polanyi with this version of Burke.[202] In so doing, I will also point out the striking similarities between Polanyi's thought and MacIntyre's, especially in the way they think about tradition. First, Polanyi does not believe that tradition opposes reason; instead, in Polanyi's view, all reason necessarily occurs within a particular tradition. Second, Polanyi's view of tradition does not imply a commitment to a static view of society; instead, for Polanyi healthy traditions are dynamic and not static. Third, Polanyi does not believe that commitment to a tradition removes all venues for conflict; instead, internal conflict—the ability to rebel against the consensus—is a fundamental element in Polanyi's theory of tradition. Fourth, MacIntyre accuses Polanyi of being a fideist. Although Polanyi is in certain respects correctly identified as such, this is not, as MacIntyre claims, because he separates tradition and reason. Polanyi believes tradition and reason are inseparable and that submission to the authority of a tradition is a prerequisite for rationality. As we saw in chapter 3, MacIntyre also embraces this view of rationality. Thus, I will argue that to the extent that Polanyi is a fideist, MacIntyre, too, falls into that category. Fifth, both MacIntyre and Polanyi are realists who believe that reality can be known, but only provisionally and fallibly; thus, for both, all inquiry is open-ended, but the truth toward which inquiry presses is timeless. Finally, the false dilemma between Enlightenment objectivism on the one hand and postmodern relativism or skepticism on the other is also identified by Polanyi. Like MacIntyre, Polanyi seeks to overcome the dilemma by offering a third alternative. Where MacIntyre offers "tradition," Polanyi gives us "personal knowledge." These two alternatives share much in common.

Tradition and Reason

Polanyi, despite MacIntyre's claim, does not believe that reason and tradition are opposed to each other. Tradition is, in fact, a necessary condition that makes the faculty of reason possible, for "no human mind can function without accepting authority, custom, and tradition: it must rely on them for the mere use of language."[203] If "all human thought comes into existence by grasping the meaning and mastering the use of language," and language is the product of a particular tradition, then it follows that all knowing is fundamentally tradition-dependent.[204] But it is not merely in relation to language that knowing depends upon tradition, for, according to Polanyi, learning is a skill that can be acquired only by submitting to the authority of one who possesses the skill. Thus, to become a scientist one must submit as an apprentice to the authority of a scientist who has mastered the art of scientific knowing. So too with any other complex field of endeavor, such as architecture, agriculture, or morality. Such a scheme implies a tradition of knowledge that is passed from one generation to the next. Thus, if knowing requires a degree of submission to the authority of an already established body of knowledge as embodied in a particular individual or school of thought, then it follows that all knowing is tradition-dependent.[205] If all knowing depends upon an underlying commitment to a particular tradition, it follows that reason is necessarily embodied in a particular tradition. Thus, reason and tradition are not opposed to each other. Instead, in Polanyi's view, tradition is logically prior to and necessary for the exercise of all rational thought.

MacIntyre, as we saw, agrees that all rationality necessarily presupposes the presence of an underlying tradition. Like Polanyi, MacIntyre recognizes that language itself requires a tradition; thus, Descartes, for example, who attempted to throw off all forms of traditional knowing, expressed himself in the idiom of a particular language and thereby embraced a tradition of thought in the very process of attempting to deny all tradition.[206] Furthermore, MacIntyre also holds that acquiring the skills necessary to participate fully in a practice or craft requires submission to the teaching authority of a master.[207] But a teaching authority and learning by apprenticeship implies the existence of a tradition in which the skills necessary for a particular practice or craft are embodied and perpetuated. Thus, complex practices depend upon the prior existence of a tradition.

MacIntyre, though, goes even further, for he argues that "the resources of adequate rationality are made available to us only in and through traditions."[208] Thus, in MacIntyre's words, "to be outside all traditions is to be a stranger to enquiry; it is to be in a state of intellectual and moral destitution."[209] Polanyi presses the point: "Mentally we are called into being by accepting an idiom of thought."[210] Thus, for both MacIntyre and Polanyi all thought occurs within the confines of a tradition. Therefore, all rationality is tradition-dependent, and, as such, pitting tradition against reason results in philosophical confusion.

Tradition and Stasis

For Polanyi, tradition is dynamic and unpredictable rather than static. This ought not to surprise us given Polanyi's background in science, for the history of science is a story of both radical change and continuity. Polanyi recognizes the fact that a tradition of inquiry provides a degree of continuity by which change can be comprehended, but at the same time he acknowledges the dynamic nature of living traditions. Traditions are dynamic on at least two levels. First, each generation reinterprets the traditions transmitted to it; thus, the tradition is altered to accommodate the particularities of those who engage it.[211] Second, each individual person who engages a tradition adds to it and alters it in the very act of engagement.[212] Because for Polanyi all inquiry entails a moral dimension, it is always possible and necessary to look from tradition as it is received and creatively strive to transpose that tradition into a better version of itself: "Processes of creative renewal always imply an appeal from tradition as it is to a tradition as it ought to be. That is to a spiritual reality embodied in tradition and transcending it."[213] Thus, tradition is dynamic as its adherents seek to pursue the transcendent ideals the tradition embodies but does not yet fully realize. Polanyi, who claims affinity with Burke on many points, argues that his theory of tradition transcends Burke's view, for Polanyi's view of tradition affirms both Burkean continuity and Paine's progressivism. It is clear that, contrary to MacIntyre's assertions, Polanyi does not advocate a static traditionalism; instead, Polanyi attempts to wed what we might term "epistemological traditionalism" with a scientist's passion for discovery. This, incidentally, is essentially MacIntyre's position.

MacIntyre's traditionalism, like Polanyi's, is dynamic within a context of continuity. The narrative nature of traditions implies that tradition is an ongoing process of composition. Since each rational person necessarily participates in a tradition, each person contributes to the content of the tradition that develops. In MacIntyre's words, "To be an adherent of a tradition is always to enact some further stage in the development of one's tradition."[214] MacIntyre's description of tradition as a narrative is useful, for it points out both the continuity and the dynamism that characterize traditions. The latest installment of a narrative is necessarily an outgrowth of that which has been written previously. Thus, the most recent articulations of a tradition are only intelligible within the larger context of the tradition as a whole. In this sense, a tradition is characterized by its continuity. On the other hand, this narrative is without conclusion; thus, it is continually the subject of the creative impulses of those who currently embody it. This is tradition's dynamism.[215] An adequate formulation of tradition requires both continuity and change. Polanyi and MacIntyre both recognize this.

Tradition and Conflict

Polanyi's version of tradition allows for significant degrees of conflict and dissent. Again, given the history of science this should not surprise us, for that history can, in large measure, be recounted as a series of radical innovations, which are initially rejected by the majority but eventually gain the status of an orthodoxy only to be overturned by another radical innovation. Although it is true both that all knowing is rooted in tradition and that entering into a tradition requires an act of submission to an authority, it is also the case that a dynamic tradition is one that acknowledges the possibility of internal dissent. As Polanyi puts it, "Since a dynamic orthodoxy claims to be a guide in search of truth, it implicitly grants the right to opposition in the name of truth."[216] For Polanyi, although all knowing is rooted in a tradition and depends in this regard on submission to authority, he does not hold that one's submission to authority needs be absolute or completely unquestioning. Instead, "every acceptance of authority is qualified by some measure of reaction to it or even against it. . . . On the other hand, even the sharpest dissent still operates by partial submission to an existing consensus."[217] Thus submission to authority is necessary for knowing, but it is never absolute, and even apparently radical dissent requires the prior existence of a tradition, for dissent implies the existence of something to which one objects. Dissent, then, is meaningless apart from an underlying consensus represented in tradition.

MacIntyre agrees. A central feature of MacIntyre's account of tradition is conflict. MacIntyre defines a "living" tradition as "an historically extended, socially embodied argument."[218] Again, "a tradition is an argument extended through time in which certain fundamental agreements are defined and redefined in terms of two kinds of conflict," one of which is internal and the other external.[219] MacIntyre can imagine traditions in which no conflict exists, but these are, in his words, "Burkean" traditions, which are either "dying or dead."[220] On the other hand, a healthy tradition necessarily includes a degree of conflict, in part about the very content of the tradition itself. This squares with the narrative feature of traditionalism, for a narrative is continuously developing at the hands of those who find themselves part of the story. Since different individuals will have different visions of where and how the narrative ought to proceed, it follows that a necessary element of any tradition is an ongoing discussion or argument about the meaning of the tradition in the past and the direction of the tradition in the future. All this goes on within the overall structure of traditionalism in which the tradition is accepted as normatively good in that it is both "my" tradition and "our" tradition, and we ought to preserve that which has been given to us and creatively build on what we have in order to pass our narrative additions to the next generation.[221]

Of course, all this may occur without the participants fully recognizing what is occurring, for at the epistemological level, much of the content of tradition goes unnoticed. As Polanyi puts it, "The adherents of a great tradition are largely unaware of their own premises, which lie deeply embedded in the unconscious foundations of practice."[222] A tradition can and does consist, at least in part, in a conflict over the very content of the tradition, but those engaged in the conflict may not fully realize the fundamental premises about which they are arguing. In other words, the conflict may be engaged on one level while on another level common premises may be held tacitly and never be explicitly articulated.

Tradition and Belief

MacIntyre accuses Polanyi of fideism, but we do well to clarify in what manner Polanyi is a fideist and the ways in which MacIntyre himself appears to follow Polanyi on this important point. Polanyi makes no apologies for attempting to push back the objectivist epistemological demands in his attempt to "restore the balance of our cognitive powers" and thereby once again create a space for the moral ideals that we know to be true but cannot establish through the application of an explicit methodology. All knowing, according to Polanyi, depends on a fiduciary framework; thus, belief necessarily precedes and undergirds all forms of knowing. In Polanyi's words, "I propose to introduce the word 'belief' in place of the word 'knowledge,' with the intention of keeping always open in our minds a broad and patent access to the personal origins of our convictions."[223] In short, we must believe before we can know, and that which we know depends, in large part, on what we initially believe. This necessary element of belief occurs on multiple levels that can be summed up in the concept of tradition. Both Polanyi and MacIntyre understand that humans are embedded linguistically, culturally, and historically, and that we must initially take these particularities as givens—they comprise the conceptual framework by which we comprehend our world, and we must initially accept them a-critically in order to employ them to the end of achieving understanding. Human rationality itself cannot exist apart from the prior acceptance of a tradition, which is necessarily embodied in a community.[224]

Polanyi's invocation of Augustine brings this point into full relief, for, according to Augustine, knowing requires antecedent belief.[225] One must submit in faith to the authority of the tradition into which one is inculcated before rational inquiry is possible. As MacIntyre puts it, "Faith in authority has to precede rational understanding."[226] Indeed, this submission is, initially at least, not a matter of choice, for language (and the culture of which it is a component part) is acquired a-critically, and language frames the particular worldview of its speakers. Thus, the language by which a person critically reflects upon the world is indwelt a-critically and provides the resources available to—and the limitations that constrain—the speaker.[227] Whereas language, as is clear, requires an initial commitment in order fully to enter into its idiom, other complex skills that are not primarily linguistic also require a similar step of faith. Because skills cannot be reduced to a set of explicit and comprehensive rules, one must learn the practical, tacit elements through engaging in a practice under the tutelage of a master.[228] The relationship of the apprentice to the master necessarily requires belief, for the novice must submit to the teaching authority of the master despite not initially grasping the meaning of the master's activity.[229]

If belief must necessarily precede knowing, we can draw some important implications. First, it appears that skepticism is ultimately untenable. Both MacIntyre and Polanyi agree on this point and offer Hume as an example. MacIntyre argues that Hume's radical doubt reduced him to asking questions similar to those asked by a young child. For example, Hume, when contemplating the implications of his theory of knowledge, asked rhetorically yet plaintively,

> Where am I, or what? From what causes do I derive my existence, and to what condition shall I return? Whose favour shall I court, and whose anger must I dread? What beings surround me? And on whom have I any influence? I am confronted with all these questions, and begin to fancy myself in the most deplorable condition imaginable, environ'd with the deepest darkness and utterly depriv'd of the use of every member and faculty.[230]

Hume's radical doubt reduced him to questioning those things that were obvious. He was reduced to this state, according to MacIntyre, because "he has set a standard for the foundation of his beliefs which could not be met."[231] This led him ultimately to radical skepticism, which in turn led him to a point in which he loses "any means of making himself—or others—intelligible to himself, let alone to others. His very scepticism itself becomes unintelligible."[232] According to Polanyi, skepticism of the Humean kind is simply unlivable, for despite Hume's talk of radical doubt, he in fact could not live his life in accord with the conclusions of his own thought. If Polanyi is correct and all knowing depends on a fiduciary element, then skepticism is disingenuous. Thus, when a skeptic insists that doubt is rational, he is actually covertly affirming his beliefs: "Since the sceptic does not consider it rational to doubt what he himself believes, the advocacy of 'rational doubt' is merely the sceptic's way of advocating his own beliefs."[233] The failure of skepticism to provide an adequate epistemological context by which to live a life points out that it is simply impossible to question simultaneously all of one's beliefs. To do so leads either, in MacIntyre's words, to "mental breakdown"[234] or to an inauthentic situation whereby one theoretically affirms skepticism while remaining committed to traditional truths in practice. Polanyi calls this duplicity "pseudo-substitution."[235]

A second implication of a theory of knowledge that depends on an initial step of belief is its obvious circularity—one must commit oneself to certain premises, and the conclusions one reaches are necessarily entailed by the premises embraced; thus, in MacIntyre's words, "the end is to some significant degree presupposed in the beginning."[236] According to Mac-Intyre, this circularity is not a flaw. It is, rather, "a feature of any large-scale philosophical system which embodies a conception of enquiry, albeit an often unacknowledged feature. And it could only be thought a flaw from a standpoint still haunted by a desire to find some point of origin for enquiry which is entirely innocent of that which can only emerge later from that enquiry."[237] Polanyi, too, recognizes the circular nature of his theory of knowledge, and like MacIntyre, rather than attempting to escape the circle, argues that this is a characteristic of all theories of knowledge. "Any enquiry into our ultimate beliefs can be consistent only if it presupposes its own conclusions. It must be intentionally circular."[238]

This element of circularity, which both MacIntyre and Polanyi recognize and affirm, is overcome by their somewhat different solutions to Meno's paradox. MacIntyre follows Thomas Aquinas, who, in his *Commentary on Aristotle's Posterior Analytics*, wrote that "before an induction or syllogism is formed to beget knowledge of a conclusion, that conclusion is somehow known and somehow not known."[239] According to MacIntyre, we must possess "within ourselves the potentiality for moving towards and achieving the relevant theoretical and practical conclusions." But that potentiality must be actualized, and that is only possible if we are taught. Thus, "there emerges a conception of a rational teaching authority."[240] In MacIntyre's solution, we possess the potentiality to know, and that potentiality can only be actualized when we submit as an apprentice to the teaching authority of a master.

Polanyi struggled with this paradox through his years of writing. He gives two versions of his solution that, though slightly different, are complementary. In *Personal Knowledge*, he speaks of the moment of illumination in which a "logical gap" is crossed between our formalizable knowledge and the new insight that comes to us. It is a gap because it cannot be crossed on the basis of a step-by-step process that follows explicit rules. The gap is crossed by achieving a new tacit integration. We do this by, in the words of Polanyi's friend G. Polya, looking at the unknown.[241] This bit of advice is not as cryptic as one might initially imagine if we begin by assuming Polanyi's theory of tacit knowing. Polanyi writes,

By fixing our attention on a focus in which we are subsidiarily aware of the data by which the solution of a problem is determined, we form a conception of this solution. The admonition to look at the unknown really means that we should look at the known data, but not in themselves, rather as clues to the unknown; as pointers to it and parts of it. We should strive persistently to feel our way towards an understanding of the manner in which these known particulars hang together, both mutually and with the unknown.[242]

Here Polanyi emphasizes the achievement of a new and improved tacit integration that reveals the solution to a problem as we discover how the particulars that we know, and also those which we do not, cohere with one another.

What we find in *The Tacit Dimension* and the essay "Creative Imagination" is quite similar to the above, although other elements are emphasized.[243] Through intuition, which Polanyi defines as skillful guessing, a person can sense a growing coherence as he searches for a solution to a problem.[244] This intuition of deepening coherence is not formalizable, for it entails a logical leap generated by an illumination that comes on the heels of a period of preparation and incubation.[245] Thus, we see him first emphasize the new meanings produced by a new tacit integration, while subsequently the emphasis lies on intuition and coherence. The two versions are complementary and merely emphasize different elements within Polanyi's theory of knowledge.

MacIntyre, though not employing a theory of tacit knowing, does look to what he calls "insight" to cross a "gap" between what we can demonstrate and what we can know. He writes,

Yet, as enquiry progresses, even in these initial stages we are compelled to recognize a gap between the strongest conclusions which such types of dialectical argument can provide and the type of judgment which can give expression to a first principle. Argument *to* first principles cannot be demonstrative, for demonstration is *from* first principles. But it also cannot be a matter of dialectic and nothing more, since the strongest conclusions of dialectic remain a matter only of belief, not of knowledge. What more is involved? The answer is an act of the understanding which begins from but goes beyond what dialectic and induction provide, in formulating a judgment as to what is necessarily the case in respect of whatever is informed by some essence, but does so under the constraints imposed by such dialectical and inductive conclusions. Insight, not inference, is involved here, but insight which can then be further vindicated if and insofar as this type of judgment provides just the premises required for causal explanations of the known empirical facts which are the subject-matter of that particular science.[246]

The similarities to Polanyi are important, for MacIntyre recognizes that something other than dialectic and induction is involved in achieving knowledge. But, and this is an important point, we must note that MacIntyre distinguishes between belief and knowledge. This is a distinction Polanyi denies. Polanyi seeks to replace the term "knowledge" with "belief," for he is convinced that all claims to knowledge ultimately depend on a fiduciary framework, and that claims to knowledge, then, must ultimately be claims of belief. The similar manner in which both MacIntyre and Polanyi deny epistemological foundationalism and construct theories of knowledge that are tradition-dependent and rely on initial belief and submission to a teaching authority all point to what Polanyi called the "fiduciary framework" upon which all knowing relies. In this regard, Polanyi is, indeed, a fideist, but at the same time it appears incorrect for MacIntyre to deny this label, for he and Polanyi are in virtual lockstep on the central points of this matter. Given the premises embraced by both, it appears that belief and knowledge are not cleanly separable, as MacIntyre seems to believe.[247] Thus, in his attempt to avoid accusations of fideism, MacIntyre appears unwilling to accept the fideistic implications of his own thought.

This point can be further explored by taking up a question we addressed in chapter 3, namely, is it possible for a person to change allegiance from one tradition to another? Recall that for MacIntyre such a move is possible, for he believes it possible to enter sympathetically into the idiom of another tradition as "a second first language" and thereby gain a position by which to judge the rational superiority of one tradition over another. The impetus for such an attempt often comes in the form of an "epistemological crisis" in which the resources of one's native tradition appear inadequate to withstand successfully the pressures of either an internal or external opposition.

In discussing Polanyi on this point, MacIntyre writes, "Since reason operates only *within* traditions and communities according to Polanyi, such a transition or a reconstruction could not be the work of reason. It would have to be a leap in the dark of some kind."[248] MacIntyre contrasts a leap in the dark—which implies fideism—with his account. In his view, a leap in the dark requires that a person necessarily abandons all of his premises and, in a sense, blindly converts to another set of premises. MacIntyre argues that this is not, in fact, how such switches are accomplished, for it is impossible to remain a rational being and at the same time put all of one's premises to question. Consequently, he believes that two options exist. First, one can make an irrational leap in the dark from one tradition or set of premises to another. In such a situation "there is no rational continuity between the situation at the time immediately preceding the crisis and any situation following it."[249] The second option is one that holds that in order to maintain one's rational existence, one must recognize that all rational inquiry takes place within a tradition and that moving from one tradition to another in response to an epistemological crisis requires that a degree of rational continuity exists between the first and the second state. The first alternative amounts to a radical conversion experience; the second represents a continuous rational inquiry.[250]

But whereas the MacIntyre of 1977's "Epistemological Crisis" criticizes Polanyi for insisting that all "reason operates only within traditions and communities," which, according to MacIntyre, indicates that Polanyi is a fideist, the MacIntyre of 1988's *Whose Justice? Which Rationality?* appears to have concluded that Polanyi is correct. Repeatedly MacIntyre insists that all rational inquiry must necessarily occur within the confines of a tradition. For example, he denies "that there is some neutral standing ground, some locus for rationality as such, which can afford rational resources sufficient for enquiry independent of all traditions."[251] Thus, for MacIntyre it is not "possible to speak except out of one particular tradition in a way which will involve conflict with rival traditions."[252] It follows, then, that "we, whoever we are, can only begin enquiry from the vantage point afforded by our relationship to some specific social and intellectual past through which we have affiliated ourselves to some particular tradition of enquiry, extending the history of that enquiry into the present: as Aristotelian, as Augustinian, as Thomist, as Humean, as post-Enlightenment liberal, or as something else."[253] In the final analysis, then, it appears that both MacIntyre and Polanyi agree that all inquiry must necessarily proceed out of a tradition upon which it is dependent for its very existence.

Polanyi agrees with MacIntyre that radically different traditions cannot even speak intelligibly to each other, for they employ different conceptual languages (and often different spoken languages as well). Thus, "formal operations relying on one framework of interpretation cannot demonstrate a proposition to persons who rely on another framework. Its advocates may not even succeed in getting a hearing from these, since they must first teach them a new language."[254] A radically different interpretational framework "represents a new way of reasoning." And so "we cannot convince others of it by formal argument, for so long as we argue within their framework, we can never induce them to abandon it. Demonstration must be supplemented, therefore, by forms of persuasion which can induce a conversion."[255] Such forms of persuasion cannot be completely formulated in terms of a rational argument the steps of which lead from commitment to one tradition to commitment to another. A logical gap intervenes that can only be crossed by an act of commitment—conversion.[256] Polanyi writes that "granting of one's personal allegiance is . . . a passionate pouring of oneself into untried forms of existence."[257] Only through a process of apprenticeship can one learn to dwell in the new tradition. Thus, whether consciously or not, we become converted when we submit to the authority of another tradition in a movement that may be motivated by rational argument but in the end requires a step of faith. Therefore, MacIntyre appears to be ignoring the essential fideistic element implied in his position.

Realism

Underlying both MacIntyre's and Polanyi's theory of knowledge is a commitment to metaphysical realism. For both, reality is independent of the knower and is knowable, albeit only imperfectly.[258] Truth, for both, is timeless, but our understanding of it is not.[259] Since we are embedded in the tradition into which we have been inculcated, we can never throw off the particularities that serve as the lens by which we conceptualize the world. Thus, our understanding of reality is always colored by the tradition in which we find ourselves. Furthermore, humans are finite and fallible. In light of the above limitations on human inquiry, both MacIntyre and Polanyi conclude that all inquiry is necessarily open-ended, and although we embrace our conclusions—in Polanyi's words, with universal intent—we may be wrong. Inquiry is ongoing and entails passionate disagreement and even apparently interminable conflicts. This is not a failure. Instead, it merely reflects the reality of human limitation and the corresponding contingency of human inquiry.[260]

The False Dilemma

Previously we encountered a dilemma that has emerged in modern philosophy. On the one hand, the intellectual heirs of such thinkers as Descartes and Bacon demand that those things we claim as true must admit of explicit formulation and submit to the requirements of an epistemological method whereby universally valid conclusions can be made with absolute certainty. This is the theory of knowledge that MacIntyre identifies as the "Enlightenment Project." This approach to knowledge has failed to meet its own rigorous demands, and such thinkers as Oakeshott, MacIntyre, and Polanyi spend considerable effort showing why this was inevitable. The reaction against this approach to knowledge came in various forms, but generally the common thread was a diminished confidence in the attainability of both universality and certainty. Whereas the optimistic Enlightenment theories of knowledge, rooted in some form of foundationalism, are identified with the Enlightenment Project, the collapse of this endeavor has given birth to a post-Enlightenment approach that is antifoundationalist. "Postmodern" is a catchall (and often abused) term sometimes employed to identify this reaction to the Enlightenment Project. Postmodern theories of knowledge are characterized by an emphasis on particularities rather than universals, which leads to doubt regarding the possibility of achieving anything resembling true or universally valid conclusions. In short, whereas Enlightenment theories of knowledge tend enthusiastically to assert the possibility of securing universal truth, postmodern theories of knowledge are skeptical of such claims, for in this view the particularities of culture, religion, language, and historical moment simply cannot be transcended and, in fact, serve to constitute reality; therefore, there is nothing beyond them toward which the knower strives.

Oakeshott criticizes what he calls the "rationalist" for demanding a "mistake-proof" method or standard of evaluation whereby moral decisions can be made with certainty. The alternative he proposes is his coherence theory of truth guided by intimations toward greater coherence. But such a solution gives away too much. Oakeshott does not fall into a wholesale relativism whereby everything is equally permitted, but his approach does not provide the conceptual tools necessary to avoid a softer form of relativism, for one can never know which among many intimations ought to be pursued or which tradition, among many, is morally preferable.

MacIntyre explicitly identifies the dilemma in his *Three Rival Versions of Moral Enquiry*, and he correctly recognizes it as a false dichotomy. In MacIntyre's idiom, the "encyclopaedists" represent the thinkers of the Enlightenment, while the "genealogists" represent the reaction against modern epistemic universalism and absolutism.[261] As MacIntyre frames it, "*Either* reason is thus impersonal, universal, and disinterested *or* it is the unwitting representative of particular interests, masking their drive to power by its false pretensions to neutrality and disinterestedness."[262] But, as MacIntyre points out, there is a third alternative, which he dubs "tradition."[263] Concepts like tradition, authority, submission, and personal commitment, all of which were rejected by the Enlightenment rationalists, are embraced by MacIntyre as necessary for human knowing. His tradition-constituted theory of knowledge is rescued from skepticism by his underlying commitment to realism, which is dedicated to the belief that there exists an external reality that is both timeless and knowable. Since humans cannot simply transcend their particularities, our knowledge of reality will always be colored by the traditions in which we are embedded and that serve as the lens by which we view reality. But despite the imperfect nature of our knowing, it is properly conceived as knowing nonetheless. This is less than the Enlightenment rationalist hoped for, but it is far more than that for which the postmodern has settled.

Polanyi's description of what he calls the "objectivist" maps directly onto MacIntyre's encyclopaedist. The objectivist rejects all appeals to tradition and begins with nothing except a commitment to doubt all that cannot be explicitly and definitely proven. He aspires to a completely dispassionate and detached stance in the hope of achieving complete objectivity. But Polanyi goes to great lengths to show that this approach to knowledge is both intellectually dishonest and morally corrupting. In other words, given its premises, it necessarily had to fail. In terms of its purely intellectual feasibility, those who advocated this form of knowledge simply could not live up to the standards imposed by their own system. Thus, we see figures such as Descartes and Hume relying on underlying commitments to tradition (in the form of language, as least) and voicing their commitments under the guise of purely rational principles.[264] But by embracing a standard of truth that admitted as knowledge only those things that could be determined with explicit certainty, religion and morality as proper subjects for knowledge were eventually relegated to the realm of subjective value, while scientific knowledge was given full authority in the realm of objective facts. This division, when pursued to its logical ends, eventually produced a skepticism about the possibility of any moral truth. But, coursing through the collective veins of the West is an impulse toward moral perfectionism, which is the remnant of its Christian heritage. This combination of moral skepticism and moral perfectionism produced a "moral inversion" that has sanctioned horrible injustices, all in the name of morality, which ironically has no real status in the objectivist's scheme.

Thus, for Polanyi, and also for MacIntyre, the dichotomy between objectivism and what Polanyi calls "nihilism" is actually a logical progression. In order to extricate ourselves from the terminal end of this downward spiral, we must "restore the balance" of our thought by recognizing that knowing requires personal participation in the form of commitment. Because knowing is a skill, we must submit ourselves to the authority of a tradition and to the mastery of one who belongs to the tradition. When we acknowledge the fiduciary nature of all knowing, the barrier that was erected between facts and values is collapsed, and once again the humane subjects can be admitted as legitimate objects of knowledge. Holding this account together is Polanyi's commitment to the existence of an independent reality—with which we can make contact—and the responsibility to embrace our conclusions with universal intent. Therefore our freedom to act is tempered by our responsibility to conform to reality as we find it. Polanyi describes the dilemma, and his solution to it is as follows:

> Objectivism seeks to relieve us from all responsibility for the holding of our beliefs. That is why it can be logically expanded to systems of thought in which the responsibility of the human person is eliminated from the life and society of man. In recoiling from objectivism, we would acquire a nihilistic freedom of action but for the fact that our protest is made in the name of higher allegiances. We cast off the limitations of objectivism in order to fulfil our calling, which bids us to make up our minds about the whole range of matters with which man is properly concerned.[265]

Thus, freedom from objectivism does not necessarily imply a retreat into nihilism, for rather than being the opposite of objectivism, nihilism is objectivism's logical end. By affirming personal knowledge, we can again regain the capacity to affirm those ideals that we know to be true but cannot prove scientifically. In so doing we commit ourselves to pursue responsibly these ideals, and we do so in submission to the reality with which we strive to make contact.

CONCLUSION

Oakeshott, MacIntyre, and Polanyi seek to overcome the failings of the modern project by transcending it. Although I have attempted to show why I believe Oakeshott does not go far enough down the path we are traveling, I have not criticized MacIntyre nearly as much. This is, in large part, because I believe MacIntyre is generally correct. He does, though, as I pointed out, fail to acknowledge the fideistic elements in his own thought, and this resistance to the conclusions implied by his premises suggests an unwarranted commitment to an ideal of rationality that cannot be sustained by his own position. Furthermore, although MacIntyre recognizes the role of unformalizable knowledge, he does not emphasize its importance. Tacit knowing, however, clearly points to the dependent nature of all knowing, for, according to Polanyi, we depend on some things in order to know other things; thus, in Polanyi's words, "all knowing is either tacit or rooted in tacit knowledge."[266]

Polanyi's conception of knowing provides us with a helpful insight that we can apply to our discussion of tradition. Polanyi argues that knowing occurs only in a from–to structure. Thus, we necessarily know by referring *from* a collection of subsidiaries *to* the object of our explicit attention. Tradition serves to constitute, in part, the complex array of subsidiarily held concepts, beliefs, and perceptions that serve as the means by which we attend to other things. We can never fully divest ourselves of tradition and at the same time remain rational beings. To engage the world rationally is to engage tradition as a subsidiary, and even though we can turn our focal attention upon particular traditions or even the concept of tradition itself, we can never eliminate the from–to structure of knowing and the fact that we are constantly depending on resources inherited from the past. Thus, the modern attempt to overthrow tradition per se is ill-fated from the start, for if it were ever fully accomplished, we would find ourselves little more than prerational, prelinguistic brutes. Emancipation from tradition is, in reality, emancipation from humanity.

Despite the obvious differences in all three thinkers, we see the inescapable role played by tradition. If they are correct on this vital point, the implications are significant, for it would seem that philosophy took a wrong turn, and the result—call it "rationalism," the "Enlightenment Project," or "objectivism"—provides a false conception of knowing and thus a false conception of the knower. The consequences, as Oakeshott, MacIntyre, and Polanyi all understand, extend far beyond the rarified air of academic philosophy. There are, in other words, social and political implications. The liberal self is born of this wrong turn. So too, the version of cosmopolitanism that has emerged as the partner of the liberal self is bolstered by an erroneous conception of the role played by tradition. In chapter 5, we will explore some of the main features of the social and political consequences of this errant view, and I will suggest some modest means by which we can begin a recovery of a more adequate view of tradition and, at the same time, a more adequate view of liberty.

CHAPTER 5

The Incoherence of Liberalism and the Response of Tradition

The only reason we are still alive is our inconsistency in not having actually silenced all tradition.

—Gerhard Krüger[1]

Having grappled with the work of Oakeshott, MacIntyre, and Polanyi, we are ready now to consider how resources developed by these thinkers (and others) can be appropriated to help us critique the liberal self and then begin the task of suggesting an alternative. It is important to recognize that those three thinkers would not necessarily approve of the way I interpret their thought or the way I apply their ideas to the problem of the liberal self. That, however, is not necessarily surprising, and it is certainly not a problem if we recall that, for MacIntyre, a healthy tradition consists in an ongoing debate about the content and meaning of the tradition itself.

Liberalism is both incoherent and unstable. The liberal cosmopolitan dream is an illusion. It is time to seriously consider the kind of society we want to create for our children. The future of freedom is not guaranteed. But we have good resources at our disposal if only we open our eyes and then submit to the limits necessary for the effective appropriation of those resources.

This chapter will oscillate between theory and practice. I will begin with an attempt to develop a working definition of tradition. I will then focus on the ways liberalism fails both theoretically and in practice. Next I will seek to outline of an alternative to liberalism not by inventing something new but by turning (or returning) to an alternative tradition that can be grasped through an engagement with the thought of Burke, Augustine, and the poetry of T. S. Eliot, along with certain theological concepts that seem unavoidable. Finally, I will consider some of the practical implications that will naturally come to light if this account of liberty (and of the human person) is embraced as an alternative to the liberal self.

Defining Tradition

Attempting to define tradition is no simple task, for the concept can be understood in various ways with different points of emphasis. For instance, Pieper distinguishes between sacred and secular traditions. He does not deny the importance of secular traditions, for "they serve an indispensable function of liberating and unburdening the individual conscience and social functions." Human interactions can occur with "less friction" when basic behaviors and practices are taken for granted.[2] Sacred tradition, however, is less concerned with fostering smooth relations between humans than the preservation of an original utterance of God.[3] Clearly the focus of this project is not sacred tradition per se but a more generic conception of tradition that may in some ways encompass sacred tradition, but it does not in the process exclude what is not specifically sacred. Our investigation of Oakeshott, MacIntyre, and Polanyi has provided us with a bevy of concepts that can serve as a framework for understanding tradition.

Tradition is, at its most simple, the transmission of a belief or conviction about reality from one generation to the next. Traditions are often embedded in practices and habits in such a way that the specific and explicit content and meaning of the tradition is not readily apparent. Tradition is that which has been inherited from the past and that which shapes the way we see the present and anticipate the future. In Polanyian terms, tradition serves subsidiarily in a *from–to* structure by which we grasp the meaning of the world. As such, we can never categorically suspend all reliance on tradition as we seek to evaluate the merits of a particular tradition. To reject any dependence upon tradition is to reject the possibility of rational thought.

Tradition is inseparable from authority, for in employing tradition in the knowing process we necessarily submit to its strictures even as we seek to grasp the meaning of the world itself. Tradition consists of a master–apprentice relationship whereby the apprentice submits to the authority of the master and in so doing enters into the world of the tradition and, at the same time, employs the tradition to see more clearly the reality to which it points. Tradition serves both to facilitate and to limit knowing. There is, however, no other means by which knowing occurs.

To be attuned to tradition is to be attuned to the past, but not the past as a dead relic waiting for dissection. Rather, the past is seen as a living reality that penetrates the present, illuminating it and giving it meaning. The person willing to submit to the authority of tradition will be open to the authority of the past—though never its slave. Such a person will not abjure memory, but will instead seek to honor and preserve that which has been received. To receive a tradition is to inherit from the past something of value that is, at the same time, characterized by its delicacy. A tradition, if neglected by one generation, is lost: replaced by another tradition or sub-merged beneath the ever-persisting onslaught of the immediate. Recovery is not impossible, but neither is it simple.

The inheritance, however, is never merely static. It is dynamic even as it maintains continuity with itself. A healthy, living tradition is supple and adaptable to changing circumstance. Furthermore, part of honoring a tra-dition entails seeking not only to preserve but also to improve that which has been inherited.[4] In the process, tradition is capable of evolving, yet its identity persists over time. This is perhaps most especially the case insofar as a tradition is true. A living tradition, in the fullest sense, is stable yet supple because it is an articulation of the real. At the very least, a living tradition must be believed to be true by those who receive it. As soon as people seek to preserve a tradition merely because it is a tradition, the sup-ple integrity of the tradition begins to ossify. The tradition becomes tradi-tionalism and thereby loses its essence.

Tradition, in this sense, serves as an icon. Jaroslav Pelikan makes this point by distinguishing between an *icon* and an *idol*.[5] An icon is a par-ticular embodiment of a universal truth. An icon points beyond itself to the real and the universal, which is the goal of knowledge, yet it is some-thing we can never attain without the mediation of particulars. When we cease to see tradition as an icon, when instead we focus upon the tradition as an end in itself, the icon becomes an idol. The aspiration to grasp the reality beyond the particularities of the specific tradition is the mark of a healthy approach to tradition. An idol, on the other hand, purports to embody truth in itself. It becomes an object of worship that misdirects the affections. When traditions become idols, they lose their ability to adapt to changing historical circumstances. They become objects of veneration—or a means of control—rather than the means of encountering truth.

When we claim that tradition acts as an icon, we are implying that a reality exists that is independent of the knower. That reality is accessed through the mediation of tradition. Thus, knowing can aspire toward truth even though the process is fraught with difficulties and potential pitfalls. When tradition becomes an idol, the reality towards which it points is ignored. Reality comes to be seen as nothing more than the particularities of competing traditions. The result is a conception of reality whereby the notion of universality is replaced by a radical particularity of competing idols. There is no reality toward which these idols point and thus no truth toward which to strive. The traditions have become merely the strongholds of power from which denizens of competing views sally forth to assert their wills over their opponents.

The connection here with Polanyi is obvious. Polanyi's account of knowing is rooted in his realist ontology. And when Pelikan speaks of tradition as an icon, he is suggesting that we look from (or through) tradition to the reality toward which it points. This echoes Polanyi's from–to structure of knowing whereby we look from the subsidiaries to the object of our explicit attention. We can, of course, shift our focus to the subsidiaries, but in so doing they become explicit and, at the same time, we invariably depend on other subsidiaries. So, too, we can examine particular traditions, or even the concept of tradition itself, but given the from–to structure of knowing, we can never extricate ourselves from dependence on tradition. The belief that there is a reality toward which we strive keeps this enterprise from descending into solipsism or mere subjectivity.

When tradition becomes traditionalism, when the icon becomes the idol, when we deny the reality toward which the tradition points, the living tradition reaches a fatal end and becomes an ideology, and rather than promoting understanding of the real it fosters a destructive relationship with the world. Idolatry leads to error, frustration, pathology, and bloodshed. At the same time, a wholesale rejection of tradition—an attempt (never full achieved) to deny the role of tradition in the knowing process—leads not only to philosophical error but to social and political disorder. In short, the consequences of an errant relationship with tradition—either by idolizing it or ignoring it—is not merely epistemological. The consequences are psychic, social, political, and invariably harmful.

An obvious question arises at this point: Why do individuals who participate in the same tradition regularly and even emphatically disagree with one another? If there is a necessary connection between rationality and tradition, should we not expect to see at least general agreement among those sharing the same tradition? There are at least five explanations for this apparent incongruity. First, individual temperaments differ. One's temperamental disposition will influence both the manner in which one views reality and the particular aspects of reality that one chooses to consider. That is not to say that temperament determines thought, but, like other elements, such as language and culture, temperament helps to form the parameters of one's thought. Second, each individual possesses a unique set of personal experiences. These experiences, which are subjected to interpretation through the lens of language, culture, and temperament, inevitably shade the manner in which one comprehends the world. This, perhaps, is merely another way of saying that human knowers are embedded in particular situations, and therefore the aspiration to a God's-eye view, unencumbered by the particularities of one's individual perspective, is merely a manifestation of the false ideal of the Enlightenment rationalist. Third, humans are fallible. The imperfectability of the human species is hard to deny. In theological terms, humans all suffer the noetic effects of the Fall. Our minds only imperfectly and provisionally grasp the truths of reality. Thus, even if all people possessed identical temperaments and identical experiences and therefore shared the same tradition, they would still likely fail to come to identical conclusions regarding the nature of reality. Such is the human situation. Fourth, it is often misleading to speak of *the* tradition of a particular culture, for often, perhaps always in pluralist modern societies, there exists a complex coalition of traditions rather than a single monolithic tradition, and even apparently monolithic traditions often, upon closer examination, reveal pluralistic aspects. For example, within the broad tradition we call the Christian tradition, we find such various subtraditions as Roman Catholicism, Eastern Orthodox, Anglican, Reformed, and Pentecostalism. Across these various subtraditions, there will be much agreement, for all adherents belong to a broad tradition of Christianity. But adherents of these various subtraditions will also disagree sharply on the basis of the assumptions tacitly or explicitly accepted by the particular subtradition. Furthermore, differences will inevitably arise within these particular subtraditions because of, at least in part, the temperamental and experiential differences of particular members. All the while, our universal fallibility provides ample possibility for disagreement. Finally, it is important to note that genuine rational disagreement requires a certain degree of agreement, for in order to disagree, opposing parties must first tacitly agree on the terms of the debate. Thus, even when disagreement appears to be sharp, a fundamental underlying agreement is necessary to facilitate the disagreement. But, of course, underlying agreement does not mitigate the severity of potential disagreements. Thus, despite the indispensability of tradition—both for its necessary epistemological role and as a repository of collective wisdom—universal agreement is an unlikely ideal the pursuit of which may at times produce more harm than good.

However, despite the differences, Polanyi argues that all free people participate in a "universal tradition" by which certain values—the reality of truth, justice, charity, and tolerance—are upheld and practiced. These values point to a common "transcendent ground" and serve to unite free people in a common enterprise. Polanyi sees this as a necessary foundation for the development of science and, more broadly, for the advance of a free society. He argues that this underlying assumption is what saves his position from nihilism: "The coherence of all men's consciences in the grounds of the same universal tradition is an integral part of my position."[6] Again, tradition points beyond itself to a reality that is fixed though never fully plumbed. Contact with this reality will, despite variations of time and culture, show a significant degree of similarity: "All contacts with spiritual reality have a measure of coherence." Such coherence may, on the surface, appear to be merely local or national. However, "this tradition may well be merely a national variant of a universal human tradition. For a similar coherence will be found between different nations when each follows a national tradition of this type. They will form a community of free peoples. They may argue and quarrel, yet will always settle each new difficulty in the end, firmly rooted in the same transcendent ground."[7] Polanyi is, of course, working under the assumption that a normative reality exists and free people are obligated—if they are to remain free—to abide by the limits of that reality. For him, any attempt to deny such limits would be to steer directly into nihilistic conclusions. Liberty, in other words, depends on submission to certain ideals that make liberty possible.

We can frame this discussion in a way that shows matters in a slightly different light. Recall that MacIntyre insists that humans are essentially storytelling creatures, and to properly understand a human life is to grasp its narrative structure. But I think we can take this further, for we not only tell stories and frame our lives in terms of stories, but also, perhaps most profoundly, we see ourselves as *inhabiting* stories. We tell each other inherited stories and come to see ourselves as part of the stories we tell. This is merely another way of saying that we inherit traditions that enter our consciousness as narrative structures, and we come to see the world through the mediation of the traditions we inherit. As such, one way of understanding a person and a society is to ask the questions: What are your stories? What are the stories you tell each other and identify with? What stories shape the contours of your understanding of yourself and the world? What stories do you *inhabit*?

When constructing his ideal city in words, Socrates places a premium on telling children the right kind of stories. Why? Because children are mimetic creatures. They imitate the models they encounter, and imitation is, as Socrates understood, transformative, for what a person imitates is what that person will become. As such, Socrates insists that the storytellers be compelled to tell the kinds of stories most conducive to forming virtuous citizens. Indeed, the entire *Republic* might be read as an attempt by Plato to replace the worn-out myths of Athens with something more adequate and salutary.

Nietzsche, too, recognizes the power and necessity of formative stories, which he calls "myth." He writes,

> Without myth every culture loses the healthy natural power of its creativity: only a horizon defined by myths completes and unifies a whole cultural movement. . . . Images of the myth have to be the unnoticed omnipresent demonic guardians, under whose care the young soul grows to maturity and whose signs help the man to interpret his life and struggles. Even the state knows no more powerful unwritten laws than the mythical foundation that guarantees its connection with religion and its growth from mythical notions.[8]

When Zarathustra descends from his mountain cave, he does so with the intent of preaching a new myth: God is dead. He seeks to replace the decadent old myth with a new myth characterized by renewed vitality and spirit.[9] Thus, the nihilism of Nietzsche is not oriented toward pure destruction, but rather destruction for the sake of creation. As he puts it, "If a temple is to be erected a temple must be destroyed: that is the law."[10] Yet, the death of God is not accomplished without a certain dread that calls for a new myth to replace the old. Nietzsche's madman recognizes the problem. After bursting into the marketplace and declaring that God is dead, he grows reflective: "What water is there to clean ourselves? What festivals of atonement, what sacred games shall we have to invent?"[11] In short, what new myths will we need to create to replace the old myth we have shattered? Nietzsche realizes better than most that at the heart of this new myth, as with all myths, is a religious core that seeks to provide an orienting story for humanity. And even though the prospect of losing a long-established myth is disconcerting and perhaps even terrifying, Nietzsche sees the possibilities inherent in being released from the moral constraints implied by theism. Indeed, for those "philosophers" and "free spirits" there is a "new dawn" that provides those who can tolerate the loss with a new range of possibilities—a blank canvas upon which the strong and creative may exercise their freedom.[12] This myth of liberation from the strictures of the past and its badly worn theism is depicted as the "sacred 'Yes'" uttered by the child who emerges only after the lion vanquishes the fierce dragon of values and clears the way for a new and creative moment where the old myths are replaced by new and more adequate ones.[13]

We inhabit inherited stories. We can either seek to live according to them or we can with Nietzsche seek to destroy the old in favor of something ostensibly new. However, we should pause when we notice that the new myth with which Nietzsche replaces the old is merely the myth of the liberated self, unconstrained by the gods of the past and insisting on the free expression of the individual. The radical rhetoric turns out to be nothing more than a cover for the familiar and conventional urge to liberation—the same urge we saw in Descartes, Bacon, and Rousseau—albeit liberation taken to its logical extreme. Nietzsche ultimately fails because tradition that does not function as an icon becomes an idol. In similar fashion, a myth that does not point to a reality beyond itself reveals its inner decadence and eventually collapses of its own weight. The myth of liberation cannot sustain itself in the light of reality.

The invention of the state of nature is a myth, introduced in the seventeenth century, that fosters a conception of the human person as essentially free. The natural human condition, according to this myth, is one of perfect freedom and perfect equality. (This outlook complements politically the philosophical methodology of Descartes and Bacon.) Political society is conceived as a work of art rather than nature, and here we see how the notion of the state of nature transforms nature from a morally structured reality to something from which to escape (as in Hobbes and Locke) or a condition from which we have unfortunately but irreversibly fallen (as in Rousseau). To live in accordance with nature is the ideal in the Aristotelian/Thomist tradition, but in this new conception, nature becomes a condition from which humans have extricated themselves. Liberation from nature allows humans to create a world limited by nothing but contract and consent. Indeed, although a state of nature and "natural man" are unknown to history, this does not matter. The myth makes it possible to imagine a person whose will is completely unfettered. To be sure, some accounts limited this expression of the will to the parameters established by natural law, but once skepticism about natural law developed, the myth remained and the will was impeded by nothing. To suggest that humans are born into a complex set of relationships that imply obligation and responsibility prior to consent is to do violence to this original freedom. The state of nature is a myth that promotes the liberal self, but to the extent that both traffic in a false conception of reality and a false conception of tradition, both collapse into their own incoherencies.

We are warranted to ask at this point what myths serve to ground and orient the American self-understanding. What are our founding myths? Of course, there are multiple stories that serve as a framework of self-understanding; however, some play a more explicit and central role. Given the pervasive influence of the biblical narrative, we should not be surprised that secular events have often been invested with biblical and even eschatological import. For instance, the Puritans frequently referred to themselves as the "new Israel" and interpreted their own experience in terms of the Exodus: they escaped the oppression of the old world, crossed a seemingly boundless wasteland, and arrived in the promised land, a land of "milk and honey." The American Revolution was also frequently framed in terms of liberation from an oppressive tyrant—sometime explicitly referred to as "Pharaoh." Abolitionism and the civil rights movement continued employing similar themes of liberation from injustice. Thus, the narrative of liberation, derived from the Bible, is written deeply into the fabric of the American consciousness. However, by the time of the American Revolution, the Lockean influence had made its way across the Atlantic and insinuated itself into the consciousness of the American colonists. The image of the isolated and free individual in a state of nature—a mythic depiction of a human who never existed—found a suitable complement in the stories of liberation rooted in the biblical tradition. Once fidelity to that tradition began to waver, an alternative myth, unencumbered by theological categories or limits, was ready and waiting to take up the banner of liberation. We should not be surprised that liberalism has found fertile soil in America, and in the West more generally.

THE CRISIS OF LIBERALISM

Before describing an alternative, let us consider the various ways liberalism fails. We have seen how a rejection of the epistemic role of tradition results in philosophical incoherence. There are also practical problems, for it does not appear that late-stage liberalism is a reliable protector of individual liberty. Consider the illiberal impulse, all too common today, to shout down or shut down, by physical or legal force, any who express disagreement with the liberal conception of the self. The language of individual rights is pervasive, but all too often rights are used as weapons to compel others rather than as a guarantor of the freedoms proper to human beings, for rights stripped of their metaphysical context—grounded in natural law and a theologically informed anthropology—descend into mere assertions of individual will. On college campuses we hear of so-called microaggressions and trigger warnings by means of which free speech is curtailed and those who do not bow to the reigning liberal orthodoxy are punished. We hear of proprietors and institutions that are legally sanctioned for refusing, as a matter of conscience, to celebrate lifestyle choices of those with whom they disagree. The freedom of religion itself is threatened under the auspices of a liberalism that refuses to acknowledge the freedom of dissenters. Such curtailment of freedom—ironically, in the name of freedom—hearkens back to Rousseau's ominous warning that those who refuse to bow to the general will will be forced to be free. We see here what seems to be the fruits of the late-stage liberalism in which all limits have been dissolved in the acid of individual emancipation.

In speaking of religious freedom, it might be helpful to recall that Rousseau advocated the abolition of historic Christianity (rooted in a complex tradition) and the adoption of what he called a "civil religion," a religion invented to consolidate the power of the state.[14] Rousseau understood what champions of a so-called secular state do not: religion is unavoidable. As Rousseau puts it, "No state has ever been founded without religion as its base." In other words, humans are unavoidably religious; they need a myth. Rousseau understood that the question is not *if* humans will worship but, rather, *what* will they worship? As such, he sought to overturn Christianity and replace it with a religion that was incorporated into the state and served its ends. This civil religion represents "a purely civil profession of faith, the articles of which it belongs to the sovereign to establish." Recall that the "sovereign" in Rousseau's scheme is merely the "private individuals who make it up." The will of the sovereign is merely the general will, which is never wrong and to which each citizen is compelled to bow. The tenets of this civil religion are "not exactly dogmas of religion" but instead are "sentiments of sociability." Without subscribing to these "sentiments of sociability" it is "impossible to be a good citizen or a faithful subject." In Rousseau's civil religion—which replaces Christianity—articles of faith rooted in a tradition that reaches back through the centuries, and by which Christians have been joined, are replaced by a novel religion of the state. Those who refuse to acknowledge or subscribe to the tenets of this civil religion will be banished from the polity "not for being impious but for being unsociable." Furthermore, "if, having publicly acknowledged these same dogmas, a person acts as if he does not believe them, he should be put to death; he has committed the greatest of crimes: he has lied before the laws." Such a religion, Rousseau insists, should have few and general dogmas that include only one "negative dogma" or prohibition: intolerance. For Rousseau, civil intolerance and theological intolerance are indistinguishable. Intolerance consists in the belief that another is fundamentally wrong: "Tolerance should be shown to all those that tolerate others, so long as their dogmas contain nothing contrary to the duties of a citizen." That final clause is frightening in its implications, which he spells out in the next sentence: "Whoever dares to say *outside the church there is no salvation* ought to be expelled from the state." There is, in other words, no place for principled disagreement at a fundamental level. There is, in this illiberal liberalism, only compulsion, exile, and even death for those who dare to oppose the "sentiments of sociability" imposed by the general will. Those who are paying attention to the American social and political scene will undoubtedly hear echoes of Rousseau in the words of the social justice warriors who are, with great self-righteousness and energy, set on compelling their opponents to be sociable.

MacIntyre, for one, suggests that the recovery of the language of virtue, rooted in the concepts of narrative, practice, and tradition, will provide the means by which a more coherent conception of liberty can be achieved. Others have argued that natural law can provide an adequate framework for understanding the connection between liberty and responsibility. Still others argue that the commands of God expressed in Holy Writ are necessary for properly understanding human flourishing and the place of liberty therein. To these arguments the liberal can simply reply that individuals can choose to limit themselves by whatever means they like (so long as they do not stray from the narrow circle of liberal orthodoxy, which means keeping their religious and metaphysical commitments to themselves), but the fact that they are *choosing* demonstrates the primacy of choice. Liberalism wins.

But perhaps that conclusion is too hastily drawn. Not all choosing is contingent upon the presence of the liberal self. Humans naturally make choices as a simple exercise of their freedom. Liberalism turns on a particular conception of the human person, one devoid of anything essential other than the capacity to choose. A normative human nature, ends proper to flourishing, divine commands—all these are denied in order to give individual choice its widest latitude. The problem is not choice per se. It is the attempt to erase or ignore any limits on the choosing self. The solitary individual, constrained by nothing save his individual will, is the basic foundation of liberalism. Consequently, all legitimate associations must be the product of individual choice. Contract, rather than nature or covenant, lies at the heart of human relations, and tradition is at best an optional accessory—and at worst a hindrance to freedom—rather than an essential part of the human experience.

The classical liberal asserts that this atomistic conception of the human person not only is true but is the best preserver of liberty. However, we should at least pause when we notice that the classical liberalism of the nineteenth century seems to have given way to (and perhaps paved the way for) the welfare-state liberalism of the twentieth century. Could it be that the autonomous individual is inadequate to resist the centralizing forces that threaten to reduce free men and women to wards of a nanny state? Could it be that, bereft of the bonds of vibrant, stable communities that acknowledge some limits, the individual naturally looks to the state to fill the void? Alexis de Tocqueville argues that autonomous individualism is the engine that facilitates the growth of the centralized state.[15] Tocqueville believed associations could help stave off the creep toward centralization, yet he knew that associations are not adequate on their own. As we saw,

Tocqueville argued that in early America the spirit of religion—and here he means Christianity—served to limit the spirit of freedom, and here we can see how religious belief created a context within which associations could exist and thrive. Tocqueville was describing what I have called first wave liberalism. However, it is not clear that today Christianity exercises the same kind of influence over American life that it did in Tocqueville's day. To the extent this is so, we have moved into liberalism's second phase, and the stage is set for its undoing.

Reversal of Liberalism

The essence of liberalism is the liberation of the individual. There is, however, a second aspect to liberalism we have not yet directly addressed: equality. For the social contract thinkers, the state of nature consists of individuals who are completely free and equal. (We see the same egalitarianism impulse in the methodologies of Descartes and Bacon). Freedom and equality are both essential to liberalism. Freedom has come to mean the eradication of limits on individual choice. This impulse to liberation initially focused on eliminating the authority of tradition but continued to eventually include the attempted elimination of the authority of nature and God. In terms of morality, this gave us emotivism. In terms of metaphysics, this led to the abandonment of classical realism in exchange for nominalism. (Nominalism, of course, has been lurking around for centuries—Ockham, after all, predates liberalism. Yet, Ockham's narrow technical point has found fertile soil in the emancipated self. Thus, it is no surprise that nominalism comes fully into its own in the modern era.) When the widest latitude for individual choice is the goal, all choices come to be seen as equally valid as long as they are freely chosen. Any notion of a hierarchy of goods is replaced by the insistence that a mere procedural framework is in place to facilitate unencumbered free choices. Equality, in this respect, becomes a corollary to a liberal conception of freedom, and any impediment to either the freedom of choice or the equality of choices becomes an affront. In this context, tolerance becomes insufficient, for tolerance implies difference—and even a tacit affirmation of hierarchy—for one only tolerates what one disapproves of. Disapproval, in other words, implies that some choices are better than others, and though I believe your choices are inferior to mine, I will tolerate your bad choices for the sake of peace, stability, or some other good. But if equality, along with freedom, is an unassailable ideal, then every hint of disapproval must be removed, for only then will complete equality be achieved. Tolerance must be replaced by approval, and approval must soon give way to celebration, which is to say that the liberal conception of the self eventually seeks to eliminate differences. Enforced diversity ends in bland uniformity. The flip side of this trajectory is that those who refuse to fall in line will be demonized as judgmental, intolerant, or, to employ Rousseau's term, unsociable. Such individuals are the heretics of the liberal order and must be purged or silenced. In the name of freedom and equality, the freedom of those who insist that not all choices are equal will be disregarded, but it becomes painfully clear at this point that, despite the protestations of the liberal ideologue, not all opinions are in fact equal and that the liberal does in fact embrace an array of substantial goods, albeit surreptitiously. Equality becomes merely a parody and freedom a charade, both in service of a self-righteous power by which the liberal order seeks to eliminate all contenders. Liberalism, in other words, consumes all rivals and then consumes itself.[16]

If liberalism is, indeed, fundamentally destructive even of itself, then it is fundamentally unstable. However, it is important to acknowledge in this context that liberal regimes have existed with a remarkable degree of stability, and this would seem to run counter to my claim. However, the stability of liberal regimes, or so my argument goes, has been due to the nonliberal cultural, philosophical, and theological grounds upon which the liberal regimes were built and which liberalism slowly but inexorably erodes.

Why, then, is liberalism failing and in so doing revealing its illiberal heart? How could the dominant political doctrine of our day become fundamentally compromised? First, liberalism is incapable of accounting for itself because of its rejection of tradition as an indispensable component of the knowing process. This results in a fundamental philosophical incoherence at the heart of the liberal project. To remove the incoherence and admit the necessary role of tradition would threaten to undermine the entire enterprise, for admitting the role of tradition implies submission and authority, both of which serve as impediments to the infinitely expansive will. Thus, it would seem that the logic of liberalism cannot accommodate tradition, and therefore liberalism is necessarily trapped in its own incoherence.

Second, the fact that the liberal order seems to be moving decidedly toward its own inversion suggests that, in addition to the philosophical incoherence, there is a logic embedded in liberalism that leads to its own practical negation. The ideals central to liberalism—freedom and equality—have been absolutized. Late state liberalism has ossified into an ideology. Ideologies lack the suppleness and flexibility necessary to accommodate changing circumstances. Ideologies reject rational discourse in the pursuit of truth in favor of power plays in pursuit of dominance. Discourse and persuasion are exchanged for the volume of the protest. Rational speech—that which Aristotle believed set us apart from other animals—is replaced by the will to power, which often manifests itself as the will to purge. It is only in light of this fact that we can grasp how the good ideals of freedom and equality can be hijacked and come to serve those who insist on curtailing the freedom of their opponents (who are conceived as enemies) to hold opinions that differ from the majority.

Finally, at the heart of the liberal project is a false conception of the human person, and out of that false conception all the pathologies of the liberal self emerge. In short, the autonomous individual is a delusion. There never has been and never will be an autonomous self. The state of nature—whether in its classical Hobbesian and Lockean or its modern Rawlsian form—presents a false depiction of the human condition. The necessity of tradition in the knowing process shows how this view of the human person is flawed.

MacIntyre argues that when a tradition—which for him is always characterized by an ongoing debate about the good—encounters an incoherence or latent contradiction that cannot be resolved in terms supplied by the tradition itself, an epistemological crisis ensues. Such a crisis will either lead to the death of the tradition or its revitalization as a result of conceptual resources that can be brought to bear that resolve the challenges that provoked the crisis. If a particular tradition is unable to resolve the challenges that it encounters, but an alternative tradition is capable of explaining why the beleaguered tradition failed, can show how to move beyond the crisis, and possesses the resources that make such progress possible, there is good reason to conclude that the tradition that can cope with the crisis is superior to the one that cannot.

It is in this context that liberalism shows itself to be in crisis: it denies the fact that rationality is constituted in the context of tradition and thereby liberalism demonstrates its own inability to grasp the nature of knowing and the role played by tradition. Liberalism, in this sense, has affirmed its foundational ideals of freedom and equality yet denied the role of tradition in upholding those ideals. Liberalism, in attempting to eradicate any limit beyond individual choice, has denied the reality toward which any healthy tradition points. As such, liberalism has become an idol rather than an icon, an ideology rather than a set of ideals to be balanced against other equally vital ideals. Furthermore, liberalism, when competitors have been vanquished, undergoes a reversal and reveals its illiberal core. Thus, there is a twofold crisis besetting liberalism: one is philosophical, the other practical; one turns on a fundamental incoherence of self-understanding, the other emerges when liberalism becomes its opposite. Liberalism is, in short, both incoherent and self-destructive.

Social Pathologies of Liberalism

Liberalism also seems to call forth certain social and political pathologies that only become apparent as liberalism becomes an increasingly pure version of itself. I want to briefly consider several.

The liberal self has an inadequate conception of time. Or, to put matters differently, the liberal self voluntarily lives with severely constricted temporal horizons. As we lose sight of the past, we also lose sight of the future. We become habitually fixated on the present and the near future, which is to say, my own future. The idea that we exist as part of a civilizational enterprise to which we contribute for a time and that continues after we are gone is lost in the myopia of presentism. We see only ourselves and, consequently, we come to focus primarily on our own pleasures, satisfactions, and grievances. The idea of sacrifice becomes difficult to justify unless the sacrifice is in service to our own future pleasures. Sacrifice—to the cause of civilization, to the distant future, to future generations—seems irrational to a mind of constricted temporal horizons.

At the same time, we lose the inclination and eventually the capacity to see ourselves as participants in an ongoing narrative. In truth, we inherit the setting, the scene, the props, and the context, and it is our role to carry on, to attempt to move the story along toward a good end without producing a rupture in the drama that makes the entire narrative arc an incoherent and therefore directionless series of utterances and actions. We forget that we are inheritors and therefore caretakers, improvisers, and potential improvers of a story. When we lose sight of the fact that we are participants in this ongoing drama, when we come to imagine that we are merely agents who can assert our wills as a means of satisfying whatever desire

2

manifests itself in the immediacy of the present, we will seek the eradication of symbols of the past that serve as reminders of our compromised and complex history.

It is no surprise that birth rates have plummeted in virtually all countries touched by liberalism. Of course, children are hardly economic assets in nonagrarian societies. But more to the point, children require significant sacrifices—both in terms of time and resources—and, what is perhaps most significant, they represent a dramatic reduction in freedom. If my conception of the best life is one with the least limits to my freedom, I will choose to drastically limit the number of children I have, if I have any at all. It should come as no surprise that those cultures and subcultures with the greatest interest in maintaining a fidelity to the past and preserving ancient traditions (often embodied in religious doctrines) are those where the birthrates are highest. If the demographic trends continue, it appears warranted in concluding that liberalism, in the form of plummeting birthrates, destroys societies.

The same can be said of marriage, for marriage—at least as conceived as a lifelong commitment to one person—represents a serious constriction of freedom. The rise of no-fault divorce signals a change in marriage law that, in turn, points to a change in our understanding of marriage. When marriage is understood in terms of a covenant or a sacrament, the union consists of two people joining together in the presence of God, who is a participant in the union. When marriage comes to be seen in merely contractual terms, consent becomes the essence of the union, and when either or both parties withdraw consent, the marriage is dissolved.[17] When the stability and permanence of marriage is reduced and when the number of children per marriage declines precipitously, the family, which is one of the foundational components of a healthy society, weakens.

In terms of politics, a loss of a sense of the past and a corresponding fidelity to the authority of inherited tradition will result in shortsighted policies. The politician will seek his own personal advantage rather than work for the common good with an eye to the long-term flourishing of the community. This can be clearly seen in the willingness of American politicians to run up a national debt beyond anyone's ability to imagine, let alone repay. The debt represents a stunning lack of concern for future generations, for with it we blithely saddle our grandchildren with debt to placate our own insatiable appetites. In effect, our freedom is purchased with theirs, for debt represents a reduction in future resources, and usable resources are one indicator of freedom. Thus, to the extent we deprive our descendants of resources, we deprive them of freedom. We are parasites on our unborn children. A society with a proper relationship to the past, and therefore a proper relationship to the future, would never countenance such cavalier pillaging of those least able to defend themselves. Yet we do, and we do so because we cannot see them, and we cannot see them because we are confined by the self-imposed *limits* of the present. (It is interesting, in this regard, to note that the liberal self apparently does, in fact, acknowledge limits. In this case, our myopia is the direct result of a self-imposed limit, namely, the present).

Capitalism complements the limitless aspirations of the liberal self. The advent of consumerism is made possible by the limitless expansion of the appetites. When Mandeville praises the public virtues that result from private vices he is extolling an optimism that market forces will produce good even if the motives of the actors are base. In such a system, unlimited avarice can happily bring about a good society. The unconstrained self, contrary to the moral teachings of centuries, is now free to indulge itself without fear of censure and, what is more, with a confidence that society will benefit. The free market serves to facilitate and accelerate the expansion of the will, and in so doing the liberal self is energized to pursue ever new heights of liberation.

Free markets evince a striking and vital difference depending on whether they are embedded in the rich soil nourished by nonliberal ingredients or exist in the desiccated soil of late modernity. When market forces, competition, and supply and demand are constrained by noneconomic limits, they are an effective means by which property can be allocated and a just means by which exchanges can be governed. However, when those same economic elements are combined with nothing more than the liberal self, the results become toxic and the liberal self is emboldened. Self-restraint is exchanged for greed, thrift for profligacy, and charity for state-sponsored welfare. People are demeaned and degraded as they relentlessly and even diligently pursue the satisfaction of their ever expanding appetites.

Our relationship to the natural world takes on a particular aspect when we lose sight of our duties both to the past and to the future. To be sure, we hear much talk about the environment today. Some express concern that we may be doing irreparable harm to our world and as a result future generations might be summarily harmed. Such a concern is proper, and those so-called conservatives who express nothing but disdain for any who speak out on behalf of the natural world are showing the stunning narrowness of their temporal horizons and corresponding irresponsibly (not to mention hubris). Alternatively, there are many who speak of the natural world as an end in itself as if there is no reality beyond the material world. Both are wrong. On the one hand, conservatives need to recover the language and practice of stewardship, which calls for a recognition of limits and a posture of loving care of that which we have received. On the other hand, the biblical writers remind us that the creation bears witness to God. The creation points to the creator. Or to put matters in another way, the creation serves as an icon pointing those who will see to the author of it all. Many who position themselves as champions of the environment (they shy away from referring to it as the "creation") fail to see the meaning toward which the created order points. The icon becomes an idol, and the discourse (and the policies) take on the hard edge of an ideology.

The Response of Tradition

Liberalism, it would seem, is a beleaguered tradition for which an alternative must be found that does not fail where liberalism does. In attempting to locate (or perhaps even cobble together) an alternative account of knowing and therefore an alternative account of the human person, we should keep several things in mind. First, a basic requirement for a healthy tradition is that it does not deny the essential role played by tradition. This seems obviously true if the tradition is to avoid veering off into incoherence from the start. Second, recovery is not simple, for to recover a lost tradition requires a serious historical study. Yet a serious engagement with history as an authoritative source of truth runs counter to the fundamental disposition of the liberal self. Thus, the problem is twofold: (1) serious historical engagement is required, and (2) the disposition to denigrate the past has to be overcome. We become open to the past when we imagine that it potentially holds answers to vexing questions. Such an intimation can propel a search that opens up the world of the past and makes it once again possible to take tradition seriously. Finally, historical research is not adequate in itself, for no tradition can simply be dragged out of the past and imposed onto the present in a cut-and-paste exercise. Instead, the recovery of a tradition requires creative appropriation, and that appropriation requires a work of imagination to recognize how the particular contours of a tradition can be adapted to one's particular cultural and historical context. Ultimately, a tradition is not adopted because it is conceived to be useful or convenient or old. A tradition is recovered and appropriated for one reason only: because it is believed to be true. It is believed to provide a means by which the real is encountered. As such, tradition requires a recognition of limits in two ways: the structure of tradition limits knowing even as it facilitates the same, and a living tradition acknowledges that individual will must subordinate itself to a given reality and to norms embedded in that reality. Such a move requires creativity, imagination, courage, and humility.

It appears that a polity in which the emancipation of the individual is held as the highest value cannot accommodate a strong view of tradition: the two positions are fundamentally incompatible. However, I am wagering that it may be possible to develop an account of liberty that both fosters and protects individual freedom while at the same time taking the fact of tradition seriously. On the one hand, this might conceivably entail recovering the conditions necessary to sustain what I have called "first wave liberalism." However, in light of the fact that first wave liberalism tends to transform into second wave liberalism and thereby become illiberal, first wave liberalism, if it is to be sustained, requires a constant infusion of nonliberal resources to keep its fiercer instincts in check. This is no easy task given the imperial nature of liberalism, which seeks to remake all contenders in its own image. On the other hand, it may be possible to imagine a nonliberal conception of liberty, one that does not depend on the myth of the liberal self. Given our current social and cultural moment, proposing such an alternative may appear to be a quixotic enterprise, one that might appeal to certain people of a theoretical bent but has no real practical prospects in the near term. However, in light of the apparent fact that liberalism eventually turns on itself, such a project might, in fact, be necessary. With that, it is important to note that what I am proposing is neither radical nor new. Indeed, if it were a radically novel idea, it would run at cross purposes to my entire project. Ultimately, I am attempting to describe—using resources latent in our own past—what we might term a "tradition-constituted liberty."

Although I am not advocating a radically new idea, at the same time neither am I advocating a return to some sort of traditional aristocratic society where social roles are determined by birth and where social—and geographical—mobility is severely restricted. Furthermore, I am not longing for some fabled past where complexity and crisis are held at bay by a common fidelity to a particular narrow set of traditions. Nor am I suggesting that tradition is a foolproof guide. But on the other hand, neither am I suggesting that tradition is an optional accoutrement, one that can be chosen as an attractive, or even useful, adornment that can be set aside at will and without consequence. Any adequate account of rationality and of liberty must include tradition as an essential ingredient.

Fortunately, the Western tradition has resources latent within it that can point to an alternative vision that does not fall victim to the fundamental incoherencies of liberalism. Aristotle, for his part, would have rejected the modern proclivity for starting political analysis with the autonomous individual in a hypothetical state of nature. Instead, he began with the basic building block of society: the family. In this view, we are naturally and unavoidably embedded in relationships that obligate us from the very start. Natural relationships, born in and sustained by traditions (a point not clearly articulated by Aristotle), precede choice. In this conception of things, duties and responsibilities receive the primary emphasis, and though the notion of individual rights can still plausibly exist, virulent rights claims are tempered by the context in which those rights now emerge.

Likewise, Burke extolled the virtues of the "little platoons" that cultivate a due sense of the responsibilities we inherit and foster a proper affection for one's country, and even for mankind in general.[18] Only by beginning with a recognition of the complex amalgam of natural affiliations and traditions that those affiliations foster and sustain can we create a context within which, as Burke puts it, a "moral and regulated liberty" exists and endures.[19] A "moral and regulated liberty" is not a denial of liberty but neither is it an endorsement of an unrestrained liberation that denies all limits. It is, rather, an acknowledgment that liberty requires limits, and tradition is a primary means by which limits are articulated. Both Aristotle and Burke offer an alternative to the liberal self, an alternative that has long been ignored but one that does not fall prey to the incoherence to which liberalism succumbs.

It seems appropriate at this point to attempt to sketch an account of liberty (and a corresponding account of the human person) that is not an extension of the liberal self and therefore avoids the errors we have been discussing. This alternative acknowledges the essential role played by tradition, and therefore it seems reasonable to call this alternative a "tradition-constituted account of liberty." A tradition-constituted liberty will consist of three key attributes. First, it will recognize that the liberty of the individual is essential, but it also will be able to accommodate conceptions of liberty that are not directly oriented toward the individual. In other words, the freedom to associate (or not) is vital, but so too is the freedom of associations to act as their members deem correct. Second, a tradition-constituted liberty will acknowledge the role of limits. It will not fall prey to the notion that any curtailment or abridgment of liberty is necessarily an offense that must be eradicated. Finally, a tradition-constituted liberty will be built upon a deep and persistent notion of inheritance—which is to say, tradition—and it is this third idea that provides the context within which the other two make sense.

Although wholesale conversion to some version of tradition-constituted liberty might be too much to expect, it is possible that resources native to this account might be appropriated in an effort to reclaim some version of first wave liberalism that characterized the American Founding. However, given the natural instability of first wave liberalism, it can only survive with a constant infusion of nonliberal ingredients. This more modest solution, despite its drawbacks, might be the best we can hope for, but in light of the crisis of liberalism we are now witnessing, the moment may be ripe to consider an alternative.

This alternative to the liberal conception of freedom insists that a legitimate and sustainable freedom is only possible in the context of limits given but not chosen. Liberalism conceives of freedom as emancipation from all constraint; it is *freedom from*. The alternative, which has deep roots in the classical and Christian world, understands freedom not as the eradication of all limits, but as *freedom to* do as one ought. Freedom, in this account, is the freedom to act within given limits in the pursuit of goods proper to human creatures.

Burke

We saw in chapter 4 that Polanyi construes the modern political scene as a confrontation between the followers of Edmund Burke and the followers of Thomas Paine.[20] Polanyi argues that although the political rhetoric in Britain and America tended toward the progressivism of Paine, in actual practice, tradition governed far more than most would admit. That is, even though many "profess the right of absolute self-determination in political theory [they rely] on the guidance of tradition in political practice."[21] Polanyi argues that a theory of progress and freedom must be rooted in an adequate account of tradition. His account "accepts Burke's thesis that freedom must be rooted in tradition, but transposes it into a system cultivating radical progress."[22] In other words, Polanyi's reading of Burke suggests that Burke emphasizes the role of tradition while remaining skeptical of the idea of progress and perhaps even resisting change. This view of Burke, though common, is not quite correct. Since we have, in the context of this project, encountered Burke frequently but only in passing, we might do well now to focus directly on his thought, especially his understanding of tradition. It should be pointed out that Burke is sometimes identified as a liberal, but this is not correct if we understand the essence of liberalism as the autonomous self liberated from all limits other that those that are explicitly chosen. In other words, Burke is a lover of liberty, but his affection for liberty is not rooted in a commitment to the liberal self. Instead, he develops an account of liberty that avoids the pitfalls of liberalism while still defending the good of individual liberty.

As is well known, Burke expressed dismay when he saw France descending into its revolution. In his *Reflections on the Revolution in France*, Burke lays out the reasons for his concerns and provides an alternative to the Jacobin attempt to refashion French society from the ground up. The Jacobins sought to destroy the old order so that a new and better one could be built. The idea that destruction could be a first step toward fashioning a good and just world was abhorrent to Burke, who asserted that "I do not like to see any thing destroyed; any void produced in society, any ruin on the face of the land."[23] He condemns those who would "destroy an old scheme of things, because it is an old one."[24] He praises the "sullen resistance to innovation" that characterized the English national temperament.[25] He insists that "no discoveries are to be made, in morality."[26] He expresses his dislike for revolutions and "the spirit of change."[27] Such claims lead readers to conclude, if they are not careful, that Burke is simply interested in maintaining the status quo, that he is fundamentally opposed to change, and therefore conservatism, at least in the Burkean vein, is synonymous with resisting any attempt to change or improve the current situation.

Burke, however, does not fall into such a trap. Instead, he notes that "a state without the means of some change is without the means of its conservation."[28] Change, then, is an essential component of Burke's thought. But what kind of change? And change for what purpose? For Burke, change is often necessary, but changes are best when they emerge organically and in continuity with the past. Thus "in what we improve, we are never wholly new; in what we retain we are never wholly obsolete."[29] In using the term "improve," Burke is acknowledging that progress is possible. Not, perhaps, progress in discovering moral truth, but, to be sure, progress is possible in the manner and consistency in which we apply those truths.[30] At the same time, improvement is not guaranteed, neither is it necessarily permanent as some of the more optimistic writers of his age insisted.[31]

What troubles Burke is an approach to improvement characterized not by respect for the past but rather by hatred: "Rage and phrenzy will pull down more in half an hour, than prudence, deliberation, and foresight can build up in an hundred years."[32] Thus, the key is to prudently introduce change in such a way that destruction is avoided and so that the resources of the past can be employed in the effort. And this, in many cases, is no easy feat. Yet, for Burke, such an approach is surely less susceptible of error than the rash and hurried attempts at reform that he witnessed in France: "At once to preserve and to reform is quite another thing." Such a process takes time. It is generally gradual, but the gentle pace allows for corrections along the way that a faster course of reform simply cannot accommodate. Some might find this a frustratingly slow process, but Burke takes precisely the opposite view: "It is one of the excellencies of a method in which time is amongst the assistants, that its operation is slow, and in some cases almost imperceptible." However, "by a slow but well-sustained progress, the effect of each step is watched; the good or ill success of the first, gives light to us in the second; and so, from light to light, we are conducted with safety through the whole series."[33]

Intentional change, even of the prudent and gradual variety, requires, among other things, the freedom of individuals to choose. The prudent statesman (and also the wise parent, employer, worker, or friend) must possess the liberty to act if the notion of improvement or innovation is to have any meaning at all. This centrality of liberty is crucial in our discussion, for it is important to see that Burke is a champion of liberty, but at the same time he is not a champion of liberty without limits. He expresses his appreciation for "a manly, moral, regulated liberty."[34] And although he admits that liberty in the abstract is undoubtedly a good thing, he insists that praise of liberty must be contingent on how that liberty is employed: "The effect of liberty to individuals is, that they may do what they please: we ought to see what it will please them to do, before we risque congratulations."[35]

What, then, are the limits to liberty that Burke recognizes? What sort of regulation does a "regulated liberty" entail? Answering these questions gets us to the crux of the issue, for liberalism, as it has developed, seems to imply a destruction of limits. At the same time, liberty with limits suggests to the liberal mind an internal tension if not an outright contradiction. A true and legitimate liberty, so the liberal argues, must entail the absence of external restraints and even the absence of any internal, psychological restraint other than sheer, unadulterated will. Anything less is a concession and a condition that must be rectified if liberty truly is to thrive.

Burke emphatically disagrees with such sentiments. For him there are several aspects of the human experience that serve to constitute the limits within which freedom can flourish. The first aspect is human nature itself. It is, of course, unfashionable today to speak of a normative human nature, but for Burke this is a category that must be acknowledged. Burke—and in this he follows the general opinion of both classical and Christian thinkers—holds that there is a nature common to all humans, and one aspect of moral and social health is acknowledging and submitting to the limits of that common nature. These limits are not simply human but rather reflect the very structure of reality. Thus, Burke argues that those whose judgment is clouded by passion deny "any fixed order of things." In the "fog and haze of confusion all is enlarged, and appears without any limit."[36]

Burke rejects the notion of a "state of nature," at least as it is conceived by thinkers such as Locke and Rousseau. Instead, "The state of civil society . . . is a state of nature; and much more truly so than a savage and incoherent mode of life. For man is by nature reasonable; and he is never perfectly in his natural state, but when he is placed where reason may be best cultivated, and most predominates. Art is man's nature. We are as much, at least, in a state of nature in formed manhood, as in immature and helpless infancy."[37] As a result, Burke insists that the prudent statesman must make it a priority to become a student of human nature. If this study is neglected, then the aspiring leader is simply unfit to public service.[38]

Humans are, for Burke, capable of ascertaining the moral law, which is "that eternal immutable law, in which will and reason are the same."[39] This formulation is suggestive, for it indicates that Burke does not seek to separate reason and the will such that one becomes the slave of the other, or so that one can be ignored while the other takes priority. Instead, reason and will find agreement in the eternal law, which, according to the tradition to which Burke is alluding, is nothing other than the natural law. This eternal law is, ultimately, located in the divine nature, so it is impossible to continue without turning to another source of limits in Burke's thought: religion. For Burke, human nature is created by God, and to adequately grasp this nature, one must recognize both that humans are creatures with a common nature and, at the same time, that one facet of human nature is a sort of inherent fallibility. Burke writes, "He that had made them thus fallible, rewarded them for having in their conduct attended to their nature."[40] Furthermore, for Burke, this inclination to root basic concepts in religious commitments is not one rational option among several. Instead, "We know . . . man is by his constitution a religious animal; that atheism is against, not only our reason, but our instincts; and that it cannot prevail long."[41] Humans are, for Burke, naturally religious, and to deny that or to live in a way that runs contrary to that fact is to court disaster. In fact, Burke argues that "nothing is more certain, than that our manners, our civilization, and all the good things which are connected with manners, and with civilization, have, in this European world of ours, depended for ages upon two principles; and were indeed the result of both combined; I mean the spirit of a gentleman, and the spirit of religion."[42] The "spirit of religion" is one of two indispensable pillars of Western civilization, and given Burke's claim to the universality of religious belief, it might be warranted to surmise that he believes that it is an indispensable pillar of any civilization. At the same time, the "spirit of the gentlemen" seems to be rooted more explicitly in a particular European social milieu than in a universal impulse.

What, then, constitutes the spirit of the gentleman? One feature is education. Formal education was kept alive by the patronage of the nobility and the practices of the clergy, and such learning "paid back what it received to nobility and to priesthood; and paid it with usury, by enlarging their ideas, and by furnishing their minds."[43] What we would call "classical education" today, Burke refers to (favorably) as "Gothic and monkish." Burke credits this education as the cause of "all the improvements in science, in arts, and in literature, which have illuminated and adorned the modern world."[44]

Burke is not, however, simply concerned with the education we commonly associate with formal schooling. There is a more pervasive aspect of education that forms the very soul of the gentleman. This is an education in the affections. It is on this point that Burke is often misunderstood. MacIntyre reads Burke as putting reason and tradition into opposition. In MacIntyre's words, Burke "wanted to counterpoise tradition and reason and tradition and revolution. Not reason, but prejudice; not revolution, but inherited precedent; these are Burke's key oppositions."[45] In *After Virtue*, MacIntyre asserts that Burke contrasted "tradition with reason and the stability of tradition with conflict. Both contrasts obfuscate." In MacIntyre's view, "all reasoning takes place within the context of some traditional mode of thought" and traditions in "good working order" always "embody continuities of conflict." Thus, "when a tradition becomes Burkean, it is always dying or dead."[46] In *Whose Justice? Which Rationality?*, MacIntyre notes in passing that "Burke theorized shoddily" and "was an agent of positive harm."[47] Burke, he continues, "ascribed to traditions in good order, the order as he supposed of following nature, 'wisdom without reflection.' So that no place is left for reflection, rational theorizing as a work of and within tradition."[48] In short, we may summarize MacIntyre's reading of Burke as follows: Burke contrasted tradition and reason, and in so doing placed stability, consensus, prejudice, and prescription on the side of tradition. On the side of reason Burke placed conflict, rational reflection, and revolution.

However, Burke is not opposed to change. He is, to be sure, opposed to revolution and revolutionary change, but he clearly affirms the possibility, and even the necessity, of reasonable, organic change. But what of the accusation that he places reason and tradition in opposition? Burke argues that he and his English contemporaries "still feel within us, and we cherish and cultivate, those inbred sentiments which are the faithful guardians, the active monitors of our duty, the true supporters of all liberal and manly morals." He and his countrymen "preserve the whole of our feelings still native and entire, unsophisticated by pedantry and infidelity." He continues, "We are generally men of untaught feelings; that instead of casting away all our old prejudices, we cherish them to a very considerable degree, and, to take more shame on ourselves, we cherish them because they are our prejudices; and the longer they have lasted, and the more generally they have prevailed, the more we cherish them."[49] These statements, when considered in isolation, seem to indicate that Burke's conception of knowledge pits sentiment and prejudice (inherited from the past) against reason. However, a closer look clearly shows that this is not the case. When considering the faulty social and political views of the Jacobins, he notes that their "barbarous philosophy" is "the offspring of cold hearts [affections] and muddy understanding [reason]."[50] Both the head and the heart, so to speak, play a role in knowing, and either or both can be dulled or mistaken. He notes that "we are afraid to put men to live and trade each on his private stock of reason; because we suspect that this stock in each man is small, and that the individuals would do better to avail themselves of the general bank and capital of nations and ages."[51] In other words, the rational faculties of each individual are rather paltry, and we would do better to supplement our individual reason with the collective wisdom of human experience, which is to say, with the resources afforded by tradition. In this light, reason and tradition are not opposed to one another; instead, they mutually support each other. This point is clearly seen when Burke writes, "Many of our men of speculation, instead of exploding general prejudices, employ their sagacity to discover the latent wisdom which prevails in them. If they find what they seek, (and they seldom fail) they think it more wise to continue the prejudice, with the reason involved, than to cast away the coat of prejudice, and to leave nothing but the naked reason."[52] In this way, "prejudice, with its reason, has a motive to give action to that reason, and an affection which will give it permanence."[53] Thus, for Burke, prejudice (affection) works in conjunction with reason to justify and motivate action. They complement each other, and to ignore one or the other is to distort our conception of knowing and action.

How, then, is affection formed? The affection proper to citizens—Burke calls these public affections—begin in what he calls the "little platoons." As he puts it, "to love the little platoon we belong to in society, is the first principle . . . of public affections."[54] Our loves begin with the small, the local, and the intimate, and extend outward from there. Not surprisingly, then, "we begin our public affections in our families. . . . We pass on to our neighborhoods."[55] In Burke's conception, human loves begin close to home and, once formed, are capable of extending to larger, more distant entities. In fact, the loves cultivated in the little platoons form "the first link in the series by which we proceed towards a love to our country and to mankind."[56] Implicit in this description is the notion that loves are properly ordered when formed in a certain manner and direction: begin close to home, make that the anchor, and move upward from there to eventually encompass one's country and even all of mankind. Duties are born of these loves and are, in fact, inseparable from them. Because we love, we recognize our duties, and we are faithful to those duties because we love. When we grasp that the affections Burke is describing is nothing more than rightly ordered loves, we can see how Burke is participating in a tradition of inquiry that extends back to Augustine, for whom the *ordo amoris* is central.

Burke's little platoons are recipients of a tradition, preservers and de-velopers of that tradition, and, finally, benefactors of future generations, who, in turn, become the recipients of an intact, and often improved, tra-dition. It is in this context that the concept of inheritance becomes an im-portant key to Burke's thought. Burke is critical of those revolutionaries who have learned "to despise all their predecessors."[57] Such despising led to "a great departure from the ancient course."[58] This wholesale rejection of the past represents, for Burke, the height of carelessness mixed with naïveté about the nature of humans and societies. He levels his attack most directly at those who willingly ignore that which they inherited: "You chose to act as if you had never been moulded into civil society, and had everything to begin anew. You began ill, because you began despising everything that belonged to you."[59] In this we see that, for Burke, what we possess in terms of social and political institutions is rooted in inheritance. Thus, to reject the inheritance is to reject the very ideas, forms, customs, practices, and institutions that constitute a people. It is a sort of social and political suicide. And, ironically, such a rejection of the past in the name of a better future is, in fact, a serious threat to the future in whose name the rejection is made, for "people will not look forward to posterity, who never look backward to their ancestors."[60] Thus, if one is truly concerned with securing a good, stable, and just future, one must begin with looking back to one's inheritance—recognize the good latent therein; lovingly improve upon that which has been received; and, in due time, pass that improved inheritance on to the next generation. In this way, "the idea of inheritance furnishes a sure principle of conservation, and a sure principle of transmission; without at all excluding a principle of improvement."[61]

Inheritance implies both benefits and duties. Liberty is one of the chief benefits Burke identifies, but this is not some abstract liberty; rather, these are liberties embodied in such documents as the Magna Carta and the Declaration of Right. These are understood as "an entailed inheritance derived to us from our forefathers, and to be transmitted to our posterity."[62] On the other hand, the revolutionaries are "unmindful of what they have received from their ancestors, or of what is due to their posterity." In ignoring their inheritance, they "cut off the entail . . . [and] commit waste on the inheritance, by destroying at their pleasure the whole fabric of their society" and in so doing "leave to those who come after them, a ruin instead of an habitation." In thus rejecting their inheritance, "the whole chain and continuity of the commonwealth would be broken. No one generation could link with the other. Men would become little better off than flies of a summer."[63]

For Burke, the notion of tradition entails loving reception, care, improvement, and transmission. The future is secured by first loving that which has been inherited from the past. The loving reformer "should approach to the faults of the state as to the wounds of a father, with pious awe and trembling solicitude." Clearly, Burke is not denying the need to improve various facets of the state, but there is a dramatic difference between the loving reformer and the revolutionary. The former will "look with horror on those children of their country who are prompt rashly to hack the aged parent in pieces, and put him into the kettle of the magicians, in hopes that by their poisonous weeds, and wild incantations, they may regenerate the paternal constitution, and renovate their father's life."[64] Such is the disposition of the revolutionary mind, or more generally, of a mind that despises tradition.

The idea of inheritance and a "chain and continuity" with the past serves to extend a person's awareness beyond the immediate present. It pushes the imagination back into the past even as it makes it possible to imagine a better future. In this context, Burke appropriates the language of contract, but he does so in a way that is dramatically different from the social contract thinkers whose influence extended from England to the Continent and beyond to the American colonies. "Society," he writes, "is indeed a contract." However, it is not simply a contract rooted in the consent of autonomous individuals for the preservation of property, the establishment of security, or the expansion of individual liberty. The social contract thinkers framed the social contract in terms of securing certain goods that were tenuous in a state of nature. Burke, on the other hand, rejects the notion of a state of nature as described by thinkers such as Locke and Rousseau. Instead, for Burke, "society [or the state] is not a partner-

ship in things subservient only to the gross animal existence of a temporary and perishable nature. It is a partnership in all science; a partnership
in all art; a partnership in every virtue, and in all perfection." But as soon
as such a lofty and extensive vision for this partnership is articulated, it
becomes clear that "the ends of such a partnership cannot be obtained in
many generations." Thus, it necessarily "becomes a partnership not only
between those who are living, but between those who are living, those who
are dead, and those who are to be born." In this sense, the intergenerational
dynamic of inheritance is embodied in the intergenerational concept of
this metaphysical contract. The contract, of course, extends beyond any
particular contract to ultimately encompass all of humanity: "Each contract of each particular state is but a clause in the great primaeval contract
of eternal society, linking the lower with the higher natures, connecting
the visible and invisible world, according to a fixed compact sanctioned
by the inviolable oath which holds all physical and all moral natures, each
in their appointed place."[65]

Because Burke rejects a pre-social state of nature, and insists that the
natural state of humanity is social and political, the notion that humans,
by virtue of reason and consent, leave the state of nature and form civil society is also rejected. Indeed, Burke conceives of something quite different,
for nature, art, necessity, and reason fall on the same side of the ledger,
while the unnatural, the perverted, and the irrational fall on the other side.
Thus, if we reduce civil society to a mere choice (as do the social contract
thinkers), we are ignoring that civil society is natural and necessary for humans to function as humans. It is to reject reason itself. As Burke puts it,
civil society is "the first and supreme necessity only, a necessity that is not
chosen but chooses. . . . This necessity itself is a part too of that moral and
physical disposition of things to which man must be obedient by consent
or force." Which is to say, one must willingly submit to the necessity
(limits) imposed by nature, or be compelled to do so either by circumstances rooted in nature itself or by those who are acting according to reason. Alternatively, "if that which is only submission to necessity should be
made the object of choice, the law is broken; nature is disobeyed; and the
rebellious are outlawed, cast forth, and exiled, from this world of reason,
and order, and peace, and virtue, and fruitful penitence, into the antago-
nistic world of madness, discord, vice, confusion, and unavailing sorrow."[66]

Given this alternative conception of contract that summarily rejects
the social contract account that has dominated Anglo-American political

thought from Hobbes to Rawls, what are the implications for liberty? In a letter written in November 1789 to a French aristocrat named Charles-Jean-François Depont, Burke lays out his conception of freedom.[67] He admits, at the outset, that such a definition is not simple: "Permit me then to continue our conversation, and to tell you what the freedom is that I love, and that to which I think all men entitled. This is the more necessary, because, of all the loose terms in the world, liberty is the most indefinite." With that caveat, he continues, "It is not solitary, unconnected, individual, selfish liberty, as if every man was to regulate the whole of his conduct by his own will. The liberty I mean is *social* freedom." Burke is not denying the place of individual liberty, but he is arguing that liberty cannot be conceived in simple individualistic terms. Given the great contract in which all humans participate, this notion of social freedom is not surprising, for freedom necessarily comes with duties and limits that are in keeping with the necessity of nature and the social reality of human existence. As such, social freedom "is that state of things in which liberty is secured by the equality of restraint." Putting liberty and restraint together seems odd to liberal sensibilities, but if we keep in mind that Burke loves a "manly, moral, regulated liberty" the connection becomes clear.[68] Liberty must be limited by internal restraint or by external power. An unconstrained liberty is at odds with the nature of things and cannot last for long: "A constitution of things in which the liberty of no one man, and no body of men, and no number of men, can find means to trespass on the liberty of any person, or any description of persons, in the society. This kind of liberty is, indeed, but another name for justice; ascertained by wise laws, and secured by well-constructed institutions." In other words, true liberty is not born in some mythical state of nature. It is realized in the context of just laws and institutions that provide the context and limits for a secure liberty. Thus, "whenever a separation is made between liberty and justice, neither is, in my opinion, safe." Apart from justice, liberty is untenable. Therefore, shorn of its moral context, liberty becomes license, which in turn results in the loss of liberty. Reason and affection must orient the will to "that eternal immutable law, in which will and reason are the same."[69]

How, then, is that immutable moral law known? Through reason constituted by and interacting with the resources inherited from tradition. We build upon the understanding we have received, seek to improve that understanding, and then pass it on to the next generation. It becomes clear, at this point, that for Burke tradition, reason, justice, and liberty go hand

in hand. They form a context within which each can flourish, and to remove any one part jeopardizes the whole. We can attempt to ignore the
resources of tradition—at our peril—but we cannot escape the fact that
human knowing is mediated by tradition. In this sense, the natural and
proper shape (both a descriptive and prescriptive aspect) of human knowing (and human society) is tradition. An account of liberty that does not
include a proper role for tradition is doomed to fail. Liberty without limits
is a mirage.

This analysis puts the American situation in clearer relief. The
American Founding occurred in the early stage of liberalism when
American colonial society was deeply rooted in a milieu of religious beliefs
and cultural traditions that extended back into a nonliberal past.
Tocqueville understood this combination as the reason freedom could
exist without running over its banks into chaos. In terms we have been
using, the American Founding occurred as a first wave liberal project.
With the continued development of liberalism, the first wave was replaced
by liberalism's second wave, which explicitly and categorically rejects the
limits imposed by religious belief or nature or the past. Thus, modern conservatives who argue that returning to the original meaning of the U.S.
Constitution will solve our many problems are misguided. That which
provided the moral and political context for the Constitution has been
dramatically altered. Russell Kirk put the matter in terms of the difference
between written and unwritten constitutions. An unwritten constitution
is the social, moral and political habits, beliefs, and practices that constitute a people.[70] All written constitutions emerge from an unwritten constitution and depend on that unwritten constitution for their sustained
success. When a people's unwritten constitution changes, the written constitution must either change to accommodate the unwritten constitution
or there will exist a fundamental tension between the two. In that conflict,
the unwritten constitution will eventually prevail. In other words, if our
original constitutional system was a project of first wave liberalism, that
system will appear very different in the context of second wave liberalism.
The solution—if there is one—is not a return to the original constitution
unless that includes a prior recovery of the tradition that animated that
document, a tradition that has been largely burned away by the caustic acid
of liberalism.

Those who argue that the United States is a propositional nation also
miss an important fact. The United States was founded by people deeply

formed by the Christian narrative who believed in a moral order that was both intelligible and obligatory. It was in this context that the Founding occurred. Jefferson's grand phrases about the "self-evident" truth that "all men are created equal, that they are endowed by their Creator with certain unalienable Rights, that among these are Life, Liberty, and the pursuit of Happiness" were written into a cultural consensus that simply does not exist today. The propositions expressed in the Declaration of Independence provide an adequate framework of self-understanding only if they are superimposed upon a background of a shared cultural vision. Tocqueville argued that laws are an important part of what gives the United States its identity, but more fundamental than laws are the mores that give shape to the moral world. Tocqueville defines mores as "habits of the heart" and "habits of the mind," or, more compactly, "the whole moral and intellectual state of a people."[71] If the mores of a people change, or, perhaps more to the point, if the mores fragment so that groups holding competing sets of mores occupy the same place and subsist under the same constitution and the same founding propositions, we should expect political chaos. Abstract propositions about the human condition are not adequate to bind a people to each other or to a common good. The idea of a propositional nation only worked when the propositions were not doing the heavy lifting required to form a people into citizens. The propositional nation was a shorthand—or perhaps better, a sleight of hand—that exchanged the thick and necessary cultural consensus necessary to bind a people for glowing abstractions that have proven inadequate once the underlying consensus collapsed.

This loss of a shared cultural consciousness is at least in part driven by the fact that the liberal self has an inadequate conception of past. If the past is seen as something from which we have managed to escape, one will find precious little reason to revisit that clammy dungeon. The result is a loss of shared cultural memories and an accompanying loss of a desire to study the past. In 1930, the Spanish philosopher José Ortega y Gasset noted that "the most 'cultured' people today are suffering from incredible ignorance of history." However, "historical knowledge is a technique of the first order to preserve and continue a civilisation already advanced."[72] An ignorance of history among a population of citizens who ostensibly govern themselves will result in nothing other than, as Ortega y Gasset put it, "the vertical invasion of the barbarians," for a people without knowledge of history is no longer capable of civilization.[73] They become their own barbarian hordes, ill-equipped to either govern themselves or to maintain a free society. In this regard, Nisbet argues that "a sense of the past is far more basic to the maintenance of freedom than hope for the future. . . . Hence the relentless effort by totalitarian governments to destroy memory."[74] However, the liberal self has accomplished with far greater efficiency (and considerably less bloodshed) what the totalitarian regimes of the twentieth century sought. We have come to view our own past with apathy, embarrassment, or even scorn. At best we see the study of history as a diversion or perhaps a place to mine for evidence of past grievances. Instead, a proper view of history sees the study of the past as a vital, living, and authoritative reality that, despite its complexity and shortcomings, exercises claims on us. Apathy, carelessness, and scorn are far more effective destroyers than outright hostility. We have become voluntary amnesiacs.

Augustine

Burke provides us with resources to begin conceptualizing an account of liberty that does not rest on a liberal anthropology. However, it is vital to recognize that Burke himself is working in a tradition that extends back into antiquity. He is not, in other words, creating a tradition; rather, he is appropriating concepts he has inherited and adopting them to his particular situation. In so doing, he is participating in the dynamic process of tradition we have been describing. In this light it is clear that the thinkers we have examined in detail—Oakeshott, MacIntyre, and Polanyi—are in important ways recipients and participants in that same tradition. Polanyi explicitly places himself in the Augustinian tradition and so too does MacIntyre. I want to turn now to Augustine and show that Burke, Oakeshott, MacIntyre, and Polanyi are, despite deviating in important ways, participating in a tradition that is identifiably Augustinian. In so doing, I want to focus on three aspects of Augustine's thought: (1) his insistence on the necessity of belief, (2) his claim that all knowledge is made possible by the divine teacher, and (3) his conception of the *ordo amoris*—the order of love(s).

Augustine's treatise *On the Profit of Believing* (*De utilitate credendi*) is written to a friend, Honoratus, who had been taken in by the Manichean heresy. The Manicheans argued that the Catholics are misguided "and are commanded to have faith before reason," whereas the Manicheans promised to provide relief from the "terror of authority" and "by pure and simple reason, they would lead within to God, and set free from all error those who were willing to be their hearers." The ideal of the Manicheans was not significantly different than the ideal of the modern rationalist: "They urge no one to have faith, without having first discussed and made clear the truth."[75]

This ideal is, according to Augustine, obviously false. There are many things we believe without explicit reasons to justify the belief. Children, for instance, believe what their parents tell them about their parentage (and much else) without demanding a reason prior to the belief. Augustine expresses this claim in a way that would resonate with Polanyi: "We believe, and believe without any doubt, what we confess we cannot know."[76] In his *Confessions*, Augustine admits that much knowledge is based on faith in authority. For instance, historical events are impossible to confirm directly. All we have are the accounts of others. He concludes, "Unless we believed what we were told, we would do nothing at all in this life."[77] He is even more explicit in a dialogue titled *The Teacher*: "What I understand I also believe, but not everything I believe I also understand. Again, everything I understand I know; not everything I believe I know. Hence, I'm not unaware how useful it is to believe even many things I do not know."[78]

Augustine argues that there is a proper order to knowing and there are, as such, preconditions to grasping truth. Of course, we can all admit that the study of difficult subjects requires a teacher: few people learn calculus or Heidegger without the benefit of a teaching authority. Augustine admits this but pushes further: "Every system of teaching, however mean and easy, requires, in order to its being received, a teacher or master."[79] If this is so, the role of authority becomes quickly apparent.

Truth is the proper object of knowledge, yet the mind must be prepared to receive that truth. When people are "moved by authority" their "life and habits" are "cleansed" and "rendered capable of receiving the truth."[80] Thus, belief (or what we might say "trust") in an authority makes possible the next move, which is understanding. It is through submission to the authority of a teacher that we become fit to receive the truth. Belief precedes understanding and makes understanding possible. Of course, there are good authorities and bad ones, so it is imperative to judge their adequacy. A good authority facilitates "a lifting up first of our mind from dwelling on the earth" and this lifting represents "a turning from the love of this world unto the True God. It is this authority alone which moves fools to hasten unto wisdom." It is therefore necessary to submit to good authority, but, one must infer, it is damnable to submit to a bad one. But, for Augustine, there is something even worse than believing a bad authority: "So long as we cannot understand pure (truths), it is indeed wretched to be deceived by authority, but surely more wretched not to be moved."[81] It seems that, for Augustine, because authority is foundational for all knowing, believing a bad authority is not as serious a problem as denying the need for authority in the first place, for the former position at least recognizes the basic structure of knowing, while the latter denies this structure and is, as a consequence, further from the truth. But even though belief in authority is necessary, Augustine is no advocate of a blind leap. Authorities can be evaluated, and he suggests that miracles are one means of validating authority, specifically, the authority of Christ. The second means is what he calls the "multitude of followers." The first seems easier to grasp than the second, for we all know it is possible for a multitude to be dead wrong. However, if we recall Burke's suggestion that the private stock of reason possessed by each person is paltry and therefore we ought to consult the collective wisdom of the past, we can perhaps read Augustine here as making the same basic point.

Faith, then, prepares the way for reason, and the proper object of reason is truth, and "God is Truth . . . no one is by any means wise, unless his mind come into contact with the Truth."[82] But faith, itself, is a gift from God. As he puts it in the opening of his *Confessions*, "My faith, Lord, calls upon you. It is your gift to me. You breathed it into me by the humanity of your Son, by the ministry of your preacher."[83] "Your preacher" likely refers to Ambrose, who was instrumental in Augustine's conversion. However, it is also plausibly an allusion to Augustine's dialogue *The Teacher*. Here Augustine argues that all knowing is made possible by illumination, and the agent of illumination is Christ. This represents a clear development of the solution to the paradox of knowledge Plato lays out in *Meno*, and it is an obvious refutation of the position carved out by Descartes centuries later. Plato, of course, ostensibly demonstrated that all knowing is recollection when he has Socrates lead a slave boy through a proof of the Pythagorean Theorem and argues that the boy clearly understood the theorem but only needed to be reminded of what he knew. Augustine attempts to ground his solution in Christian theology rather than in a doctrine of the preexistence of souls. When we come to know a truth, our minds are illuminated, and "therefore, when I'm stating truths, I don't even teach the person who is looking upon these truths. He's taught not by my words but by the things themselves made manifest within when God discloses them."[84] If this is true, then "we should not call anyone on earth our teacher, since *there is one in heaven Who is the Teacher of all*."[85] Thus, it is "He alone who teaches us whether what is said is true."[86] God, it turns out, is both the proper object of knowledge, the giver of the faith that makes understanding possible, and the One by whom all things are known. He is truly the alpha and omega of the knowing process, the initiator and the goal and also that which provides light along the way.

If God is the giver of faith, He is also the giver of love, that greatest of the theological virtues. And it would be no exaggeration to suggest that love is at the center of Augustine's thought. Indeed, Augustine's personal longing for love frames his search for truth, which culminates in his dramatic conversion. As a young man, "the single desire that dominated my search for delight was simply to love and to be loved."[87] Yet, the search was unsatisfying until he found love in God. As he so famously puts it, "you have made us for yourself, and our heart is restless until it rests in you."[88] In retrospect Augustine realizes that his vain search for love was in reality a search for God, who is the only one able to satisfy the deepest longings of the soul. The problem was that he loved the creation rather than the creator, and therefore his will was directed downward rather than up toward the highest things.[89] This is not to suggest that the lower things are not proper objects of love or that the higher cancels out the lower. The problem emerges when in preference to "those things which are at the bottom end of the scale of good, we abandon the higher and supreme goods, that is you, Lord God, and your truth and your law."[90]

All things that exist are good by virtue of their very existence. God created and sustains physical bodies just as He created and sustains souls. Therefore, *everything* that exists is a proper object of love. However, all objects of love are only properly loved if they remain situated in the divine order. The good in everything is from God. If we, instead, love the created thing at the exclusion of Him who made the thing good by giving it being, "it will justly become bitter, for all that comes from him is unjustly loved if he has been abandoned."[91] Furthermore, there are "gradations according to the order of nature."[92] Thus, the living is above the nonliving, the sentient above the nonsentient, the rational above the nonrational, and the immortal above the mortal.[93] Each is a proper object of love so long as the loves are arranged ordinately beneath an ultimate love for God. This proper order of loves is, according to Augustine, a simple but true definition of virtue, and it was this order of love that is "disturbed" by sin.[94] Sin disrupts the proper ordering of love, and "things which are not in their intended position are restless." Rest is only found when our loves are properly ordered. Furthermore, for Augustine, liberty is "the fit companion of virtue."[95] If virtue is nothing other than a proper ordering of loves and liberty is a proper companion of virtue, it follows that liberty is only possible when loves are well ordered. The alternative is slavery to the disorder and restlessness of malformed loves. As with Burke, liberty and virtue are inseparable. Neither countenances a conception of liberty without moral limits.

Augustine understands that it is love, not reason, that moves us most profoundly. As he puts it, "My weight is my love. Wherever I am carried, my love is carrying me."[96] And again, "The specific gravity of bodies is, as it were, their love, whether they are carried downwards by their weight, or upwards by their levity."[97] In other words, we will arrive where our loves carry us, and if our loves are well ordered, we will be carried to understanding of God and His truth and therein find rest. Alternatively, if our loves are disordered, we will be carried in various directions where our loves are never satisfied and our hearts will remain restless. Ironically, this assent, via love, requires the virtue of humility, for "it is humility which has access to the highest regions."[98] Humility is a proper recognition of one's place in the order of being. When we understand ourselves properly, we will grasp that we are completely dependent on God, not only for our creation but also for our ongoing existence. We are dependent, contingent creatures who have sinned and therefore introduced a disturbance in the order of being. Indeed, Augustine suggests that sin, because it is a turning away of the creature from the creator, resulted in a loss of being so that "his being became more contracted than it was when he clave to Him who supremely is."[99] It is only by grace that we are sustained, by faith that we are led to truth, and by love that we are lifted to God.

It should be clear that Polanyi, MacIntyre, Oakeshott, and Burke are, in important ways, working within the Augustinian tradition of inquiry. Without belaboring the point, here are some salient examples: When Oakeshott speaks of practical knowledge as rooted in connoisseurship, he is suggesting that one's tastes must be ordinately arranged so that the good can be distinguished from the bad. And though taste is not identical with love, the underlying kinship is clear. Polanyi acknowledges his debt to Augustine but is also critical of him in important ways—a conflict which, as MacIntyre points out, is a sign of a healthy tradition. Polanyi accuses Augustine of denying the spiritual usefulness of the natural sciences and as a consequence destroying interest in science for a millennium.[100] Nevertheless, he argues that a return to Augustine is necessary—not in terms of a rejection of science but in a restored recognition that belief necessarily precedes understanding.[101] He again cites the authority of Augustine when he argues for the necessity of a teaching authority.[102] Furthermore, Polanyi argues that "science exists only to the extent to which there lives a passion for its beauty, a beauty believed to be universal and eternal."[103] A passion for beauty is, perhaps, another way of conceiving of love, and a passion for a universal and eternal beauty certainly evokes theological connotations that resonate with Augustine's theologically informed account of knowledge.

Although Burke's terminology is different, the underlying meaning is clearly Augustinian. He speaks of "prejudices" that are inherited and of the inadequacy of reason and hence the need for dependence on the wisdom of tradition, which is another way of naming a teaching authority. When men of reason investigate prejudices, they generally find truth buried within, which is to say that faith precedes understanding. When he speaks of the "heart" and "the whole of our feelings" and the "affections," he is not abandoning understanding in favor of a sort of postmodern subjectivity, nor is he elevating the passions above reason, as did Hume. Rather he is participating in this Augustinian tradition that, in some respects, continues back to Plato. It was, after all, Plato who argued that musical training tutored the affections so that a person could learn to appreciate that which was beautiful and good and to feel "distaste" toward the things that were not. All this, Plato argued, occurred "before he is able to grasp the reason."[104] In other words, rightly ordered affections, proper taste, belief, and a teaching authority all precede understanding.

Burke conceives of liberty—and civilization itself—as a precious inheritance to be cared for with a kind of loving tenderness. Although tradition is not a central part of Augustine's thought (one could argue tradition was so pervasive as to be invisible until it was systematically attacked in the seventeenth century), the concept of inheritance is present. Augustine describes the "true religion" as "what hath been handed down from our blessed forefathers, this is what hath been preserved even unto us."[105] The inheritance has been preserved and received intact, and those who have participated in this multigenerational process indeed deserve the epithet "blessed." Again, the *concept* of tradition per se as well as the *content* of a specific tradition are obvious. This tradition we are tracing offers a clear alternative to liberalism, and, crucially, it does not seem to encounter the same philosophical incoherencies or create the same social pathologies.

Eliot's Four Quartets: *A Poetic Affirmation*

We have traced the lineaments of an alternative to the liberal self back through Burke to Augustine. But if this is, in fact, a living (though neglected) tradition, we should expect to find a remnant, an array of positive artifacts indicating that the tradition is alive. Indeed, if this tradition is true, it should continue to bear on reality itself, illuminating the real in ways that are satisfying, though perhaps not anticipated. Furthermore, we might expect that insights derived from the tradition would not be confined to the philosophical and theological realms but instead pour out into literature, poetry, and the arts. Armed with that intimation, I want to turn to a work of poetry that is both a work of modern innovation and one deeply embedded in the great tradition. It is, in other words, evidence that the author is participating in the dynamic process of tradition and contributing to its development even as he steadfastly stewards that which he has received. It is, furthermore, an example of a writer deeply aware of the fact that he is working within a particular tradition and at the same time reflecting on the nature of tradition itself. Since that is essentially the twofold goal of this entire book, it will be helpful to briefly consider the *Four Quartets* by T. S. Eliot.

The *Four Quartets* represents Eliot at his most mature and most profound. Having shaken the world of poetry with his groundbreaking early poems, including "Prufrock" and *The Waste Land*, Eliot, now converted to Christianity, embarks on an extended reflection on time that ultimately turns on the miracle of Christ's incarnation wherein time and eternity meet and, in the process, time is redeemed from its heretofore endless cycle of repetitions. I want to briefly identify some of the key themes in Eliot's poem that indicate that he is working within the tradition we have been tracing.

The theme of time is introduced in the opening lines, but the juxtaposition is cryptic:

> Time present and time past
> Are both perhaps present in time future,
> And time future contained in time past.

If all time is eternally present
All time is unredeemable.[106]

We have here at the start the relationship between the past, the present, and the future. However, their relationship is a puzzle. Somehow an eternal present (which is how Augustine understands God's relationship with time) is unredeemable. But why does time need redeeming? The opening lines present more of a mystery than a clear direction. But this, it seems, is part of the point. Our attempts to make true statements about the meaning of time and existence are constantly thwarted. We seek to describe reality and are constantly frustrated with the fragile limits of language.

Words strain,
Crack and sometimes break, under the burden,
Under tension, slip, slide, perish,
Decay with imprecision, will not stay in place,
Will not stay still.[107]

Yet we continue,

Trying to learn to use new words, and every attempt
Is a wholly new start, and a different kind of failure . . .[108]

Perhaps, though, the problem is not language itself. Perhaps we can, as Polanyi puts it, know more than we can tell. Perhaps reality is not something that can be neatly reduced to words and propositions. If so, our efforts to articulate reality will always come up short.

And so each venture
Is a new beginning, a raid on the inarticulate
With shabby equipment always deteriorating
In the general mess of imprecision of feeling,
Undisciplined squads of emotion.[109]

Yet, by the final stanza of the final quartet, something has changed. Somehow the words fit. Somehow they stay put.

And every phrase
And sentence that is right (where every word is at home,
Taking its place to support the others. . . .
The complete consort dancing together).[110]

And what is more, that which was unsayable is remembered, and instead of being a source of frustration, there is an air of peace and contentment.

And the end of all our exploring
Will be to arrive where we started
And know the place for the first time.
Through the unknown, remembered gate
When the last of earth left to discover
Is that which was the beginning.[111]

How can something be unknown yet remembered? Meno's paradox lurks in the background. Eliot offers a solution that, in poetic terms, mirrors something of what we saw in both MacIntyre and Polanyi. "East Coker," the second of the quartets, begins and ends with two sentences that rather cryptically suggest a direction. The quartet begins with this line:

In my beginning is my end.[112]

Then after reflecting on various aspects of human life, we conclude with this:

In my end is my beginning.[113]

Perhaps beginnings and ends are not so easily separated. Perhaps a resolution to the puzzle of time is only possible when we grasp how the two are implied in each other.

Ultimately, the resolution to the perplexity of time and the flux and froth of shifting meanings and broken words is found only in love.

Love is itself unmoving,
Only the cause and end of movement . . .[114]

Here we begin to grasp one way Eliot is profoundly in debt to Augustine (and through Augustine to Dante). Love is both the cause of and the telos of movement. Love is that which draws us up toward the highest things. It is love that directs and leads us to that which we seek.

> With the drawing of this Love, and the voice of this Calling . . .[115]

Note that Love, expressed using an uppercase "L," becomes something more than the expression of human affection. Indeed, love transitions from the mundane to the transcendent in a steady expansion and elevation. We begin with what we know.

> Thus, love of a country
> Begins as attachment to our own field of action . . .[116]

Here Eliot strikes a distinctly Burkean note that evokes the love that begins in the "little platoons" and extends upward and outward. This love draws us out of ourselves and, it turns out, this love is not simply a subjective expression but that which is both cause and end. It draws us to itself. Or, perhaps more properly, to Himself. For Love becomes the agent of our transformation—the agent by which time is redeemed and, in the process, the agent by which we are redeemed. But this process is not without pain, for the image of fire permeates the quartets, and Christian theology sees fire in two aspects: destroyer and purifier.

> The only hope, or else despair
> Lies in the choice of pyre or pyre—
> To be redeemed from fire by fire.[117]

However, we are not able to accomplish this on our own. The "wounded surgeon" becomes the agent of redemption, and His name is Love.[118]

> Who then devised the torment? Love.
> Love is the unfamiliar Name
> Behind the hands that wove
> The intolerable shirt of flame
> Which human power cannot remove.
> We only live, only suspire
> Consumed by either fire or fire.[119]

It is Christ whose incarnation represents the "point of intersection of the timeless with time," that makes possible the redemption of time's heretofore meaningless cycles.[120] The Incarnation is the key to the puzzle of time. Yet such an insight is not obvious, and it is surely not easily gained, especially by one who rests content in the sufficiency of temporality. Humility is required.

> The only wisdom we can hope to acquire
> Is the wisdom of humility: humility is endless.[121]

It is Augustine who notes that "it is humility which has access to the highest regions."[122] It is only by going down that one can ascend. It is only by submission to authority that one can become a master.

Frequently making allusion to Dante's *Divine Comedy*, Eliot puts himself (or the narrator)

> in the middle, not only in the middle of the way
> But all the way, in a dark wood . . .[123]

And later the same person encounters

> . . . one walking. . . .
> . . . .
>   some dead master
> Whom I had known, forgotten, half recalled . . .[124]

As Dante encounters Virgil in a dark wood in the middle of his life and submits to his guidance, so Eliot's persona encounters a dead master, who tells him, with an air of both confidence and a hint of sadness, that one cannot simply return to some past time or some way of understanding that was, perhaps, efficacious in another age.

>   Last season's fruit is eaten
> And the fullfed beast shall kick the empty pail.
> For last year's words belong to last year's language
> And next year's words await another voice.[125]

Yet Eliot recognizes a paradox that we, too, must see. For although the past is indeed past, it is also continually present. However, those who would seek to conserve must recognize that

we cannot revive old factions
We cannot restore old policies
Or follow an antique drum.[126]

Nevertheless, this is not the entire story. We cannot shuck the past as a snake sluffs its skin and begin wholly anew, even though modern philosophic prejudices facilitate just that conceit. The mature thinker does not fall for such notions.

It seems as one becomes older,
That the past has another pattern, and ceases to be a mere sequence—
Or even development: the latter a partial fallacy,
Encouraged by superficial notions of evolution,
Which becomes, in the popular mind, a means of disowning the
past.[127]

Superficial notions of evolution. The Whig theory of history. Hegelian dialectic. All foster the idea that the past is superseded by the present, which will in turn be replaced by the next present. This is, according to Eliot, not true, or more precisely, a "partial fallacy." It is partly true and partly false, for any notion of progress or development depends on advancing beyond the past, but the unavoidable and persistent presence of the past in every moment shows the point where the idea of progress stumbles into fallacy.

Instead, the human condition consists in constantly appropriating from the past in order to function in the present.

There is only the fight to recover what has been lost
And found and lost again and again: . . .[128]

But the recovery is never static, for progress is possible, though never guaranteed. But in the same way that ascent requires the decent of humility, so progress requires a return.

And the way up is the way down, the way forward is the way back.[129]

Tradition is the living presence of the past that we can deny or ignore but never fully shake off. It is the union of the living and the dead in a great cosmic dance where past, present, and the future meet in agreement, not opposition.

> At the still point of the turning world. Neither flesh nor fleshless;
> Neither from nor towards; at the still point, there the dance is,
> But neither arrest nor movement. And do not call it fixity,
> Where past and future are gathered. Neither movement from nor
>   towards,
> Neither ascent nor decline. Except for the point, the still point,
> There would be no dance, and there is only the dance.[130]

Furthermore, it is this union that facilitates knowledge of the highest things.

> And what the dead had no speech for, when living,
> They can tell you, being dead: the communication
> Of the dead is tongued with fire beyond the language of the living.[131]

We learn from the dead, for they are both dead and not dead. The past is never lost, though it may be forgotten. But that which is learned from the dead may be beyond the limits of language. It is fire that cannot be reduced to "the language of the living." It is that which purifies or destroys. There are no other alternatives, for time and eternity become one, and we are, whether we like it or not, part of the dance.

> The moment of the rose and the moment of the yew-tree
> Are of equal duration.[132]

In the end, the apparent tension between past and present dissolves. We see "an easy commerce of the old and the new."[133] The tension of time is subsumed in the dance of eternity.

> And all shall be well and
> All manner of thing shall be well
> When the tongues of flame are in-folded
> Into the crowned knot of fire
> And the fire and the rose of one.[134]

Past and present are unavoidably joined, and the present is only under-standable in light of that which has gone before. The structure of our lives and the means of our knowing is inextricably tied to the dynamic process of tradition.

The Deformation of Christianity

This tradition that we traced back to Augustine in various ways acknowl-edges the indispensable and salutary role played by tradition. Furthermore, as the Augustinian roots of this tradition suggest, perhaps theology is simply unavoidable. What, then, of liberalism? What, then, of liberalism's two primary contemporary expressions: cosmopolitanism and identity politics? How are these to be understood in light of the tradition we are tracking? It is my contention that we cannot adequately grasp the mean-ing of these movements apart from Christian categories. They represent, or so I will argue, partial and often badly deformed articulations of Chris-tian themes. Why? Despite various attempts at eliminating the public in-fluence of the Christian tradition, the residue of Christianity is not so easily effaced. In other words, it is no easy task to repaganize a society once it has had a deep encounter with Christianity.

Liberalism and its modern corollaries—cosmopolitanism and identity politics—are rooted in impulses that seek to replace Christianity. How-ever, they are compelling because they traffic in Christian themes and symbols. First, though, let us go back. It is Nietzsche who reminds us that there is no modern liberal democracy apart from Christianity. As he puts it, "The democratic movement is the heir of the Christian movement."[135] What, specifically, is the connection? Equality, the idea of which has deeply embedded itself "into the tissue of modernity."[136] Tocqueville agrees and argues that the single most important idea animating the modern world is equality, which is the offspring of Christianity.[137] Liber-alism, it seems, is unimaginable apart from Christianity.

In this light, we should not be surprised if we hear the echo of Chris-tianity in modern political ideologies. Yet, these biblical themes have been stripped of their spirit, and have come to serve human rather than divine ends. First, the theme of liberation finds its roots in the Exodus of Israel where God delivers the Hebrew children from the oppression of slavery in Egypt. Slavery represents an unjust limit on freedom. Yet, when the no-tion of justice is separated from its divine source, liberation from all limits becomes the ideal. Any limit is seen as oppression. And oppression, as we all know, is undesirable and must be removed. Liberalism represents the impulse of the Exodus bereft of God, and in such a context the promised land is illusory.

Cosmopolitanism represents, on one level, a replaying of the Tower of Babel story wherein humans long for unity and seek to create it on their own apart from God. It also traffics, perhaps more specifically, in an eschatological longing for the peace and unity found in the kingdom of God at the end of days. But again, the concepts have been immanentized. Where the kingdom of God is properly understood to be deferred to the *parousia*, and therefore believers wait in hopeful expectation, an immanentized version depends on our active efforts to bring it about in cooperation with the "logic of history," which is a secularized version of divine providence. This explains how the cosmopolitans can talk about the "inevitability" of globalization (which is an economic and political theory often covering up a theological aspiration) and at the same time work diligently for that end and see any who resist as both irrational and working against "history," which is a heresy against the faith in "progress."

Identity politics is rooted in a profound intuition about the human condition that Nietzsche understood better than most. As he put it, "Every sufferer instinctively seeks a cause for his suffering; more exactly, an agent; still more specifically, a guilty agent who is susceptible to suffering— in short, some living thing upon which he can, on some pretext or other, vent his affect, actually or in effigy."[138] The categories of debt and guilt are deeply embedded in the human psyche. For the Christian, this is irrevocably tied to the Fall and presages the need for divine grace. But even if we claim that there is no sin that binds us all together and points to our need of "outside" help, the experience of guilt remains along with an urge to punish. Identity politics takes up the idea of guilt and specifies a debtor. Rather than guilt extending to the human race per se, guilt is directed at a particular class (currently some combination of white, male, heterosexual, Christian). A "chosen people," rendered guiltless by historical or appropriated grievance, is justified in punishing the guilty. But there is no Christ and therefore no grace. The punishment does not remove the stain of guilt; therefore, no punishment is sufficient. One side is justified by its status as victim; the other is perpetually guilty and therefore deserving of punishment. The cycle is relentless and the logic unassailable.

However, the identity politics that has grown out of the Left is fostering a mirror image of itself on the Right. It is not surprising that some young white males would eventually react to the hopeless situation of being forever stained by guilt. The response is seen in the rise of white nationalism and neo-Nazism. But this is where the narrative diverts from Christian categories and plunges directly to the end Nietzsche envisioned. The language of blood and soil is not Christian. It represents a return to a pre-Christian pagan understanding of membership. It denies the legitimacy of guilt and therefore of mercy or justice. It does not look for grace. Without apology or qualification it embraces the will to power. These two versions of identity politics will feed off of each other as each seems to legitimate the existence of the other. As leftist identity politics focusing on race and gender continues to insist on punishing the guilty and, among other things, seeks to erase the past by destroying monuments that recall a complex and compromised history, the identity politics of the Right will find more sympathizers and adherents as it engages in "active forgetfulness," which accords with Nietzsche's claim that there is "no happiness, no cheerfulness, no hope, no pride, no present, without forgetfulness."[139] The Left will justify violence in response, and its armed wing, Antifa, is already mobilized.

What we see in all this is that modern political movements are motivated by something deeper than politics. Furthermore, what we are witnessing today is the cessation of democratic politics—which depends on debate, compromise, and respect—and the rise of naked power that is expressed as self-righteousness. We have the vestiges of Christian categories but without Christ. We have, as a consequence, the absence of grace and instead a works-based salvation—a sort of neo-Pelagianism—that must be achieved in time rather than realized in eternity. We must, it turns out, save ourselves. This theologically malnourished self-understanding was clearly on display in the election of 2008. Candidate Obama preached to adoring crowds, "We are the ones we've been waiting for." What is that other than the outlines of a works-based soteriology that puts ourselves in the messianic role? But temporal salvation is a dangerous business, for we moderns tend to be characterized by nothing so much as our impatience. We want salvation and we want it now. Or to put the matter in terms of a common chant of the social justice warriors: "What do we want? Justice! When do we want it? Now!" Of course, justice is a good thing, but as Christians have long understood, the best we can do is approximate justice in our imperfect and bumbling attempts to right wrongs, help the hurting, and repair damaged institutions. However, when politics becomes religious, gaining the reins of power becomes the sole obsession of both parties, for power becomes the only prize worth pursuing. In this age of immantenized religion, the theological virtues are transformed to facilitate and justify the power of the state. Charity (love) becomes state welfare; hope deferred to the Day of the Lord becomes a demand for immediate action by the state; and faith in God is transmuted into a faith in state power to create a just world. Politics, in short, has become religious. Or to put it more provocatively, politics has become too Christian, albeit a badly deformed version of Christianity.

Secularization, then, is not the primary problem we face today. However, there is one sense in which our contemporary politics have become re-paganized, which is not exactly the same as secularized. In the classical, pagan world, politics was seen in ultimate terms. The quest for a perfect constitution was paramount, for it was believed that a perfect constitution would render the best citizens. Augustine relegates politics to a position of secondary importance by introducing the category of eternity. If the exclusive—or even primary—locus of human concerns is the temporal realm, politics will naturally be of utmost import. However, when the earthly city is situated in terms of the City of God, temporal affairs dim in relation to matters of eternity. The importance of politics is reduced but not eliminated, for in this veil of tears, justice still matters, order is necessary, and peace is sought by all. As fidelity to the orthodox Christian faith continues to wane, politics is once again being elevated to paramount importance. However, the fervor, born of a Christian expectation of perfection in eternity, is not so easily discarded. Liberation, equality, concern for others—all rooted in Christian beliefs—are unmoored from the patience that characterizes Christian hope. Eternity is discarded, but the hopeful fervor remains untempered by the category of eternity.

In this age of Christian categories bereft of eternity, two likely options emerge. The first is an anti-Christian reaction that seeks to blame social and political pathologies on the fact that vestiges of Christianity remain. The accusations are familiar. Christians want to impose their values on others; Christians think that some forms of sexuality are approved by God and some are condemned; Christianity is the source of ongoing injustice, restrictions, and inequalities, and these barriers can be demolished with the destruction of Christianity (or, in a more gentle disposition, in the liberalization of Christianity). Christianity becomes the scapegoat par excellence, and this despite the fact that the ideals the liberal champions and accuses Christianity of opposing are historically unimaginable apart from Christianity.[140] Much of Nietzsche's writing exemplifies this anti-Christian sentiment, yet he rarely, and perhaps never, breaks through to a denouement whereby his anti-Christianity resolves into a simple nonreactive post-Christian posture. The second option will likely emerge when (or if) the anti-Christian impulse has exhausted itself. This will result in a post-Christian moment where the Christian church is no longer seen as a serious competitor, a live option, or even an uncomfortable reminder of limits. The longings born of the Christian past will give way to a sort of cultural despondency in which a great ennui will envelope citizens. Without the hope of eternity or the energy to pursue justice in time, the future itself becomes a problem. What will join us together as a people? What will we pursue together if the old ideals and passions have dissipated? When the old myths fail, old dreams die as well. Nietzsche's Last Man must be revitalized by a new animating myth. The *Übermensch* is precisely this alternate myth with which Nietzsche hoped to replace the Christian myth. Today some in the West are embracing the will to power and the language of blood and soil, and this represents an attempt to reenchant the world along neopagan lines. It is the attempt to make the world tolerable, to make living meaningful, in a world from which Christianity has been banished.

There is a deep irony that should not go unnoticed. The cosmopolitans tend to be deeply suspicious of religious belief in general and Christianity in particular. Those in the vanguard of identity politics tend to see Christianity in particular as an ongoing source of oppression that would deny equality to some group in preference to others, thus solidifying historic inequalities and setting up a confrontation between Christianity (at least in its historic and orthodox forms) and those who champion absolutized versions of equality and liberation. However, the ideal of universal equality is historically rooted in Christianity. So too is an aspiration to liberation from oppression. The universalization of concern for others—a concern that extends beyond tribe or proximity—is also impossible to separate from its roots in a Christian past.[141] What, then, becomes of equality, liberation from oppression, and a universalized concern for others if Christianity is removed, destroyed, or subverted? Can those ideals persist and thrive apart from the theological soil that gave them life? Upon what can we justify equality apart from some account of a human nature endowed with essential dignity? There is nothing left but the bald assertion of equality as a function of collective will. But will is not the same as intrinsic right. Will is merely another name for power, and when an adequate grounding for equality and other good ideals is removed, the will to power is all that remains. Thus, the demise of Christianity will likely signal the end of equality and the rise of a new age of power. Even lip service to equality will be swept away in a furious move of "active forgetfulness," and those who today claim power and preference by virtue of their status as victims will feel the full implications of a new world where brute force is the only currency. Thus a post-Christian paganism will enter the scene where the concern for the weak and downtrodden will be replaced by the will to power. The weak, the disenfranchised, the marginal, and the victims: all will be crushed or ignored unless they, too, learn to operate in terms of power bereft of right, which is—double irony—precisely what some are now seeking to do, all while cloaking their power plays in the language of equality, respect, and tolerance.

There is, of course, an alternative.

Theological Anthropology

The incoherencies of liberalism have deformed the very tradition that gave it birth, and they have led to a dead end. If the deformation of the Christian tradition is the cause of the pathologies of liberalism, perhaps a recovery of basic theological insights could assist us as we attempt to frame an alternative to liberalism. I want to briefly touch on three concepts—creation, the Trinity, and realism—that will, in conjunction, provide us with a picture of reality and humanity that is more adequate than the liberal framework.

First, when we speak of creation, our thoughts tend to be drawn back to the beginning where God speaks the world into existence. Over the centuries Christian theologians have spent a great amount of time discussing the supposed dates and sequences of events and whether or not the opening chapters of Genesis should be read literally, figuratively, mythically, or allegorically. This focus has been, in many ways, an unfortunate distraction. By focusing attention on the event of creation at some remote time in the past, we foster the impression that the world is a self-sustaining machine, a sort of Newtonian mechanism that God brought into existence at a particular time and, though He has intervened on occasion, the structure itself is autonomous and self-sufficient. This is an incorrect, or at least an incomplete, view of creation. Rather than center our reflections on the Genesis account, we would do better to begin with the paean to the *logos* in the Gospel according to John and the great Christological hymn in St. Paul's letter to the Colossians. St. John writes, "In the beginning was the Word [*logos*], and the Word was with God, and the Word was God. The same was in the beginning with God. All things were made by him; and without him was not any thing made that was made. In him was life; and the [that] life was the light of men."[142] Christ is the *logos*, "the word" or, as it can be translated, "the rational principle." He is not only with God, He is God. The two are, in fact, one. (As Christian theology becomes clearer, three come to be seen as one.) Nonetheless, it is through the *logos* that all things were made. He is the agent of creation, which suggests that the world is infused with a kind of rational order, which incidentally provides a basis for investigation into the natural order. The *logos* is the source of life, and the life of Christ is that which makes the world intelligible (gives light). Knowing is dependent upon light, and light, which is inseparable from the life of Christ, is a gift from the One who created all things. It is not hard to see here the silhouette of Augustine's doctrine of illumination wherein Christ is the teacher of all that is known.

St. Paul writes of Christ that "he is before all things, and by him all things consist."[143] Christ precedes, both temporally and ontologically, all that is not God, and what is more, all things "consist" in Him, which is to say, all things depend on Christ at every moment for their being. If He withheld His sustaining power from the creation even for a moment, all things would cease to be. As Augustine puts it, "He did not create and then depart; the things derived from him have their being in him."[144] In this light, we can see that creation is not a one-off event that happened at some point in the distant past but rather creation is happening continually as Christ's will and power sustains all according to His good pleasure. From this perspective it is readily seen how the idea of a mechanistic creation dovetails with the idea of an autonomous self, and how focusing on the singular event of creation helps foster the former and make plausible the latter. However, when we view creation Christologically, both temptations are deflected. The creation is not ontologically self-sustaining, and neither is the self autonomous. Instead, the creation in general and humans specifically are essentially, necessarily, and perpetually contingent.

Indeed, we owe every aspect and every moment of our being to Christ through whom all things were made and by whom all things consist. There is no existence apart from that ongoing ontological sustenance.

When we see Christ and creation in these terms, the consequences ripple outward in suggestive ways. The implications for stewardship are immense. If Christ is understood as holding the creation together in an ongoing act of loving care, He is practicing an ongoing stewardship of creation without which the creation itself could not exist. As imitators of Christ, humans should work as stewards of that which we have been given. This, of course, includes the natural world, but our discussion of tradition as an inheritance should make it clear how tradition and stewardship are inseparable. We steward that which we receive as an act of faithful imitation of our Lord. Our ongoing acts of loving care are the means by which the inheritance is preserved, improved, and transmitted. Culture and stewardship go hand in hand, and when we neglect the responsibility that naturally comes with the gift of culture, when we neglect to steward that which we have received, the gift begins to atrophy. It takes only one generation of careless disregard to derail the delicate process of reception, care, and transmission by which any culture is sustained.

Second, the autonomous liberal self is an assertion that tacitly challenges Trinitarian theology. According to orthodox Christianity, God exists eternally as three persons. There was no point in eternity where God consisted of one person and, through some act of self-division, two more persons were created. God in His eternality consists of a plurality and a unity: one God, three persons. God is eternal, self-sustaining, and non-contingent. Yet, in His tri-unity, God exists as a community—not as a community of independent gods, but rather as a community of persons within a unified Godhead. Thus, at the very center of reality is not an autonomous self but a divine communion characterized by loving mutuality and self-giving.

This triune God created all that exists as an act of gratuitousness. In His divine independence, He did not need a creation, yet in His divine will and creative joy He called all things into existence. In the creation account in Genesis, God saves the creation of humans until the last, as if this moment represents the crescendo to the divine symphony. And in this specific act of creation, God imparts His own image.[145] If humans are created in the image of God, and if God is in His very essence a divine communion, then it seems to follow that humans, by nature, are not simply autonomous beings. Like God, we are essentially communal beings. Unlike God, we do not in ourselves constitute a community. Rather, we find ourselves naturally and necessarily embedded in relationships from the very start. We are members before we are individuals. Which is to say, we are members of a family, a community, a parish, a neighborhood before we can even begin to conceive of ourselves as individuals. The act of individuation always occurs in the context of memberships that are given and exist before we possess the ability to encounter the world rationally or to even imagine that we are autonomous selves.

We are built for community. We are built to love. We are equipped with the capacity to creatively engage the world in acts of love by which we bring out the latent potentialities of a world created to complement our natural desires and ends. To be human is to be a member of natural communities into which we are born. We can, of course, choose to abandon these. Yet to abandon them, we first must exist in them; thus, membership precedes rejection and is therefore more fundamental. We are, in other words, essentially creatures of community. Attempts to imagine or create a condition of autonomy is to do violence to the order of reality to which we must submit if we are to flourish. The liberal self is, in short, an affront to reality. However, contrary to the aspiration of the liberal self, we can never fully extricate ourselves from memberships that reflect the divine order, and to attempt such an extrication is to rend the lineaments of reality.

The doctrine of the Trinity not only insulates against the idea of the autonomous self, it also deflects an account of society in which the person is subsumed by the larger community. The Trinity maintains individual personality in the context of divine community. Both are essential, and theories of human nature or human communities that do violence to either the essential reality of the person or of the community are contrary to the divine nature and therefore run at odds to the very structure of reality. Both individualism and communism are heresies.

Finally, at the heart of the liberal project lies a nominalist conception of reality and specifically a nominalist conception of the human person. Of course, nominalism is not new. Most thinkers trace it back to William of Ockham, the fourteenth-century Franciscan, who argued that universals are impositions of the mind rather than actual realities. All that is outside the mind is mere particularity. The consequences of this shift went far beyond what Ockham could have imagined or desired. If there are no universals, there are no universal natures. Universal terms are not pointing to real existents but are merely categories of mind. This being the case, language is merely a means by which humans impose their will on the vast particularity of reality. For the nominalist, there is no "human nature" in which all humans participate. There is no teleological structure of reality that orders, guides, and limits human affairs. Will rather than nature becomes the primary feature of human existence, and choice becomes the locus of our humanness. Furthermore, if there is no human nature, then there are no choices that are by nature better than other choices. The idea of natural law becomes incoherent in the nominalist framework, for natural law presupposes the existence of a normative human nature that is ordered to certain goods that are proper to human beings, who, by virtue of their humanness, participate in that nature.

Hobbes, by some accounts the founder of liberalism, understood quite well the implications of this conception of reality. He is unambiguous in his affirmation of the nominalist position: "There being nothing in the world universal but names; for the things named are every one of them individual and singular."[146] If all things are individual and singular, if there is no universal human nature, then our understanding of morality has to be retooled. Hobbes makes moral claims merely the subjective preferences of individuals. People call "good" those things they desire, and they call "evil" those things they hate. The words "good" and "evil" are merely what individuals determine based on desire, for there is nothing good or evil per se. Nor is there "any common rule of good and evil, to be taken from the nature of the objects themselves."[147] Thus, in the state of nature, there is no right or wrong, no just and unjust, for nature does not consist of universals that would bind all humans together into a common moral world. In this state of nature, "the notions of right and wrong, justice and injustice have there no place. Where there is no common power, there is no law: where no law, no justice."[148] Law only comes into being in the wake of a contract whereby power is granted to an individual or body tasked with making law.[149]

The implications of nominalism bear on such topics as the relation of faith and reason, divine voluntarism, and other issues, but our concern here is limited to how nominalism plays out in our understanding of the human person and how that disposition complements and even helps drive the development of the liberal self. If there is no human nature, persons are radically individuated. They are not intrinsically linked to each other.

Because there is no normative nature by which our desires and decisions can be guided, the unencumbered will becomes not only the ideal but also the de facto reality. There are no intrinsic limits on the individual will. External laws, of course, may limit what choices a person makes, but this is merely an exercise in power, and, given the absence of any normative nature, this power is arbitrary and thus changeable even if the arbitrary law is ultimately handed down from God Himself.

This account of the human person recalls our earlier discussion of Bacon and Descartes. Descartes sought to reduce all of knowledge to principles that were ultimately rooted in mathematics. He insisted that all knowledge must consist of "clear and distinct" ideas and that once an indubitable first principle is ascertained, the knowing process continues in a deductive fashion from certainty to certainty. This requires that all objects of knowledge are commensurable and equally discrete individuated particles. The notion that there is a hierarchy of reality or that some things are related to each other analogically rather than univocally is rejected by Descartes. We see his nominalist bent in his insistence that the proper condition for knowing is an individual isolated with his own thoughts unhampered by others. Bacon, too, evinces a nominalist disposition when he describes nature in purely adversarial terms. In so doing, he reduces nature to merely physical power to be thwarted or harnessed. This is a dramatic shift from seeing nature as normative and salutary, albeit, for the Christian, blemished by sin.

The alternative to nominalism is some form of realism. We saw that tradition, when conceived as an icon, points beyond itself to a reality that exists independently of the knower yet can only be known via the mediation of particulars. The tradition of classical realism holds that all things are imbued with a nature that they share with other similar things. Humans, too, have a nature, and to flourish is to live in conformity with the limits and ends indicated by that nature. There are, in other words, ends proper to humans, and to approximate those ends is to approximate flourishing. On the other hand, to ignore, deny, or thwart those ends is to undercut one's ability to flourish. For the Christian theist, these ends make up part of the divine order hierarchically arranged under the Lordship of Christ, who creates and sustains all things. Thus, to deny, reject, or thwart ends proper to human flourishing is to pit oneself against God, the creator. Furthermore, the individualism of nominalism also stands contrary to the doctrine of the Trinity, which affirms a community in the Godhead characterized by a divine nature that is holy. An orthodox understanding of both creation and Trinitarianism challenges the nominalist conception of the self.

Practical Implications

When we come to see that we inhabit a cosmos imbued with limits, that we are built for membership in community, that we possess human natures entailing certain normative ends, and that we necessarily inhabit traditions that shape our self-understanding and our view of the world, practical alternatives to the various pathologies of the liberal self come into focus. Our relationship with the past will be transformed. Our interest in history will come alive, for we will recognize that the past is a trove of knowledge bequeathed to us if we will but receive it. T. S. Eliot puts it this way: "Some one said: 'The dead writers are remote from us because we *know* so much more than they did.' Precisely, and they are that which we know."[150] We will come to recognize that through the study of the past we can better understand our particular role and how that fits into the larger narratives of which we are a part. Rather than being apathetic to the past, we will come to see ourselves as active participants in an ongoing drama to which we can contribute. Simultaneously, we will come to see the future in light of the past rather than as an abstraction lacking context, continuity, or any meaning other than the desires we impose upon it.

In this light we can see how both cosmopolitanism and identity politics misuse history, each in a particular way. The cosmopolitan sees history as a story of progress toward liberation and unity. As such, the past is merely a stepping stone to the present, which represents the high point of history. At best, the past is a necessary means to the ends we seek. At worst, it is an embarrassment that is best ignored or forgotten. Identity politics sees history as a source of grievances—a constantly festering wound—that must be mined for instances of injustice that will, in turn, be credited to some convenient scapegoat who will be made to suffer punishment for the wrongdoing. The temptation in this case is to simplify history into a singular narrative of oppression, for to encounter the past in all its complexity would be to cloud the self-assured confidence required to mete out punishment upon the guilty.

Alternatively, when we come to see ourselves as necessarily part of a community and a participant in an ongoing narrative, when we are no longer blinkered by the conceit of autonomy imposed by the liberal self, we can see history for what it is: a complex, challenging, and frequently compromised accounting of fellow humans who have, like us, attempted to make their way in a world that often presents us with conflicting narratives, competing goods, and judgments that are too often clouded by imperfection and partial understanding. In studying history sympathetically, we glean understanding of human nature and its weaknesses along with its strengths. We learn empathy. We learn humility as we recognize aspects of ourselves in the lives we study. In the process, we gain the wisdom without which a good life is impossible.

Once we extricate ourselves from the cave of the liberal self, we can see that marriage is not simply a contractual arrangement between two autonomous individuals that can be nullified when either member decides that the liabilities outweigh the benefits. Instead, as Wendell Berry puts it, "The marriage of two lovers joins them to one another, to forebears, to descendants, to the community, to Heaven and earth. It is the fundamental connection without which nothing holds."[151] Berry strikes an Aristotelian note when he insists that marriage is the fundamental connection that holds the rest of society together. Berry insists that when two people wed, they are saying yes to each other, but also to their respective families that extend back into the mists of the past and forward into the future as people long dead and children yet unborn bear witness to the union of two lovers. Indeed, when two people marry, they, through their offspring, change the course of history. Their fateful decision to say yes to one person (and no to the rest) sets in motion a line of descendants who, in turn, will each make choices that in their own way will alter forever the human story. When seen from this vantage point, marriage is no light and transient union sealed by a contract and broken at a whim. Instead, marriage is a covenant binding the two lovers to each other, but also to their separate pasts now joined and to their shared future anticipated in the affirmation of their vows to each other and realized with the birth of each child.

Parenthood, likewise, appears differently when our perspective changes. Rather than being impediments to my freedom, children come to be seen as gifts from God that transform my life, that alter my self-understanding, and that, in short, induce me to see myself as a responsible caretaker rather than an individual without care. When we grasp that we are fundamentally members, we recognize that parenthood is, itself, a reversal of roles, for once I was the helpless child in need of care, and now I am the one who can provide the same care to another. As a parent I recognize my responsibility to inculcate in my children a sense of what is important, a sense of what is vital to living well, and a practical set of skills that makes it possible to pursue the good life. Rather than a curse or a burden, children can be seen as a means by which I participate in the great narrative of human history, playing my role, first as a child and next as a parent, and in so doing I come fully into the meaning of living responsibly as a member of a family, a community, and of the universal human story.

When political leaders orient their priorities and decisions beyond their immediate interests, their perspective shifts dramatically. They will concern themselves with the long-term good of their communities. Love of a particular place—a love that encompasses both a knowledge of the past and hope for the future—transforms political action into acts of stewardship. Even when ambition serves as a driver of action, an expansive temporal horizon can induce noble behavior with the hope that future generations will recognize and honor that noble behavior. In this sense, ambition can be turned to good account.

It goes without saying that our willingness to put future generations into debt would be diminished by a healthy relationship to the future. If we saw our children and their children (and beyond) as our responsibilities rather than as anonymous (or more likely invisible) abstractions to whom we owe nothing, we would be loath to burden them with the cost of our comfort and diversions. In fact, we would be willing to sacrifice on their behalf. We would be willing to live within our means so we could provide something to our children as a sort of down payment on our hope that they will, in turn, care well for the generations they beget.

Our relationship with the natural world would change dramatically if we saw ourselves as a small (though vital) part of a larger story. We would see ourselves as caretakers rather than exploiters, and we would seek to care for and improve the world in such a way that we would leave it better than we found it. In short, we would see ourselves as stewards rather than mere recipients of a boon. We would recognize our responsibility to tend well the world we have inherited and pass it along to our children as a healthy whole rather than broken and fragmented.

Our role as stewards extends beyond our relationship to the natural world, for as members of a particular civilization we are inheritors and therefore necessarily caretakers. Our task is to handle with care that which we have received, cultivate it as best we can, and transmit it to our children.

Such is the manner in which civilization is preserved and improved. The fact that this cultural stewardship occurs in a process of reception, care, and transmission—that is, in the mode of tradition—is no coincidence. To be a participant in a culture is to be an active participant in the process of tradition. There is no other option.

Cosmopolitanism, Tribalism, or Humane Localism

Liberal cosmopolitanism is derived from a radically different view of the human condition than the one embraced by those who affirm the essential role of tradition. We live in a society that elevates the autonomous individual and celebrates individual choice as the apex of human existence. Despising limits and asserting one's freedom is a theme that pervades our cultural consciousness and manifests itself everywhere, from advertising to film, from education to religion.

One motive of the liberal rejection of tradition is the fear that tradition is a carrier of religious belief, and religious belief has been the source of much injustice (so goes the accusation) throughout human history. As Nussbaum makes clear, her ideal conception of society shuns any reliance on "comprehensive ethical or metaphysical doctrines that could not be endorsed by reasonable citizens holding a wide range of comprehensive doctrines."[152] One is left wondering what room that claim leaves for any comprehensive ethical or metaphysical doctrines at all or what, in Nussbaum's mind, constitutes a reasonable citizen. One might be tempted to argue that Nussbaum's metaphysically austere liberalism amounts to a comprehensive ethical and metaphysical doctrine that many reasonable citizens would summarily reject. On the other hand, the ethical cosmopolitanism of the classical and Christian variety was rooted firmly in a religious view of reality that, either tacitly or explicitly, acknowledged the role of tradition in perpetuating and cultivating its continued existence. At the very least, the classical and Christian view can accommodate the role played by tradition, while Nussbaum and her allies find little positive space for it in their conception of human affairs, unless, of course, by tradition we mean merely trivial lifestyle preferences.

To be sure, there are plenty of examples of religious belief promoting not ethical cosmopolitanism but aggressive tribalism. This fact is not to be ignored, but neither should we ignore the fact that the twentieth century demonstrated with bloody clarity the violent frenzy of an aggressively anti-religious political vision.[153] It seems that neither religion per se nor secularism immediately offers a superior vantage point from which to evaluate cosmopolitanism. On the one hand, religious belief can promote an ethical cosmopolitanism and, further, a common religious belief can serve as the primary impetus for a common culture that extends as far as the religious belief is shared. On the other hand, Nussbaum and other contemporary secular cosmopolitans argue that comprehensive beliefs tend to divide people in a world where a plurality of religious beliefs and convictions (traditions) exists. Their solution, then, is to privatize religious belief (if it can not be eradicated) and attempt to articulate a universalist vision bereft of metaphysically controversial views. Needless to say, in such a scheme, the role of tradition is readily dispensed with, for tradition and religious beliefs are difficult to disentangle, and, besides, who needs the resources (and constraints) of tradition when we have, instead, rational, enlightened individuals?

Both the religious and secular versions of cosmopolitanism seem to offer promise and danger. Ethical cosmopolitanism, political cosmopolitanism, and aggressive tribalism have all been rooted in both religious conviction and secular commitments. The power and scope of the medieval Church suggests at least an aspiration toward political cosmopolitanism, which at times included forced conversions and exile of unbelievers. At the same time, for much of Church history, the political vision has been deferred to the eschatological Day of the Lord at the end of time, and therefore political cosmopolitanism is defanged in the process. On the other hand, today the most enthusiastic supporters of political cosmopolitanism tend to be the secular liberals, who are wary of, as Nussbaum puts it, "comprehensive ethical or metaphysical doctrines." This is not surprising to many Christian thinkers who have noted that when God is removed from the political and moral calculus of a people, the state naturally steps in to assume the universalizing role once occupied by God. It is not hard to see how this universalizing impulse would naturally extend to the world as a whole, thus promoting political cosmopolitanism as an ideal. Secularism, it would seem, is ultimately impossible to maintain, and if the natural religious impulse is not channeled toward God, it will break out in pseudo-religious movements—such as liberalism, cosmopolitanism, identity politics—where the fervor of religious passion is combined with an aggressive and self-righteous political and social vision.[154]

At least some forms of what we have been calling ethical cosmopolitanism affirm that human beings are united by a common nature or by knowledge of common moral truth—mediated by a particular tradition—and as a consequence are obligated to treat all human beings with respect. This form of ethical universalism is fully compatible with the claim that we owe special duties to certain individuals either by virtue of a unique relationship or proximity. According to this rather modest form of cosmopolitanism, we owe all humans respect and ought to affirm the inherent dignity of each person. In this sense, we all participate in a universal tradition (reminiscent of Burke's "great primaeval contract of eternal society"). However, a more expansive form of ethical cosmopolitanism—the form advanced by Nussbaum—asserts that we owe positive duties to all humans regardless of relationship or proximity. This strong version of ethical cosmopolitanism seems to warrant some form of political cosmopolitanism capable of facilitating the expansive ends of this sweeping ethical vision. It is for this reason that at least one writer has argued that cosmopolitanism in this form is at heart an imperialist doctrine.[155] It seeks to dispense with particular traditions in an attempt to unify all under a single liberal conception of the person and the state. The specter of Rousseau clearly haunts this version of cosmopolitanism. Furthermore, it seeks to extend human love beyond its proper dimensions. But to love humanity is to love an abstraction. To put matters in terms of the biblical tradition, God in His infinitude loves the world, and humans ought to imitate Him as is appropriate to finite beings. We do this by loving our neighbor. The parable of the Good Samaritan suggests that neighborliness and proximity are connected, and although our attention and even concern can move out beyond our embodied limits, our capacity (and duty) to love is in some way limited by physical proximity.

If a modest ethical cosmopolitanism is warranted, what of the other forms of cosmopolitanism we have discussed? Both ethical and political cosmopolitanism, on their faces, plausibly avoid the degradations of tribalism with its insularity and easy recourse to violence. However, in practice it is not at all clear that political cosmopolitanism, with its attendant centralization of power, or cultural cosmopolitanism, with its attendant centralization of consciousness, are any less fraught with peril than the blinkered existence of the tribe. Let me suggest four arguments against political and cultural cosmopolitanism, each of which in one way or another bears on tradition.

First, humans have a deep and abiding longing to belong. We quite naturally frame our identities, at least in part, according to our various relationships and associations. I am a son, brother, husband, father, neighbor, citizen. These identities help to me to situate myself in terms of self-understanding and in terms of action, for a life of virtue is unintelligible if it is abstracted away from the concrete relationships that form the contours of my existence. Furthermore, my need to belong is not fully realized only in terms of human relationships. My relationships with cultural artifacts help to frame my understanding of myself and others. A particular language, a particular cuisine, a particular geography, climate, manners, stories, songs, metaphors—in other words a particular set of traditions—these all serve to make me who and how I am. Although I can imagine my abstracted self as a global citizen or as a brother to all humanity, such an extension requires significant effort and is as unlivable as it is unnatural. The limits of my belonging are determined by the limits of my love, and love, not an abstract feeling of good will, has limits. My imagination can reach beyond my love; however, my need to belong is only satisfied when it is coextensive with my capacity to love. Thus, it appears that local political institutions and local cultures—which is to say, a particular set of traditions—are best suited to human needs and desires. Bereft of these kinds of affiliations, people will seek belonging in alternative communal forms: religious cults, the tribalism of identity politics, or even the expansive religion of globalization.

Second, neither political cosmopolitanism nor cultural cosmopolitanism is suited to human scale. Human scale is the idea that there exists a scale that is fitting for human flourishing. Depart from the proper scale, and the potential for flourishing correspondingly diminishes. One feature of scale is simply biological: we are embodied creatures, therefore we occupy a particular space and time. We are limited, placed creatures, and, therefore, our existence is in some respects necessarily local. If this is the case, then politics, economics, education, and other vital elements of society must be centered on the local and the placed. This is not to say that components of these institutions cannot extend beyond the local; however, if the local is subsumed by the national or international, the centrality of the local is lost and the principle of human scale is disregarded.[156] In this light, the principle of subsidiarity clearly emerges as one naturally suited to addressing matters of human scale while at the same time acknowledging the possibility that some institutions must exceed the local if they are to function as they should. As long as flourishing individuals and healthy local communities are understood to justify the existence of institutions that extend beyond them, a proper perspective can be maintained—and this, incidentally, is what Burke argues in the context of the "little platoons." If, however, it ever comes to pass that national and global institutions are thought to be primary and individuals and local communities mere parts or servants of the whole, then the principles of human scale and subsidiarity will have been violated and the damage will manifest itself in deformed alternatives. Thus, whatever else political and cultural cosmopolitanism represent, they are not suited to humans, for they ignore the limits imposed by human scale, which is to say, they ignore the limits of embodied tradition.

Third, political cosmopolitanism is not suited to the complex and dangerous aspect of human nature. In a certain sense, political cosmopolitanism seems altogether desirable if we hold that humans are essentially good and perhaps even perfectible. If power consolidated is nothing to be feared or, at worst, a problem that can be mitigated by proper education, liberal institutions, or sheer optimism, then the putative good that such power can accomplish clearly outweighs the potential danger. Nussbaum and Kant share the same dream: a cosmopolitan world of happiness, peace, and justice where autonomous individuals embrace common ethical norms and universal political institutions promote the peaceful interaction of all. However, the history of political affairs should lead to caution. A world community requires an enforcement arm that encompasses the globe. Without absolutely trustworthy leaders, such a power would represent a threat to freedom like no other. But where are such leaders to be found? Until they are found, we do well to keep power relatively diffuse. If the centralization of political power is a legitimate concern, we would do well to foster political institutions scaled to human needs and human nature. At the same time, cultural cosmopolitanism would clearly facilitate political cosmopolitanism, for cultural variance is one of the main blocks against political unity. Thus, to the extent that political cosmopolitanism is to be avoided, cultural cosmopolitanism should be resisted in favor of the local.

Finally, there is an aesthetic appeal to variety and vibrant difference that cultural cosmopolitanism tends to diminish even as ethical cosmopolitanism equips us with the moral vision to appreciate the vastly different ways other humans shape their particular places. As with liberalism, cultural cosmopolitanism—liberalism's natural counterpart—inevitably leads to a flatness and banality even as its champions celebrate the tolerance they see as integral to it. But tolerance is not the same as universal platitudes about equality or the value-free rhetoric of the enlightened. One only tolerates what one does not approve. In other words, true tolerance is only a possibility in a world of real difference. Real difference helps provide the kind of texture that makes the world the stunningly beautiful place that it is. Even when the beauty is admittedly absent, its absence is noticeable and therefore regrettable. Local traditions, particularities, and personalities are what constitute "local color," and color, after all, is one feature of beauty. Remove the local color and something is lost. Remove the local songs, stories, businesses, cuisine, dialects, and games, and something very good has been lost, and when lost, it is likely gone forever.

We can see this concern expressed by Pieper, who notes that "it is really one of the most pernicious things happening on this planet that a secularizing global civilization, which seems to have its mind set on deserting and betraying definitively the basis of its great tradition, is compelling all remaining cultures to surrender their own *tradita* and so to uproot themselves."[157] However, as Pelikan argues, "an abstract cosmopolitanism [is] no substitute for our real traditions."[158] Our inquiry has shown that this is true on two levels: tradition is a necessary facilitator of knowing, and tradition provides the resources by which individuals and societies can wisely navigate the world. Or to put the matter differently, the great tradition provides a coherent array of resources that can both account for itself and can explain how the liberal project failed. At the same time, local and particular traditions frame our lives in a way that complements—and points toward—the great tradition and paves the way for our embrace of loves that aspire toward the universal without abandoning the particular.

Tradition is, then, an essential and unavoidable aspect of the human condition. It is a necessary condition for rational thought, for language, and for the cultivation of a distinctly human culture. Furthermore, tradition provides an alternative to the liberal cosmopolitan conception of the human person that is built upon an incoherent conception of rationality and fosters a view of the human condition that is at odds with our lived experience. If this is the case, it might be helpful to briefly offer some suggestions on how to practically live in such a way that the particular traditions we inhabit are attended to with the care and respect they deserve.

Place-Making

We are all deeply implicated in the liberal project and thus inhabit what is essentially an empire of individual choice. By practice and consciousness we tend to resist affiliations that demand long-term commitment. Choice is elevated to the highest of values, and freedom is identified with unadulterated choice. To the extent that our lives are constituted by the primacy of choice or the perception thereof, we are liberals, and if our tastes run toward the universal and the eradication of local traditions and practices, then we are cosmopolitans. The communities and traditions we inhabit are understood to be chosen, embraced, and rejected based primarily on an act of individual will. We tend to be consumers of traditions, not inheritors or caretakers or stewards. We view traditions as a smorgasbord of alternatives each potentially tantalizing, each one an option to be accepted or rejected or tried on for a while in a provisional fashion and replaced when it becomes threadbare or when our interests are diverted by something else. We are eclectics and dabblers, and our philosophical anthropology, our lifestyle, and our economy encourage this very outlook.

However, not all cultures are (or have been) confined by this anthropology of liberation. In other words, liberalism, though advertising itself as a traditionless posture that judges the world from a neutral standpoint (a Cartesian residue that hovers over much of the liberal project), is incoherent to the extent that its advocates depend on something they explicitly deny, for rationality itself is embedded in tradition. If our deepest longings are best fulfilled in the context of vibrant local communities—in the context of the little platoons and their respective traditions—we do well to consider how best to foster a more rooted existence. We do well to cultivate the art of place-making, for place-making and tradition are intimately connected. The vast majority of this book has focused on theoretical issues tied up with tradition. Here are some practical suggestions for making places and thereby practically inhabiting the traditions we have inherited.

First, a sense of limits is essential. As I have argued, political limits are an essential means by which power is controlled, and local traditions are a vital means by which humans participate in and perpetuate particular goods. Our embodiment indicates another facet of our limitedness, and so, too, the fact that we exist in time and are therefore subject to the limits of temporality. The reality that we all will die is another limit that must be acknowledged. Culture itself can be understood as a set of limits around which a group of people agree to live. If we understand culture in these terms, those who aspire to eradicate all limits are, in fact, seeking to eradicate culture—and their own humanity.

Second, we must come to orient our lives around long-term commitments and a recognition of natural duties. This runs at odds with a culture that celebrates mobility and encourages citizens to keep their options open. Commitment-free relationships, a rootless nomadism, and the demand for an ever expanding range of options foster habits that undermine the stability of local communities that necessarily depend on long-term affiliations grounded in a commitment to cultivating the traditions inherited from the past. A person committed to assiduously keeping his options open will, in the process of avoiding commitments, miss out on the very best kinds of human goods that are only found in the wake of commitment.

Third, limits and long-term commitments can be better realized if we recover the language and sense of providence, vocation, and stewardship. Providence, of course, implies some form of theism, which includes at the very least a God who is both concerned and in some way involved in human affairs. The belief that God has created a world infused with moral norms necessarily implies that certain actions are prohibited while others are enjoined. There exists, prior to any human will, limits on human action. The theological doctrine of vocation requires the antecedent notion of providence, for vocation is the doctrine of calling whereby God calls each person to a particular set of tasks and, as a consequence, to a particular place. Again, the idea of vocation implies a sort of positive limitation, a natural suitability that is unique to each person. Finally, the idea of stewardship implies that the places and traditions we have inherited are gifts to be wisely tended and lovingly passed on to the next generation. But one can only tend well what one understands and ultimately loves. Understanding and love are limited, for only God can understand the entire world or love it in a way that does not become merely an abstraction. Stewardship, then, is necessarily rooted in local affections and particular commitments; it is rooted in the traditions we inherit and inhabit.

Finally, place-making is an art that requires time and practice, and it is desperately needed if the temptation of both cultural and political cosmopolitanism are to be countered. What are some of the features of place-making? Neighborliness is one facet. As one becomes a good neighbor, one helps to create the small fibers that bind people and places together. Related to neighborliness is friendship, one of the sweetest goods in life and one that is only fully realizable in terms of particularity. One cannot be friends with the world, and Facebook friends are at best a parody of the kind of friendship described by Aristotle, who argued that friends must live in proximity to each other, for only then can they truly know each other and fully appreciate their shared virtues. Place-making also entails education in local traditions, stories, practices, flora and fauna. As one becomes familiar with the particulars of one's place, one is better equipped to act as a steward and therefore better able to pass on to the next generation that which one has inherited and tended.[159]

What I am suggesting represents a third way that avoids the liberal cosmopolitan temptation while at the same time shunning a descent into aggressive tribalism or identity politics. This third alternative, what we might call *humane localism*, appreciates the variety and differences between cultures and the traditions born of those cultures and thus resists the homogenizing impulse that is so strong in modern liberal democracies. It recognizes that the language of the global village represents an abstraction that will never satisfy human longings. Humane localism is characterized by a love for one's particular place, traditions, and the people who inhabit them. Yet at the same time humane localism is not animated by fear or hatred of the other, for by an act of imagination it sees through the inevitable differences and recognizes the common humanity we all share. It recognizes that we are all living souls with needs and longings that bind us together even as the particulars of our own places and traditions remind us of our distinctness. In short, humane localism is rooted in respect, not in homogeneity, in love of one's traditions, not hatred of other traditions, in a recognition that liberty is sustainable only with limits, and in the realization that human flourishing is best realized in the company of friends and neighbors sharing a common place in the world.

Afterword

A Conservatism Worth Conserving, or
Conservatism as Stewardship

Some might be tempted to suggest that what I have described is some version—albeit a strange one—of conservatism. The accusation is warranted, but not simply answered, for the term "conservative" has in recent decades become badly frayed and promiscuously applied. Today in the popular mind "conservative" denotes a fairly standard litany of progrowth, promilitary individualism that claims to despise "Big Government" while championing the limitless upward mobility of the most talented and energetic. The language of tradition and limits do not come naturally to these "conservatives." The ideas they espouse and the policies those ideas spawn are not conservative in any coherent fashion. In fact, they represent a variation of the liberal self that, I have argued, is fundamentally incoherent and unstable.

Our cultural standard-bearers chafe against the notion of limits. We are told that freedom and limits are incompatible, and that freedom is only real if limits are ignored. We are told by advertisers that our limitless appetites are normal and their satisfaction is an indicator of our success. Appetites, however, are boundless, and some might recall that the virtue of self-control has, in earlier times, been deemed an important feature of a well-formed character. Self-control and limitlessness do not readily mix.

We are told that the solution to our economic woes is growth. We need steady and sustained growth in order to ensure that our standard of living continues to improve indefinitely. No one seems interested in asking whether infinite growth is even possible. No one seems inclined to ask whether our standard of living is sufficient or even sustainable. No one is willing to point out that limitless growth is best facilitated by the limitless expansion of the appetites, or that consumerism stands in stark contrast to stewardship.

Americans have always been a restless people. We believe that to be in motion is the key to productivity, and productivity is an indicator of worth. The idea of upward mobility is especially attractive to those who find themselves twice blessed with both talent and opportunity. To improve one's position, to continue to steadily mount the ladder of success, one must relocate or at least be ready to do so. Any commitment to a particular place or a particular community—and to the traditions that constitute those places and communities—must come in a distant second behind the ambition to succeed. The notion that a person might forgo opportunities in order to stay rooted, in order to stay home, smacks of parochialism, shiftlessness, and misplaced priorities. Traditions, in other words, are seen to be part of the problem, for they necessarily imply, and even impose, limits and in so doing impede progress.

Mobility is encouraged by (and in turn helps cultivate) a conception of the human person as primarily an individual and only accidentally a member of a community, a parish, or even a family. On the surface, this conception of the person would seem to carve out the maximal space for individual freedom, for if all of my relationships are purely elective and transient, then I am much freer than if at least some of my relationships are natural, durable, and bring with them obligations. Ironically, this conception of the autonomous individual helps to facilitate the growth of the centralized state. Robert Nisbet, in his classic work *The Quest for Community*, argues that as intermediate institutions eroded under pressure from both the state and changing social patterns, the natural longing for community remained as a constant feature of the human constitution. While virtually all means of satisfying that longing were breaking up, the monolithic state emerged as the one enduring institution. People naturally began looking to the state to fulfill their desire for community, and as a result the state enjoyed a burst of energy that only aided in the centralization of its power. In short, the atomized individual, far from being a means to maximizing freedom, was and is instrumental in the growth and empowerment of the centralized state.[1]

Today the role of the government in the economy is generally accepted as necessary and good, and the lines between Washington, DC, and Wall Street are increasingly blurred. The inevitable outcome is the concentration of both economic and political power.[2] Is anyone still naïve or blind enough to deny the incestuous relationship between Big Business and Big Government? In fact, both helped to create the other and both need each other to exist. Many "conservatives" rail against Big Government, but this is only part of a complex problem. Through regulatory capture, tax "incentives," and the specter of "too big to fail," Big Business continues to exercise power far beyond what is legitimate or safe. To ignore this is to ignore a crucial aspect of the problem of concentration and, incidentally, to prevent an effective reduction in the scope and power of Big Government.

The recent "conservative" penchant for elective foreign wars plays readily into the hand of Big Government, for war has always served to concentrate power. Thus, when lawmakers and presidents champion intervention (which is to say, war) in troubled areas around the world, they are, for all their self-satisfied idealism, participating in a charade: in the name of universal democracy, or the cessation of tyranny, or individual freedom, or universal rights they are working to expand the scope and power of the central government. They are, in other words, pursuing a policy derived from naturally limitless abstractions (which is to say, ideologies) rather than policies rooted in traditions that are necessarily particular, concrete, limited, and often local.

Thus, the ideas of mainstream "conservatives," far from inhibiting the centralization and growth of power, actually facilitate it. Big Government is not going away, because virtually everything politicians do helps promote it. At the same time, the mores that animate many (and perhaps most) Americans—individualism, mobility, a suspicion of limits, and a general hostility to tradition—contribute to the same end.

So what can be done? First, it should be clear that the term "conservative" has been hijacked. What is called conservative today is a far cry from the concepts espoused by earlier conservatives for whom the language of tradition and limits came naturally. But regardless of whether or not the term itself is salvageable in our current cultural and political climate, the family of concepts toward which any legitimate conservatism points remains intact. We need merely to reacquaint ourselves with these concepts that have been so badly neglected.

Conservatism is about concrete realities, not abstract ideals. The cosmopolitan ideal whereby we come to think that being a citizen of the world is preferable to being a citizen of a particular place with its particular little platoons is an error rooted in an abstraction. Individuals too often prefer perfect imagined places to the real, though imperfect, places we inhabit. Yet it is, at least in part, our love for a particular place that makes it lovely. And love for a particular place is only possible when we commit ourselves to living in that place in the company of its people. To live a life of perpetual possibility is to live a life without the reality of love. Because we are embodied creatures, our love is properly conceived in terms of particular places, people, and traditions. To claim to love the whole world but to lack commitment to a particular place is a false and bloodless version of love, for love must be rooted in particular places, people, and traditions, and love only becomes itself in light of these basic and concrete commitments.

Discussion of particular places leads us to consider the issue of human scale. There is a scale suited to human flourishing, and to exceed that scale is to undermine the possibility of human happiness. Yet we live in a world where bigger is often considered better, and things of modest scale are seen as backward, stunted, or inadequate. We admire large buildings, large institutions, large corporations, megachurches, multi-million-dollar budgets, and those who preside over them. However, we too often fail to ask a simple though indispensable question: What is the optimal scale? In lieu of this, we automatically think that if big is good, bigger must be better, and continually expanding must be best. Once we begin asking questions about quality rather than simply thinking in terms of quantity, the problem of thinking merely in terms of quantity becomes painfully obvious. There is, of course, a countervailing trend where the small and modest is preferred. Consider the enthusiasm in some circles for simplifying, downsizing, farmers' markets, local food, and local art. On the one hand, such impulses can represent a sort of boutique rebellion against the prevailing spirit of the age that is little more than one more "lifestyle choice" that appeals to a select group of well-heeled consumers. On the other hand, those same impulses may be rooted in a suspicion that bigger is not necessarily better and that human flourishing turns on human-scale artifacts, institutions, and dispositions. Insofar as the latter is the case, there is good reason to hope.

Talk of human scale highlights the issue of limits. In a world where limits are seen as an affront, a willingness to accept limits seems to represent a retreat from the freedom of unfettered autonomy. Yet most humans throughout history have been aware of and willing to submit to social, natural, and divine limits. We are bound by traditions that provide meaning and context to particular human communities. We are bound by norms rooted in nature that inform us, if we pay attention, to ways that humans can flourish in an uncertain world. We are bound by the commands of God, who is the ultimate source of all good things. All of these limits are made known to us, in one way or another, by virtue of the traditions that we inhabit.

When we properly conceive of place and limits, our understanding of liberty will be constituted in a way that is both sustainable and liberating. Whereas the autonomous individual seeks absolute freedom but unwittingly promotes the growth of the centralized (and ultimately illiberal) state, a person deeply committed to a particular place and willing to acknowledge the many ways humans are limited will, ironically, find that "a moral and regulated" liberty emerges in the wake of these commitments. A liberty worthy of human beings is one where individuals act freely in pursuit of goods that can only be realized in the context of a healthy, human-scaled community. In other words, only when human lives are lived in submission to limits known through tradition and embodied in local communities can a sustainable and rich conception of liberty be secured.

To champion liberty but to denigrate tradition and to shun limits is to undermine the possibility of liberty itself. Only when those claiming to be conservative recommit themselves to traditions embodied in particular places and willingly submit to the limits that are proper to human beings will their pursuit of liberty have a chance of lasting success. Only when those claiming to be conservative become willing caretakers of gifts long cultivated and faithfully transmitted, only when they freely accept the responsibility entailed in stewarding the delicate and hard-won gifts of civilization, will they live up to their name. A conservative is, above all else, a faithful steward.

NOTES

PREFACE

1. https://www.insidehighered.com/news/2017/03/03/middlebury
-students-shout-down-lecture-charles-murray.
2. https://en.wikipedia.org/wiki/Google%27s_Ideological_Echo
_Chamber.
3. https://www.washingtonpost.com/graphics/2017/local/charlottes
ville-timeline/?utm_term=.9ed2e077965d.

INTRODUCTION: Surveying the Landscape and Defining Terms

1. Two recent books, published after the completion of mine, argue along somewhat similar lines. See Patrick J. Deneen, *Why Liberalism Failed* and D. C. Schindler, *Freedom From Reality*.
2. Rawls, *A Theory of Justice*, 12.
3. Rawls, *A Theory of Justice*, 13.
4. Manent, *An Intellectual History of Liberalism*, 32.
5. Locke, *Second Treatise*, §4.
6. Locke, *Second Treatise*, §95.
7. Locke, *Second Treatise*, §§129, 130.
8. Locke, *Second Treatise*, §119.
9. Locke, *Second Treatise*, §97.
10. Locke, *Second Treatise*, §§6, 12.
11. Rousseau, *The Social Contract*, 1.6.
12. Rousseau, *The Social Contract*, 1.6.
13. Rousseau, *The Social Contract*, 1.6.
14. Rousseau, *The Social Contract*, 1.7.

15. Rousseau, *The Social Contract*, 2.3.

16. Rousseau, *The Social Contract*, 4.2.

17. Rousseau, *The Social Contract*, 1.7.

18. Rousseau, *The Social Contract*, 1.9.

19. Rousseau, *The Social Contract*, 2.5.

20. Rousseau, *The Social Contract*, 2.6.

21. Hallowell, *The Moral Foundations of Democracy*, 66. Of course, Hobbes denied the possibility of any notion of justice (higher law) that preceded the contract, so again, at the very inception of liberalism we see the seeds sown (Hobbes, *Leviathan*, 1.13).

22. Jouvenel, *On Power*, 15.

23. Rousseau, *The Social Contract*, 2.3.

24. Rousseau, *The Social Contract*, 4.1.

25. Nisbet, *The Present Age*, 54.

26. Sabine, *A History of Political Theory*, 432.

27. Nisbet, *The Quest for Community*, 205.

28. Sandel, *Democracy's Discontent*, 12.

29. See the SCOTUS decision at http://caselaw.findlaw.com/us-supreme -court/505/833.html.

30. T. S. Eliot understood this characteristic feature embedded in liberalism: "That Liberalism may be a tendency towards something very different from itself, is a possibility in its nature. For it is something which tends to release energy rather than accumulate it, to relax, rather than to fortify. It is a movement not so much defined by its end, as by its starting point; away from, rather than towards, something definite. . . . Liberalism can prepare the way for that which is its own negation" (Eliot, *The Idea of a Christian Society*, 12).

31. Rousseau, *The Social Contract*, 3.1.

32. Cicero, *Republic* 3.33.

33. Marcus Aurelius, *Meditations* 4.4.

34. Kant, *Perpetual Peace*, 107–8.

35. See Habermas, "Kant's Idea of Perpetual Peace, with the Benefit of Two Hundred Years' Hindsight," 130.

36. Habermas, *Between Facts and Norms*, 515.

37. Nussbaum, "Patriotism and Cosmopolitanism," 4.

38. Nussbaum, "Patriotism and Cosmopolitanism," 13.

39. Nussbaum, "Patriotism and Cosmopolitanism," 13.

40. Nussbaum, "Patriotism and Cosmopolitanism," 15.

41. Nussbaum, "Toward a Globally Sensitive Patriotism," 80.

42. Nussbaum, "Toward a Globally Sensitive Patriotism," 79–80.

43. Nussbaum, "Toward a Globally Sensitive Patriotism," 82.

44. Nussbaum, "Toward a Globally Sensitive Patriotism," 83.

45. The "logic of history" is, itself, a confusing notion, for it suggests that history has a particular normative direction. Yet such a determinative direction runs counter to the belief that freedom consists of the infinite expansion of my personal choice. The logic of history is determinate; infinite freedom is not. Both cannot be true.

46. See the text of Obama's speech at https://obamawhitehouse.archives .gov/the-press-office/2016/09/20/address-president-obama-71st-session -united-nations-general-assembly.

47. Giddens, *Runaway World*, 57.

48. Giddens, *Runaway World*, 59.

49. Giddens, *Runaway World*, 62–63.

50. Giddens, *Runaway World*, 64.

51. Giddens, *Runaway World*, 62, 67.

52. Pieper, *Tradition: Concept and Claim*, 9.

53. Pieper, *Tradition: Concept and Claim*, 17.

54. Pieper, *Tradition: Concept and Claim*, 26.

55. Pieper, *Tradition: Concept and Claim*, 47.

56. Pelikan, *The Vindication of Tradition*, 65.

57. Pelikan, *The Vindication of Tradition*, 54.

58. Shils, "Tradition and Liberty," 104–5.

59. Shils, "Tradition and Liberty," 107.

60. Shils, "Tradition and Liberty," 109.

61. Shils, *Tradition*, 14–15.

62. Much of the literature of tradition is written by Catholic theologians and focuses specifically on Roman Catholic theology. A good example of this is Yves Congar, *The Meaning of Tradition*.

63. Tocqueville, *Democracy in America*, 429.

64. Tocqueville, *Democracy in America*, 431.

65. Tocqueville, *Democracy in America*, 431.

CHAPTER 1   The Seventeenth-Century Denigration of Tradition and a
Nineteenth-Century Response

1. Descartes, *Discourse on Method*, 33.

2. Luther, "An Open Letter to the Christian Nobility," 146–47.

3. Bacon, *Novum Organum*, 129.

4. Bacon, *The Great Instauration*, 1.

5. Bacon, *Novum Organum*, 129. Bacon understood himself in these very terms. He prays that God will "vouchsafe through my hands to endow the human family with new mercies." And when his method of investigation is

properly employed he anticipates that "knowledge being now discharged of that venom which the serpent infused into it, and which makes the mind of man to swell, we may not be wise above measure and sobriety, but cultivate truth in charity" (Bacon, *The Great Instauration*, 15).

6. Bacon, *The Great Instauration*, 27, 29.

7. Bacon, *The Great Instauration*, 21.

8. Bacon, *The Great Instauration*, 16.

9. Bacon, *Essays*, 5.

10. Bacon, *Essays*, 6. The Latin phrase is a reference to Luke 2:29, the prayer of Simeon, which reads, "Sovereign Lord, as you have promised, you now dismiss your servant in peace."

11. Bacon, *Novum Organum*, 129.

12. Bacon, *The Great Instauration*, 1. Note that Bacon was Baron of Verulam.

13. Hobbes, too, is motivated by his fear of death. See *Leviathan*, 1.13.

14. Bacon, *The Great Instauration*, 8.

15. Bacon, *Novum Organum*, 44. Bacon is specifically critical of traditional Aristotelian logic, which he believes is only useful for winning arguments rather than asserting human power over nature, which is his goal. See *Novum Organum*, 11–15, 61, 62–63; *The Great Instauration*, 12, 21, 22.

16. Bacon, *Essays*, 63.

17. Bacon, *Essays*, 7.

18. In an essay titled "Of Atheism," Bacon again makes this point: "The causes of atheism are: divisions in religion, if they be many; for any one main division addeth zeal to both sides, but many divisions introduce atheism" (Bacon, *Essays*, 43).

19. Bacon, *Essays*, 45.

20. Bacon, *Novum Organum*, 55.

21. Bacon, *Novum Organum*, 50.

22. Bacon, *The Great Instauration*, 24.

23. Bacon, *The Great Instauration*, 25.

24. Bacon, *Novum Organum*, 31.

25. Bacon, *The Great Instauration*, 2.

26. Bacon, *The Great Instauration*, 7, 11.

27. Bacon, *Novum Organum*, 32.

28. Bacon, *Novum Organum*, 130.

29. Bacon, *The Great Instauration*, 16.

30. Bacon, *The Great Instauration*, 12.

31. Bacon, *Novum Organum*, 18.

32. Bacon, *Novum Organum*, preface.

33. Bacon, *Novum Organum*, 14; cf. *The Great Instauration*, 24.

34. Bacon, *Novum Organum*, 37.

35. Bacon, *Novum Organum*, 129.

36. Bacon, *The Great Instauration*, preface.

37. Bacon, *New Atlantis*, 43.

38. Bacon, *New Atlantis*, 59n171.

39. Bacon, *New Atlantis*, 62.

40. Bacon, *New Atlantis*, 69.

41. Bacon, *New Atlantis*, 70.

42. Bacon, *New Atlantis*, 80.

43. Bacon, *New Atlantis*, 81.

44. Bacon, *New Atlantis*, 81.

45. Bacon, *Essays*, 61.

46. The connection between power and knowledge has been frequently touched upon in subsequent works both philosophical and literary. See, for example, C. S. Lewis, *The Abolition of Man*; Aldous Huxley, *Brave New World*; and George Orwell, *1984*.

47. Descartes writes that "the controversies of the Schools which, insensibly rendering those who practice them more wrangling and obdurate, are perhaps the prime cause of the heresies and dissensions which now afflict the world" ("Letter from the Author," 186).

48. Descartes, *Discourse on Method*, 39.

49. Descartes, *Discourse on Method*, 50.

50. Descartes, *Discourse on Method*, 49.

51. Descartes, *Discourse on Method*, 88.

52. Descartes, "Letter from the Author," 173.

53. Descartes, "Letter from the Author," 186.

54. Descartes, *Discourse on Method*, 35.

55. Descartes, *Discourse on Method*, 84.

56. Descartes, *Discourse on Method*, 44.

57. Descartes, *Meditations*, 95. Of course, for Descartes, science entailed both what we would classify as science and philosophy.

58. Descartes, "Letter from the Author," 187. Hobbes, too, blames the philosophy of the ancients for the deplorable state of philosophy (see *Leviathan*, 1.4–5).

59. See Descartes, *Rules for the Direction of the Mind*, rule #4, p. 16. Cf. "Letter from the Author," 175.

60. Descartes, "Letter from the Author," 179.

61. Descartes, "Letter from the Author," 183. Cf. *Discourse on Method*, 40; *Rules for the Direction of the Mind*, rule #2, p. 11.

62. Descartes, *Rules for the Direction of the Mind*, rule #3, p. 13.

63. The word "knowledge" in the sense in which Descartes uses it is a translation of the Latin *scientia*, which he intends to indicate systematic knowl-

edge based on indubitable foundations (*Rules for the Direction of the Mind*, 10n1). Thus, for Descartes, "all knowledge is certain and evident cognition" (*Rules for the Direction of the Mind*, rule #2, p. 10).

64. Descartes, *Discourse on Method*, 32; cf. 29, 36.

65. Descartes, *Discourse on Method*, 33; cf. 85, 91.

66. Descartes, *Discourse on Method*, 53. Cf. *Meditations*, 96; *Rules for the Direction of the Mind* rule #3, p. 14; *Principles of Philosophy*, 194.

67. Descartes, *Discourse on Method*, 53. Descartes also casts doubt upon "my deceptive memory" (*Meditations*, 102).

68. Descartes, *Meditations*, 95.

69. Descartes, *Meditations*, 102.

70. Descartes, *Principles of Philosophy*, 193.

71. Descartes, *Discourse on Method*, 32; cf. *Principles of Philosophy*, 193.

72. Descartes, *Discourse on Method*, 31.

73. Descartes, *Discourse on Method*, 43; cf. *Rules for the Direction of the Mind*, rule #2, p. 10–13.

74. Gilson and Langan note that "the whole philosophy of Descartes is conditioned by the fact that it was born of the faith of its author in the universal validity of mathematical reasoning" (Gilson and Langan, *Modern Philosophy*, 55).

75. Descartes, *Rules for the Direction of the Mind*, rule #4, p. 16.

76. Descartes, *Discourse on Method*, 41.

77. Descartes, *Discourse on Method*, 53–54.

78. Descartes, *Rules for the Direction of the Mind*, rule #2, p. 12.

79. Descartes, *Discourse on Method*, 42–43.

80. Descartes, *Rules for the Direction of the Mind*, rule #4, p. 19.

81. Descartes, "Letter from the Author," 183.

82. Descartes, *Rules for the Direction of the Mind*, rule #7, p. 25.

83. Descartes, *Rules for the Direction of the Mind*, rule #8, p. 32.

84. Descartes, "Letter from the Author," 182.

85. Descartes, "Letter from the Author," 182.

86. Descartes, *Discourse on Method*, 35.

87. Descartes, *Discourse on Method*, 51–52.

88. Descartes, *Discourse on Method*, 39.

89. Descartes, *Discourse on Method*, 38.

90. Descartes, *Meditations*, 113.

91. Tocqueville, *Democracy in America*, 403, 404.

92. Tocqueville, *Democracy in America*, 11.

93. Tocqueville, *Democracy in America*, 507.

94. Tocqueville, *Democracy in America*, 508.

95. Tocqueville, *Democracy in America*, 508.

96. Tocqueville, *Democracy in America*, 47.

97. Tocqueville, *Democracy in America*, 435.
98. Tocqueville, *Democracy in America*, 673.
99. Tocqueville, *Democracy in America*, 672n1.
100. Tocqueville, *Democracy in America*, 673.
101. Tocqueville, *Democracy in America*, 670.
102. Tocqueville, *Democracy in America*, 439.
103. Tocqueville, *Democracy in America*, 672.
104. Tocqueville, *Democracy in America*, 693.
105. Tocqueville, *Democracy in America*, 703.
106. Tocqueville, *Democracy in America*, 691.
107. Tocqueville, *Democracy in America*, 691–92.
108. There is a serious philosophical tension between the claim that all reality is merely material and the assertion of the autonomy of the will. Materialism seems to imply determinism, and in that sense, freedom is merely an illusion.

CHAPTER 2   Michael Oakeshott and the Epistemic Role
of Tradition

1. Oakeshott, *Rationalism in Politics*, 226.
2. Oakeshott, *Religion, Politics and the Moral Life*, 117.
3. See, for example, Pitkin, "The Roots of Conservatism," 497n5; Greenleaf, *Oakeshott's Philosophical Politics*, 3, 83. Neal Wood recognizes some of the un-Burkean aspects of Oakeshott's thought, namely, his rejection of natural law and his skepticism (see Wood, "A Guide to the Classics: The Skepticism of Professor Oakeshott").
4. Burke, *Reflections on the Revolution in France*, 182.
5. Chesterton remarks, "Tradition may be defined as an extension of the franchise. Tradition means giving votes to the most obscure of all classes, our ancestors. It is the democracy of the dead. Tradition refuses to submit to the small and arrogant oligarchy of those who merely happen to be walking around. All democrats object to men being disqualified by the accident of birth; tradition objects to their being disqualified by the accident of death. Democracy tells us not to neglect a good man's opinion, even if he is our groom; tradition asks us not to neglect a good man's opinion, even if he is our father" (Chesterton, *Orthodoxy*, 47–48).
6. Oakeshott, "On Misunderstanding Human Conduct," 364.
7. See, for example, Peter J. Stanlis, *Edmund Burke and the Natural Law*.
8. Oakeshott, *On Human Conduct*, 41. Cranston believes it is misguided to link Oakeshott with Burke and finds in Oakeshott's thought much that is

Humean. Cranston writes, "This emphasis of Oakeshott's on the 'politics of repair' and on statesmanship as 'choosing the least evil' has prompted some readers to see him as another Edmund Burke. But this is a mistake. Burke, like most conservative political theorists, is a champion of the Christian Order, of Natural Law, of the Right to Property, and so forth. Oakeshott, who carries the scepticism of his philosophy into his politics, has no belief in such metaphysical abstractions. His kindred spirit is not Burke, but David Hume. Like Hume, Oakeshott is conservative as a result of his doubt. Hume relied on tradition, habit and custom precisely because he could see nothing else to rely on: no God, no Natural Law, no Rights. But Hume did not make the mistake of elevating custom and tradition into sacred substitutes for God and Natural Law. His sceptical conservatism was open, undogmatic, and splendidly tolerant" (Cranston, "Michael Oakeshott's Politics," 84). For a detailed discussion of Oakeshott's skepticism, see Botwinick, *Michael Oakeshott's Skepticism*.

Oakeshott, himself, makes the same point in a review of Russell Kirk's *The Conservative Mind*. Oakeshott writes, "But this broad survey of the conservative disposition does not avoid a certain confusion. What I think Mr. Kirk never makes clear is that the conservative disposition in *politics* (that is, in respect of government and the instruments of government) does not need to be buttressed by the kind of speculative beliefs (such as a belief in a Providential Order) which the conservative in general has often favoured. . . . There is indeed no inconstancy in being conservative in politics and 'radical' in everything else. Mr. Kirk is not responsible for this confusion; Burke himself, more than anyone else, impressed it upon modern conservatism. And on account of his speculative moderation and his clear recognition of politics as a specific activity, it would perhaps have been more fortunate if the modern conservative had paid more attention to Hume and less to Burke" (Oakeshott, "Conservative Political Thought," 474). Again, in his essay "On Being Conservative," Oakeshott writes that "in my opinion, there is more to be learnt about [the conservative disposition] from Montaigne, Pascal, Hobbes and Hume than from Burke or Bentham" (*Rationalism in Politics*, 435).

9. Paul Franco, *The Political Philosophy of Michael Oakeshott*, 1–2. Franco's is a good book-length study of Oakeshott, and there are others, including Franco's more recent *Michael Oakeshott: An Introduction*. Whereas Franco emphasizes the continuity in Oakeshott's thought throughout his lengthy career, others attempt to point out the discontinuities. See, for example, Charles Covell, *The Redefinition of Conservatism: Politics and Doctrine*.

10. Collingwood, review of *Experience and Its Modes*, by Michael Oakeshott, 249–50.

11. Oakeshott, *Experience and Its Modes*, 6.

12. Oakeshott, *Experience and Its Modes*, 9.

13. Oakeshott, *Experience and Its Modes*, 69.

14. Oakeshott writes, "It seems that philosophers (and others) have considered reality so important that to conceive of it as situated within experience appeared to offer it an affront. Consequently it has become almost a tradition to begin by postulating a gulf between experience and reality, a gulf which many have declared impassable, but which some have believed themselves to have bridged. Such a point of departure, however, appears to me misconceived, and I must beg to be allowed another from which to consider this subject. Instead of constructing a view of experience on the basis of a conception of reality, I propose to derive my view of the character of reality from what I conceive to be the character of experience. And what I have first to suggest is that reality is experience" (Oakeshott, *Experience and Its Modes*, 49).

15. Oakeshott, *Experience and Its Modes*, 42.

16. Oakeshott, *Experience and Its Modes*, 81.

17. Oakeshott, *Experience and Its Modes*, 49.

18. Oakeshott, *Experience and Its Modes*, 34.

19. Oakeshott, *Experience and Its Modes*, 69.

20. In a later essay, he expands the list to include poetry. See Oakeshott, "Poetry and the Conversation of Mankind," in *Rationalism in Politics*.

21. Oakeshott, *Experience and Its Modes*, 75.

22. Oakeshott, *Experience and Its Modes*, 84.

23. Oakeshott, *Experience and Its Modes*, 74.

24. Oakeshott, *Experience and Its Modes*, 74.

25. Oakeshott, *Experience and Its Modes*, 76. "All abstract worlds of experience are wholly independent of one another. Between them there can be no passage of argument whatever without the grossest fallacy" (Oakeshott, *Experience and Its Modes*, 311).

26. This view has significant implications for the modern dominance of science. Oakeshott realizes this and thrusts hard against so-called scientism: "We have too long been accustomed to the notions that science is a guide to life, that science is the only true guide to life, and that the world of practical experience (and particularly moral and religious ideas) must submit themselves to the criticism of scientific thought, for any other view not to appear false or reactionary or both. But there is little in the history of folly to which one may compare the infatuation which the modern mind has conceived for 'science'" (Oakeshott, *Experience and Its Modes*, 312).

27. Oakeshott, *Experience and Its Modes*, 91.

28. Oakeshott, *Experience and Its Modes*, 93.

29. Oakeshott, *Experience and Its Modes*, 74.

30. Oakeshott, *Experience and Its Modes*, 169–70. Oakeshott does not believe that all knowledge—even all scientific knowledge—is fully communicable, for there is knowledge that can only be acquired through practice.

31. Oakeshott, *Experience and Its Modes*, 172.
32. Oakeshott, *Experience and Its Modes*, 221.
33. Oakeshott, *Experience and Its Modes*, 243.
34. Oakeshott, *Experience and Its Modes*, 296.
35. Oakeshott, *Experience and Its Modes*, 296.
36. Oakeshott, *Experience and Its Modes*, 308–11.
37. Oakeshott, *Rationalism in Politics*, 509.
38. Oakeshott, *Rationalism in Politics*, 513.
39. Oakeshott, *Experience and Its Modes*, 82.
40. Oakeshott, *Experience and Its Modes*, 84–85.
41. Oakeshott, *Experience and Its Modes*, 330.
42. Oakeshott, *Experience and Its Modes*, 354.
43. Oakeshott, *Rationalism in Politics*, 6.
44. Oakeshott, *Rationalism in Politics*, 6.
45. Oakeshott, *Rationalism in Politics*, 8–9.
46. Oakeshott, *Rationalism in Politics*, 10.
47. Oakeshott, *Rationalism in Politics*, 10.
48. Oakeshott, *Rationalism in Politics*, 11.
49. Oakeshott, *Rationalism in Politics*, 12.
50. Oakeshott, *Rationalism in Politics*, 12.
51. Oakeshott, *Rationalism in Politics*, 12.
52. Oakeshott, *Rationalism in Politics*, 16.
53. Oakeshott, *Rationalism in Politics*, 16.
54. Oakeshott, *Rationalism in Politics*, 18.
55. Oakeshott, *Rationalism in Politics*, 16.
56. Oakeshott, *Rationalism in Politics*, 27.
57. Oakeshott, *Rationalism in Politics*, 22.
58. Oakeshott, *Rationalism in Politics*, 39.
59. Oakeshott, *Rationalism in Politics*, 40.
60. Oakeshott, *Rationalism in Politics*, 41.
61. Oakeshott, *Rationalism in Politics*, 23.
62. Oakeshott, *Rationalism in Politics*, 101.
63. Oakeshott, *Rationalism in Politics*, 101–2.
64. Oakeshott, *Rationalism in Politics*, 102.
65. Oakeshott, *Rationalism in Politics*, 103.
66. Oakeshott, *Rationalism in Politics*, 104. As we will see in chapter 4, Polanyi insists on the personal element in all knowledge.
67. Oakeshott, *Rationalism in Politics*, 104.
68. Oakeshott, *Rationalism in Politics*, 104.
69. Oakeshott, *Rationalism in Politics*, 105.
70. Oakeshott, *Rationalism in Politics*, 105.
71. Oakeshott, *Rationalism in Politics*, 106.

72. This subject/object dualism is attacked by Gilbert Ryle, *The Concept of Mind*, chap. 2, and Ryle, "Knowing How and Knowing That," 1–16. Polanyi's epistemology, like Oakeshott's, attempts to rethink the subject/object dichotomy presumed by the rationalist.

73. Oakeshott, *Experience and Its Modes*, 69.

74. Oakeshott, *Rationalism in Politics*, 110.

75. Oakeshott, *Rationalism in Politics*, 110, cf. 108.

76. Oakeshott, *Rationalism in Politics*, 112. Oakeshott frequently employs the example of cooking to illustrate this point. A novice may follow the instructions in a cookbook and produce a decent product, but it is only the expert who employs skills that are not reducible to written instructions who will produce the masterpiece. Cf. Oakeshott, *Rationalism in Politics*, 27, 52. Polanyi, *Personal Knowledge*, chap. 4, also speaks in these terms.

77. Oakeshott, *Rationalism in Politics*, 115–16.

78. Oakeshott, *Rationalism in Politics*, 120.

79. Oakeshott writes, "I must try to show the relevance of this view of things to what may be called the general moral and social conduct of human beings: for I do not admit that scientific activity is, in this respect, a special case" (*Rationalism in Politics*, 124). As we will see in chapter 4, Polanyi, too, uses science as a paradigmatic example representing all knowledge.

80. Oakeshott, *Rationalism in Politics*, 120.

81. Oakeshott, *Rationalism in Politics*, 123.

82. Oakeshott, *Rationalism in Politics*, 227.

83. Oakeshott, *Rationalism in Politics*, 123.

84. Oakeshott, *Rationalism in Politics*, 122.

85. In Polanyi's words, "We can know more than we can tell" (*The Tacit Dimension*, 4).

86. Oakeshott, *Rationalism in Politics*, 127–28.

87. Oakeshott, *Rationalism in Politics*, 127.

88. Oakeshott, *Rationalism in Politics*, 128.

89. Oakeshott, *Rationalism in Politics*, 128–29.

90. Oakeshott, *Rationalism in Politics*, 130.

91. Oakeshott, *Rationalism in Politics*, 68.

92. Oakeshott, *Rationalism in Politics*, 46.

93. Oakeshott, *Rationalism in Politics*, 46.

94. Oakeshott, *Rationalism in Politics*, 46.

95. Oakeshott, *Rationalism in Politics*, 47.

96. Oakeshott, *Rationalism in Politics*, 48.

97. This, of course, is nothing other than the technical knowledge about which we have already heard much.

98. Oakeshott, *Rationalism in Politics*, 51.

99. Oakeshott, *Rationalism in Politics*, 52.

100. Oakeshott, *Rationalism in Politics*, 53.

101. Oakeshott, *Rationalism in Politics*, 54–55.

102. Oakeshott, *Rationalism in Politics*, 55.

103. Oakeshott, *Rationalism in Politics*, 56.

104. Oakeshott, *Rationalism in Politics*, 57.

105. Oakeshott, *Rationalism in Politics*, 60. The allusion to "a boundless and bottomless sea" seems plausibly directed at Descartes, who in his Second Meditation expresses concern about the doubts that have arisen in his mind: "I do not see how I shall be able to resolve them; and, as though I had suddenly fallen into very deep water, I am so taken unawares that I can neither put my feet firmly down on the bottom nor swim to keep myself on the surface" (*Meditations*, 102). Here we can see, expressed in metaphor, Oakeshott's antifoundationalism contrasted with Descartes's foundationalism, for where Oakeshott is content with existence in this bottomless sea, Descartes sought to establish an indubitable foundation. In his first published article (republished as a book) Oakeshott voices the same sentiment regarding morality: "Morality is this endless search for the perfect good; an endless, practical endeavour resulting in momentary personal failures and achievements and in a gradual change of moral ideas and ideals, a change which is perhaps more than mere change, a progress towards a finer sensibility for social life and a deeper knowledge of its necessities. But, nevertheless, a battle with no hope of victory" (*Religion, Politics and the Moral Life*, 44).

106. Oakeshott, *Rationalism in Politics*, 61.

107. Oakeshott, *Rationalism in Politics*, 61; cf. Oakeshott, *Rationalism in Politics*, 227.

108. Oakeshott, *Rationalism in Politics*, 60.

109. Oakeshott, *Rationalism in Politics*, 64.

110. Oakeshott, *Rationalism in Politics*, 66.

111. Oakeshott, *Rationalism in Politics*, 67.

112. Oakeshott, *Rationalism in Politics*, 67.

113. Oakeshott, *Rationalism in Politics*, 68.

114. Oakeshott, *Rationalism in Politics*, 69.

115. Oakeshott, *Rationalism in Politics*, 466.

116. Oakeshott, *Rationalism in Politics*, 467.

117. Oakeshott, *Rationalism in Politics*, 467; italics in the original.

118. Oakeshott, *Rationalism in Politics*, 468.

119. Oakeshott, *Rationalism in Politics*, 468.

120. Oakeshott, *Rationalism in Politics*, 468.

121. Oakeshott, *Rationalism in Politics*, 469.

122. Oakeshott, *Rationalism in Politics*, 471. Oakeshott writes, "There is a freedom and inventiveness at the heart of every traditional way of life, and

deviation may be an expression of that freedom, springing from a sensitiveness to the tradition itself and remaining faithful to the traditional form" (*Rationalism in Politics*, 472).

123. Oakeshott, *Rationalism in Politics*, 471.

124. Oakeshott, *Rationalism in Politics*, 472; italics in the original.

125. Oakeshott, *Rationalism in Politics*, 473.

126. Since both "Rational Conduct" and "Political Education" were written after "The Tower of Babel," we can tentatively conclude that Oakeshott came to believe that rather than being merely an error, purely ideological action is actually an impossibility.

127. Oakeshott, *Rationalism in Politics*, 474.

128. Oakeshott, *Rationalism in Politics*, 475.

129. Oakeshott, *Rationalism in Politics*, 9–10.

130. Oakeshott, *Rationalism in Politics*, 476.

131. Oakeshott, *Rationalism in Politics*, 476.

132. Oakeshott, *Rationalism in Politics*, 466. This account obviously owes much to Aristotle's notion of *phronesis*, "practical knowledge."

133. Himmelfarb misreads Oakeshott at this point when she argues that Oakeshott believes that true morality depends exclusively on the habit of affection and conduct (see Himmelfarb, "The Conservative Imagination," 416).

134. Oakeshott, *Rationalism in Politics*, 477.

135. Oakeshott, *Rationalism in Politics*, 480.

136. Oakeshott, *Rationalism in Politics*, 477–78.

137. Oakeshott, *Rationalism in Politics*, 478.

138. Oakeshott, *Rationalism in Politics*, 478.

139. Oakeshott, *Rationalism in Politics*, 478.

140. Oakeshott, *Rationalism in Politics*, 479.

141. Oakeshott, *Rationalism in Politics*, 481. This state of affairs is, in many respects, similar to that described by Alasdair MacIntyre in the first two chapters of *After Virtue*, in which he uses the striking metaphor of destruction and partial recovery of the fragments of a once whole moral philosophy to explain the "interminable" nature of modern moral conflicts.

142. Oakeshott, *Rationalism in Politics*, 483.

143. Oakeshott, *Rationalism in Politics*, 484.

144. Oakeshott, *Rationalism in Politics*, 484.

145. Oakeshott, *Rationalism in Politics*, 485.

146. Oakeshott, *Rationalism in Politics*, 486.

147. Oakeshott, "On Misunderstanding Human Conduct," 364.

148. Oakeshott, *On Human Conduct*, 55.

149. Oakeshott, *On Human Conduct*, 55–56.

150. Oakeshott, *On Human Conduct*, 56.

151. Oakeshott, *On Human Conduct*, 58.

152. Oakeshott, *On Human Conduct*, 59.

153. Oakeshott, *On Human Conduct*, 63.

154. Oakeshott, *On Human Conduct*, 64.

155. Oakeshott, *On Human Conduct*, 68.

156. See, for example, Blumer, "Politics, Poetry, and Practice," 355–61; Watkins, "Political Tradition and Political Theory," 323–37; Pitkin, "The Roots of Conservatism," 496–525.

157. Although he may not have had this completely worked out when writing "The Tower of Babel," his later essays are quite emphatic and express the point clearly.

158. Oakeshott, *Rationalism in Politics*, 48.

159. Oakeshott, *Rationalism in Politics*, 477.

160. Oakeshott writes that if the "self-consciously conditional theorist . . . is concerned to theorize moral conduct or civil association he must forswear metaphysics" (*On Human Conduct*, 25).

161. Oakeshott, *Rationalism in Politics*, 57.

162. Raphael, "Professor Oakeshott's *Rationalism in Politics*," 213.

163. Oakeshott, *Rationalism in Politics*, 69.

164. Oakeshott, *Rationalism in Politics*, 59.

165. Oakeshott, *Rationalism in Politics*, 67.

166. Oakeshott, "*Rationalism in Politics*: A Reply to Professor Raphael," 91.

167. Raphael, "Professor Oakeshott's *Rationalism in Politics*," 213.

168. Wood, "A Guide to the Classics," 660.

169. Wood, "A Guide to the Classics," 661.

170. Wood, "A Guide to the Classics," 662.

171. Pitkin, "The Roots of Conservatism," 509; Gray, *End Games: Questions in Late Modern Thought*, 88. See also Spitz, "A Rationalist *Malgre Lui*: The Perplexities of Being Michael Oakeshott," 339–40; Himmelfarb, "The Conservative Imagination," 417–20; Mackenzie, "Political Theory and Political Education," 361.

172. Oakeshott, *Rationalism in Politics*, 65.

173. Oakeshott, *Rationalism in Politics*, 60.

174. In chapter 3, we will see that this is an important part of MacIntyre's solution.

175. Oakeshott, *Rationalism in Politics*, 60.

CHAPTER 3   Alasdair MacIntyre's Tradition-Constituted Inquiry

1. MacIntyre, *After Virtue*, 126–27.

2. MacIntyre, *Whose Justice? Whose Rationality?*, 10.

3. MacIntyre, *Dependent Rational Animals*, xi.

4. MacIntyre, "How Can We Learn What *Veritatis Splendor* Has to Teach?," 172.

5. MacIntyre, "Natural Law in Advanced Modernity," 93–94.

6. Gellner, *The Devil in Modern Philosophy*, 193.

7. MacIntyre is generally committed to this broad tradition, but it appears clear that the MacIntyre of *After Virtue* is primarily an Aristotelian, while in subsequent works Thomas Aquinas becomes increasingly prominent.

8. Hittinger, *A Critique of the New Natural Law Theory*, 1.

9. Anscombe, "Modern Moral Philosophy," 1.

10. See Kuhn, *The Structure of Scientific Revolution*.

11. These examples are found in *After Virtue*, 6–7.

12. More that twenty years before *After Virtue* was published, MacIntyre expressed concern about the moral "miasma" in Western society: "I do not doubt that in this country [Great Britain] there is widespread agreement in condemning murder and theft, just as there is widespread disagreement on capital punishment, divorce and nuclear weapons. What I am equally certain about is that these clear agreements take place against a background of a larger confusion in our moral thinking. Few of us are able to say to what criteria we ought to appeal in making up our minds; the commonest moral sentiment in public houses and Senior Common Rooms alike is a vague goodwill. Where classical nonconformity found clearly formulated principles in its Bible, where Bentham and James Mill had the test of Utility, we have a miasma of inherited muddle" ("The Irrelevance of the Church of England," 1054).

13. MacIntyre, *After Virtue*, 11–12.

14. MacIntyre, *After Virtue*, 19.

15. MacIntyre, *After Virtue*, 21.

16. MacIntyre, *After Virtue*, 49–51.

17. See Hume, *A Treatise of Human Nature*, 3.1.1.

18. MacIntyre, *After Virtue*, 60.

19. MacIntyre, *After Virtue*, 60.

20. MacIntyre, *After Virtue*, 69. MacIntyre finds the notion of "inalienable human rights" fraught with "overwhelming objections" (251); elsewhere he calls them "pseudo-concepts"(258). In particular MacIntyre focuses on the rights theory of Alan Gewirth, who most fully makes his case in *Human Rights: Essays on Justification and Application* and *Reason and Morality*. Gewirth responds directly to MacIntyre's criticism in Gewirth, "Rights and Virtues," 739–62.

21. MacIntyre, *After Virtue*, 62–64.

22. MacIntyre, *After Virtue*, 68.

23. MacIntyre, *After Virtue*, chap. 9.

24. MacIntyre, *After Virtue*, 169–70.

25. For a sustained argument in justification of a teleological approach to inquiry, see MacIntyre, *First Principles*.

26. MacIntyre, *Dependent Rational Animals*, 93, 111.

27. MacIntyre, *Three Rival Versions*, 139; cf. MacIntyre, *First Principles*, 42.

28. MacIntyre, *After Virtue*, 236; also *After Virtue*, 152.

29. MacIntyre, *Three Rival Versions*, 139.

30. MacIntyre, *After Virtue*, 150.

31. Aristotle, *Nichomachean Ethics* 1134b18–19.

32. MacIntyre, *After Virtue*, 150.

33. Aristotle, *Politics* 1252a25–1253a40. Aristotle calls the *polis* "naturally prior" to the individual "since the whole is necessarily prior to the part" (*Politics* 1253a19–20).

34. Cf. MacIntyre, *After Virtue*, 229.

35. MacIntyre, *After Virtue*, 148, 162–63, 196.

36. MacIntyre, *Dependent Rational Animals*, x.

37. MacIntyre, *After Virtue*, 159.

38. MacIntyre, *After Virtue*, 3. Recall that Oakeshott listed Hegel (along with Bradley) as those from whom he had learned the most (Oakeshott, *Experience and Its Modes*, 6), and that Collingwood called Oakeshott's philosophical approach to history "the most penetrating analysis of historical thought that has ever been written."

39. MacIntyre, *A Short History of Ethics*, 1. "We all too often still treat the moral philosophers of the past as contributors to a single debate with a relatively unchanging subject matter, treating Plato and Hume and Mill as contemporaries of ourselves and of each other. This leads to an abstraction of these writers from the cultural and social milieus in which they lived and thought, and so the history of their thought acquires a false independence from the rest of the culture" (MacIntyre, *After Virtue*, 11).

40. See, for example, MacIntyre, *After Virtue*, 126–30; MacIntyre, *Whose Justice? Which Rationality?*, 6; MacIntyre, *Three Rival Versions*, 172, 203–4.

41. MacIntyre, *Whose Justice? Which Rationality?*, 371–72.

42. MacIntyre, *Whose Justice? Which Rationality?*, 387. This conceit, according to MacIntyre, underlies so-called Great Books courses, which seek to sample a variety of canonical texts without concern for the historical and linguistic tradition of which they are the products (*Whose Justice? Which Rationality?*, 385–86).

43. This is in radical opposition to the Rawlsian notion of the original position, which supposes that a person can actually extricate himself conceptually from the accidentals of history and society. See Rawls, *A Theory of Justice*.

44. MacIntyre, *After Virtue*, 221.

45. MacIntyre, *Whose Justice? Which Rationality?*, 363; cf. MacIntyre, *Three Rival Versions*, 66.

46. MacIntyre, *After Virtue*, 268.

47. MacIntyre notes that ignoring the limitations of human inquiry not only produces incorrect philosophical understanding but also has potentially dangerous social and political consequences: "When men and women identify what are in fact their partial and particular causes too easily and too completely with the cause of some universal principle, they usually behave worse than they would otherwise" (MacIntyre, *After Virtue*, 221).

48. MacIntyre, *After Virtue*, 186.

49. MacIntyre, *After Virtue*, 187.

50. MacIntyre, *After Virtue*, 275; italics in original.

51. MacIntyre, *After Virtue*, 187.

52. MacIntyre, *After Virtue*, 187.

53. MacIntyre, *After Virtue*, 187–88.

54. MacIntyre, *After Virtue*, 188.

55. MacIntyre, *After Virtue*, 190–91.

56. MacIntyre, *After Virtue*, 190.

57. MacIntyre, *After Virtue*, 190–91.

58. MacIntyre, *Three Rival Versions*, 61–63; MacIntyre, *Dependent Rational Animals*, 88–92.

59. MacIntyre, *Dependent Rational Animals*, 92.

60. MacIntyre, *After Virtue*, 191; italics in original.

61. MacIntyre, *After Virtue*, 191.

62. MacIntyre, *Dependent Rational Animals*, 88–89.

63. MacIntyre, *After Virtue*, 193.

64. MacIntyre, *After Virtue*, 193–94.

65. MacIntyre, *After Virtue*, 194.

66. MacIntyre, *After Virtue*, 194.

67. MacIntyre, *After Virtue*, 205.

68. MacIntyre, *After Virtue*, 206–7.

69. MacIntyre, *After Virtue*, 209. Cf. Oakeshott on cooking and tradition in *Rationalism in Politics*, 52.

70. Oakeshott whimsically suggests that conversation is the very act that distinguishes humans from other creatures: "Indeed, it seems not improbable that it was the engagement in this conversation (where talk is without a conclusion) that gave us our present appearance, man being descended from a race of apes who sat in talk so long and so late that they wore out their tails" (*Rationalism in Politics*, 490).

71. MacIntyre, *After Virtue*, 211.

72. MacIntyre, *After Virtue*, 213.

73. MacIntyre, *After Virtue*, 216.

74. MacIntyre, *After Virtue*, 216.

75. MacIntyre, *After Virtue*, 219.

76. MacIntyre, *After Virtue*, 222.

77. MacIntyre, *Whose Justice? Which Rationality?*, 12. Stephen Mulhall and Adam Swift describe MacIntyre's conception of tradition as follows: "A tradition is constituted by a set of practices and is a mode of understanding their importance and worth; it is the medium by which such practices are shaped and transmitted across generations. Traditions may be primarily religious or moral (for example Catholicism or humanism), economic (for example a particular craft or profession, trade union or manufacturer), aesthetic (for example modes of literature or painting), or geographical (for example crystallising around the history and culture of a particular house, village or region)." (Mulhall and Swift, *Liberals and Communitarians*, 90).

78. MacIntyre, *Whose Justice? Which Rationality?*, 11.

79. MacIntyre, *Whose Justice? Which Rationality?*, 369. "Just because at any particular moment the rationality of a craft is justified by its history so far, which has made it what it is in that specific time, place, and set of historical circumstances, such rationality is inseparable from the tradition through which it was achieved" (MacIntyre, *Three Rival Versions*, 65).

80. MacIntyre, *Whose Justice? Which Rationality?*, 361. "To appeal to tradition is to insist that we cannot adequately identify either our own commitments or those of others in the argumentative conflicts of the present except by situating them within those histories which made them what they have now become" (MacIntyre, *Whose Justice? Which Rationality?*, 13).

81. MacIntyre, *Whose Justice? Which Rationality?*, 361. Cf. MacIntyre, *After Virtue*, 93, 270, 277; MacIntyre, *Whose Justice? Which Rationality?*, 100–101, 172; MacIntyre, *Three Rival Versions*, 125, 142.

82. MacIntyre, *Whose Justice? Which Rationality?*, 360.

83. MacIntyre, *Whose Justice? Which Rationality?*, 360–61. MacIntyre writes, "I am irremediably anti-Hegelian in rejecting the notion of an absolute standpoint, independent of the particularity of all traditions" ("A Partial Response to My Critics," 295).

84. MacIntyre, *After Virtue*, 270.

85. MacIntyre, *Whose Justice? Which Rationality?*, 355; cf. MacIntyre, *Three Rival Versions*, 116.

86. MacIntyre, *After Virtue*, 223.

87. MacIntyre, *After Virtue*, 222.

88. MacIntyre, *Whose Justice? Which Rationality?*, 12.

89. MacIntyre, *Whose Justice? Which Rationality?*, 362.

90. MacIntyre, *Whose Justice? Which Rationality?*, 362; cf. MacIntyre, "Epistemological Crises, Dramatic Narrative and the Philosophy of Science," 453–72.

91. MacIntyre, *After Virtue*, 221. MacIntyre appears emphatic when he writes that "no way of conducting rational enquiry from a standpoint independent of the particularities of any tradition has been discovered and . . . there is good reason to believe that there is no such way" ("Precis of *Whose Justice? Which Rationality?*," 152).

92. MacIntyre, *Whose Justice? Which Rationality?*, 393.

93. MacIntyre, *Whose Justice? Which Rationality?*, 395.

94. Robert P. George comments in some detail about this apparent incongruity in MacIntyre's work in George, "Moral Particularism, Thomism, and Traditions," 593–605. Haldane, too, finds problems with this part of MacIntyre's thought and finds an inevitable relativism at its heart; see Haldane, "MacIntyre's Thomist Revival: What Next?" Haldane argues that if traditionless addressees exist, then either (1) they can appeal to some tradition-independent source of rationality by which to rationally choose which tradition to embrace, or (2) one's commitment to a tradition is ultimately irrational. If the former, then all rationality is not tradition-dependent, and MacIntyre's thesis is severely truncated. If the latter, then no tradition can claim rational superiority.

95. MacIntyre, *Whose Justice? Which Rationality?*, 367.

96. MacIntyre, *Whose Justice? Which Rationality?*, 401. It goes without saying that if this account of tradition and rationality is correct, it would be quite futile to address a book on practical rationality to individuals who have not yet committed themselves to a tradition (see MacIntyre, *Whose Justice? Which Rationality?*, 393). Perhaps MacIntyre intends his book for those who have not yet *consciously* and *explicitly* committed themselves to a tradition in spite of the fact that all rational persons are *tacitly* committed to a tradition. If this is the case, then (1) MacIntyre would do well to clarify this point, and (2) the conceptual tools afforded us by Polanyi will serve to make this position more comprehendible.

97. Some commentators have taken issue with this strong view of tradition. See, for example, Schneewind, "MacIntyre and the Indispensability of Tradition," 165–68; Boyle, "Natural Law and the Ethics of Traditions," 3–30.

98. MacIntyre, *After Virtue*, 277.

99. MacIntyre, "Epistemological Crises, Dramatic Narrative and the Philosophy of Science," 458. In his *City of God*, Augustine writes, "They say, 'Suppose you are mistaken?' I reply, 'If I am mistaken, I exist.' A non-existent being cannot be mistaken; therefore, I must exist if I am mistaken. Then since my being mistaken proves that I exist, how can I be mistaken in thinking that I

exist, seeing that my mistake establishes my existence? Since therefore I must exist in order to be mistaken, then even if I am mistaken, there can be no doubt that I am not mistaken in my knowledge that I exist" (*City of God* 11.26, p. 460).

100. MacIntyre, *Whose Justice? Which Rationality?*, 458–59.

101. "There is no standing ground, no place for enquiry, no way to engage in the practices of advancing, evaluating, accepting, and rejecting reasoned argument apart from that which is provided by some particular tradition or another" (MacIntyre, *Whose Justice? Which Rationality?*, 350). "The resources of adequate rationality are made available to us only in and through traditions" (369).

102. Many commentators have focused on this point in MacIntyre's thought, arguing that relativism is difficult if not impossible to avoid in light of MacIntyre's strong view of tradition. See, for example, Wachbroit, "A Genealogy of Virtues," 564–76; Dahl, "Justice and Aristotelian Practical Reason," 153–57; Haldane, "MacIntyre's Thomist Revival: What Next?," 91–107; Graham, "MacIntyre's Fusion of History and Philosophy," 161–75. MacIntyre replies specifically to these four critics in "Postscript to the Second Edition," in *After Virtue*; "Reply to Dahl, Baier and Schneewind," 169–78; and "A Partial Response to My Critics," 283–304, esp. 294–98.

103. MacIntyre, *Whose Justice? Which Rationality?*, 328.

104. MacIntyre, *Whose Justice? Which Rationality?*, 352.

105. MacIntyre, *Whose Justice? Which Rationality?*, 352.

106. MacIntyre, *Whose Justice? Which Rationality?*, 353.

107. Cf. MacIntyre, *Three Rival Versions*, 66–67.

108. MacIntyre, *Whose Justice? Which Rationality?*, 365.

109. MacIntyre, *Whose Justice? Which Rationality?*, 368. MacIntyre scoffs at the notion held by perspectivists that "suppose that one could temporarily adopt the standpoint of a tradition and then exchange it for another, or as one might wear first one costume and then another, or as one might act one part in one play and then a quite different part in a quite different play. But genuinely to adopt the standpoint of a tradition thereby commits one to its view of what is true and false and, in so committing one, prohibits one from adopting any rival standpoint" (MacIntyre, *Whose Justice? Which Rationality?*, 367).

110. MacIntyre, *Whose Justice? Which Rationality?*, 367.

111. MacIntyre, *Whose Justice? Which Rationality?*, 369.

112. MacIntyre, *Whose Justice? Which Rationality?*, 374.

113. MacIntyre, *Whose Justice? Which Rationality?*, 327.

114. MacIntyre, *Three Rival Versions*, 180–81.

115. MacIntyre, *First Principles*, 9.

116. Plato, *Meno* 80e. Cf. MacIntyre, *Three Rival Versions*, 63, 84, 130.

117. This, of course, is contrary to Locke's theory of knowledge in which the mind is a *tabula rasa* and a passive receptor of sense impressions.

118. MacIntyre, *First Principles*, 15.

119. MacIntyre, *Three Rival Versions*, 63.

120. MacIntyre, *Three Rival Versions*, 84.

121. MacIntyre, *Three Rival Versions*, 84.

122. MacIntyre, *Three Rival Versions*, 95. He continues, "To understand the required concept adequately the mind must already be directed by faith toward its true perfection. The rational justification of belief in the object of faith is internal to the life of faith" (MacIntyre, *Three Rival Versions*, 95–96).

123. MacIntyre, "The Idea of a Social Science," 95–114.

124. Winch, *The Idea of a Social Science*.

125. Winch, *The Idea of a Social Science*, 54–65. Winch's bibliography lists three essays by Oakeshott: "The Tower of Babel," "Rational Conduct," and "Political Education."

126. Oakeshott, *Rationalism in Politics*, 44.

127. See Postan, "The Revulsion from Thought," 395–408. Postan accuses Oakeshott of "conservative anti-rationalism" (395); Martha Nussbaum claims that MacIntyre unwisely subordinates his reason to authority, in Nussbaum, "Recoiling from Reason," 36–41.

128. Oakeshott, *Rationalism in Politics*, 8, 39; MacIntyre, *Three Rival Versions*, 63, 84.

129. MacIntyre, *After Virtue*, 193.

130. MacIntyre, *Three Rival Versions*, 225.

131. Oakeshott, *Rationalism in Politics*, 39–41.

132. MacIntyre, *Whose Justice? Which Rationality?*, 12.

133. MacIntyre, *After Virtue*, 222.

134. MacIntyre, *After Virtue*, 221.

135. Oakeshott, *On Human Conduct*, 58; MacIntyre, *After Virtue*, 223; MacIntyre, *Whose Justice? Which Rationality?*, 326.

136. Oakeshott, *On Human Conduct*, 56.

137. MacIntyre, *After Virtue*, 187–89.

138. MacIntyre, *Three Rival Versions*, 66–67.

139. MacIntyre, *After Virtue*, 156–57, 229.

140. Oakeshott, *On Human Conduct*, 41.

141. Oakeshott, *On Human Conduct*, 25.

142. Oakeshott, *On Human Conduct*, 53; cf. Oakeshott, *On Human Conduct*, 61–62.

143. Oakeshott, *On Human Conduct*, 62.

144. Oakeshott, *Rationalism in Politics*, 64.

145. Oakeshott, *Rationalism in Politics*, 64–65.

146. Of course, Oakeshott would argue that such a claim assumes a rationalist theory of mind in which the mind can be separated from what it knows.

147. Oakeshott, *Experience and Its Modes*, 69.

148. MacIntyre, *Three Rival Versions*, 59.

149. MacIntyre, *Three Rival Versions*, 59–60. The centrality of commitment and the personal element in all inquiry will come to full light in the next chapter.

CHAPTER 4   Michael Polanyi and the Role of Tacit Knowledge

1. Polanyi, *Personal Knowledge*, 266.

2. A short account of Polanyi's life is given by William Taussig Scott, "At the Wheel of the World: The Life and Times of Michael Polanyi," 10–23. For an interesting description of the Polanyi family, see Peter F. Drucker, *Adventures of a Bystander*, 123–40. For the definitive biography, see William Taussig Scott and Martin X. Moleski, *Michael Polanyi: Scientist and Philosopher*. For a shorter introduction to his life and thought, see Mark T. Mitchell, *Michael Polanyi: The Art of Knowing*.

3. Polanyi, *Personal Knowledge*, 18, 269.

4. Polanyi, *The Tacit Dimension*, 4.

5. Polanyi, *Personal Knowledge*, 56–57, cf. vii.

6. Polanyi, *The Tacit Dimension*, 6.

7. Polanyi, *The Tacit Dimension*, 6; cf. *The Study of Man*, 28–29.

8. Polanyi, *The Tacit Dimension*, 4–6; Polanyi, *Knowing and Being*, 123.

9. Polanyi, "Logic and Psychology," 29.

10. Polanyi, *Personal Knowledge*, 55–56; *Knowing and Being*, 127–28; "Logic and Psychology," 30.

11. Polanyi, *Personal Knowledge*, 56; *Knowing and Being*, 125–26.

12. Polanyi, *Personal Knowledge*, 56.

13. Polanyi, *Knowing and Being*, 128; italics in the original.

14. Polanyi, *Personal Knowledge*, 57; "Logic and Psychology," 30.

15. Polanyi, *Knowing and Being*, 197.

16. Polanyi, *The Tacit Dimension*, 11; italics in the original.

17. Polanyi, *The Tacit Dimension*, 13.

18. Polanyi, *The Tacit Dimension*, 13.

19. Polanyi briefly discusses the aspects of tacit knowing (minus the ontological) in *Knowing and Being*, 212.

20. Polanyi, *Personal Knowledge*, vii.

21. Polanyi, *The Tacit Dimension*, 15. The body as an instrument of knowing is a central component of Merleau-Ponty's phenomenological approach; see Merleau-Ponty, *The Phenomenology of Perception*.

22. Polanyi, "Science and Religion," 8.

23. Polanyi, *Knowing and Being*, 144, cf. 195.

24. Polanyi, *Knowing and Being*, 195; cf. Polanyi, *Study of Man*, 18.

25. Polanyi, *Knowing and Being*, 152. "*All* knowing is personal knowing—participation through indwelling" (Polanyi and Prosch, *Meaning*, 44; italics in the original).

26. Polanyi, "Logic and Psychology," 31.

27. Polanyi, "Logic and Psychology," 31.

28. Polanyi, "The Stability of Beliefs," 217.

29. Polanyi, *Science, Faith and Society*, 75. "Throughout the formative centuries of modern science, the rejection of authority was its battle-cry" (*Knowing and Being*, 65).

30. Polanyi, *Science, Faith and Society*, 76.

31. Polanyi, *Personal Knowledge*, 286.

32. Polanyi, *Science, Faith and Society*, 26.

33. Polanyi, *Personal Knowledge*, 141.

34. Polanyi, *Personal Knowledge*, 266. Polanyi translates the Latin: "Unless ye believe, ye shall not understand." At other points Polanyi employs a similar Latin phrase, *fides quaerens intellectum*, which translates "faith seeking understanding." However, in one passage, he offers a more creative translation: "to believe in order to know" (*Science, Faith and Society*, 15, cf. 45; *The Tacit Dimension*, 61).

35. Polanyi, *Personal Knowledge*, 266; cf. "Faith and Reason," 237–39.

36. Polanyi, *The Tacit Dimension*, 56.

37. Polanyi and Prosch, *Meaning*, 28.

38. Polanyi, "Faith and Reason," 238–39. "And I think that to-day we can feel the balance of mental needs tilting back once again" (*Science, Faith and Society*, 27).

39. Polanyi, *Personal Knowledge*, 266. For a useful discussion of Polanyi and Augustine, see Grant, "Michael Polanyi: The Augustinian Component." Also see Keiser, "Inaugurating Postcritical Philosophy: A Polanyian Meditation on Creation and Conversion in Augustine's *Confessions*."

40. This directly contradicts Bacon's view that if only his method were applied, all people will "fall into our way of interpretation without the aid of any art" (Bacon, *Novum Organum*, 130).

41. Polanyi, *Personal Knowledge*, 50, cf. 31.

42. Polanyi, *Personal Knowledge*, 53. Polanyi notes that the word "uncritically" is more precisely rendered "a-critically" (*Personal Knowledge*, 264n2; *Study of Man*, 17).

43. Polanyi, *The Tacit Dimension*, 61.

44. Polanyi, *Knowing and Being*, 160.

45. Polanyi, *Knowing and Being*, 41.

46. Polanyi, *The Tacit Dimension*, 61–62.

47. Polanyi calls this discrepancy "pseudo-substitution." I will touch on this more below.

48. Polanyi, *Knowing and Being*, 68.

49. Polanyi, *Knowing and Being*, 68.

50. Polanyi, *Knowing and Being*, 70.

51. Polanyi, *Knowing and Being*, 71.

52. Polanyi, *Personal Knowledge*, 160.

53. Polanyi, *Science, Faith and Society*, 72.

54. Polanyi, *Personal Knowledge*, 208; cf. *Science, Faith and Society*, 69.

55. Polanyi, *Science, Faith and Society*, 73, cf. 64, 81.

56. Polanyi, *Science, Faith and Society*, 76.

57. Polanyi, *Personal Knowledge*, 203.

58. See Plato, *Meno* 80d-e.

59. Polanyi, *The Tacit Dimension*, 22.

60. Polanyi, *Personal Knowledge*, 121; cf. *Science, Faith and Society*, 34.

61. Polanyi, *Personal Knowledge*, 123.

62. Polanyi, *Personal Knowledge*, 9–15; "Creative Imagination," 117.

63. Polanyi, "Creative Imagination," 116.

64. Polanyi, *Personal Knowledge*, 127–28.

65. Cf. Polanyi, *Knowing and Being*, 119.

66. Polanyi, "Creative Imagination," 116.

67. Polanyi, "Creative Imagination," 117.

68. Polanyi, *Knowing and Being*, 118.

69. Polanyi, "Creative Imagination," 121.

70. There is an ongoing discussion among Polanyi scholars regarding the nature of Polanyi's realism. See, for example, the journal *Tradition & Discovery* 26 no. 3 (1999–2000). The entire issue is dedicated to exploring this topic.

71. Polanyi, *Knowing and Being*, 133.

72. Polanyi, *The Tacit Dimension*, 23.

73. Polanyi, *The Tacit Dimension*, 19.

74. Polanyi, *The Tacit Dimension*, 33.

75. Polanyi, *Knowing and Being*, 151.

76. Polanyi, *Knowing and Being*, 168.

77. Polanyi, *Personal Knowledge*, 269.

78. Polanyi, *Personal Knowledge*, 295.

79. Polanyi, *Personal Knowledge*, 295.

80. Polanyi, *Personal Knowledge*, 69–70. Aristotle also alludes to this. See *Politics* 1253a8–18. Humans, unlike other animals, possess *logos*, rational discourse.

298 Notes to Pages 154–158

81. Polanyi, *Knowing and Being*, 160.

82. "Human thought grows only within language and since language can exist only in a society, all thought is rooted in society" (Polanyi, *The Study of Man*, 60).

83. Polanyi, "Stability of Beliefs," 221; cf. *Personal Knowledge*, 80.

84. Polanyi, *Personal Knowledge*, 287.

85. Even an adult who aspires to learn a second language must exhibit trust, for "no one can learn a new language unless he first trusts that it means something" (Polanyi, *Personal Knowledge*, 151).

86. Polanyi, *Personal Knowledge*, 295.

87. Polanyi, *Science, Faith and Society*, 72.

88. Polanyi, *The Study of Man*, 39.

89. See Polanyi, *Personal Knowledge*, 171, 324.

90. "I cannot speak except from inside a language" (Polanyi, *Personal Knowledge*, 253).

91. Polanyi, *Knowing and Being*, 133.

92. Polanyi, *Personal Knowledge*, 267.

93. Polanyi, *Personal Knowledge*, 252, cf. 266–67, 318–19; *Science, Faith and Society*, 83.

94. Polanyi, *Personal Knowledge*, 303.

95. Polanyi, *Personal Knowledge*, 381.

96. Polanyi, *Personal Knowledge*, 314.

97. Polanyi, *Personal Knowledge*, 27.

98. Polanyi, *Personal Knowledge*, 256.

99. Polanyi, *Personal Knowledge*, 28.

100. Polanyi, *Personal Knowledge*, 256. Polanyi refers to Popper's emphasis on falsifiability as a contemporary example of the objectivist ideal of dispassionate pursuit of knowledge. "There is indeed an idealization of this [dispassionate nature of science] current today, which deems the scientist not only indifferent to the outcome of his surmises, but actually seeking their refutation. This is not only counter to experience, but logically inconceivable. The surmises of a working scientist are *born of the imagination seeking discovery*. Such effort risks defeat but never *seeks* it; it is in fact his craving for success that makes the scientist take the risk of failure. There is no other way. Courts of law employ two separate lawyers to argue opposite pleas, because it is only by a passionate commitment to a particular view that the imagination can discover the evidence that supports it" (*The Tacit Dimension*, 78–79; italics in the original; cf. Polanyi and Prosch, *Meaning*, 195).

101. Polanyi, *Personal Knowledge*, 253; cf. Oakeshott, *Rationalism in Politics*, 60.

102. Polanyi, *Personal Knowledge*, 301; *Knowing and Being*, 314, 316.

103. Polanyi, *Study of Man*, 36; cf. *Personal Knowledge*, 313.

104. Polanyi, *Personal Knowledge*, 311; italics in the original.

105. Polanyi, *Personal Knowledge*, 150. This is not to be confused with those who insist on converting others or killing them.

106. Polanyi, *Personal Knowledge*, 150.

107. Polanyi, *Personal Knowledge*, 318.

108. Polanyi, *Personal Knowledge*, 151.

109. Polanyi, *Science, Faith and Society*, 81.

110. Polanyi, *Science, Faith and Society*, 66–67.

111. Polanyi, *Science, Faith and Society*, 67. Cf. MacIntyre "Epistemological Crisis," 465–66; MacIntyre, *Whose Justice? Which Rationality?*, 396.

112. Polanyi and Prosch, *Meaning*, 179–80. Cf. Thomas Kuhn on "gestalt switch," in Kuhn, *The Structure of Scientific Revolution*.

113. "As Saint Augustine viewed it, a religious belief cannot be achieved by our deliberate efforts and choice. It is a gift of God and may remain inexplicably denied to some of us" (Polanyi and Prosch, *Meaning*, 180; cf. *Science, Faith and Society*, 67; *Personal Knowledge*, 324).

114. Polanyi, *Personal Knowledge*, 286, 381.

115. Polanyi, *Personal Knowledge*, 266.

116. Polanyi, *Personal Knowledge*, vii, 18.

117. Polanyi, *Personal Knowledge*, 268.

118. Polanyi, *Personal Knowledge*, 3. Polanyi notes that "the degree of our personal participation varies greatly within our various acts of knowing" (*Personal Knowledge*, 36).

119. Polanyi, *Personal Knowledge*, 288; italics added.

120. Polanyi, *Personal Knowledge*, 297.

121. Polanyi, *Personal Knowledge*, 299.

122. Polanyi, *Personal Knowledge*, 267.

123. Polanyi, *Personal Knowledge*, 299.

124. Polanyi, *Personal Knowledge*, 300.

125. Polanyi, *Personal Knowledge*, vii, cf. 403.

126. Polanyi, *Personal Knowledge*, 17; cf. *The Tacit Dimension*, 77–78.

127. Polanyi, *Personal Knowledge*, vii. "Subjective knowing is classed as passive; only knowing that bears on reality is active, personal, and rightly to be called objective" (*Personal Knowledge*, 403).

128. Polanyi, *Personal Knowledge*, 303; italics and bold in original.

129. C. S. Lewis makes a somewhat similar distinction is his "Meditation in a Toolshed."

130. Polanyi, *Study of Man*, 38.

131. Polanyi, *Study of Man*, 72; cf. *Personal Knowledge*, 133–34, 249.

132. Polanyi, *Personal Knowledge*, 265. Polanyi writes, "The great movement for independent thought instilled in the modern mind a desperate refusal of all knowledge that is not absolutely impersonal, and this implied in its turn a mechanical conception of man which was bound to deny man's capacity for independent thought" (*Personal Knowledge*, 214).

133. Polanyi and Prosch, *Meaning*, 65.

134. Polanyi, *Personal Knowledge*, 316. "I accept the responsibility for drawing an ever indeterminate knowledge from unspecifiable clues, with an aim to universal validity; and this belief includes the acknowledgment of other persons as responsible centres of equally unspecifiable operations, aiming likewise at universal validity" (*Personal Knowledge*, 336).

135. Polanyi, *Personal Knowledge*, 316.

136. Polanyi, *Study of Man*, 89.

137. Polanyi, *Personal Knowledge*, 323.

138. Polanyi, *Personal Knowledge*, 249.

139. Polanyi, *Personal Knowledge*, 315. "There remains therefore only one truth to speak about" (*Personal Knowledge*, 316; cf. *Science, Faith and Society*, 70, 71, 73).

140. Polanyi, *Personal Knowledge*, viii.

141. Polanyi, *Personal Knowledge*, 109, 145, 214, 306.

142. Polanyi, *Personal Knowledge*, 309; italics in the original.

143. Polanyi, *Personal Knowledge*, 324; cf. "Faith and Reason," 247.

144. Polanyi, *Personal Knowledge*, 324.

145. Polanyi, *Science, Faith and Society*, 75.

146. Polanyi, *The Tacit Dimension*, 17.

147. Polanyi, *Study of Man*, 28.

148. Polanyi, *Personal Knowledge*, 214.

149. Polanyi, *Personal Knowledge*, 183.

150. Polanyi, *Science, Faith and Society*, 83.

151. Polanyi, *Personal Knowledge*, 242–43.

152. Polanyi, *Science, Faith and Society*, 83.

153. Polanyi, *Science, Faith and Society*, 83.

154. Polanyi, *Personal Knowledge*, 183.

155. Polanyi, "Creative Imagination," 122. There is an ongoing debate among Polanyi scholars regarding Polanyi's view of the status of moral, religious, and artistic reality. On the one hand, there are those who, like me, argue that a central theme of Polanyi's thought is showing how all fields of inquiry are essentially the same in epistemological terms. On the other hand, there are those (represented primarily by Harry Prosch, who collaborated with Polanyi in his last book, *Meaning*) who argue that Polanyi maintained a distinction between scientific reality, which is independent of the knower, and moral, re-

ligious, and artistic reality, which is ontologically dependent upon the creative imagination of the human knower. For examples of the first position, see Gelwick, *The Way of Discovery*; Poirier, "Harry Prosch's Modernism." For examples of the second approach, see Prosch's response to Gelwick in Prosch, review of *The Way of Discovery*, and his response to Poirier in Prosch, "Those Missing 'Objects'"; also see Prosch, *Michael Polanyi: A Critical Exposition*, esp. chaps. 17 and 18; and Prosch, "Polanyi's Ethics." See also Meek, *Contact with Reality: An Examination of Realism in the Work of Michael Polanyi*, and Meek, "'Recalled to Life': Contact with Reality." See also the issue of *Zygon* 17 (1982), which focuses on Polanyi's thought. This topic comes up with some regularity in the journal *Tradition & Discovery*. See, for example, the issue on Polanyi's realism, *Tradition & Discovery* 26, no. 3 (1999–2000).

156. Prosch, "Polanyi's Ethics," 91.

157. Polanyi, *Knowing and Being*, 65; *Science, Economics, and Philosophy*, 215; *The Tacit Dimension*, 63; *Logic of Liberty*, 10, 18.

158. Polanyi, *Science, Economics, and Philosophy*, 79; cf. *Knowing and Being*, 8, 65.

159. Polanyi, *Science, Economics, and Philosophy*, 79.

160. Polanyi, *Knowing and Being*, 46.

161. Polanyi and Prosch, *Meaning*, 20.

162. Polanyi and Prosch, *Meaning*, 18.

163. Polanyi, *Knowing and Being*, 10; cf. *The Tacit Dimension*, 57–60, 85–87.

164. There is significant overlap between Polanyi's concept of moral inversion and what Eric Voegelin called "Gnosticism." See Voegelin, *New Science of Politics*, and Voegelin, *Science, Politics and Gnosticism*. See also Mitchell, "Personal Participation," esp. 69–75.

165. Polanyi, *Personal Knowledge*, 228.

166. Polanyi, *The Tacit Dimension*, 58.

167. Polanyi, *The Tacit Dimension*, 58.

168. See, for instance, Legutko, *The Demon in Democracy*.

169. Polanyi, *Personal Knowledge*, 233.

170. Polanyi, *Knowing and Being*, 22, cf. 67–69; *Logic of Liberty*, 121–22.

171. In this overview of Polanyi's thought I have neglected to include a discussion of his doctrine of emergence, which I find to be the least attractive part of his work and quite outside the concerns of the present project.

172. Oakeshott, "The Human Coefficient."

173. Oakeshott, "The Human Coefficient," 77.

174. Oakeshott, "The Human Coefficient," 79.

175. Oakeshott, "The Human Coefficient," 79.

176. Oakeshott, "The Human Coefficient," 79.

177. Oakeshott, "John Locke," 72.

178. Polanyi, *Personal Knowledge*, 270.

179. Oakeshott, *Rationalism in Politics*, 13n4.

180. Oakeshott, "Science and Society," 692n1.

181. Polanyi, *Science, Faith and Society*, 33.

182. Oakeshott, *Rationalism in Politics*, 15.

183. Polanyi, *Personal Knowledge*, 269–98.

184. It should be pointed out that in the two notes in which Oakeshott refers to the parallels between his concepts of practical and technical knowledge and Polanyi's discussion of similar concepts, he is referring exclusively to Polanyi's early *Science, Faith and Society*. In that work Polanyi does not develop his theory of tacit knowing with the distinction between the focal and subsidiary elements. Thus, although Oakeshott is quite correct to see the similarities between his work and Polanyi's at this stage, Polanyi develops this area of his thought much more thoroughly than Oakeshott; thus the similarities are unmistakable, but Polanyi's later work is significantly more complex and supersedes Oakeshott's conception by virtue of that more complex development.

185. Cf. Oakeshott, *Rationalism in Politics*, 54–55, 68, 111–12, 121, 123.

186. Polanyi, *The Tacit Dimension*, 4.

187. Polanyi, *Personal Knowledge*, 71.

188. Polanyi, *Science, Faith and Society*, 76.

189. Oakeshott, *Rationalism in Politics*, 51–52; Polanyi, *Personal Knowledge*, 30.

190. Oakeshott, *Rationalism in Politics*, 52.

191. Polanyi frequently speaks of "intimations of coherence," but unlike Oakeshott, he is referring to contact with an external reality and not to the internal coherence of a world of experience.

192. Oakeshott, *Rationalism in Politics*, 10.

193. Oakeshott, *Rationalism in Politics*, 484.

194. Oakeshott, *Rationalism in Politics*, 484.

195. Polanyi, *Personal Knowledge*, 294; italics in original; cf. *Personal Knowledge*, 288–94.

196. For a helpful treatment of Oakeshott's thought from the perspective of Polanyi's, see Walter B. Mead, "Michael Oakeshott as Philosopher: Beyond Politics, a Quest for Omniscience."

197. Polanyi, who died in 1976, did not have the opportunity to comment on MacIntyre's virtue trilogy, upon which we focused in chapter 3. He did, though, write a brief review of MacIntyre's first book, *Marxism: An Interpretation*. It is a generally favorable review, but Polanyi chides the youthful MacIntyre for lacking "political maturity" (Polanyi, "Marx and Saint Paul," 4).

198. For an accusation that MacIntyre is promoting irrationalism, see Nussbaum, "Recoiling from Reason," 36–41. Recall that Oakeshott is also ac-

cused of irrationalism. See Postan, "The Revulsion from Thought," 395–408. The fact that all three of these thinkers have faced this same accusation indicates something important about their thought collectively: despite their differences, all three are attempting to conceptualize reason in a way that breaks out of the constraints imposed by modern philosophy.

Marjorie Grene finds important similarities between MacIntyre and Polanyi. See Grene, "Response to Alasdair MacIntyre." Grene is especially qualified to discuss Polanyi's work. In addition to editing the collection of Polanyi essays published under the title *Knowing and Being*, she worked directly with Polanyi, who expresses his gratitude in the acknowledgments of *Personal Knowledge*: "This work owes much to Dr. Marjorie Grene. The moment we first talked about it in Chicago in 1950 she seemed to have guessed my whole purpose, and ever since she has never ceased to help its pursuit. Setting aside her own work as a philosopher, she has devoted herself for years to the service of the present enquiry. Our discussions have catalysed its progress at every stage and there is hardly a page that has not benefited from her criticism" (Polanyi, *Personal Knowledge*, ix). Interestingly, MacIntyre also expresses gratitude to Marjorie Grene in the preface to *After Virtue*.

For a comparison of MacIntyre and Polanyi, see Flett, "Alasdair MacIntyre's Tradition-Constituted Enquiry in Polanyian Perspective."

199. MacIntyre, "Epistemological Crises," 465.

200. MacIntyre, "Objectivity in Morality," 27.

201. MacIntyre, *After Virtue*, 221.

202. This is not to say that Polanyi is hostile to Burke. Indeed, Polanyi refers positively to Burke on several occasions. See *The Tacit Dimension*, 62–63; *Knowing and Being*, 67–69; *Personal Knowledge*, 54; *Science, Economics, and Philosophy*, 204–5.

203. Polanyi, *Knowing and Being*, 41.

204. Polanyi, *Knowing and Being*, 160.

205. Cf. Polanyi, *Knowing and Being*, 66; *The Tacit Dimension*, 61–62; *Science, Faith and Society*, 56.

206. MacIntyre writes, "It was perhaps because the presence of his language was invisible to the Descartes of the *Discours* and the *Meditationes* that he did not notice either what Gilson pointed out in detail, how much of what he took to be the spontaneous reflections of his own mind was in fact a repetition of sentences and phrases from his school textbooks" ("Epistemological Crises," 458).

207. MacIntyre, *After Virtue*, 190–91; *Three Rival Versions*, 61–63; *Dependent Rational Animals*, 88–92.

208. MacIntyre, *Whose Justice? Which Rationality?*, 369. Cf. *After Virtue*, 221; *Whose Justice? Which Rationality?*, 13, 367, 401–2; "Precis of *Whose Justice? Which Rationality?*," 152.

209. MacIntyre, *Whose Justice? Which Rationality?*, 367.

210. Polanyi, *Personal Knowledge*, 376.

211. Polanyi, *Personal Knowledge*, 160.

212. Polanyi writes, "Submission to a consensus is always accompanied to some extent by the imposition of one's views on the consensus to which we submit. Every time we use a word in speaking and writing we both comply with usage and at the same time somewhat modify the existing usage; every time I select a programme on the radio I modify a little the balance of current cultural valuations; even when I make my purchase at current prices I slightly modify the whole price system. Indeed, whenever I submit to a current consensus, I inevitably modify its teaching; for I submit to what I myself think it teaches and by joining the consensus on these terms I affect its content" (*Personal Knowledge*, 208).

213. Polanyi, *Science, Faith and Society*, 56–57.

214. MacIntyre, *Whose Justice? Which Rationality?*, 11.

215. MacIntyre, *After Virtue*, 223; *Whose Justice? Which Rationality?*, 326.

216. Polanyi, *Knowing and Being*, 70.

217. Polanyi, *Personal Knowledge*, 208.

218. MacIntyre, *After Virtue*, 222.

219. MacIntyre, *Whose Justice? Which Rationality?*, 12.

220. MacIntyre, *After Virtue*, 222.

221. MacIntyre holds that "a high degree of homogeneity in fundamental belief" is necessary for establishing a community of rationality (*Three Rival Versions*, 223).

222. Polanyi, *Science, Faith and Society*, 76.

223. Polanyi, "Stability of Beliefs," 219.

224. MacIntyre, *Whose Justice? Which Rationality?*, 396; MacIntyre, *Three Rival Versions*, 65; MacIntyre, "Epistemological Crises," 461; Polanyi, *Personal Knowledge*, 151; Polanyi, *The Tacit Dimension*, 61–62.

225. Polanyi, *Science, Faith and Society*, 15, 45; *Personal Knowledge*, 266; *The Tacit Dimension*, 61.

226. MacIntyre, *Three Rival Versions*, 84, cf. 95–96, 99.

227. MacIntyre, *Whose Justice? Which Rationality?*, 371–72; Polanyi, *Personal Knowledge*, 112.

228. MacIntyre, *Three Rival Versions*, 139, 225; MacIntyre, *Dependent Rational Animals*, 93, 111; MacIntyre, *First Principles*, 41–42; Polanyi, *Science, Faith and Society*, 14; Polanyi, *Personal Knowledge*, 30–31, 49–50; Polanyi and Prosch, *Meaning*, 61.

229. MacIntyre, *After Virtue*, 190–91; MacIntyre, *Three Rival Versions*, 61–62, 63–64, 65–66, 82, 91–92; Polanyi, *Science, Faith and Society*, 15, 45–46, 64–65; Polanyi, *The Tacit Dimension*, 61; Polanyi, *Personal Knowledge*, 207–9.

230. Hume, *Treatise of Human Nature*, 1.4.7; quoted in MacIntyre, "Epistemological Crises," 462.

231. MacIntyre, "Epistemological Crises," 462.

232. MacIntyre, "Epistemological Crises," 462.

233. Polanyi, *Personal Knowledge*, 297.

234. MacIntyre, "Epistemological Crises," 462, 466.

235. Polanyi, *The Tacit Dimension*, 60; *Personal Knowledge*, 233, 294, 315; *Knowing and Being*, 22, 67–69; *Logic of Liberty*, 121–22.

236. MacIntyre, *First Principles*, 15.

237. MacIntyre, *First Principles*, 16. Cf. *Whose Justice? Which Rationality?*, 4, 175, 252; *Dependent Rational Animals*, 77; *First Principles*, 13–16.

238. Polanyi, *Personal Knowledge*, 299.

239. *Commentary on the Posterior Analytics*, lib. 1, lect. 3; quoted in MacIntyre, *First Principles*, 14.

240. MacIntyre, *Three Rival Versions*, 63, cf. 84, 130.

241. Polanyi, *Personal Knowledge*, 127.

242. Polanyi, *Personal Knowledge*, 127–28.

243. In his introduction to *The Tacit Dimension*, Polanyi writes, "It took me three years to feel assured that my reply to the *Meno* in the Terry Lectures was right. [The Terry Lectures, delivered in 1962, were published as *The Tacit Dimension* in 1966.] This has at last been cleared up to my satisfaction in my essay 'The Creative Imagination.' . . . It appears now also that what I have said in the Terry Lectures about our capacity for seeing and pursuing problems had been said long ago in *Science, Faith and Society*" (*The Tacit Dimension*, ix–x). Thus, despite refinements in his solution, Polanyi recognizes a continuity between his early and later work on the subject.

244. Polanyi, "Creative Imagination," 116.

245. Polanyi, *Personal Knowledge*, 121–23.

246. MacIntyre, *First Principles*, 35–36.

247. See, for example, this: "Faith in authority has to precede rational understanding" (MacIntyre, *Three Rival Versions*, 84).

248. MacIntyre, "Epistemological Crises," 465.

249. MacIntyre, "Epistemological Crises," 466.

250. Regarding the first, MacIntyre writes that "the language of evangelical conversion would indeed be appropriate" ("Epistemological Crises," 466).

251. MacIntyre, *Whose Justice? Which Rationality?*, 367.

252. MacIntyre, *Whose Justice? Which Rationality?*, 401.

253. MacIntyre, *Whose Justice? Which Rationality?*, 401–2.

254. Polanyi, *Personal Knowledge*, 151.

255. Polanyi, *Personal Knowledge*, 151; cf. *Science, Faith and Society*, 66–67; *Meaning*, 179–80.

256. "The process of choosing between positions based on different sets of premises is thus more a matter of intuition and finally conscience, than is a decision between different interpretations based on the same or closely similar sets of premises. It is a judgement of the kind involved in scientific discovery. Volition may play an important part in such judgements. We recall that an inflexible will is essential in scientific research if intimations of discovery are ever to reach the state of maturity; and that very often it is right to persist in certain intuitive expectations, even though a series of facts are apparently at variance with it. Yet through all these struggles our volition must never finally determine our judgement which must remain ultimately guided by the quiet voice of conscience. Similarly, the mental crisis which may lead to conversion from one set of premises to another are often dominated by strong impulses of will-power. Conversion may come to us against our will (as when faithful communists were overcome by doubts and broke down almost overnight at the aspect of the Russian trials), or—see the example of St. Augustine—it may be vainly sought for years by the whole power of our volition. Whether our will-power be evoked by our conscience to assist its arguments or drive us on the contrary in a direction opposed both to argument and conscience, no honest belief can be made or destroyed—but only self-deception induced—by will-power alone. The ultimate decision remains with conscience" (Polanyi, *Science, Faith and Society*, 67).

257. Polanyi, *Personal Knowledge*, 208.

258. MacIntyre, *Three Rival Versions*, 66; MacIntyre, *First Principles*, 47; Polanyi, *Science, Faith and Society*, 81; Polanyi, *Study of Man*, 35; Polanyi, *The Tacit Dimension*, 23–25; Polanyi, *Personal Knowledge*, 148, 316, 395–96; Polanyi, *Knowing and Being*, 133.

259. MacIntyre, *Whose Justice? Which Rationality?*, 363; MacIntyre, *Three Rival Versions*, 66; Polanyi, *Science, Faith and Society*, 70–71, 73, 82–83; Polanyi, *Personal Knowledge*, 147, 315–16; Polanyi, *Knowing and Being*, 172.

260. MacIntyre, *After Virtue*, 93, 270, 272, 277; MacIntyre, *Whose Justice? Which Rationality?*, 100–101, 172, 361; MacIntyre, *Three Rival Versions*, 74–77, 125, 142; MacIntyre, *First Principles*, 39, 45–46; "Epistemological Crises," 455; Polanyi, *Science, Faith and Society*, 53, 61; Polanyi, *Personal Knowledge*, 93, 95, 143, 169, 173, 250, 313, 314–16, 397, 404; Polanyi, *Knowing and Being*, 57, 70, 118.

261. This reaction was, in MacIntyre's view, inevitable, for, given the premises of the Enlightenment, it had to fail. See *After Virtue*, chap. 5, "Why the Enlightenment Project of Justifying Morality Had to Fail."

262. MacIntyre, *Three Rival Versions*, 59; italics in the original.

263. MacIntyre, *Three Rival Versions*, 59–60.

264. Polanyi, *Personal Knowledge*, 269–98.

265. Polanyi, *Personal Knowledge*, 323–24.

266. Polanyi, *Knowing and Being*, 144.

CHAPTER 5   The Incoherence of Liberalism and the Response of Tradition

1. Quoted in Pieper, *Tradition*, 67–68.

2. Pieper, *Tradition*, 37.

3. Pieper, *Tradition*, 23–35.

4. Pieper, who focuses upon sacred tradition, argues that sacred tradition is the transmission of an original utterance of God. Thus, the role of tradition in this context is preservation, not improvement.

5. Pelikan, *The Vindication of Tradition*, 54–57.

6. Polanyi, *Science, Faith and Society*, 82.

7. Polanyi, *Logic of Liberty*, 56–57.

8. Nietzsche, *The Birth of Tragedy*, §23.

9. Nietzsche, *Thus Spoke Zarathustra*, prologue.

10. Nietzsche, *On the Genealogy of Morals*, Second Essay, §24.

11. Nietzsche, *The Gay Science*, §125.

12. Nietzsche, *The Gay Science*, §343.

13. Nietzsche, *Thus Spoke Zarathustra*, 25–27.

14. Quotations from Rousseau in this paragraph come from *The Social Contract*, 4.8.

15. For twentieth-century writers who make the same kind of argument, see, for example, Nisbet, *The Quest for Community*, and Jouvenel, *On Power*.

16. It must be acknowledged that freedom and equality are both admirable ideals. They are valuable additions to any reflection on persons and societies. The problem comes, as with any ideal, when one or both are isolated and absolutized. The ideal becomes an ideology, and disorder (and often bloodshed) ensues.

17. At the same time, it must be acknowledged that before the twentieth century, divorce laws tended to be so restrictive and unfair to women that women trapped in abusive marriages had little recourse. Any adequate conception of marriage must be capable of addressing such injustices.

18. Burke, *Reflections on the Revolution in France*, 136.

19. Burke, *Reflections*, 92–93.

20. Yuval Levin's 2014 book *The Great Debate: Edmund Burke, Thomas Paine, and the Birth of Right and Left* makes the same basic point.

21. Polanyi, *Knowing and Being*, 68.

22. Polanyi, *Knowing and Being*, 71.

23. Burke, *Reflections*, 241.

24. Burke, *Reflections*, 183.

25. Burke, *Reflections*, 180.

26. Burke, *Reflections*, 181.

27. Burke, *Reflections*, 113.

28. Burke, *Reflections*, 108.

29. Burke, *Reflections*, 122.

30. Burke, *Reflections*, 181.

31. See, for example, Condorcet, *Sketch for a Historical Picture of the Progress of the Human Mind*.

32. Burke, *Reflections*, 274.

33. Burke, *Reflections*, 274, 275.

34. Burke, *Reflections*, 92–93.

35. Burke, *Reflections*, 94.

36. Burke, *Reflections*, 137.

37. Burke, *Further Reflections on the Revolution in France*, 168–69.

38. Burke, *Reflections*, 238.

39. Burke, *Reflections*, 190.

40. Burke, *Reflections*, 364.

41. Burke, *Reflections*, 186.

42. Burke, *Reflections*, 172–73.

43. Burke, *Reflections*, 173.

44. Burke, *Reflections*, 197.

45. MacIntyre, "Epistemological Crises," 461.

46. MacIntyre, *After Virtue*, 221–22.

47. MacIntyre, *Whose Justice? Which Rationality?*, 8, 353. MacIntyre writes, in 1977, that "Polanyi is the Burke of the philosophy of science." As he puts it, "all my earlier criticisms of Burke now become relevant to the criticism of Polanyi" ("Epistemological Crises," 465).

48. MacIntyre, *Whose Justice? Which Rationality?*, 353.

49. Burke, *Reflections*, 181–82.

50. Burke, *Reflections*, 171.

51. Burke, *Reflections*, 182.

52. Burke, *Reflections*, 182.

53. Burke, *Reflections*, 182.

54. Burke, *Reflections*, 136.

55. Burke, *Reflections*, 307.

56. Burke, *Reflections*, 136–37.

57. Burke, *Reflections*, 126.

58. Burke, *Reflections*, 130–31.

59. Burke, *Reflections*, 124.

60. Burke, *Reflections*, 120.

61. Burke, *Reflections*, 121–22.

62. Burke, *Reflections*, 121.

63. Burke, *Reflections*, 191.

64. Burke, *Reflections*, 192.

65. Burke, *Reflections*, 193.

66. Burke, *Reflections*, 195.

67. Unless otherwise noted, all quotations in this paragraph are from *Further Reflections*, 7–8.

68. Burke, *Reflections*, 92–93.

69. Burke, *Reflections*, 190.

70. Kirk, *The Roots of American Order*, 416.

71. Tocqueville, *Democracy in America*, 275.

72. Ortega y Gasset, *The Revolt of the Masses*, 91.

73. Ortega y Gasset, *The Revolt of the Masses*, 53.

74. Nisbet, *The Quest for Community*, 184–85.

75. Augustine, *On the Profit of Believing* §2.

76. Augustine, *On the Profit of Believing* §26.

77. Augustine, *Confessions* 6.5.7.

78. Augustine, *The Teacher* 11.37.36–39.

79. Augustine, *On the Profit of Believing* §35.

80. Augustine, *On the Profit of Believing* §33.

81. Augustine, *On the Profit of Believing* §34.

82. Augustine, *On the Profit of Believing* §33.

83. Augustine, *Confessions* 1.1.1.

84. Augustine, *The Teacher* 12.40.36–38.

85. Augustine, *The Teacher* 13.46.21–22; italics in original. Augustine is paraphrasing Matthew 23:9–10.

86. Augustine, *The Teacher* 13.46.37–38.

87. Augustine, *Confessions* 2.1.1.

88. Augustine, *Confessions* 1.1.1.

89. Augustine, *Confessions* 2.3.6.

90. Augustine, *Confessions* 2.5.10.

91. Augustine, *Confessions* 4.12.18.

92. Augustine, *City of God* 11.16.

93. Augustine, *City of God* 11.16.

94. Augustine, *City of God* 15.22.

95. Augustine, *City of God* 1.31.

96. Augustine, *Confessions* 8.9.10.

97. Augustine, *City of God* 11.28.

98. Augustine, *City of God* 2.7.

99. Augustine, *City of God* 14.13.

100. Polanyi, *Personal Knowledge*, 141.

101. Polanyi, *Personal Knowledge*, 266.

102. Polanyi, *The Tacit Dimension*, 61.

103. Polanyi, *Personal Knowledge*, 267.

104. Plato, *Republic*, 401e–402a.

105. Augustine, *The Profit of Believing*, §24.

106. Eliot, *Four Quartets*, 117. All citations are to the page numbers in *Complete Poems*.

107. Eliot, *Four Quartets*, 121.

108. Eliot, *Four Quartets*, 128.

109. Eliot, *Four Quartets*, 128.

110. Eliot, *Four Quartets*, 144.

111. Eliot, *Four Quartets*, 145.

112. Eliot, *Four Quartets*, 123.

113. Eliot, *Four Quartets*, 129.

114. Eliot, *Four Quartets*, 122.

115. Eliot, *Four Quartets*, 145.

116. Eliot, *Four Quartets*, 142.

117. Eliot, *Four Quartets*, 144.

118. Eliot, *Four Quartets*, 127.

119. Eliot, *Four Quartets*, 144.

120. Eliot, *Four Quartets*, 136.

121. Eliot, *Four Quartets*, 126.

122. Augustine, *City of God* 2.7.

123. Eliot, *Four Quartets*, 125.

124. Eliot, *Four Quartets*, 140.

125. Eliot, *Four Quartets*, 141.

126. Eliot, *Four Quartets*, 143.

127. Eliot, *Four Quartets*, 132.

128. Eliot, *Four Quartets*, 128.

129. Eliot, *Four Quartets*, 134.

130. Eliot, *Four Quartets*, 119.

131. Eliot, *Four Quartets*, 139.

132. Eliot, *Four Quartets*, 144.

133. Eliot, *Four Quartets*, 144.

134. Eliot, *Four Quartets*, 145.

135. Nietzsche, *Beyond Good and Evil*, §202.

136. Nietzsche, *The Will to Power*, §765.

137. Tocqueville, *Democracy in America*, 439.

138. Nietzsche, *On the Genealogy of Morals*, 3.15.

139. Nietzsche, *On the Genealogy of Morals*, 2.1.

140. René Girard has written extensively on the concept of scapegoat. See Girard, *Violence and the Sacred*; Girard, *Things Hidden since the Foundations of the World*; and Girard, *I See Satan Falling Like Lightning*.

141. See Girard, *I See Satan Falling*, esp. chaps. 12 and 13.

142. John 1:1–4 (KJV).

143. Colossians 1:17 (KJV).

144. Augustine, *Confessions* 4.12.18.

145. Genesis 1:26–27.

146. Hobbes, *Leviathan*, 35.

147. Hobbes, *Leviathan*, 48–49.

148. Hobbes, *Leviathan*, 101.

149. Hobbes, *Leviathan*, 101.

150. Eliot, "Tradition and the Individual Talent," 40.

151. Berry, *Sex, Economy, Freedom & Community*, 139.

152. Nussbaum, "Toward a Globally Sensitive Patriotism," 79–80.

153. Of course, the secularism was often aspirational rather than actual, for modern ideological politics is often a deformed variant of Christianity rather than an actually secular regime. Even when traditional religious belief is removed, the state itself becomes the locus of religious-like devotion.

154. This should bring to mind Polanyi's discussion of moral inversion.

155. Miller, "Cosmopolitanism: A Critique," 84.

156. For a book-length treatment of the subject, see Kirkpatrick Sale, *Human Scale*.

157. Pieper, *Tradition*, 55.

158. Pelikan, *Vindication of Tradition*, 54.

159. Although they are outside the parameters of this book, religious bodies are a vital part of the concept of community. In the West, the Christian church, both local and universal, has been the primary, but not exclusive religious community. A focused examination of the role religious communities play in the preservation and transmission of tradition would be a helpful complement to my argument.

AFTERWORD: A Conservatism Worth Conserving, or Conservatism as Stewardship

1. Nisbet, *The Quest for Community*. See also Tocqueville, *Democracy in America*.

2. It is interesting to note that Marx identified this same dynamic: "The bourgeoisie keeps more and more doing away with the scattered state of

the population, of the means of production, and of property. It has agglomer-ated population, centralised means of production, and has concentrated prop-erty in a few hands. The necessary consequence of this was political centralisation" (Marx, "The Communist Manifesto," in *The Marx–Engles Reader*, 477).

BIBLIOGRAPHY

Anscombe, G. E. M. "Modern Moral Philosophy." *Philosophy* 33 (1958): 1–19.

Aristotle. *Nichomachean Ethics*. 2nd ed. Translated by Terence Irwin. Indianapolis: Hackett, 2000.

———. *Politics*. Translated by C. D. C. Reeve. Indianapolis: Hackett, 1998.

Augustine. *City of God*. Translated by Henry Bettenson. New York: Penguin, 1984.

———. *Confessions*. Translated by Henry Chadwick. New York: Oxford University Press, 1998.

———. *On the Profit of Believing*. In *Nicene and Post-Nicene Fathers*, edited by Philip Schaff; translated by C. L. Cornish. Peabody, MA: Hendrickson, 1994.

———. *The Teacher*. In *Against the Academicians and The Teacher*, translated by Peter King. Indianapolis: Hackett, 1995.

Aurelius, Marcus Antoninus. *Meditations*. Translated by C. R. Haines. London: Heinemann, 1958.

Bacon, Francis. *Essays*. Edited by Michael J. Hawkins. London: Everyman, 1994.

———. *The Great Instauration*. In *The Great Instauration and New Atlantis*, edited by J. Weinberger. Arlington Heights, IL: AHM, 1980.

———. *New Atlantis*. In *The Great Instauration and New Atlantis*, edited by J. Weinberger. Arlington Heights, IL: AHM, 1980.

———. *Novum Organum*. In *The Physical and Metaphysical Works of Lord Bacon*, edited by Joseph Devey. London, 1853.

Berry, Wendell. *Sex, Economy, Freedom & Community*. New York: Pantheon, 1992.

Blumer, J. G. "Politics, Poetry, and Practice." *Political Studies* 12 (1964): 355–61.

Botwinick, Aryeh. *Michael Oakeshott's Skepticism*. Princeton, NJ: Princeton University Press, 2011.

Boyle, Joseph. "Natural Law and the Ethics of Traditions." In *Natural Law Theory: Contemporary Essays*, edited by Robert P. George, 3–30. New York: Oxford University Press, 1992.

Burke, Edmund. *Further Reflections on the Revolution in France*. Edited by Daniel E. Ritchie. Indianapolis: Liberty Fund, 1992.

———. *Reflections on the Revolution in France*. Indianapolis: Liberty Fund, 1999.

Chesterton, G. K. *Orthodoxy*. Wheaton, IL: Harold Shaw, 1994.

Cicero. *Republic*. Translated by N. Rudd. Oxford: Oxford University Press, 1998.

Collingwood, R. G. Review of *Experience and Its Modes*, by Michael Oakeshott. *The Cambridge Review* 55 (1934): 249–50.

Condorcet, Marquis de. *Sketch for a Historical Picture of the Progress of the Human Mind*. New York: Noonday Press, 1955.

Congar, Yves. *The Meaning of Tradition*. New York: Hawthorn Books, 1964.

Covell, Charles. *The Redefinition of Conservatism: Politics and Doctrine*. New York: St. Martin's Press, 1986.

Cranston, Maurice. "Michael Oakeshott's Politics." *Encounter* 28 (January 1967): 82–86.

Dahl, Norman O. "Justice and Aristotelian Practical Reason." *Philosophy and Phenomenological Research* 50 (1991): 153–57.

Deneen, Patrick J. *Why Liberalism Failed*. New Haven, CT: Yale University Press, 2018.

Descartes, René. *Discourse on Method*. In *Discourse on Method and the Meditations*, translated by F. E. Sutcliffe. New York: Penguin, 1968.

———. "Letter from the Author to the Translator of the Principles of Philosophy, to serve as a Preface." In *Discourse on Method and the Meditations*, translated by F. E. Sutcliffe. New York: Penguin, 1968.

———. *Meditations*. In *Discourse on Method and the Meditations*, translated by F. E. Sutcliffe. New York: Penguin Books, 1968.

———. *Principles of Philosophy*. In *The Philosophical Writings of Descartes*, Vol. 1, translated by John Cottingham, Robert Stoothoff, and Dugald Murdoch. New York: Cambridge University Press, 1984.

———. *Rules for the Direction of the Mind*. In *The Philosophical Writings of Descartes*, Vol. 1, translated by John Cottingham, Robert Stoothoff, and Dugald Murdoch. New York: Cambridge University Press, 1984.

Donagan, Alan. *The Theory of Morality*. Chicago: University of Chicago Press, 1977.

Drucker, Peter F. *Adventures of a Bystander*. New York: Harper & Row, 1980.

Eliot, T. S. *Christianity and Culture*. New York: Harcourt, 1976.

————. *Four Quartets*. In *The Complete Poems and Plays 1909–1950*. New York: Harcourt, Brace & World, 1971.

————. "Tradition and the Individual Talent." In *Selected Prose of T. S. Eliot*, edited by Frank Kermode. New York: Harvest, 1975.

Flett, John. "Alasdair MacIntyre's Tradition-Constituted Enquiry in Polanyian Perspective." *Tradition & Discovery* 26, no. 2 (1999–2000): 6–20.

Franco, Paul. *Michael Oakeshott: An Introduction*. New Haven, CT: Yale University Press, 2004.

————. *The Political Philosophy of Michael Oakeshott*. New Haven, CT: Yale University Press, 1990.

Gellner, Ernest. *The Devil in Modern Philosophy*. London: Routledge and Kegan Paul, 1974.

Gelwick, Richard. *The Way of Discovery: An Introduction to the Thought of Michael Polanyi*. New York: Oxford University Press, 1977.

George, Robert P. "Moral Particularism, Thomism, and Traditions." *Review of Metaphysics* 42 (1989): 593–605.

Gewirth, Alan. *Human Rights: Essays on Justification and Application*. Chicago: University of Chicago Press, 1982.

————. *Reason and Morality*. Chicago: University of Chicago Press, 1978.

————. "Rights and Virtues." *Review of Metaphysics* 38 (June 1985): 739–62.

Giddens, Anthony. *Runaway World*. New York: Routledge, 2000.

Gilson, Etienne, and Thomas Langan. *Modern Philosophy: Descartes to Kant*. New York: Random House, 1963.

Girard, René. *I See Satan Falling Like Lightning*. Translated by James G. Williams. Maryknoll, NY: Orbis, 2001.

————. *Things Hidden since the Foundations of the World*. Translated by Stephen Bann and Michael Metter. Stanford, CA: Stanford University Press, 1987.

————. *Violence and the Sacred*. Translated by Patrick Gregory. Baltimore: Johns Hopkins University Press, 1972.

Graham, Gordon. "MacIntyre's Fusion of History and Philosophy." In *After MacIntyre*, edited by John Horton and Susan Mendus, 161–75. Notre Dame, IN: University of Notre Dame Press, 1994.

Grant, Patrick. "Michael Polanyi: The Augustinian Component." *New Scholasticism* 48 (1974): 438–63.

Gray, John. *End Games: Questions in Late Modern Thought*. Cambridge: Polity, 1997.

Greenleaf, W. H. *Oakeshott's Philosophical Politics*. New York: Barnes & Noble, 1996.

Grene, Marjorie. "Response to Alasdair MacIntyre." In *Morals, Science and Sociality*, edited by H. Tristram Engelhardt Jr., and Daniel Callahan, 40–47. Hastings-on-Hudson, NY: Hastings Center, 1978.

Habermas, Jürgen. *Between Facts and Norms: Contributions to a Discourse Theory of Law and Democracy.* Cambridge: Polity, 1996.

———."Kant's Idea of Perpetual Peace, with the Benefit of Two Hundred Years' Hindsight." In *Perpetual Peace: Essays on Kant's Cosmopolitan Ideal*, edited by James Bohman and Matthias Lutz-Bachmann, 113–54. Cambridge, MA: MIT Press, 1997.

Haldane, John. "MacIntyre's Thomist Revival: What Next?" In *After MacIntyre*, edited by John Horton and Susan Mendus, 91–107. Notre Dame, IN: University of Notre Dame Press, 1994.

Hallowell, John H. *The Moral Foundations of Democracy.* Indianapolis: Liberty Fund, 1954.

Himmelfarb, Gertrude. "The Conservative Imagination." *American Scholar* 44, no. 3 (1975): 405–20.

Hittinger, Russell. *A Critique of the New Natural Law Theory.* Notre Dame, IN: University of Notre Dame Press, 1987.

Hobbes, Thomas. *Leviathan.* Edited by Michael Oakeshott. New York: Simon & Schuster, 1962.

Hume, David. *A Treatise of Human Nature.* Mineola, NY: Dover, 2003.

Jouvenel, Bertrand de. *On Power.* Indianapolis: Liberty Fund, 1993.

Kant, Immanuel. *Perpetual Peace.* Edited by Hans Reiss. Translated by H. B. Nisbet. Cambridge: Cambridge University Press, 1991.

Keiser, R. Melvin. "Inaugurating Postcritical Philosophy: A Polanyian Meditation on Creation and Conversion in Augustine's *Confessions*." *Zygon* 22, no. 3 (1987): 317–37.

Kirk, Russell. *The Roots of American Order.* Wilmington, DE: ISI Books, 2003.

Kuhn, Thomas. *The Structure of Scientific Revolution.* Chicago: University of Chicago Press, 1962.

Legutko, Ryszard. *The Demon in Democracy.* New York: Encounter, 2016.

Levin, Yuval. *The Great Debate: Edmund Burke, Thomas Paine, and the Birth of Right and Left.* New York: Basic Books, 2014.

Lewis, C. S. *The Abolition of Man.* New York: Simon & Schuster, 1996.

———. "Meditation in a Toolshed." In *God in the Dock*, edited by Walter Hooper, 212–15. Grand Rapids, MI: William B. Eerdmans, 1970.

Locke, John. *Second Treatise.* In *Two Treatises of Government*, edited by Peter Laslett. Cambridge: Cambridge University Press, 1960.

Luther, Martin. "An Open Letter to the Christian Nobility." In *Works of Martin Luther*, vol. 2. Philadelphia: A. J. Holman Company and The Castle Press, 1915.

MacIntyre, Alasdair. *After Virtue.* 2nd ed. Notre Dame, IN: University of Notre Dame Press, 1984.

———. *Dependent Rational Animals.* Chicago: Open Court, 2000.

———. "Epistemological Crises, Dramatic Narrative and the Philosophy of Science." *The Monist* 60 (1977): 453–72.

———. *First Principles, Final Ends and Contemporary Philosophical Issues.* Milwaukee: Marquette University Press, 1990.

———. "How Can We Learn What *Veritatis Splendor* Has to Teach?" *The Thomist* 58 (1994): 171–95.

———. "The Idea of a Social Science." *Aristotelian Society* (Supplementary Volume) (1967): 95–114.

———. "The Irrelevance of the Church of England." *Listener* 59 (1958): 1054–55, 1058.

———. "Natural Law in Advanced Modernity." In *Common Truths: New Perspectives on Natural Law,* edited by Edward B. McLean, 91–115. Wilmington, DE: ISI Books, 2000.

———. "Objectivity in Morality and Objectivity in Science." In *Morals, Science and Sociality,* edited by H. Tristram Engelhardt Jr. and Daniel Callahan, 21–39. Hastings-on-Hudson, NY: Hastings Center, 1978.

———. "A Partial Response to My Critics." In *After MacIntyre,* edited by John Horton and Susan Mendus, 283–304. Notre Dame, IN: University of Notre Dame Press, 1994.

———. "Precis of *Whose Justice? Which Rationality?*" *Philosophy and Phenomenological Research* 51 (1991): 149–52.

———. "Reply to Dahl, Baier and Schneewind." *Philosophy and Phenomenological Research* 51 (1991): 169–78.

———. *A Short History of Ethics.* New York: Macmillan, 1966.

———. *Three Rival Versions of Moral Enquiry.* Notre Dame, IN: University of Notre Dame, 1990.

———. *Whose Justice? Which Rationality?* Notre Dame, IN: University of Notre Dame Press, 1988.

Mackenzie, W. J. M. "Political Theory and Political Education." *Universities Quarterly* 9 (1955–56): 351–63.

Manent, Pierre. *An Intellectual History of Liberalism.* Princeton, NJ: Princeton University Press, 1995.

Marx, Karl. *The Communist Manifesto.* In *The Marx–Engles Reader,* edited by Robert C. Tucker. New York: W. W. Norton, 1978.

Mead, Walter L. "Michael Oakeshott as Philosopher: Beyond Politics, a Quest for Omniscience." *Political Science Reviewer* 32 (2003): 221–68.

Meek, Esther L. "Contact with Reality: An Examination of Realism in the Work of Michael Polanyi." Ph.D. diss., Temple University, 1983.

———. "'Recalled to Life': Contact with Reality." *Tradition & Discovery* 26, no. 3 (1999–2000): 72–83.

Merleau-Ponty, Maurice. *The Phenomenology of Perception.* New York: Routledge, 2002.

Miller, David. "Cosmopolitanism: A Critique." *Critical Review of International Social and Political Philosophy* 5, no. 3 (2002): 80–85.

Mitchell, Mark T. *Michael Polanyi: The Art of Knowing.* Wilmington, DE: ISI Books, 2006.

———. "Personal Participation: Michael Polanyi, Eric Voegelin, and the Indispensability of Faith," *Journal of Religious Ethics* 33.1 (2005): 65–89.

Mulhall, Stephen, and Adam Swift. *Liberals and Communitarians.* Oxford: Blackwell, 1992.

Nietzsche, Friedrich. *Beyond Good and Evil.* In *Basic Writings of Nietzsche,* translated by Walter Kaufmann. New York: The Modern Library, 1992.

———. *The Birth of Tragedy.* Translated by Walter Kaufman. New York: Vintage, 1967.

———. *The Gay Science.* Translated by Walter Kaufman. New York: Vintage, 1974.

———. *On the Genealogy of Morals.* In *Basic Writings of Nietzsche,* translated by Walter Kaufmann. New York: The Modern Library, 1992.

———. *Thus Spoke Zarathustra.* Translated by Walter Kaufmann. New York: The Modern Library, 1995.

———. *The Will to Power.* Translated by Walter Kaufmann and R. J. Hollingdale. New York: Vintage, 1968.

Nisbet, Robert. *The Present Age.* Indianapolis: Liberty Fund. 1988.

———. *The Quest for Community.* Wilmington, DE: ISI Books, 2010.

Nozick, Robert. *Anarchy, State and Utopia.* New York: Basic Books, 1974.

Nussbaum, Martha. "Patriotism and Cosmopolitanism." In *For Love of Country,* edited by Joshua Cohen, 3–19. Boston: Beacon Press, 1996.

———. "Recoiling from Reason." *The New York Review,* December 7, 1989, 36–41.

———. "Toward a Globally Sensitive Patriotism." *Daedalus* (Summer 2008): 78–93.

Oakeshott, Michael. "Conservative Political Thought." *The Spectator,* October 15, 1954, 473–74.

———. *Experience and Its Modes.* Cambridge: Cambridge University Press, 1933.

———. "The Human Coefficient." *Encounter* 11 (1958): 77–80.

———. "John Locke." *The Cambridge Review* 54 (1932–33): 72–73.

———. *On Human Conduct.* Oxford: Clarendon, 1975.

———. "On Misunderstanding Human Conduct." *Political Theory* 4 (1976): 353–67.

———. *Rationalism in Politics.* Indianapolis: Liberty Fund, 1991.

———. "Rationalism in Politics: A Reply to Professor Raphael." *Political Studies* 13 (1965): 89–92.

———. *Religion, Politics and the Moral Life.* Edited by Timothy Fuller. New Haven, CT: Yale University Press, 1993.

———. "Science and Society." *The Cambridge Journal* 1 (1947–48): 689–97.

Ortega y Gasset, José. *The Revolt of the Masses.* New York: Norton, 1932.

Pelikan, Jaroslav. *The Vindication of Tradition.* New Haven, CT: Yale University Press, 1984.

Pieper, Joseph. *Tradition: Concept and Claim.* Translated by E. Christian Kopff. Wilmington, DE: ISI Books, 2008.

Pitkin, Hanna Fenichel. "The Roots of Conservatism." *Dissent* 20 (1973): 496–525.

Plato. *Meno.* Translated by G. M. A. Grube. Indianapolis: Hackett, 1981.

———. *Republic.* Translated by C. D. C. Reeve. Indianapolis: Hackett, 2004.

Poirier, Maben Walter. "Harry Prosch's Modernism." *Tradition & Discovery* 16, no. 2 (1998): 32–39.

Polanyi, Michael. "Creative Imagination." *Tri-Quarterly* (Fall 1966): 111–23. Also published in *Chemical and Engineering News* 44 (1966): 85–93.

———. "Faith and Reason." *The Journal of Religion* 41, no. 4 (1961): 237–47.

———. *Knowing and Being.* Edited by Marjorie Grene. London: Routledge & Kegan Paul, 1969.

———. "Logic and Psychology." *American Psychologist* 23 (1968): 27–43.

———. *Logic of Liberty.* Indianapolis: Liberty Fund, 1998.

———. "Marx and Saint Paul." *The Manchester Guardian*, March 17, 1953, 4.

———. *Personal Knowledge: Toward a Post-Critical Philosophy.* Chicago: University of Chicago Press, 1958.

———. "Science and Religion." *Philosophy Today* 7 (1963): 4–14.

———. *Science, Faith, and Society.* Chicago: University of Chicago Press, 1964.

———. *Society, Economics, and Philosophy: Selected Papers.* Edited by R. T. Allen. New Brunswick, NJ: Transaction, 1997.

———. "The Stability of Beliefs." *British Journal for the Philosophy of Science* 3, no. 11 (1952): 217–32.

———. *The Study of Man.* Chicago: University of Chicago Press, 1958.

———. *The Tacit Dimension.* Garden City, NY: Doubleday, 1966.

Polanyi, Michael, and Harry Prosch. *Meaning.* Chicago: University of Chicago Press, 1975.

Postan, M. "The Revulsion from Thought." *The Cambridge Journal* 2 (1948): 395–408.

Prosch, Harry. *Michael Polanyi: A Critical Exposition.* Albany: State University of New York Press, 1986.

———. "Polanyi's Ethics." *Ethics* 82 (1972): 91–113.

———. Review of *The Way of Discovery,* by Richard Gelwick. *Ethics* 89 (1979): 211–16.

———. "Those Missing 'Objects.'" *Tradition & Discovery* 17, no. 1–2 (1990): 17–20.

Raphael, D. D. "Professor Oakeshott's Rationalism in Politics." *Political Studies* 12 (1964): 202–15.

Rawls, John. *A Theory of Justice.* Cambridge, MA: Harvard University Press, 1971.

Rousseau, Jean-Jacques. *The Social Contract.* Translated by Donald A. Cress. Indianapolis: Hackett, 2011.

Ryle, Gilbert. *The Concept of Mind.* London: Hutchinson of London, 1949.

———. "Knowing How and Knowing That." *Proceedings of the Aristotelian Society for the Systematic Study of Philosophy* 46 (1945–46): 1–16.

Sabine, George H. *A History of Political Theory.* 3rd ed. New York: Holt, Rinehart and Winston, 1961.

Sale, Kirkpatrick. *Human Scale.* White River Junction, VT: Chelsea Green, 2017.

Sandel, Michael J. *Democracy's Discontent.* Cambridge, MA: Harvard University Press, 1996.

Schindler, D. C. *Freedom from Reality.* Notre Dame, IN: University of Notre Dame Press, 2017.

Schneewind, J. B. "MacIntyre and the Indispensability of Tradition." *Philosophy and Phenomenological Research* 51 (1991): 165–68.

Scott, William Taussig. "At the Wheel of the World: The Life and Times of Michael Polanyi." *Tradition and Discovery* 25, no. 3 (1998–9): 10–23.

Scott, William Taussig, and Martin X. Moleski. *Michael Polanyi: Scientist and Philosopher.* Oxford: Oxford University Press, 2005.

Shils, Edward. *Tradition.* Chicago: University of Chicago Press, 1981.

———. "Tradition and Liberty." In *The Virtue of Civility,* 103–22. Indianapolis: Liberty Fund, 1997.

Spitz, David. "A Rationalist *Malgre Lui*: The Perplexities of Being Michael Oakeshott." *Political Theory* 4 (1976): 335–52.

Stanlis, Peter J. *Edmund Burke and the Natural Law.* Shreveport, LA: Huntington House, 1986.

Tocqueville, Alexis de. *Democracy in America.* Edited by J. P. Mayer. Translated by George Lawrence. New York: Harper Perennial, 1988.

Voegelin, Eric. *The New Science of Politics.* Chicago: University of Chicago Press, 1952.

———. *Science, Politics and Gnosticism.* Washington, DC: Regnery, 1968.

Wachbroit, Robert. "A Genealogy of Virtues." *Yale Law Journal* 92 (1983): 564–76.

Watkins, J. N. W. "Political Tradition and Political Theory." *Philosophical Quarterly* 2 (1952): 323–37.

Winch, Peter. *The Idea of a Social Science.* London: Routledge & Kegan Paul, 1958.

Wood, Neal. "A Guide to the Classics: The Skepticism of Professor Oakeshott." *Journal of Politics* 21 (1959): 647–62.

INDEX

American Founding, 7, 207–8, 220, 231
    as a propositional nation, 231–32
Anscombe, G. E. M., 96–97
Anselm, 125
apprenticeship, 125
    See also MacIntyre, Alasdair; Oakeshott, Michael; Polanyi, Michael
Aquinas, Thomas, 189
Aristotle, 99, 100, 102, 103, 219
    rejection of, 25–27, 37, 56, 85
    See also MacIntyre, Alasdair
Augustine
    anticipates Descartes' *cogito*, 292n99
    authority and, 234–35
    compared with Burke, 238
    creation and, 252
    faith and reason, 233–36
    humility and, 237
    ordo amoris and, 227, 236–37
    See also Burke, Edmund; Polanyi, Michael
Aurelius, Marcus, 12

Bacon, Francis, 23, 66
    beginning anew, 31–32
    doubt and, 29–31
    equality and, 33

method and, 32–33, 296n40
    New Atlantis and, 33–35
    power and, 27–29
    scientific power and, 34
Berry, Wendell, 258
Brexit, 16, 17
Burke, Edmund, 58–59, 146–47, 181–82, 219, 220–31
    affections and, 225–27
    on change, 221–22, 225
    compared with Augustine, 238
    contract and, 228–29
    education and, 224
    freedom and, 230, 238
    gentleman and, 224–25
    human nature and, 223
    inheritance, 227–29
    limits to liberty, 223–24
    moral law and, 224, 230
    religion and, 224
    state of nature and, 223
    See also MacIntyre, Alasdair; Polanyi, Michael

Chesterton, G. K., 59, 280n5
Christianity
    deformations of, 246–51
    democracy and, 246
    equality and, 246

322

MARK T. MITCHELL

is the chair of the government department at
Patrick Henry College.

Printed in the USA
CPSIA information can be obtained
at www.ICGtesting.com
LVHW020726031223
765381LV00005B/141